W-w-w-w-whoa...

KOYOHARU GOTOUGE

I'm Gotouge—welcome to volume 15! Thank you to everyone who has supported me. The anime is really coming together. I got to see a sneak peek! The visuals are so stunning, and the music is so beautiful that it made me tremble. Back when I was new to being a manga author, I never even dreamed that Ufotable, creators of the anime I was absorbed in at the time, would end up making my show too. But no matter how great the anime is, if the original manga doesn't stay interesting, a lot of people are going to be upset! So I'll keep on working hard!

DEMON SLAYER:
KIMETSU NO YAIBA
VOLUME 15
Shonen Jump Edition

Story and Art by
KOYOHARU GOTOUGE

KIMETSU NO YAIBA
© 2016 by Koyoharu Gotouge
All rights reserved. First published in Japan
in 2016 by SHUEISHA Inc., Tokyo. English
translation rights arranged by SHUEISHA Inc.

TRANSLATION John Werry
ENGLISH ADAPTATION Stan!
TOUCH-UP ART & LETTERING Evan Waldinger
DESIGN Jimmy Presler
EDITOR Mike Montesa

Printed in the U.S.A

Published by VIZ Media, LLC
P.O. Box 77010
San Francisco, CA 94107

10 9 8 7 6 5 4 3 2 1
First printing, August 2020

viz.com

shonenjump.com

KIMETSU NO YAIBA

DAYBREAK
AND
FIRST LIGHT

**KOYOHARU
GOTOUGE**

CHARACTERS

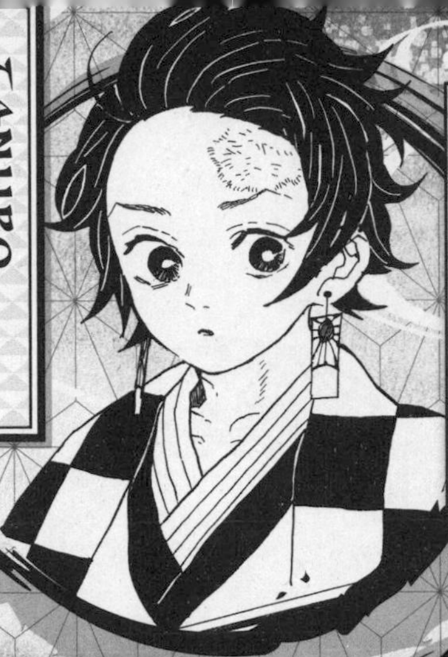

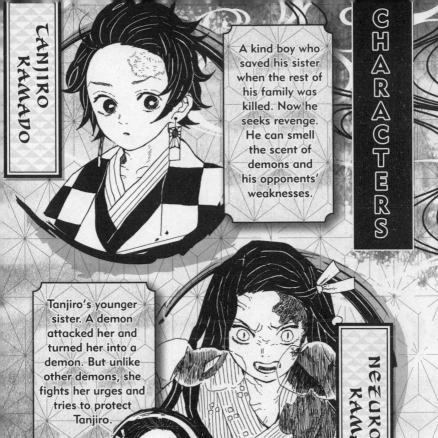

TANJIRO KAMADO

A kind boy who saved his sister when the rest of his family was killed. Now he seeks revenge. He can smell the scent of demons and his opponents' weaknesses.

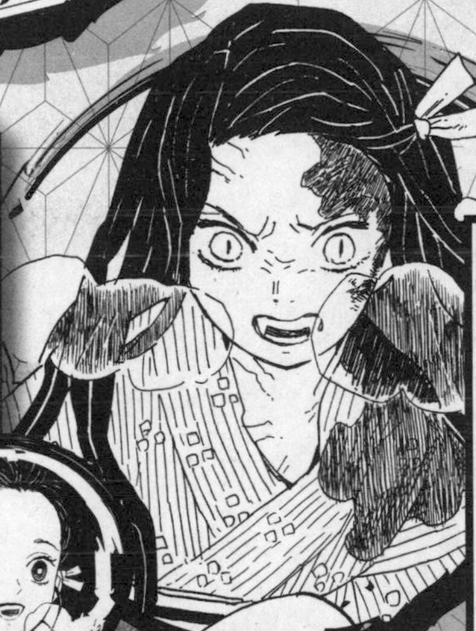

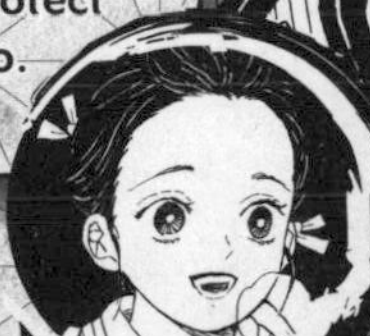

NEZUKO KAMADO

Tanjiro's younger sister. A demon attacked her and turned her into a demon. But unlike other demons, she fights her urges and tries to protect Tanjiro.

STORY

In Taisho-Era Japan, young Tanjiro makes a living selling charcoal. One day, demons kill his family and turn his younger sister Nezuko into a demon. Tanjiro and Nezuko set out to find a way to return Nezuko to human form and defeat Kibutsuji, the demon who killed their family!

After joining the Demon Slayer Corps, Tanjiro meets Tamayo and Yushiro—demons who oppose Kibutsuji—who provide a clue to how Nezuko may regain her humanity. In search of a new katana, Tanjiro visits a village of swordsmiths, but the upper-rank demons Hantengu and Gyokko attack. The Mist Hashira, Tokito, wins a hard-fought victory against Gyokko and the Love Hashira, Kanroji, takes on Hantengu's spawn. Meanwhile, Tanjiro and Genya pursue Hantengu's actual miniature form!!

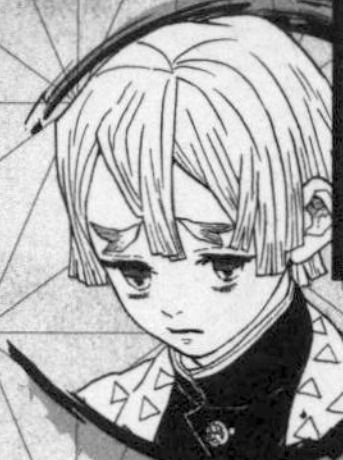

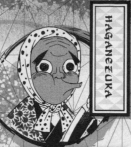

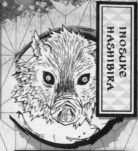

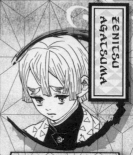

ZENITSU AGATSUMA

He went through Final Selection at the same time as Tanjiro. He's usually cowardly, but when he falls asleep, his true power comes out.

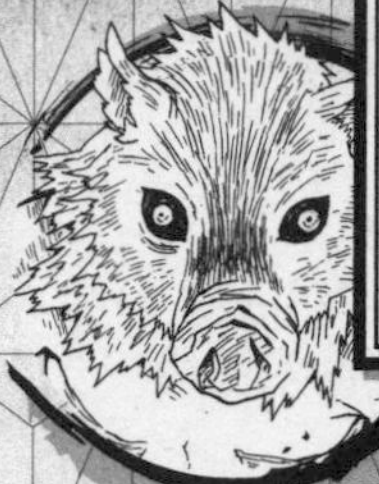

INOSUKE HASHIBIRA

He also went through Final Selection at the same time as Tanjiro. He wears the pelt of a wild boar and is very belligerent.

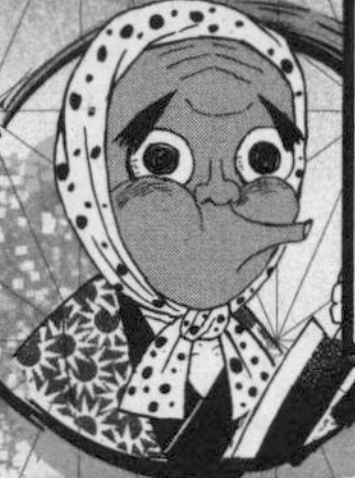

HAGANEZUKA

The swordsmith who makes Tanjiro's katanas. He has the soul of an artist, so he gets angry when a katana is treated poorly.

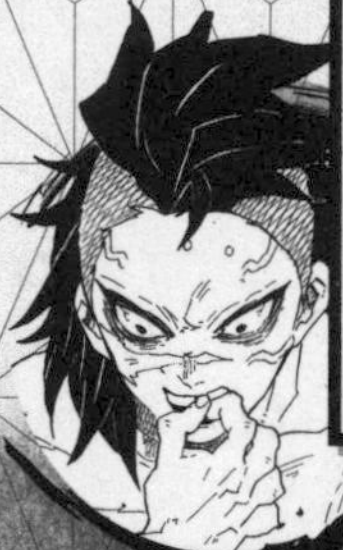

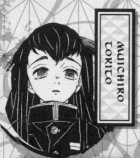

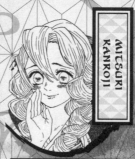

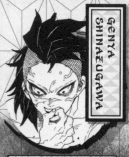

GENYA SHINAZUGAWA

He went through Final Selection at the same time as Tanjiro. His elder brother is Sanemi, the Wind Hashira. He and Tanjiro meet again in the village of swordsmiths.

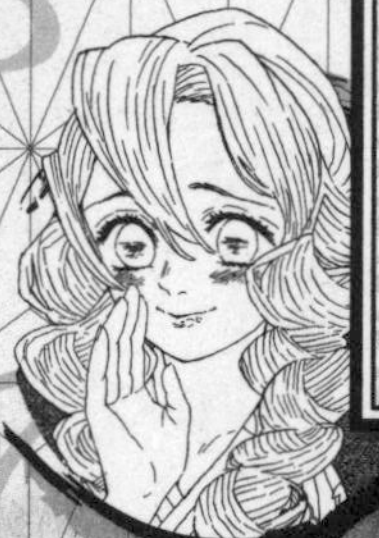

MITSURI KANROJI

Love Hashira in the Demon Slayer Corps. She joined the Demon Slayer Corps to find a man to marry.

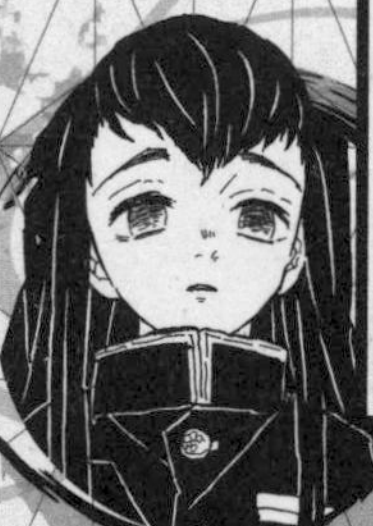

MUICHIRO TOKITO

The Mist Hashira in the Demon Slayer Corps. He's the descendant of users of Sun Breathing—the first breathing technique.

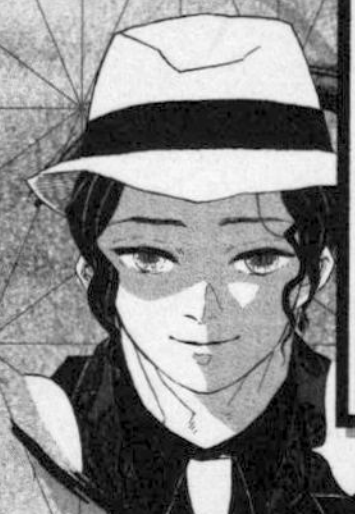

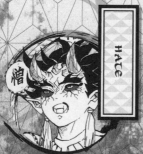

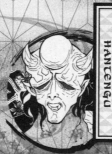

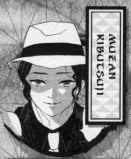

MUZAN KIBUTSUJI

Kibutsuji turned Nezuko into a demon. He is Tanjiro's enemy and hides his nature in order to live among human beings.

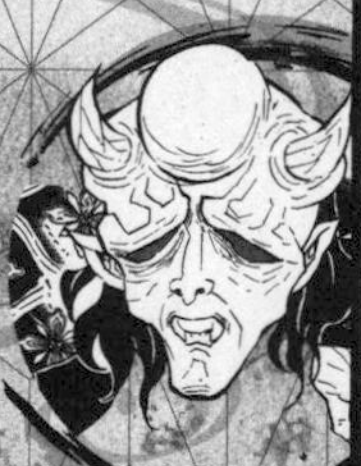

UPPER RANK 4: HANTENGU

Together with Gyokko, he has infiltrated the village of swordsmiths on orders from Muzan Kibutsuji.

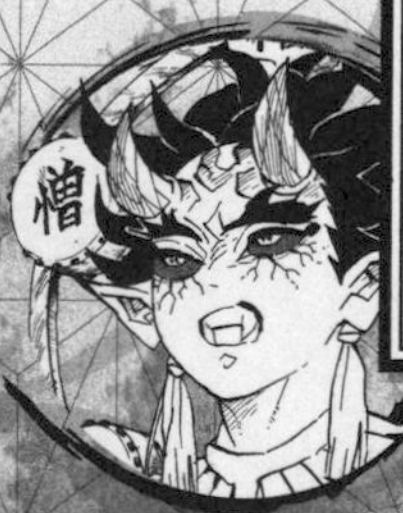
憎

HATE

Hantengu's Other Self. An alter ego of Hantengu who is a combination of that demon's separate Kidoairaku bodies. He displays the kanji for hate.

CONTENTS

DEMON SLAYER
KIMETSU NO YAIBA

15

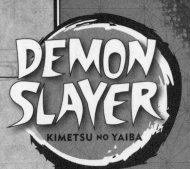

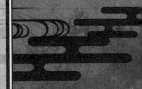

DAYBREAK AND FIRST LIGHT

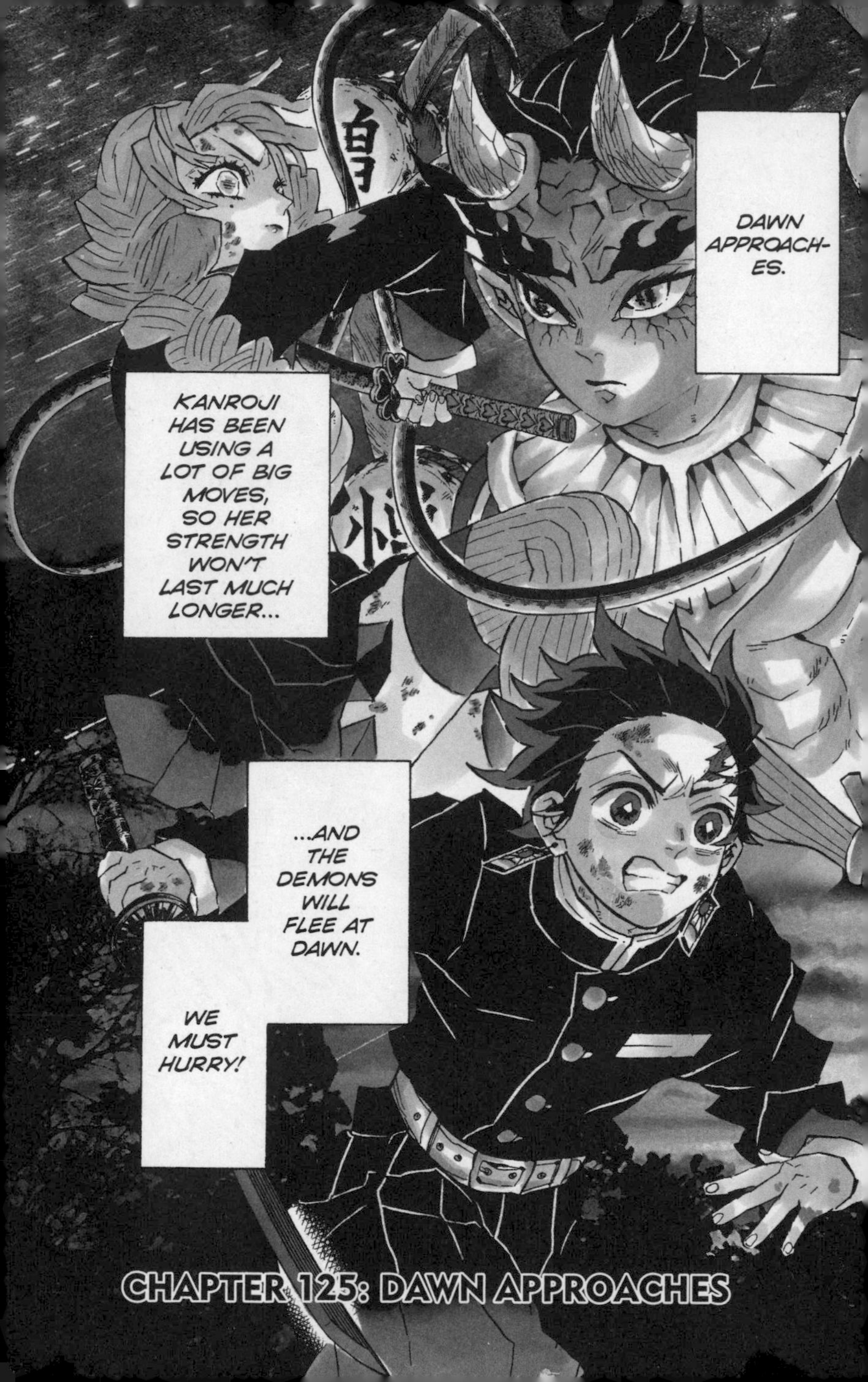
DAWN APPROACHES.
KANROJI HAS BEEN USING A LOT OF BIG MOVES, SO HER STRENGTH WON'T LAST MUCH LONGER...
...AND THE DEMONS WILL FLEE AT DAWN.
WE MUST HURRY!
CHAPTER 125: DAWN APPROACHES

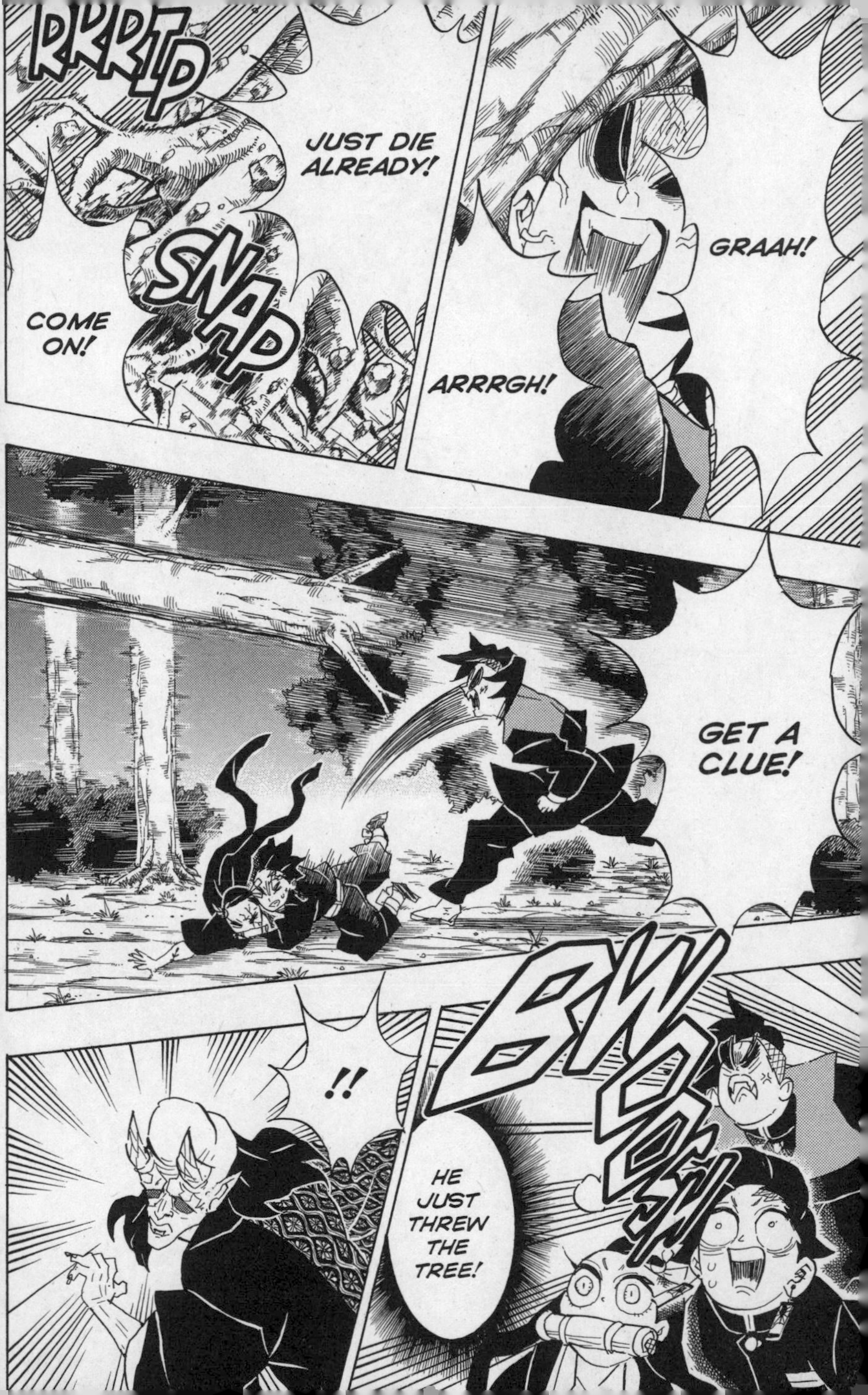
GRAAH!
ARRRGH!
RRRIP
JUST DIE ALREADY!
SNAP
COME ON!
GET A CLUE!
BWOOSH
!!
HE JUST THREW THE TREE!

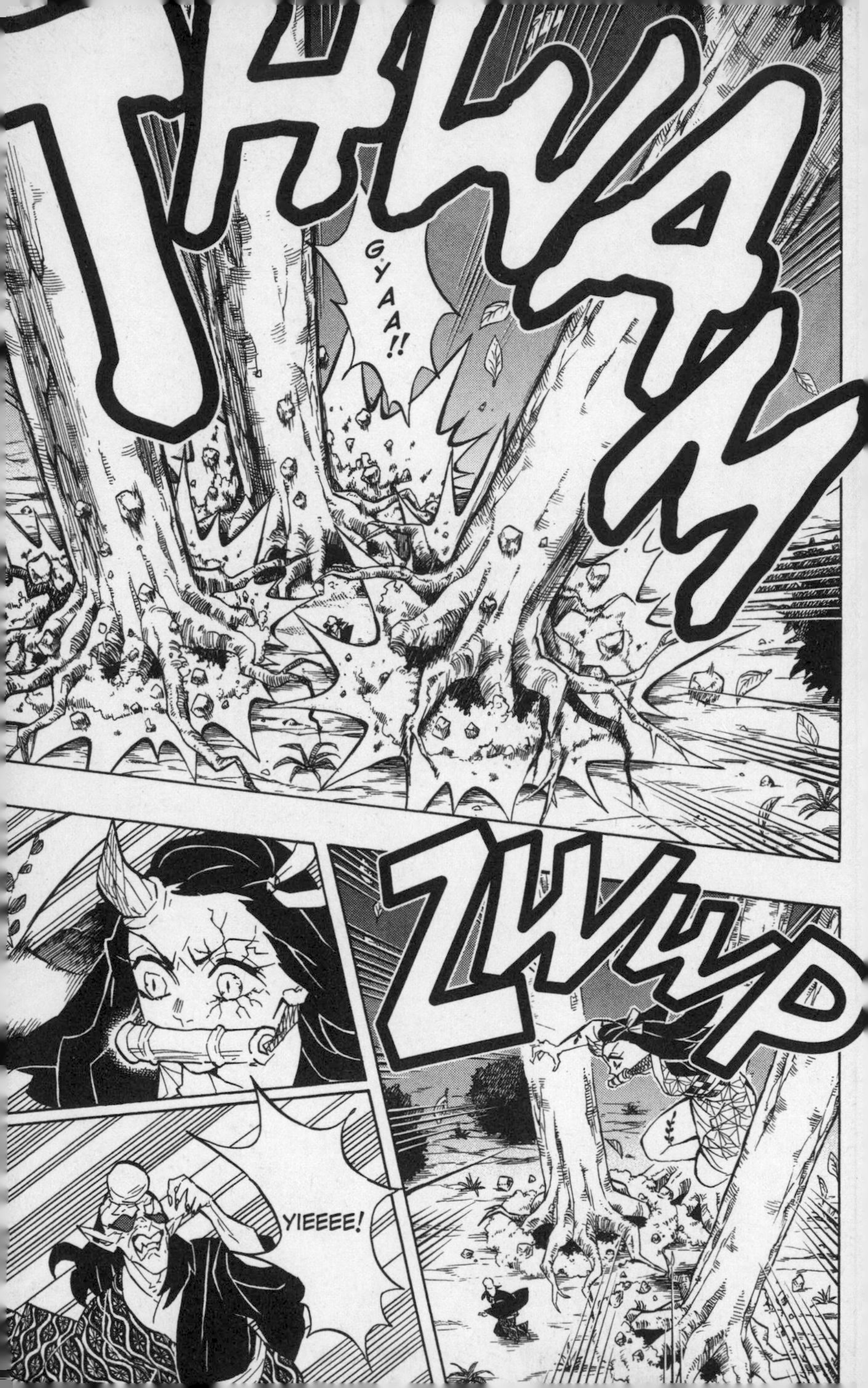
GYAA!!
ZWIP
YIEEEE!

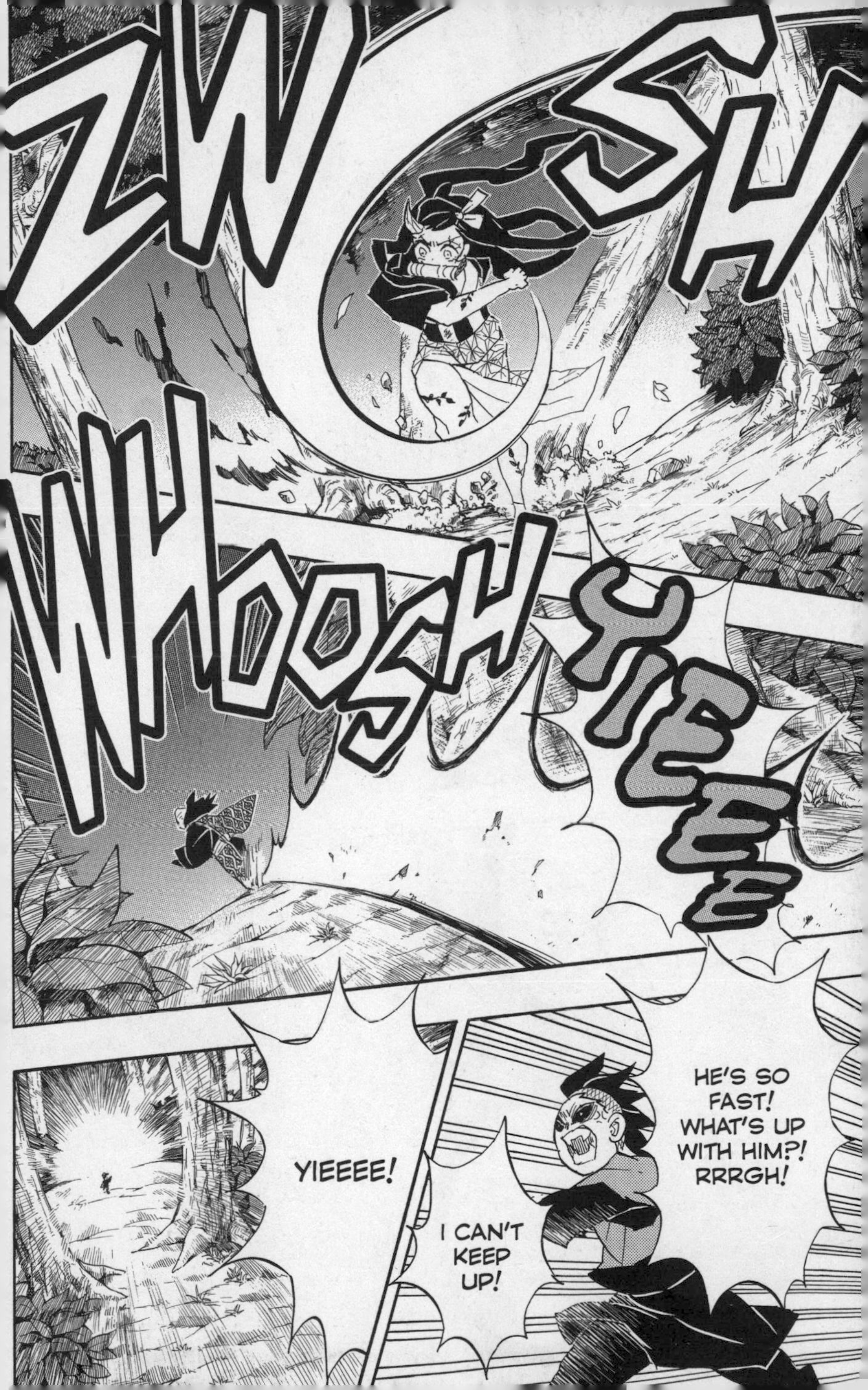
ZWOOSH
WHOOSH
YIEEEE
HE'S SO FAST! WHAT'S UP WITH HIM?! RRRGH!
I CAN'T KEEP UP!
YIEEEE!

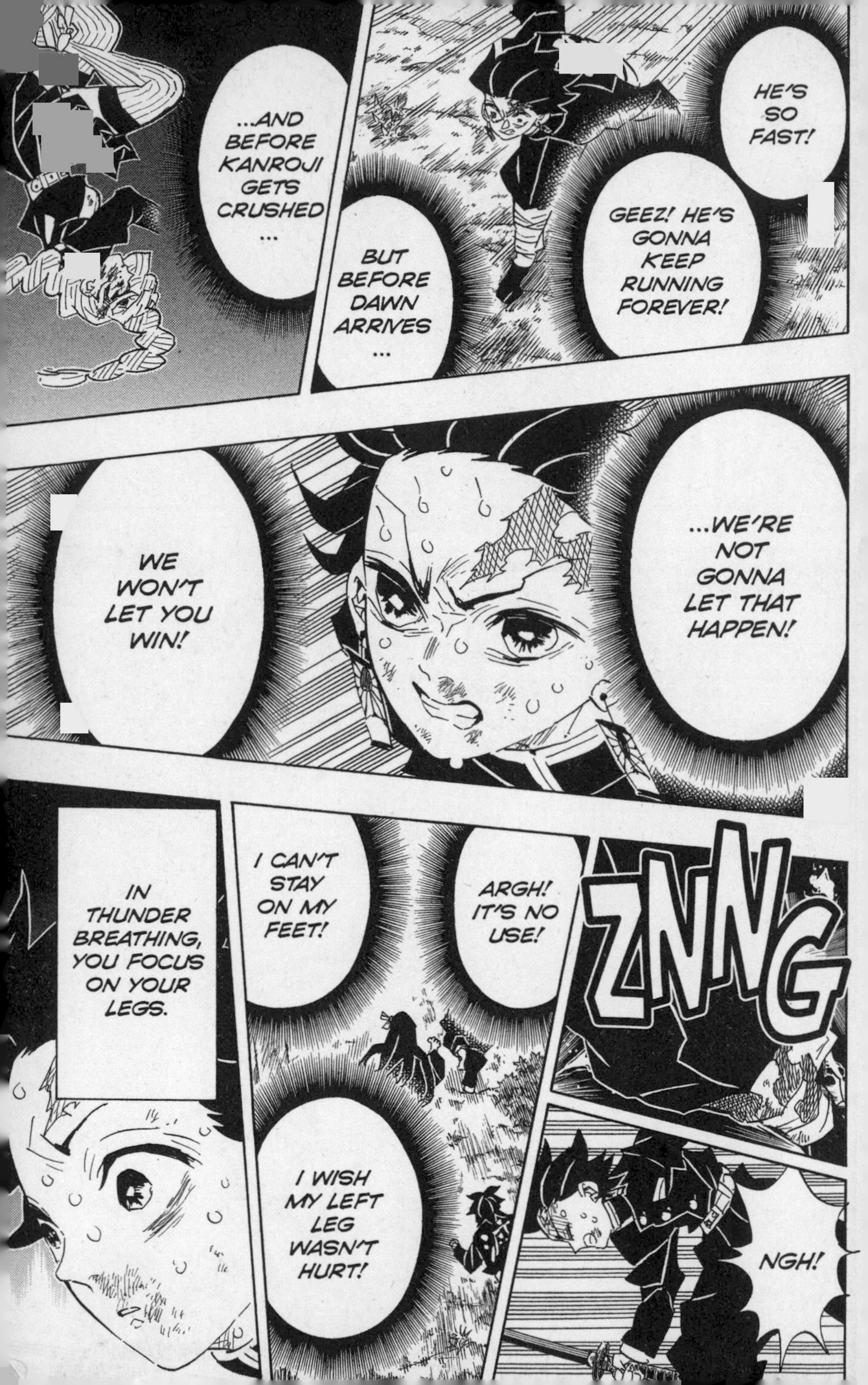
HE'S SO FAST!
GEEZ! HE'S GONNA KEEP RUNNING FOREVER!
BUT BEFORE DAWN ARRIVES ...
...AND BEFORE KANROJI GETS CRUSHED ...
...WE'RE NOT GONNA LET THAT HAPPEN!
WE WON'T LET YOU WIN!
ZNNG
NGH!
ARGH! IT'S NO USE!
I CAN'T STAY ON MY FEET!
I WISH MY LEFT LEG WASN'T HURT!
IN THUNDER BREATHING, YOU FOCUS ON YOUR LEGS.

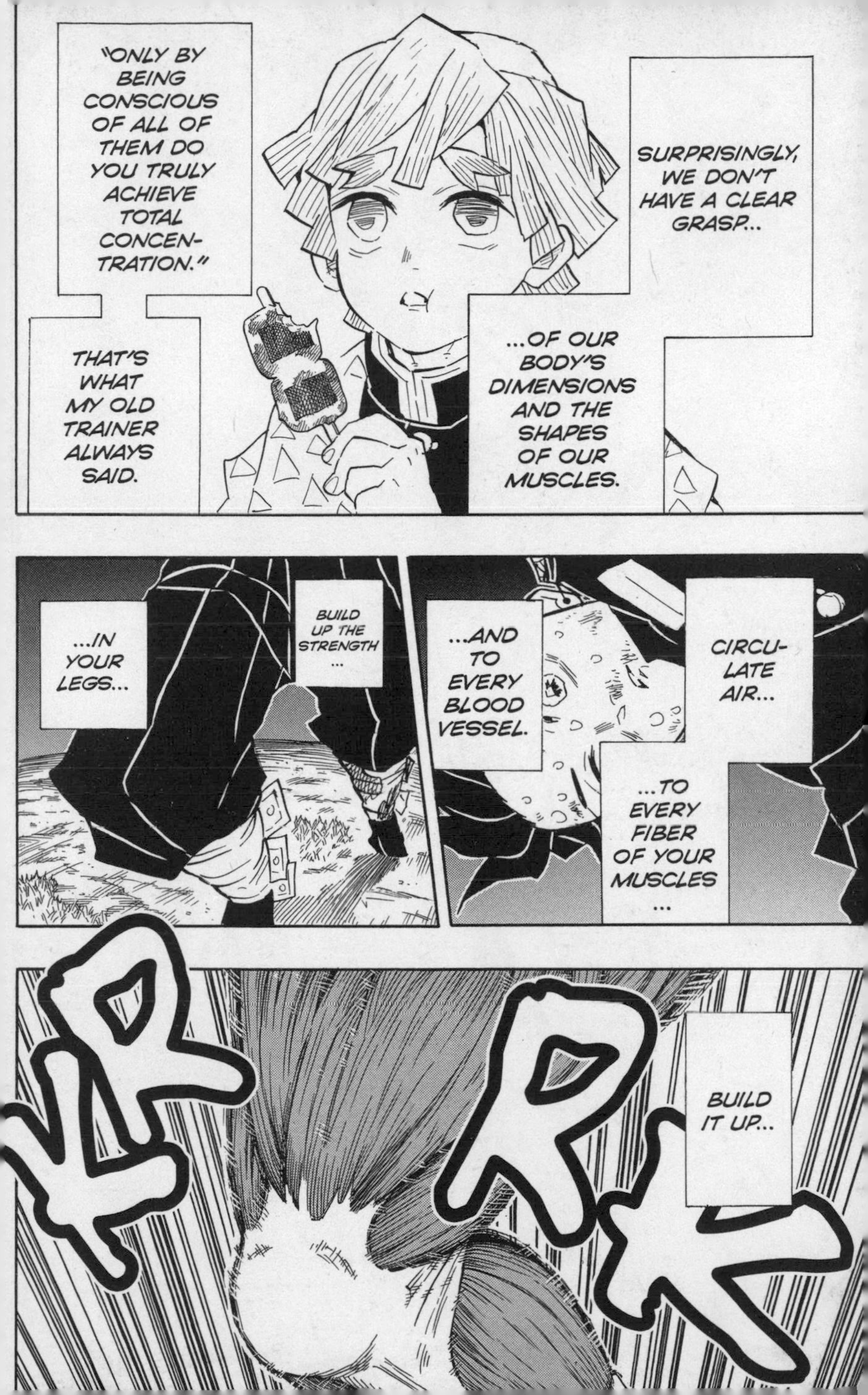
SURPRISINGLY, WE DON'T HAVE A CLEAR GRASP...
...OF OUR BODY'S DIMENSIONS AND THE SHAPES OF OUR MUSCLES.
"ONLY BY BEING CONSCIOUS OF ALL OF THEM DO YOU TRULY ACHIEVE TOTAL CONCEN- TRATION."
THAT'S WHAT MY OLD TRAINER ALWAYS SAID.
CIRCU- LATE AIR...
...TO EVERY FIBER OF YOUR MUSCLES...
...AND TO EVERY BLOOD VESSEL.
BUILD UP THE STRENGTH...
...IN YOUR LEGS...
BUILD IT UP...

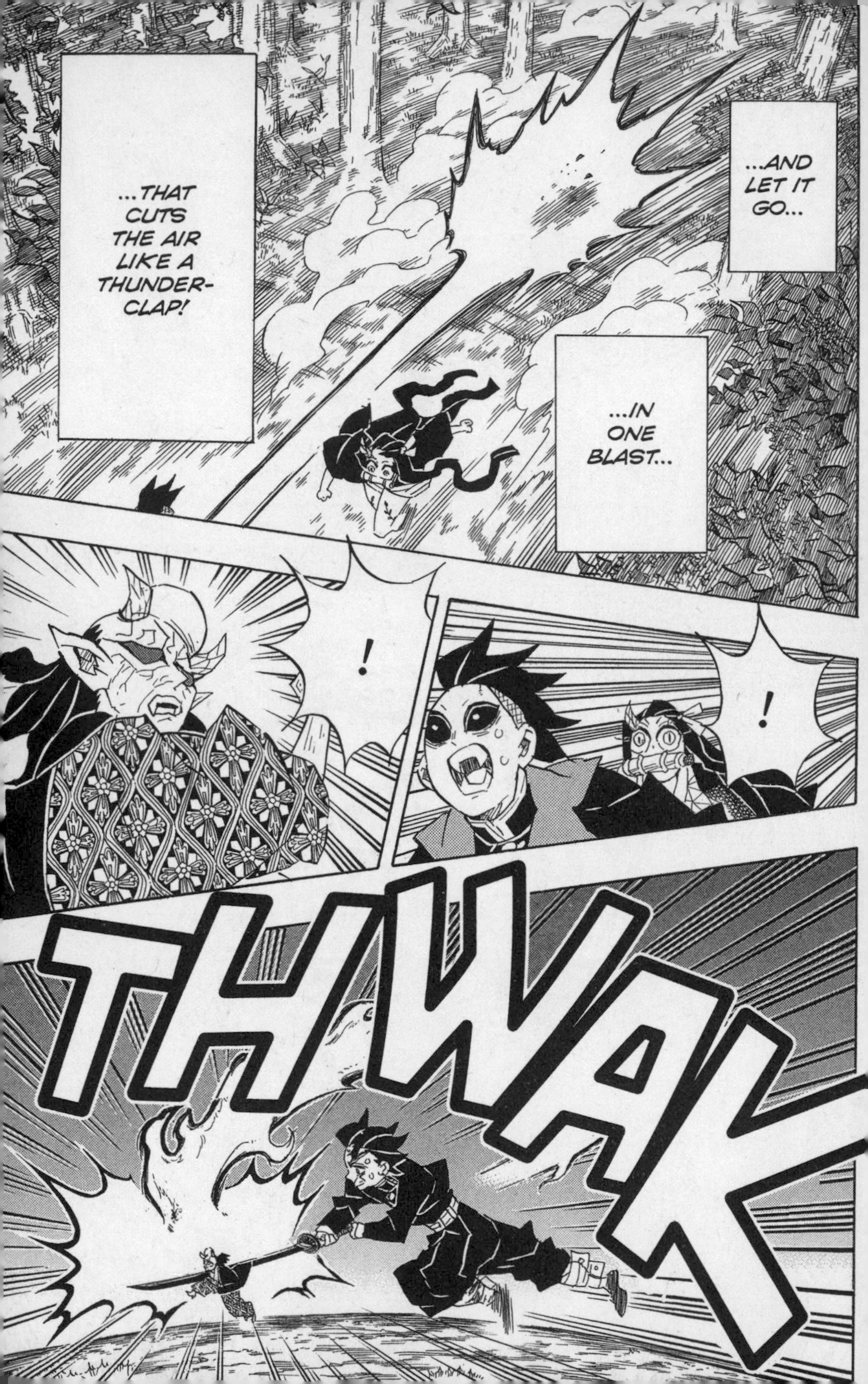
...AND LET IT GO...
...IN ONE BLAST...
...THAT CUTS THE AIR LIKE A THUNDER-CLAP!
!
!
THWAK

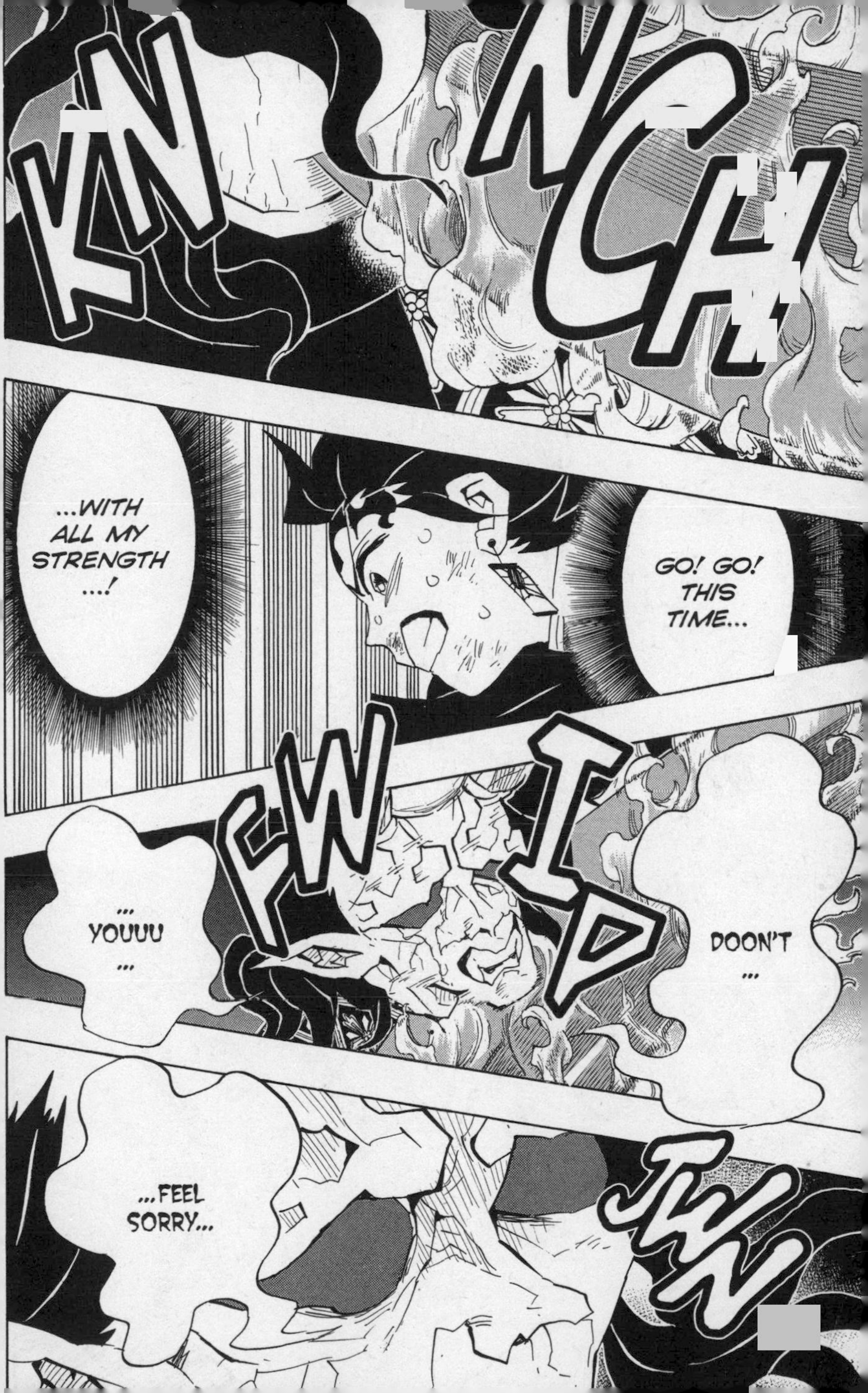
KNNCH
GO! GO! THIS TIME...
...WITH ALL MY STRENGTH ...!
FWIP
DOON'T ...
... YOUUU ...
...FEEL SORRY...

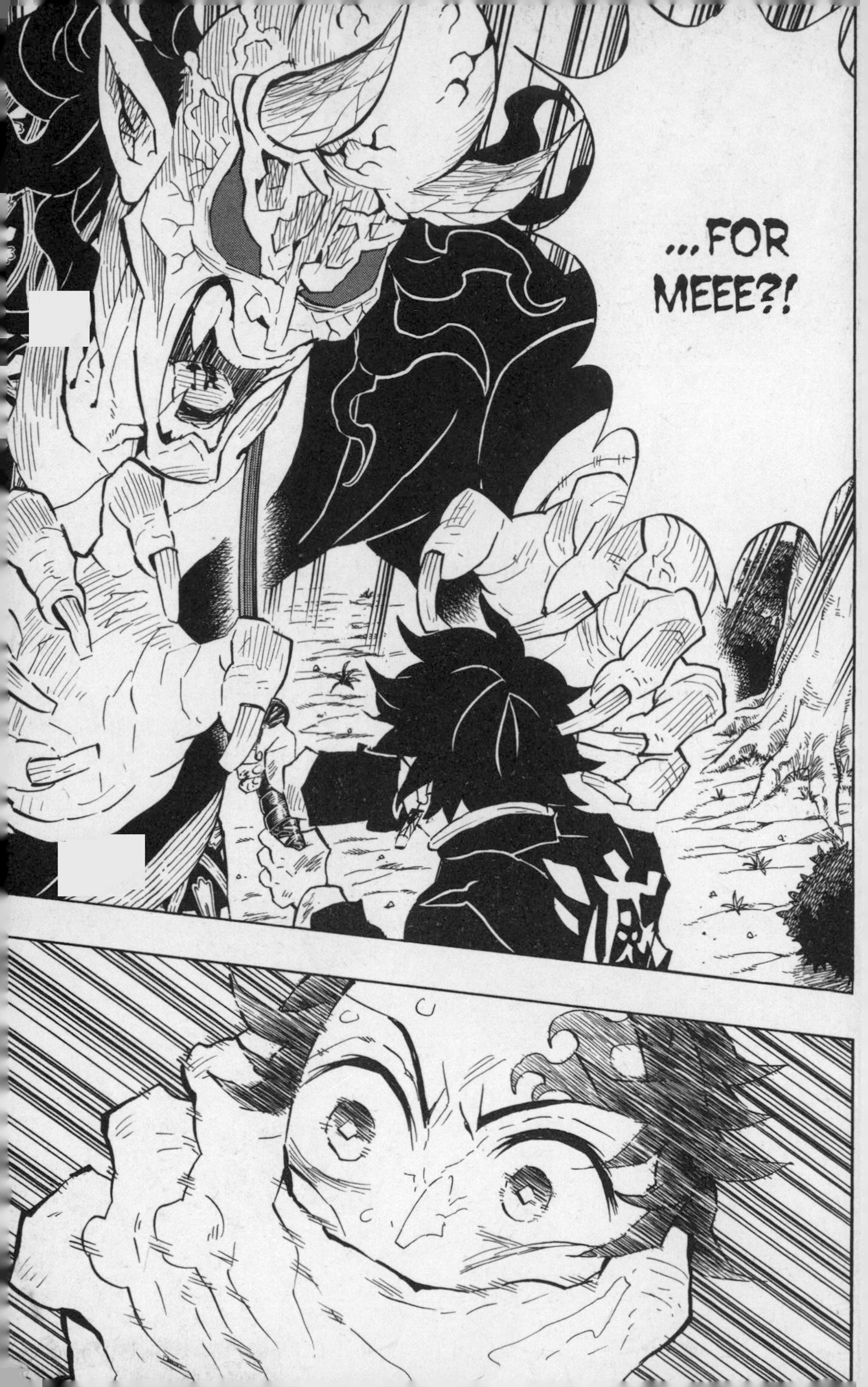
...FOR MEEE?!

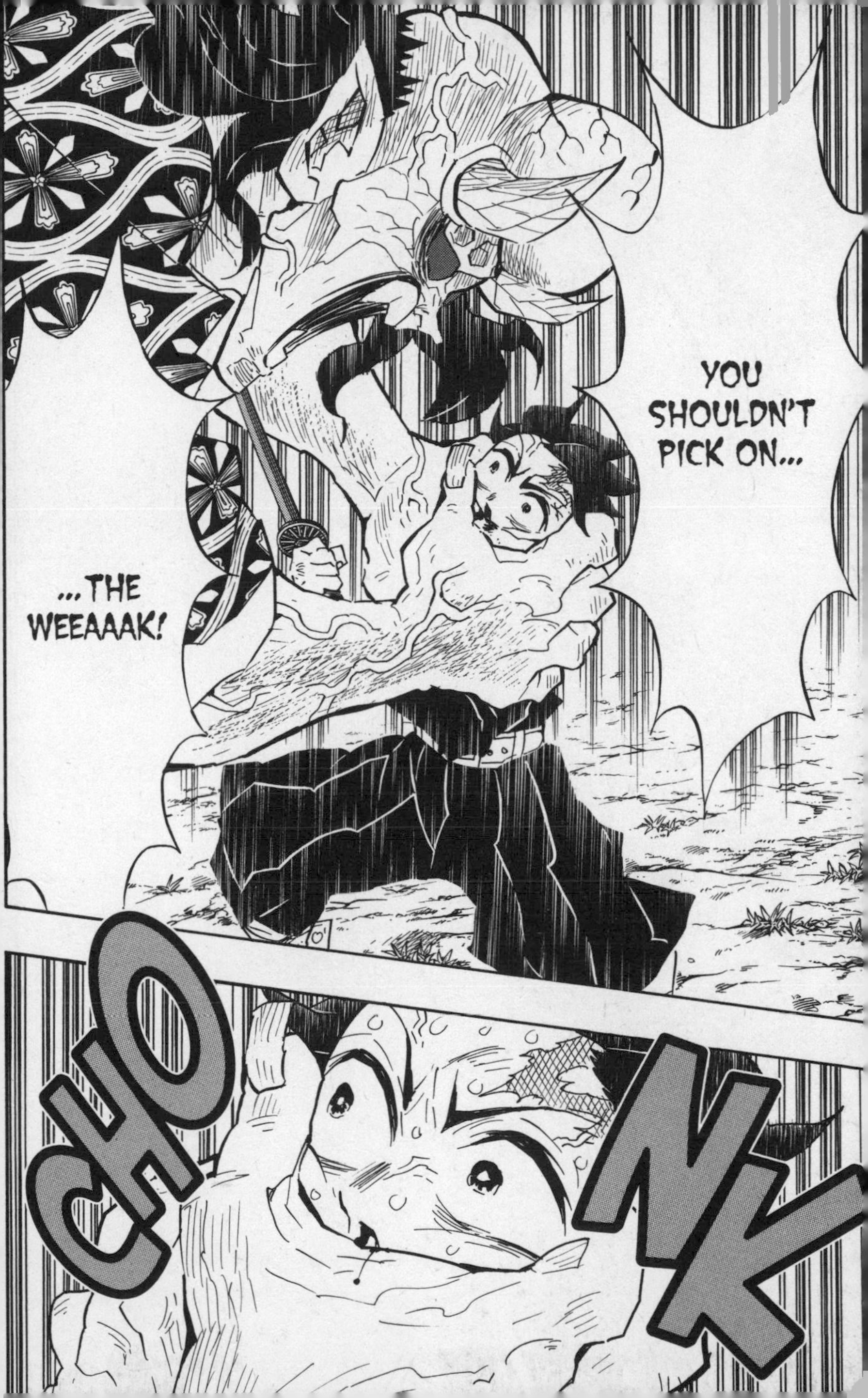
YOU SHOULDN'T PICK ON...
...THE WEEAAAK!
CHONK

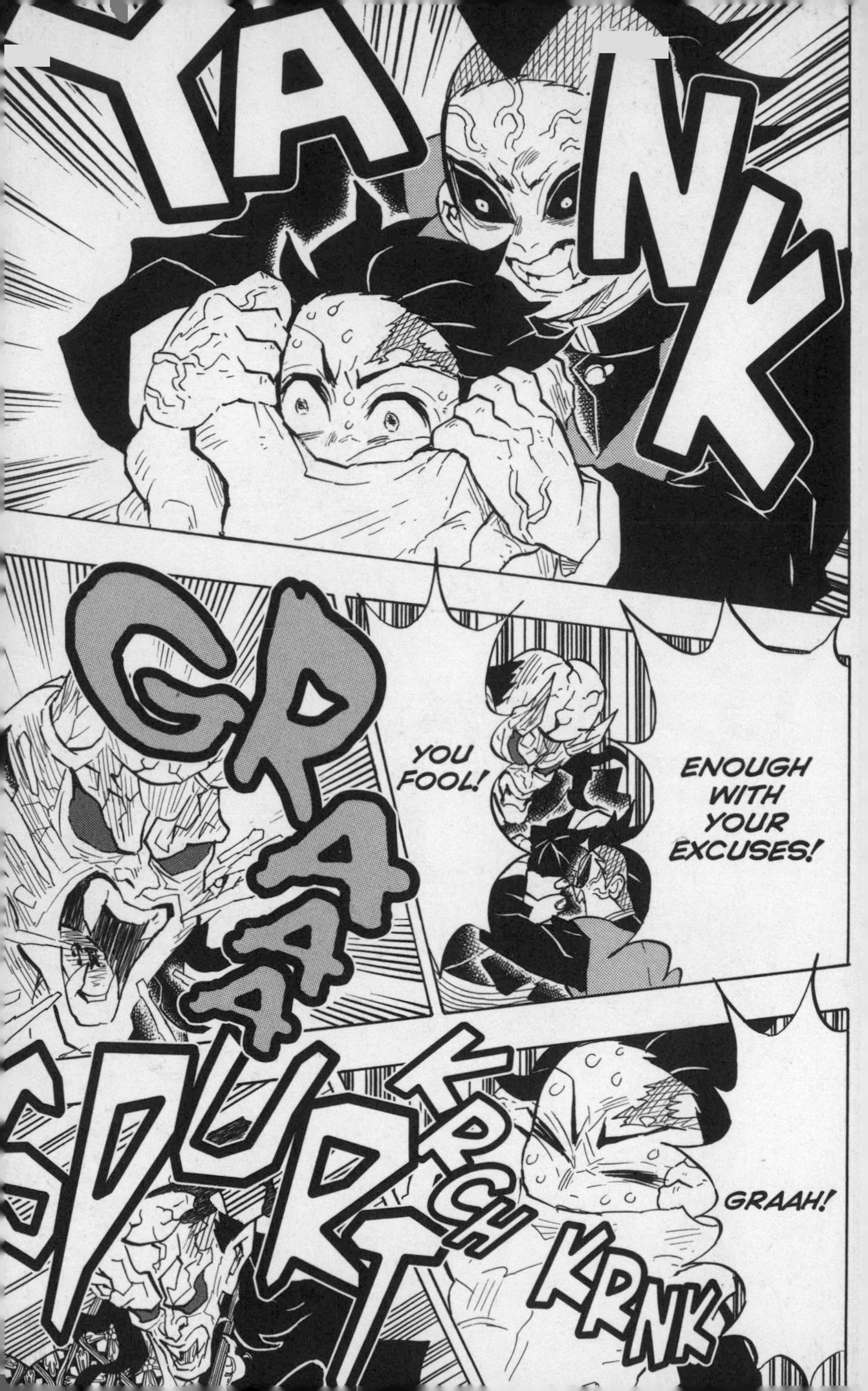
YANK
ENOUGH WITH YOUR EXCUSES!
YOU FOOL!
GRAAH!
KRNK
KRCH

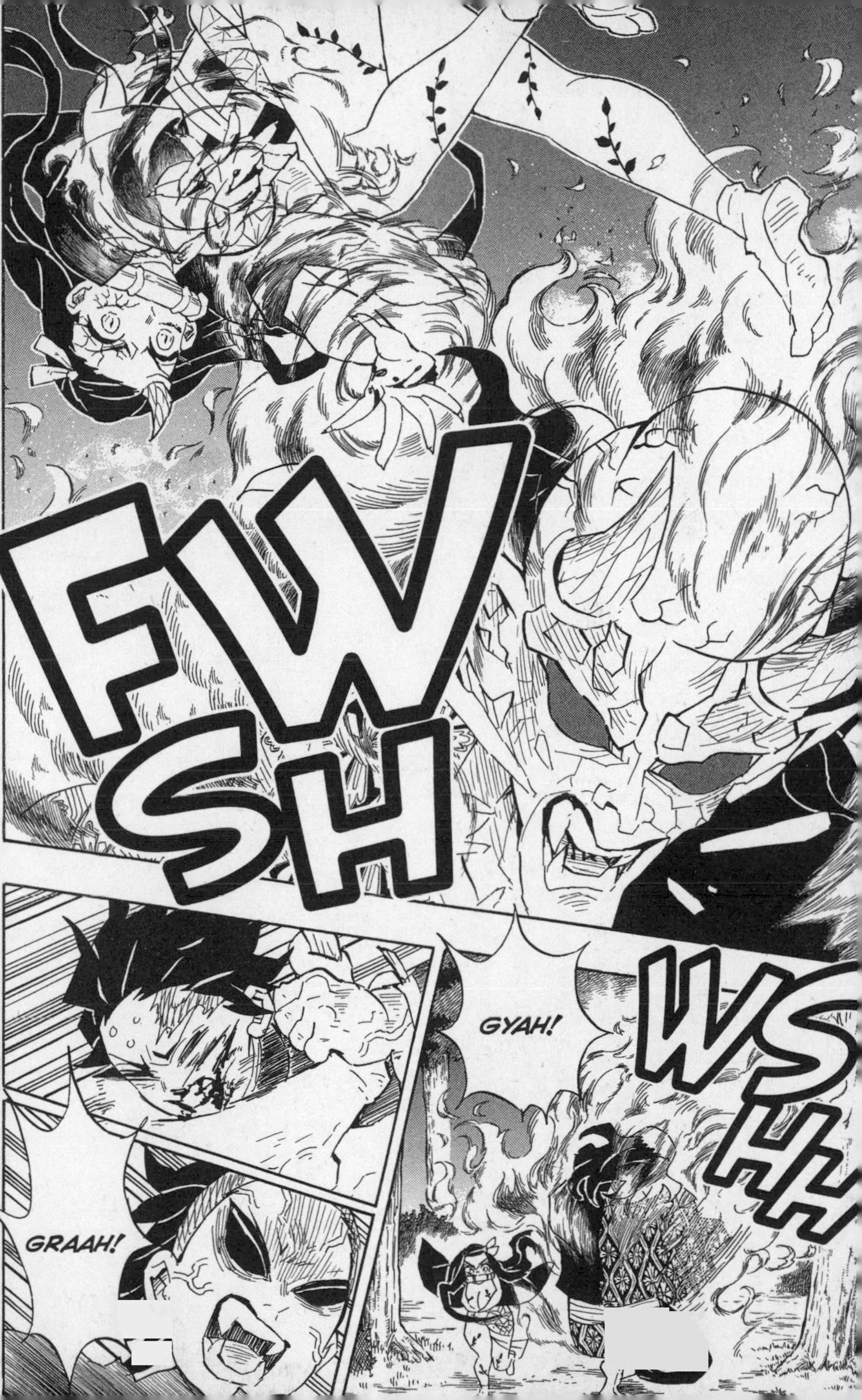
FWSH
WSHH
GYAH!
GRAAH!

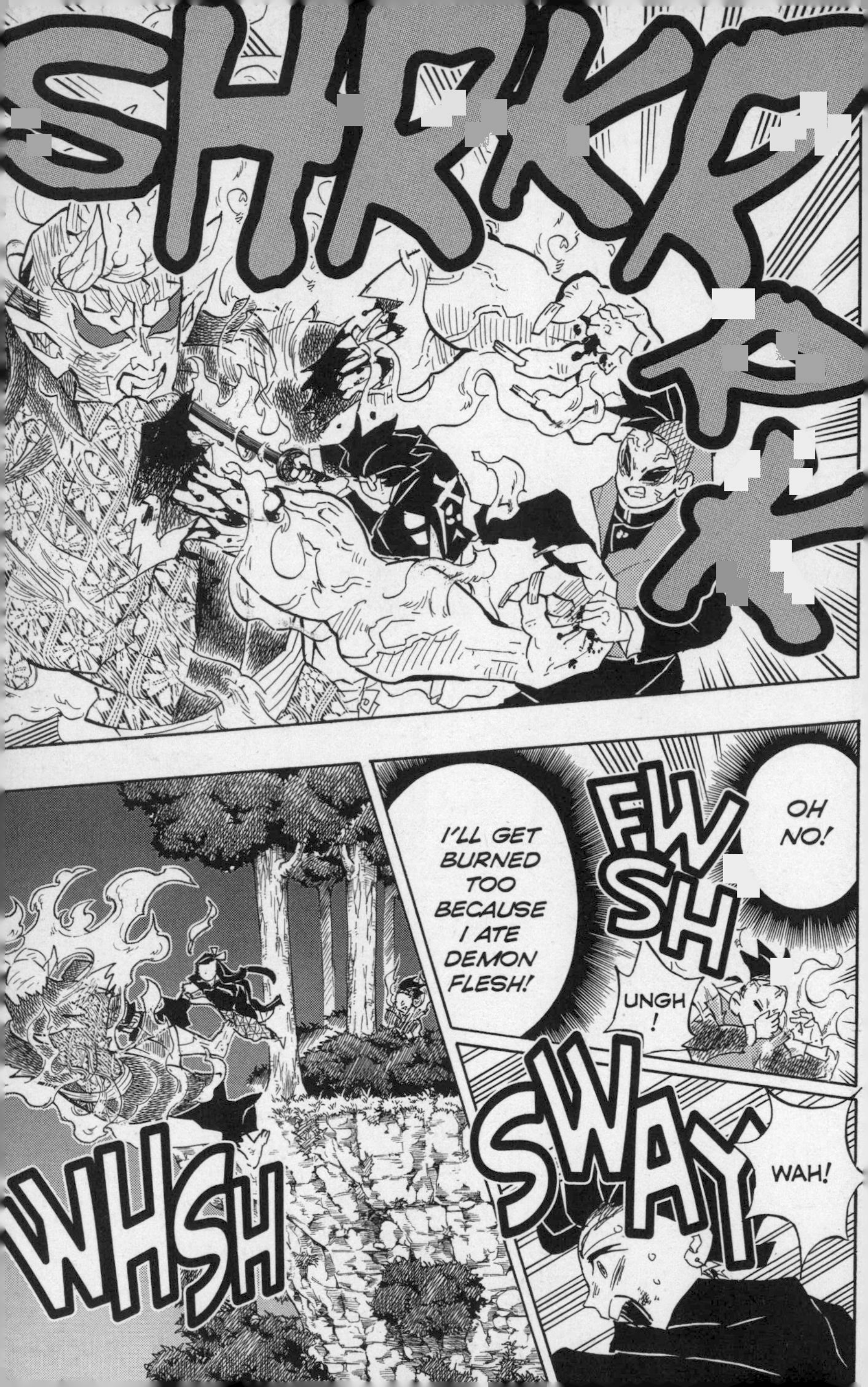
OH NO!
FWSH
I'LL GET BURNED TOO BECAUSE I ATE DEMON FLESH!
UNGH!
WAH!
SWAY
WHSH

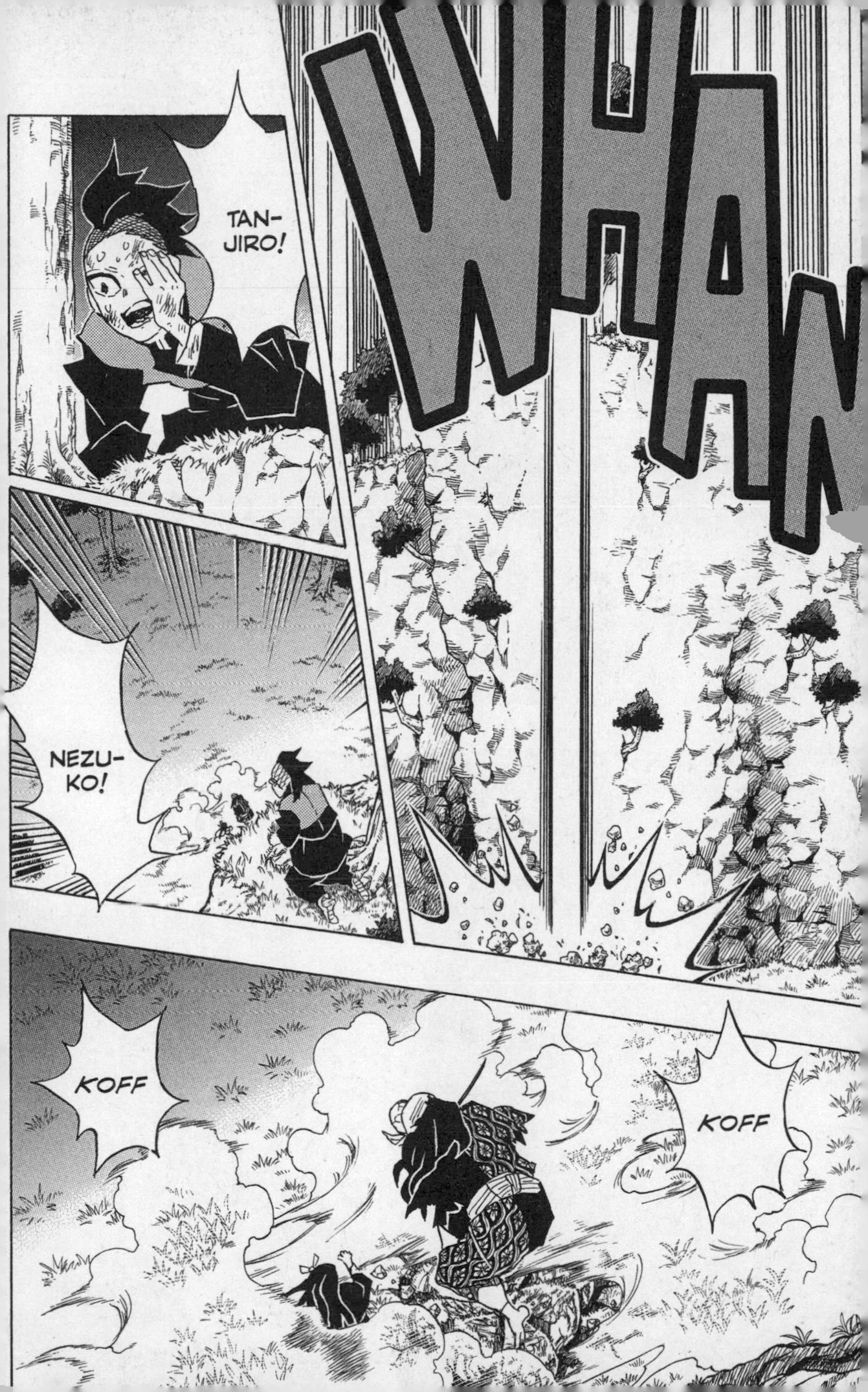
WHA
TAN-
JIRO!
NEZU-
KO!
KOFF
KOFF

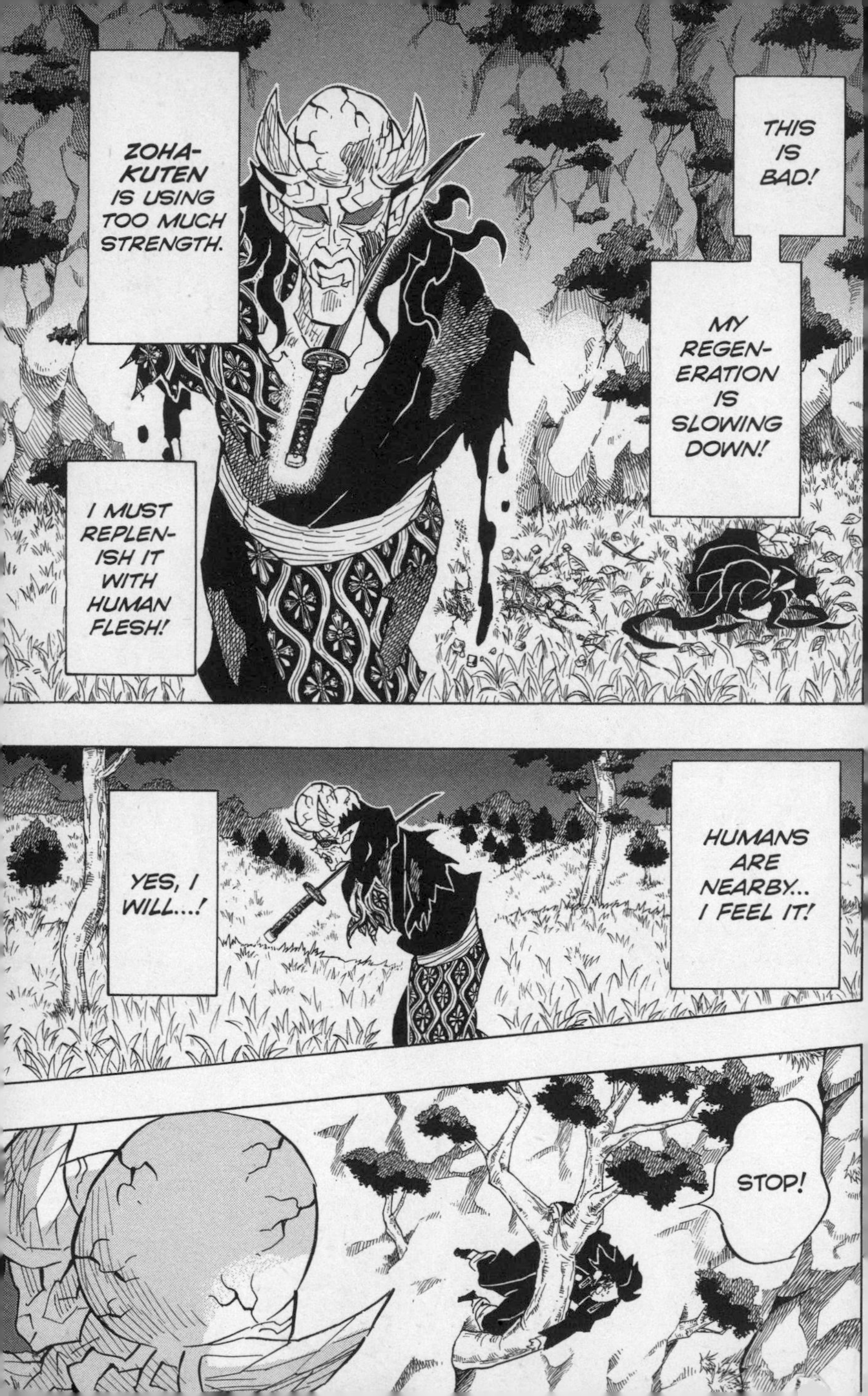
THIS IS BAD!
MY REGENERATION IS SLOWING DOWN!
ZOHAKUTEN IS USING TOO MUCH STRENGTH.
I MUST REPLENISH IT WITH HUMAN FLESH!
HUMANS ARE NEARBY... I FEEL IT!
YES, I WILL...!
STOP!

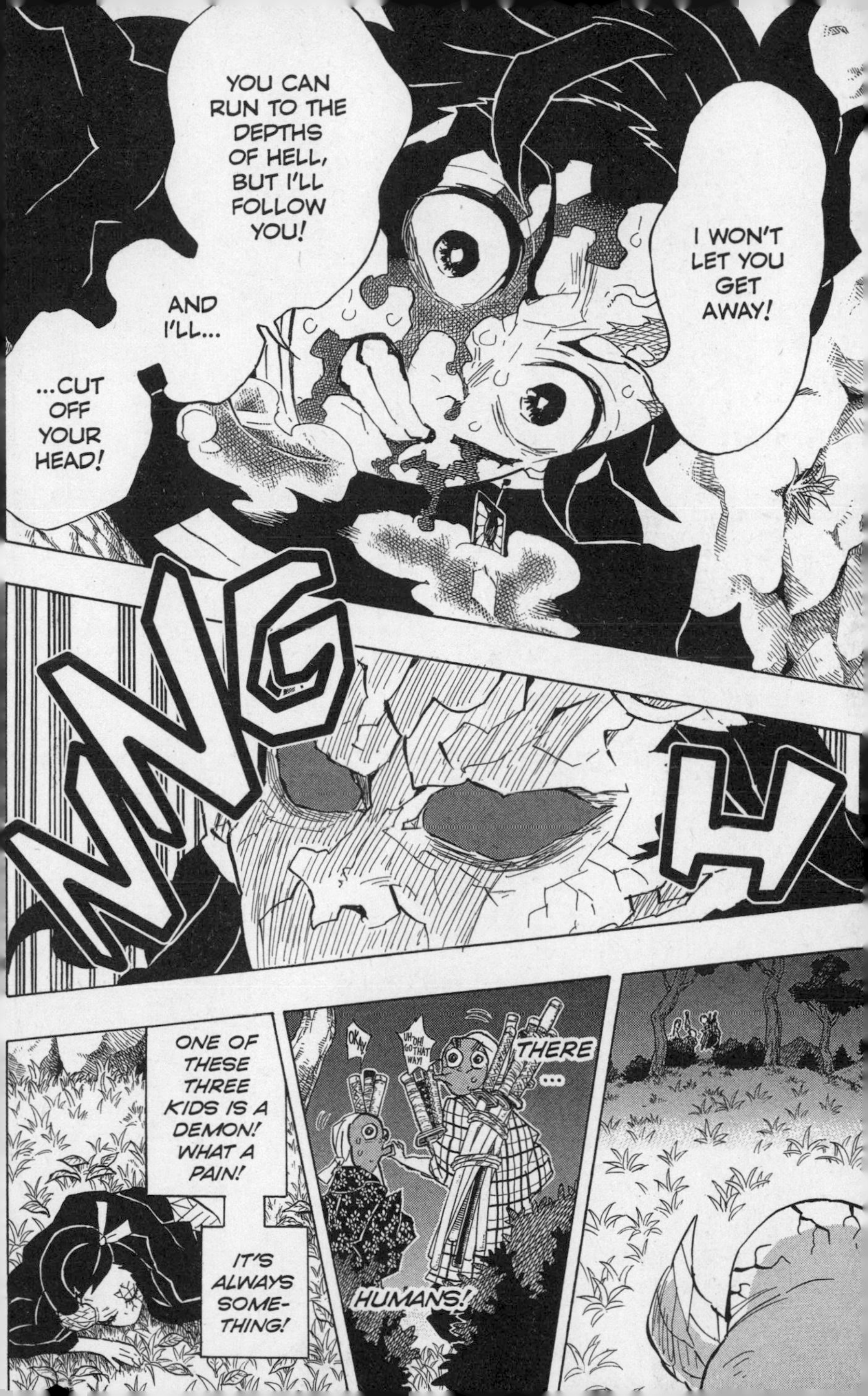
I WON'T LET YOU GET AWAY!
YOU CAN RUN TO THE DEPTHS OF HELL, BUT I'LL FOLLOW YOU!
AND I'LL...
...CUT OFF YOUR HEAD!
THERE...
UH OH! GO THAT WAY!
OKAY
HUMANS!
ONE OF THESE THREE KIDS IS A DEMON! WHAT A PAIN!
IT'S ALWAYS SOME-THING!

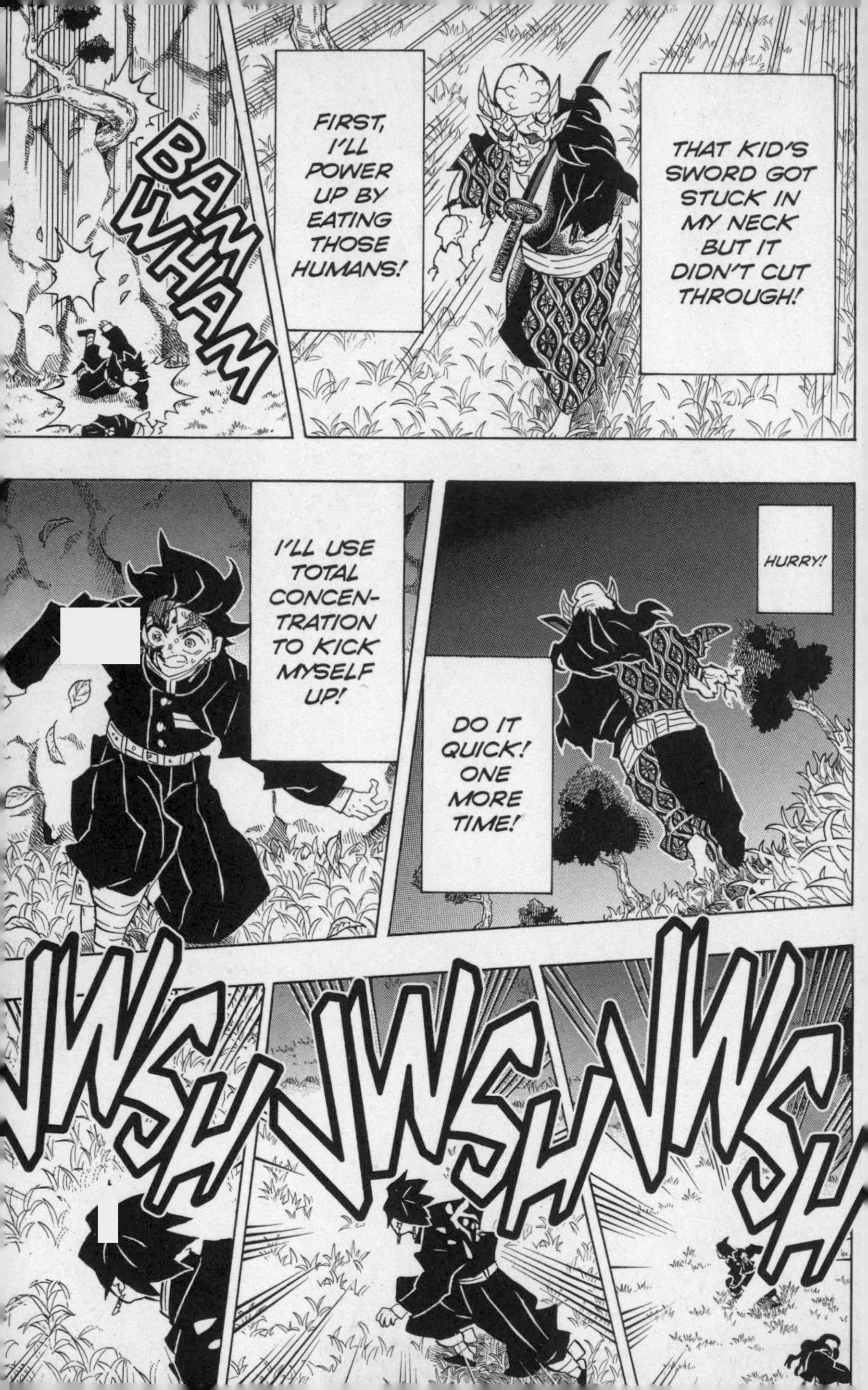
THAT KID'S SWORD GOT STUCK IN MY NECK BUT IT DIDN'T CUT THROUGH!
FIRST, I'LL POWER UP BY EATING THOSE HUMANS!
BAM WHAM
HURRY!
DO IT QUICK! ONE MORE TIME!
I'LL USE TOTAL CONCEN-TRATION TO KICK MYSELF UP!
WSH WSH WSH WSH

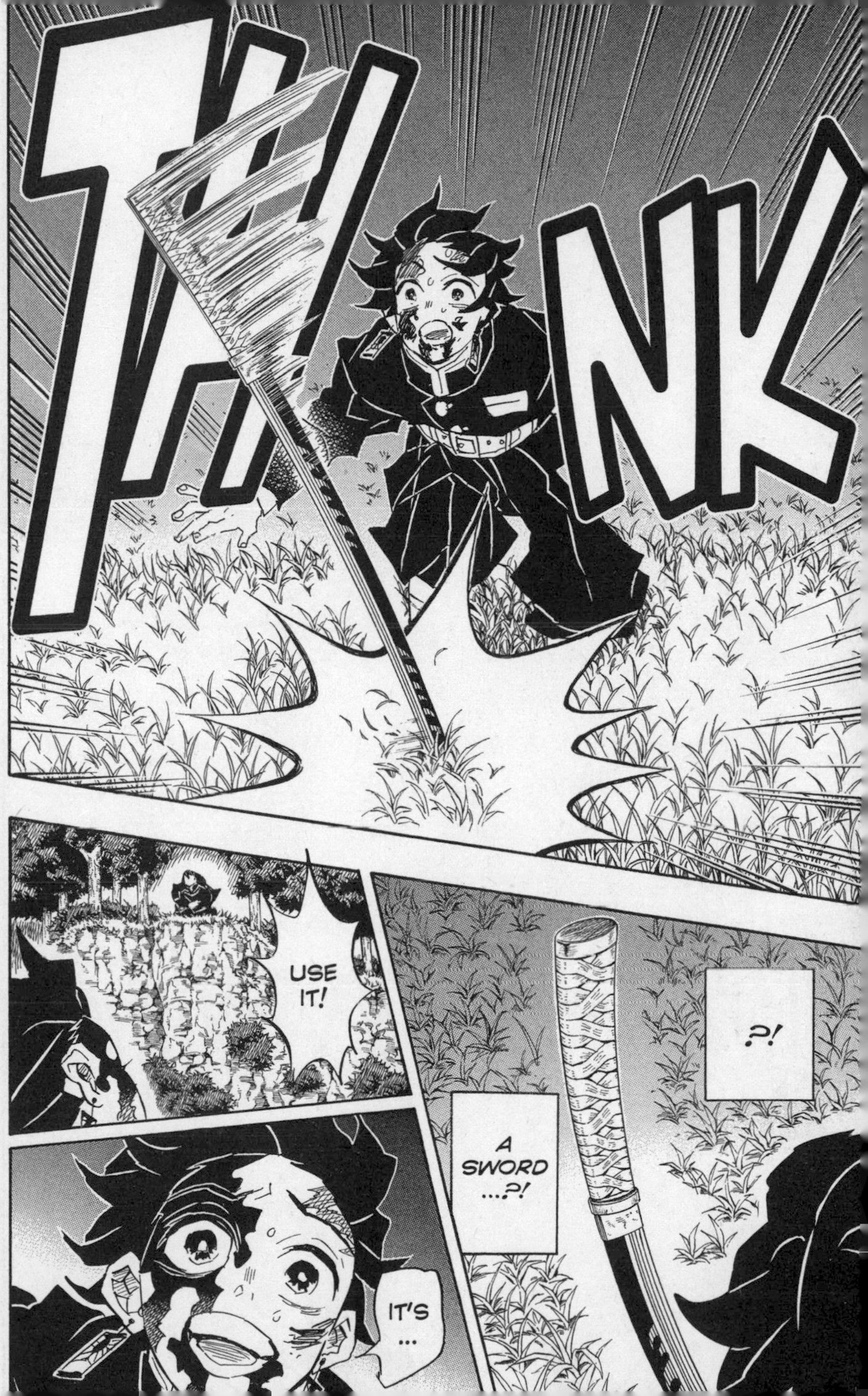
?!
A SWORD ...?!
USE IT!
IT'S ...

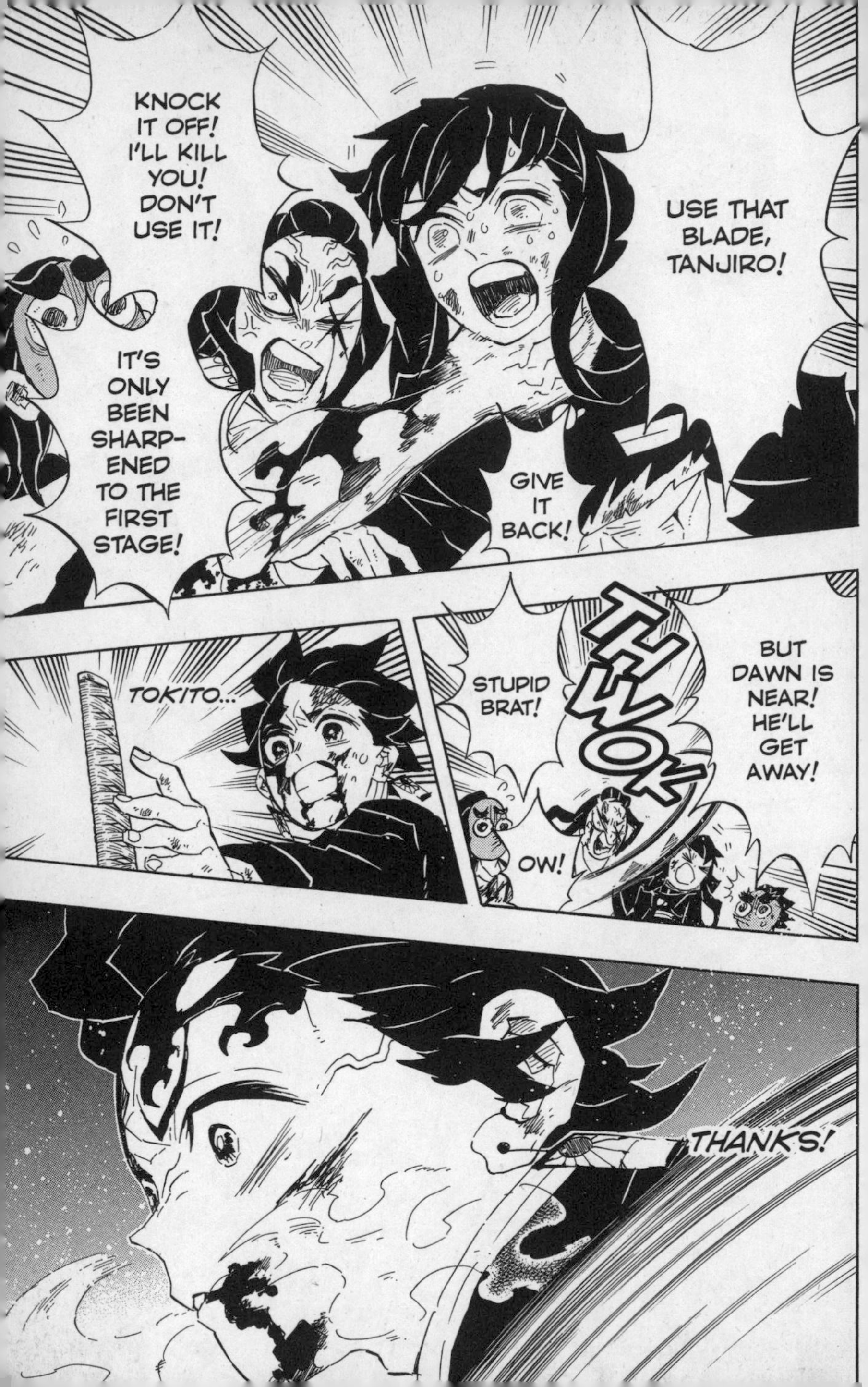
USE THAT BLADE, TANJIRO!
KNOCK IT OFF! I'LL KILL YOU! DON'T USE IT!
GIVE IT BACK!
IT'S ONLY BEEN SHARPENED TO THE FIRST STAGE!
BUT DAWN IS NEAR! HE'LL GET AWAY!
THWOK
STUPID BRAT!
OW!
TOKITO...
THANKS!

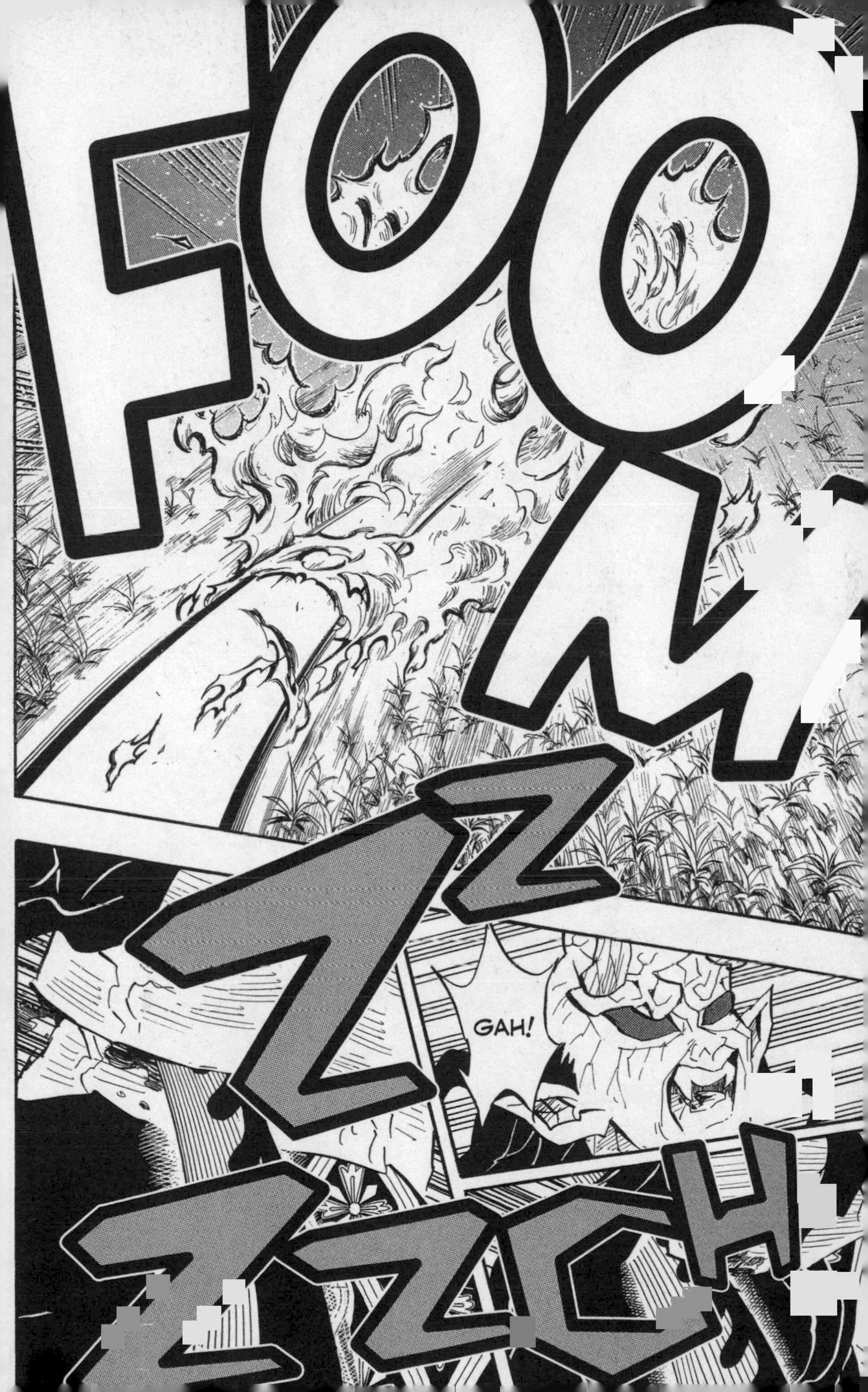
FOOM
ZZZZCH
GAH!

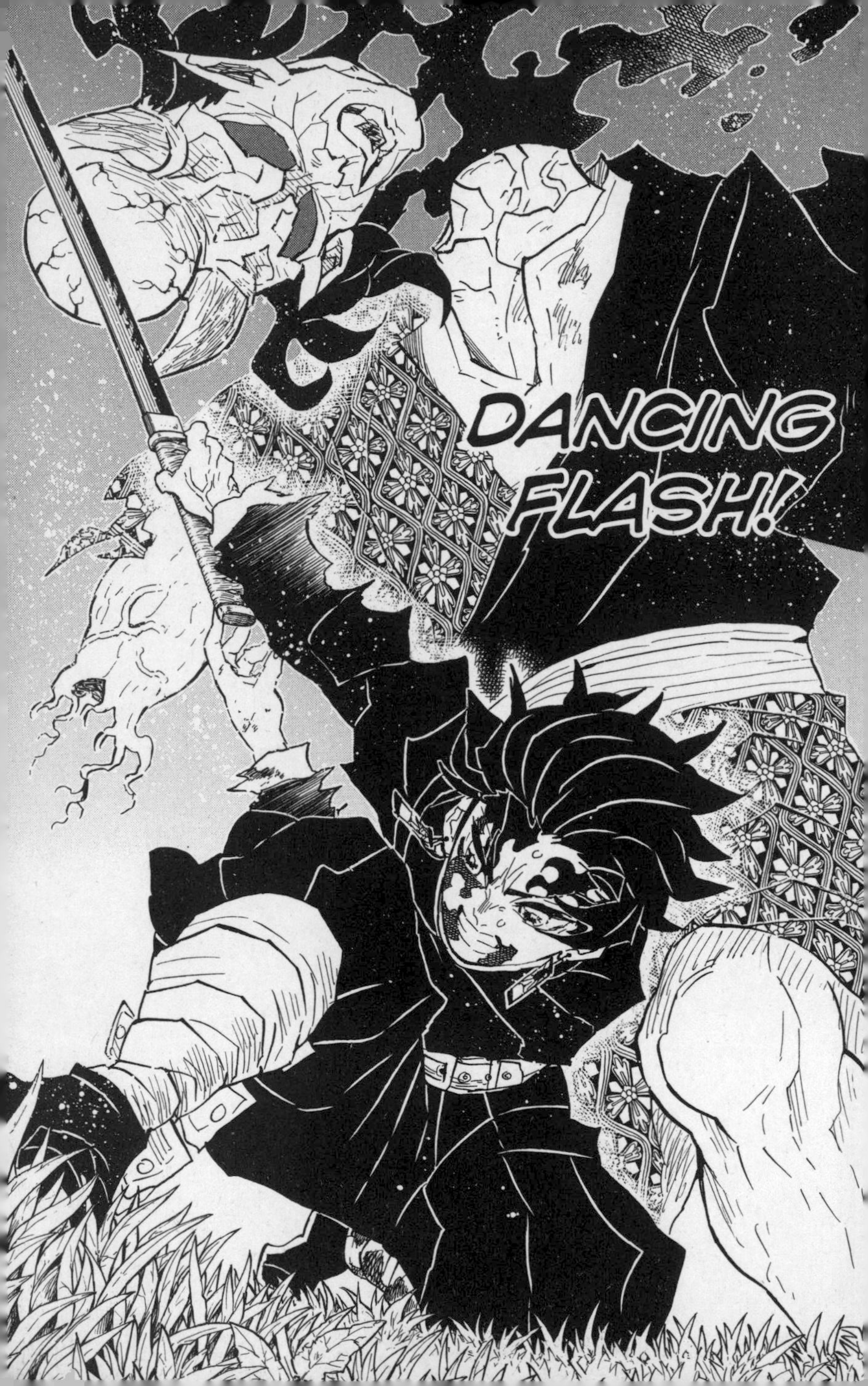
DANCING FLASH!

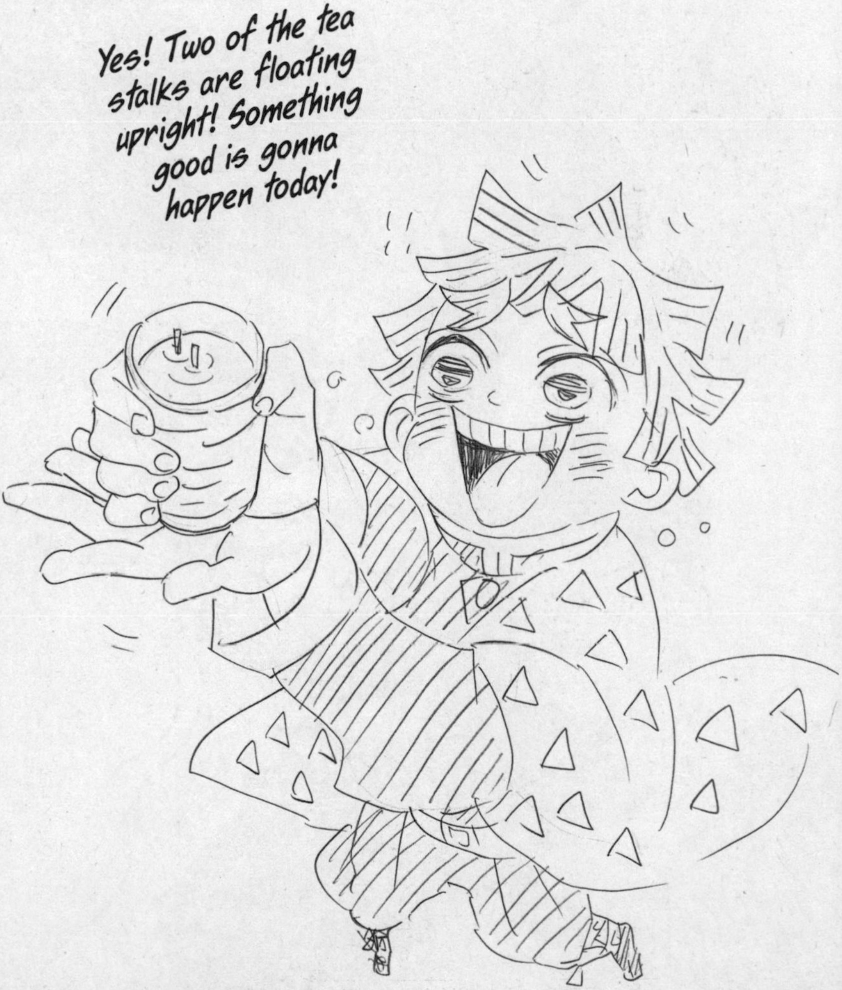
Yes! Two of the tea stalks are floating upright! Something good is gonna happen today!

CHAPTER 126: DAYBREAK AND FIRST LIGHT

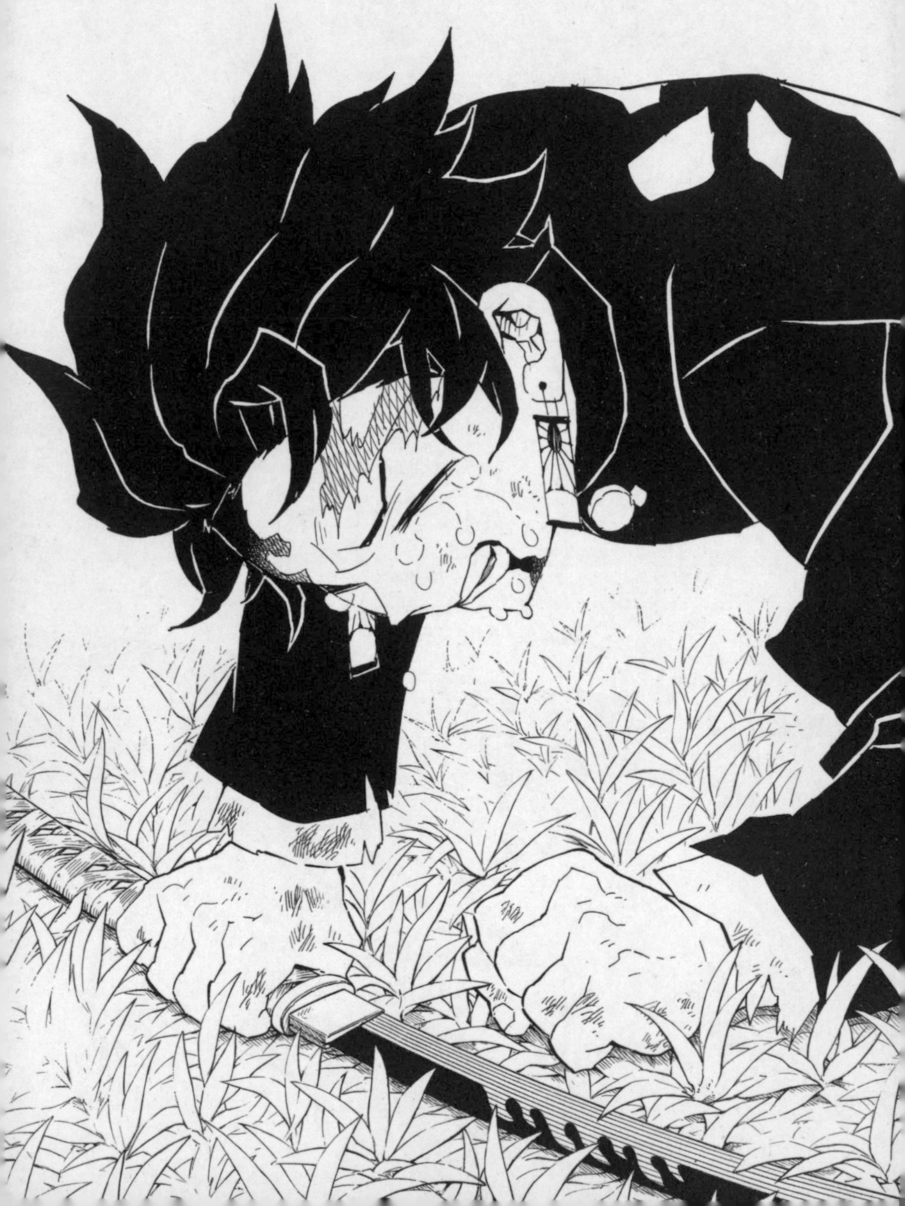

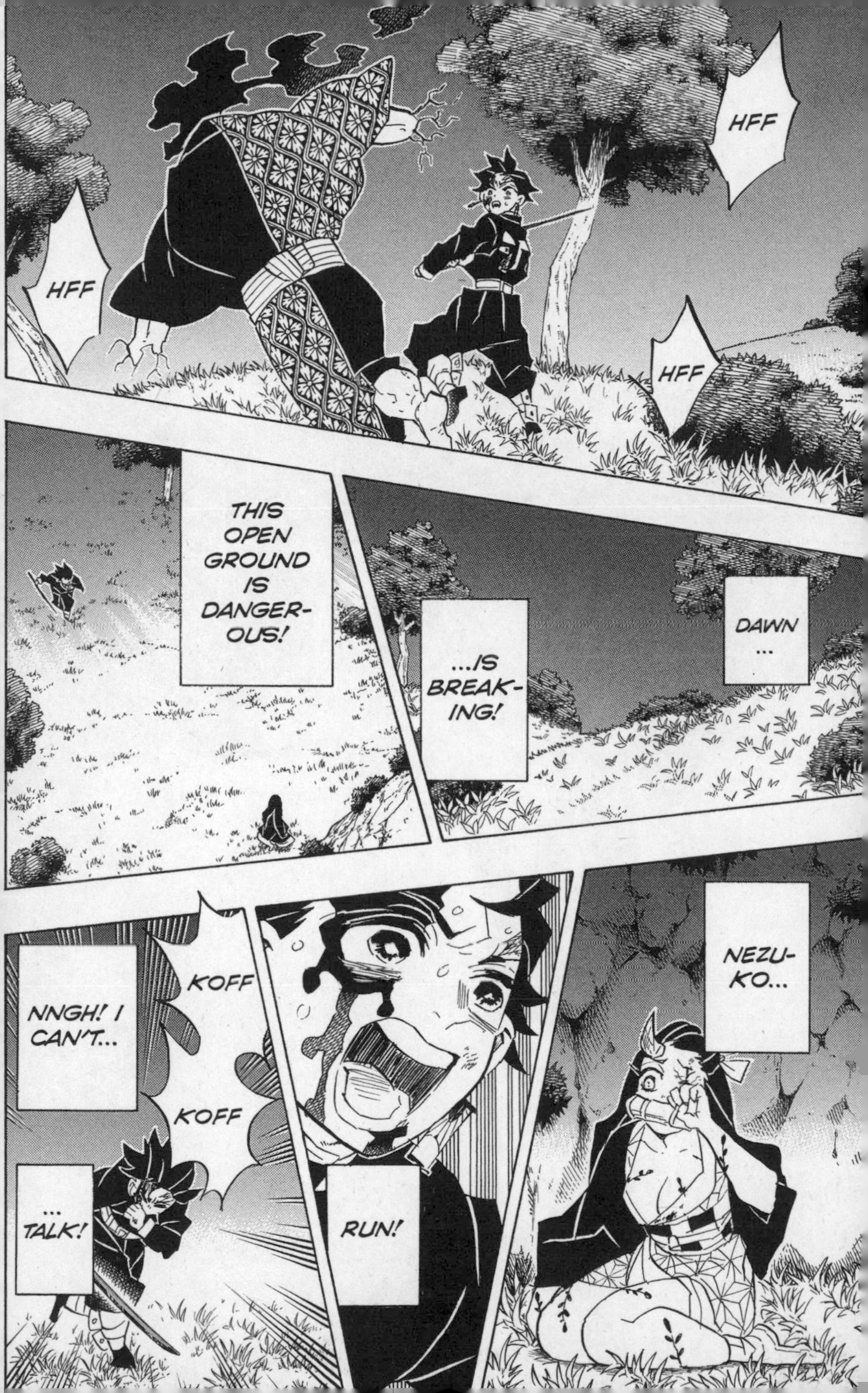
HFF
HFF
HFF
DAWN ...
...IS BREAK-ING!
THIS OPEN GROUND IS DANGER-OUS!
NEZU-KO...
RUN!
KOFF
NNGH! I CAN'T...
KOFF
... TALK!

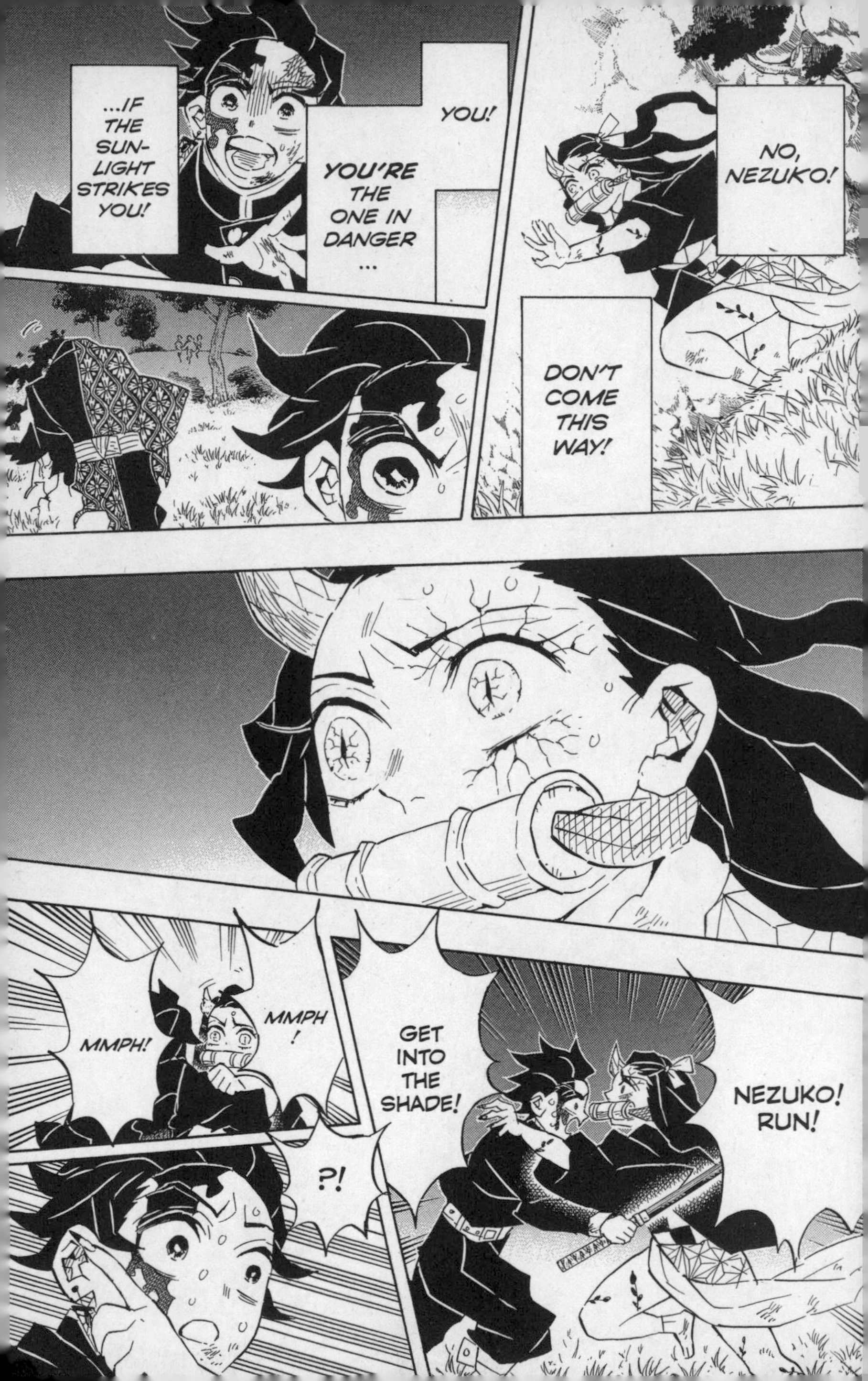
NO, NEZUKO!
DON'T COME THIS WAY!
YOU!
YOU'RE THE ONE IN DANGER ...
...IF THE SUN-LIGHT STRIKES YOU!
NEZUKO! RUN!
GET INTO THE SHADE!
MMPH!
MMPH!
?!

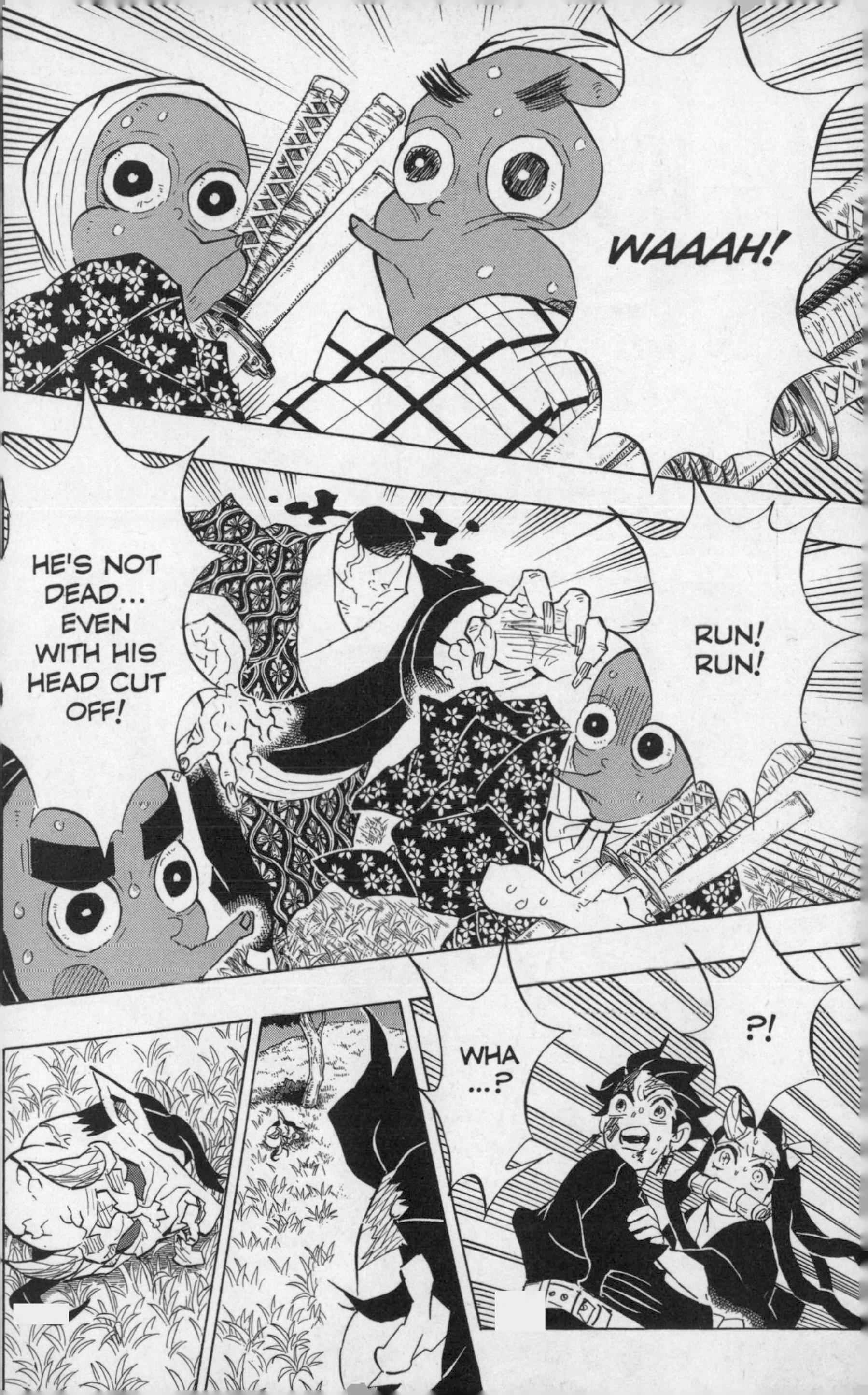
WAAAH!
RUN! RUN!
HE'S NOT DEAD... EVEN WITH HIS HEAD CUT OFF!
?!
WHA ...?

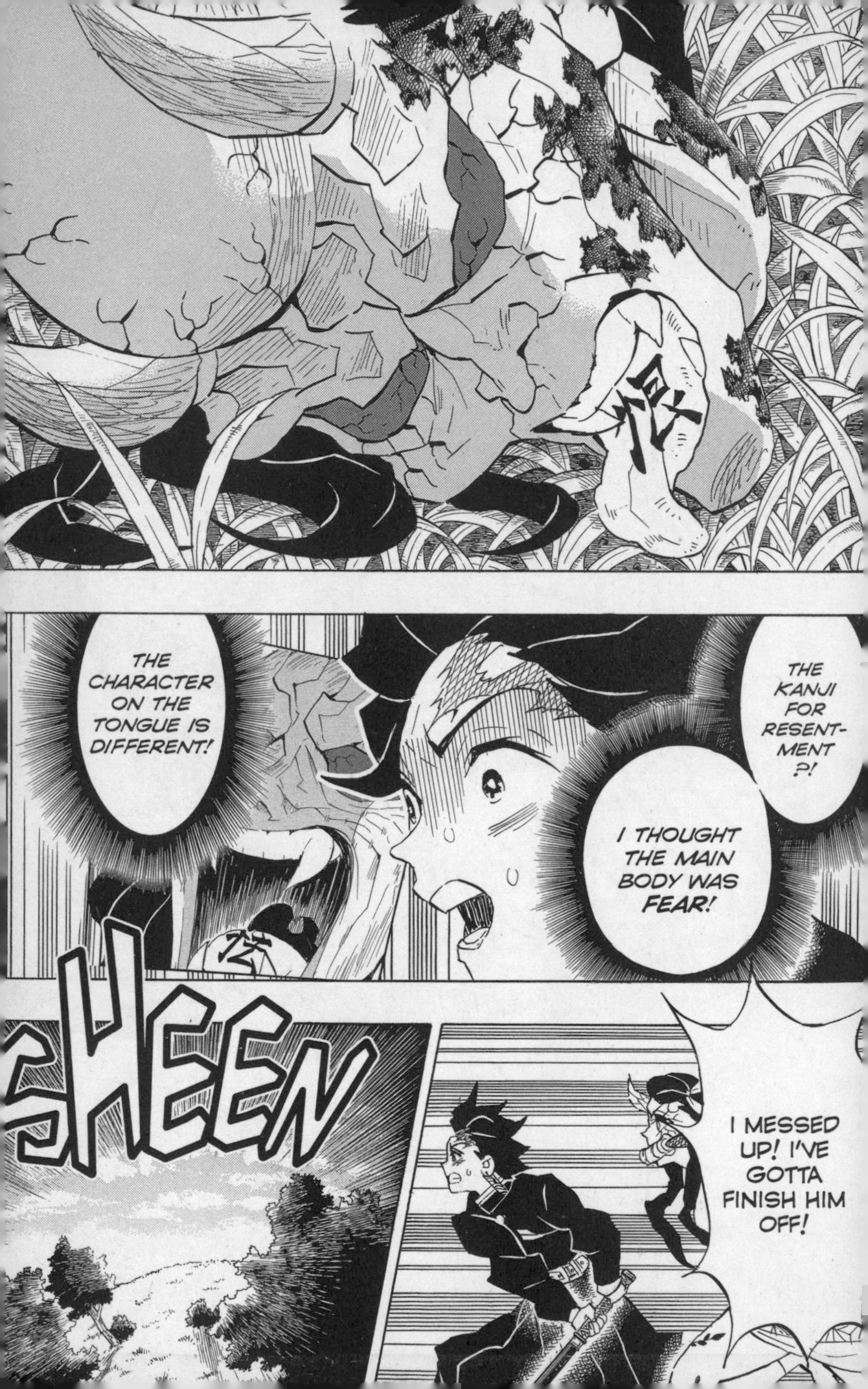
THE KANJI FOR RESENT-MENT ?!
I THOUGHT THE MAIN BODY WAS FEAR!
THE CHARACTER ON THE TONGUE IS DIFFERENT!
I MESSED UP! I'VE GOTTA FINISH HIM OFF!
SHEEN

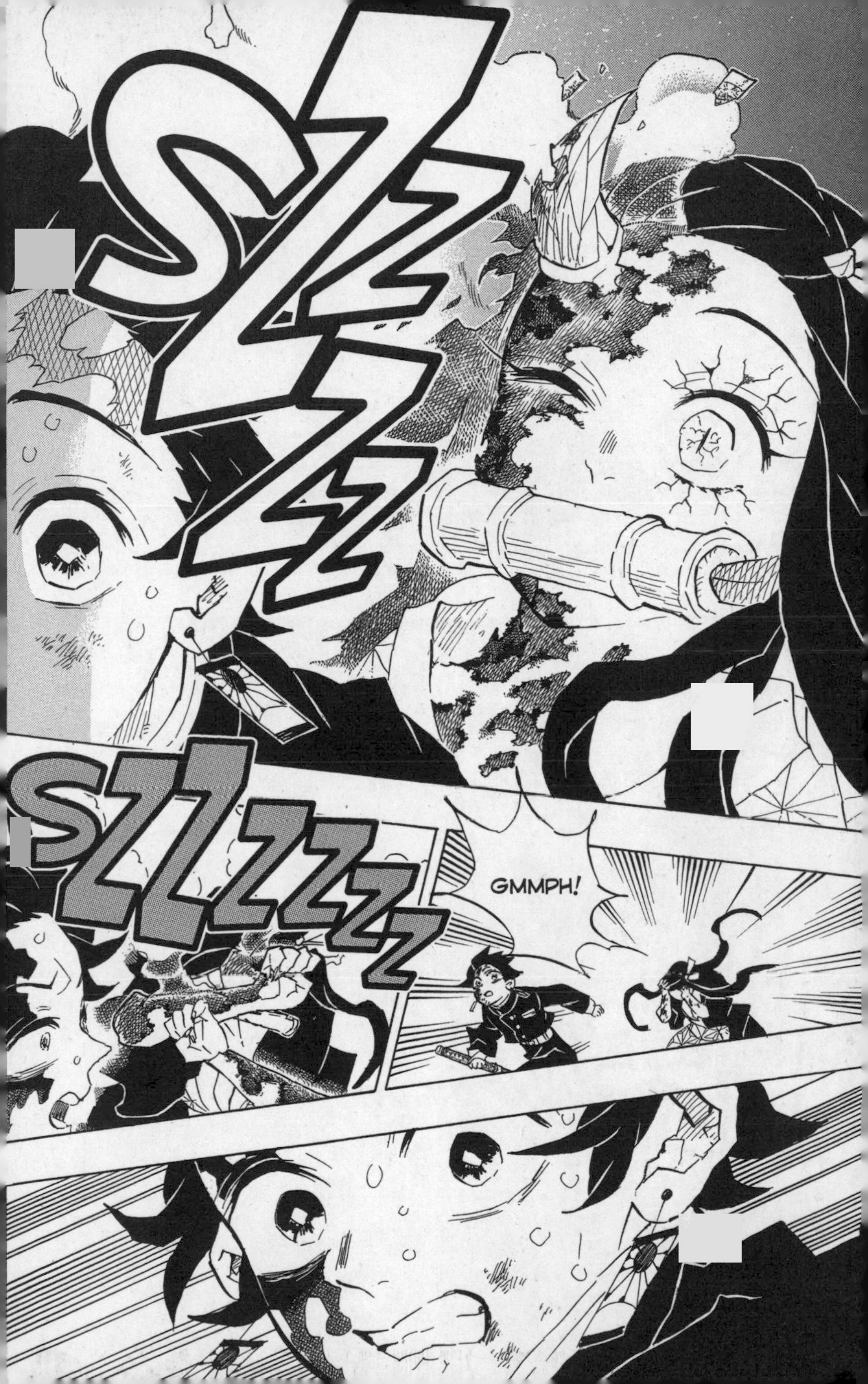
SIZZZZ
SIZZZZZ
GMMPH!

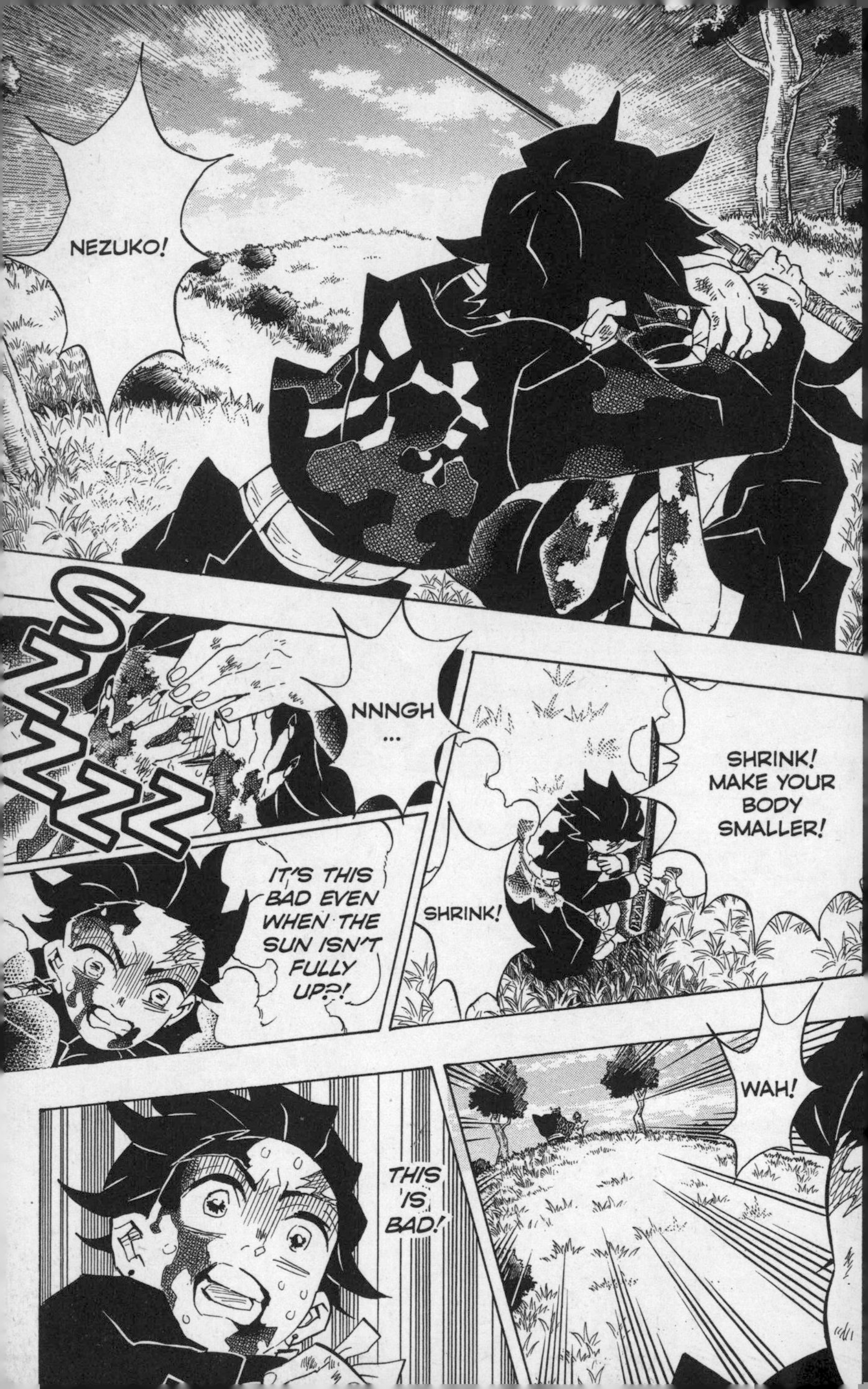
NEZUKO!
SHRINK! MAKE YOUR BODY SMALLER!
SHRINK!
NNNGH ...
IT'S THIS BAD EVEN WHEN THE SUN ISN'T FULLY UP?!
WAH!
THIS IS BAD!

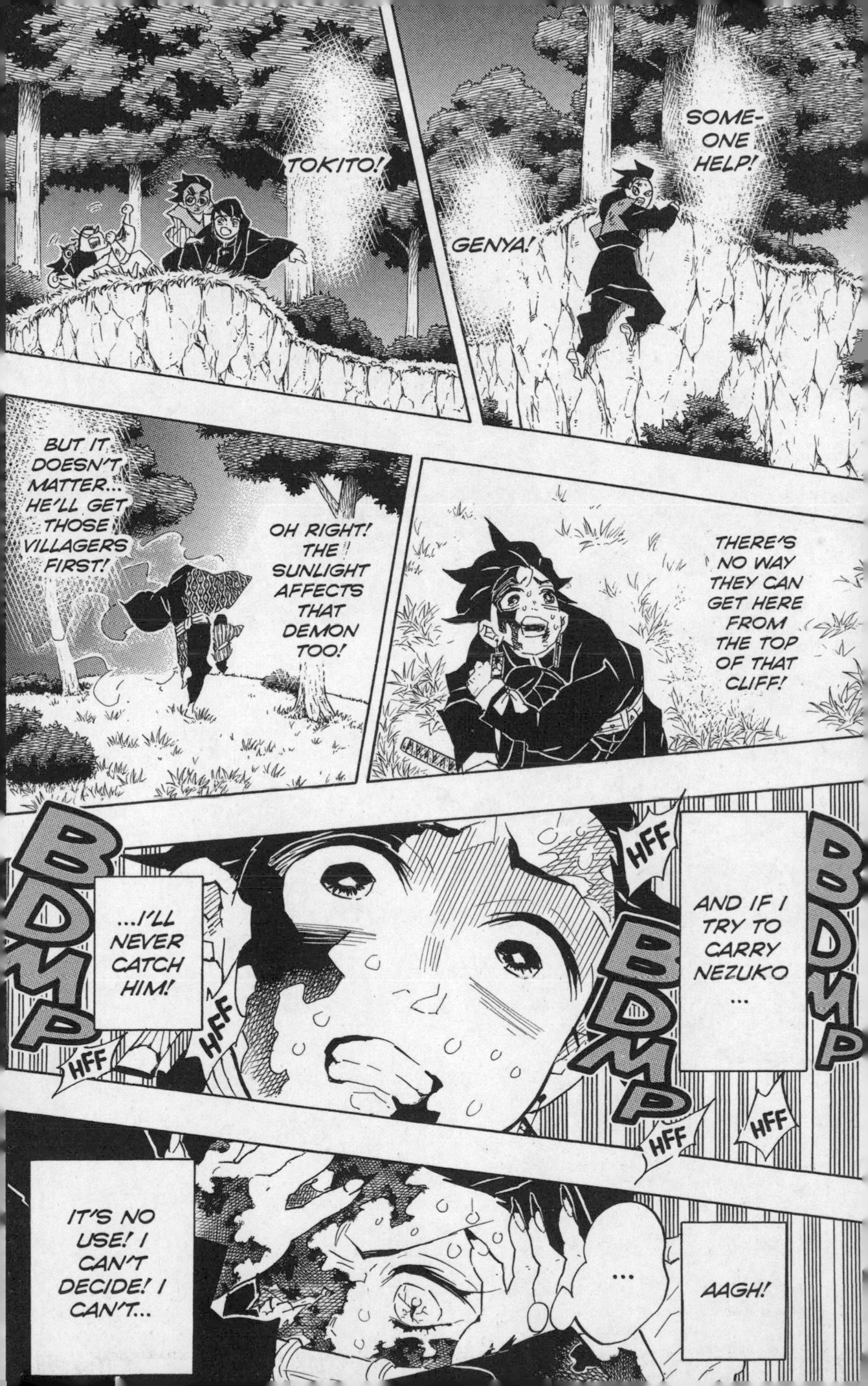
SOME-ONE HELP!
GENYA!
TOKITO!
THERE'S NO WAY THEY CAN GET HERE FROM THE TOP OF THAT CLIFF!
OH RIGHT! THE SUNLIGHT AFFECTS THAT DEMON TOO!
BUT IT DOESN'T MATTER... HE'LL GET THOSE VILLAGERS FIRST!
BDMP
AND IF I TRY TO CARRY NEZUKO ...
HFF
HFF
BDMP
HFF
HFF
...I'LL NEVER CATCH HIM!
HFF
HFF
BDMP
AAGH!
...
IT'S NO USE! I CAN'T DECIDE! I CAN'T...

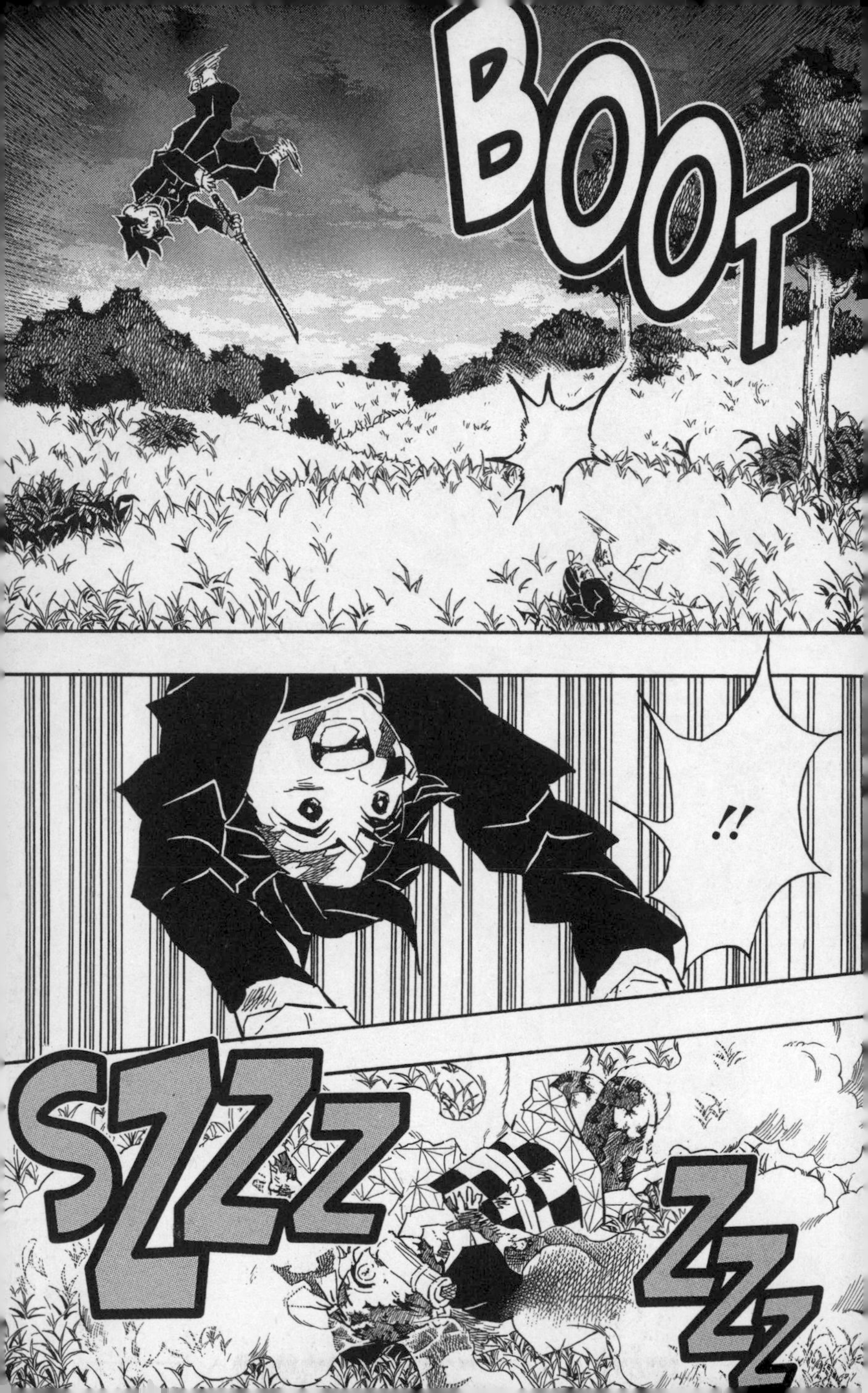
BOOT
!!
SZZZ
ZZZ

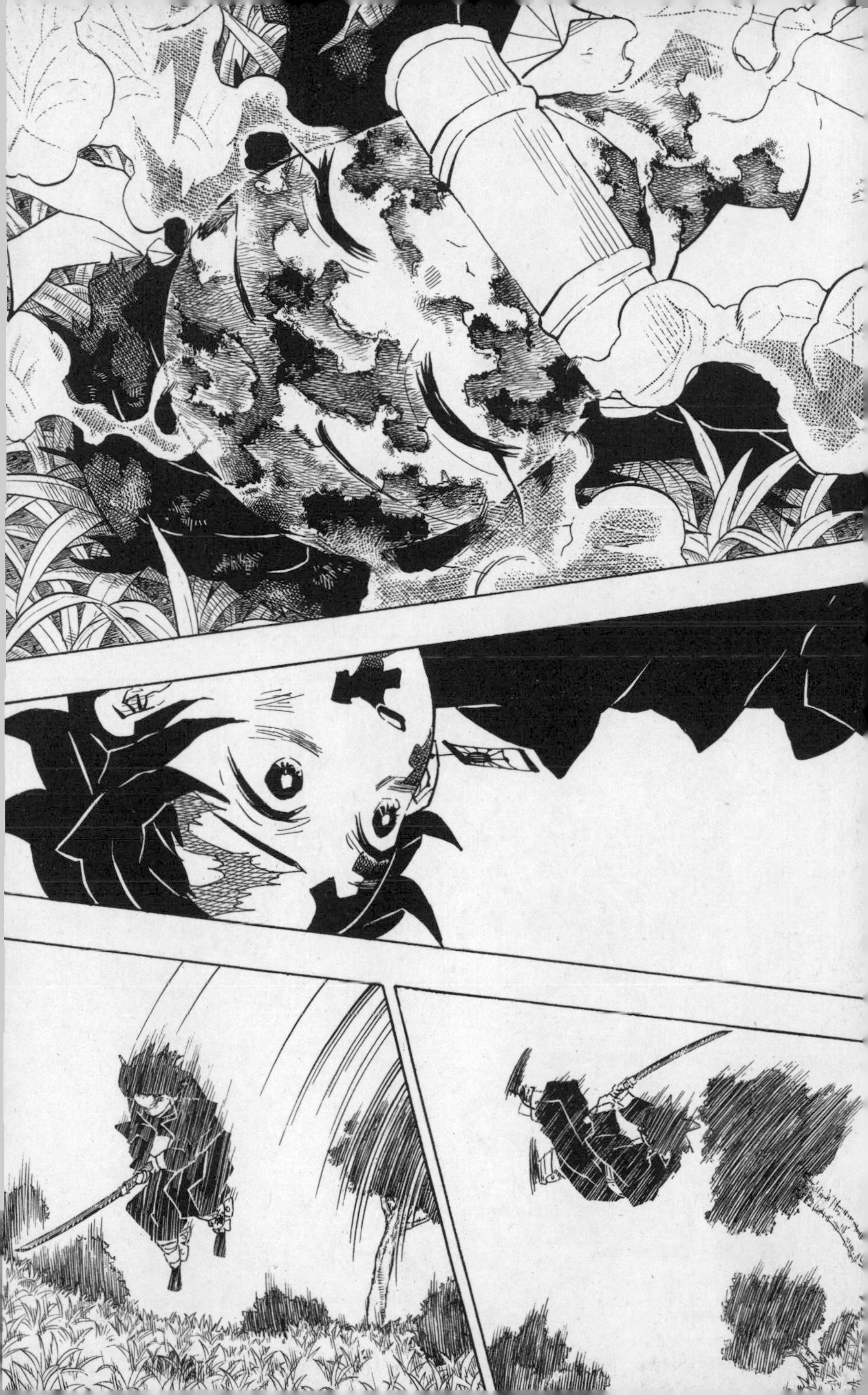

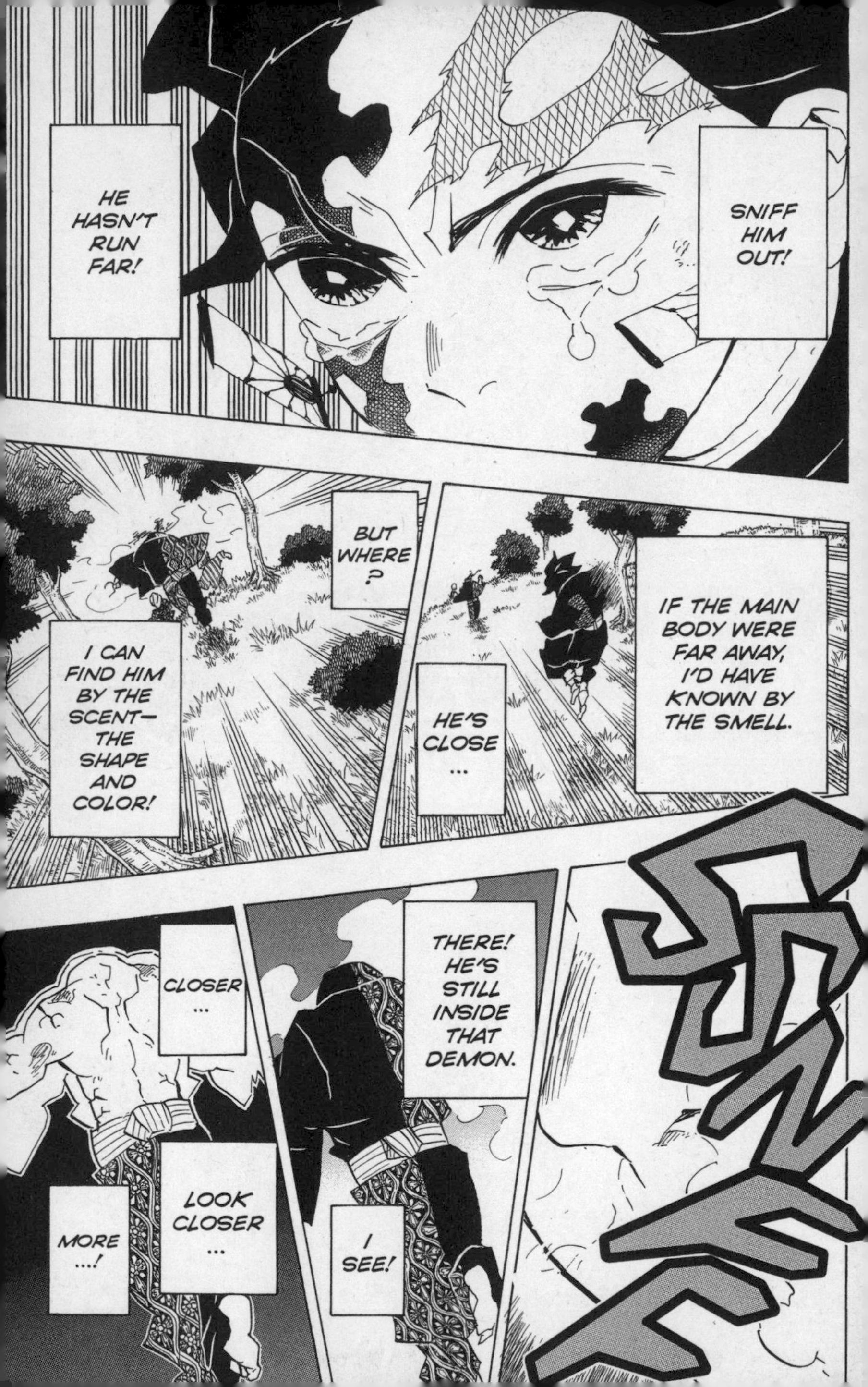
SNIFF HIM OUT!
HE HASN'T RUN FAR!
IF THE MAIN BODY WERE FAR AWAY, I'D HAVE KNOWN BY THE SMELL.
HE'S CLOSE ...
BUT WHERE?
I CAN FIND HIM BY THE SCENT—THE SHAPE AND COLOR!
THERE! HE'S STILL INSIDE THAT DEMON.
I SEE!
CLOSER ...
LOOK CLOSER ...
MORE ...!

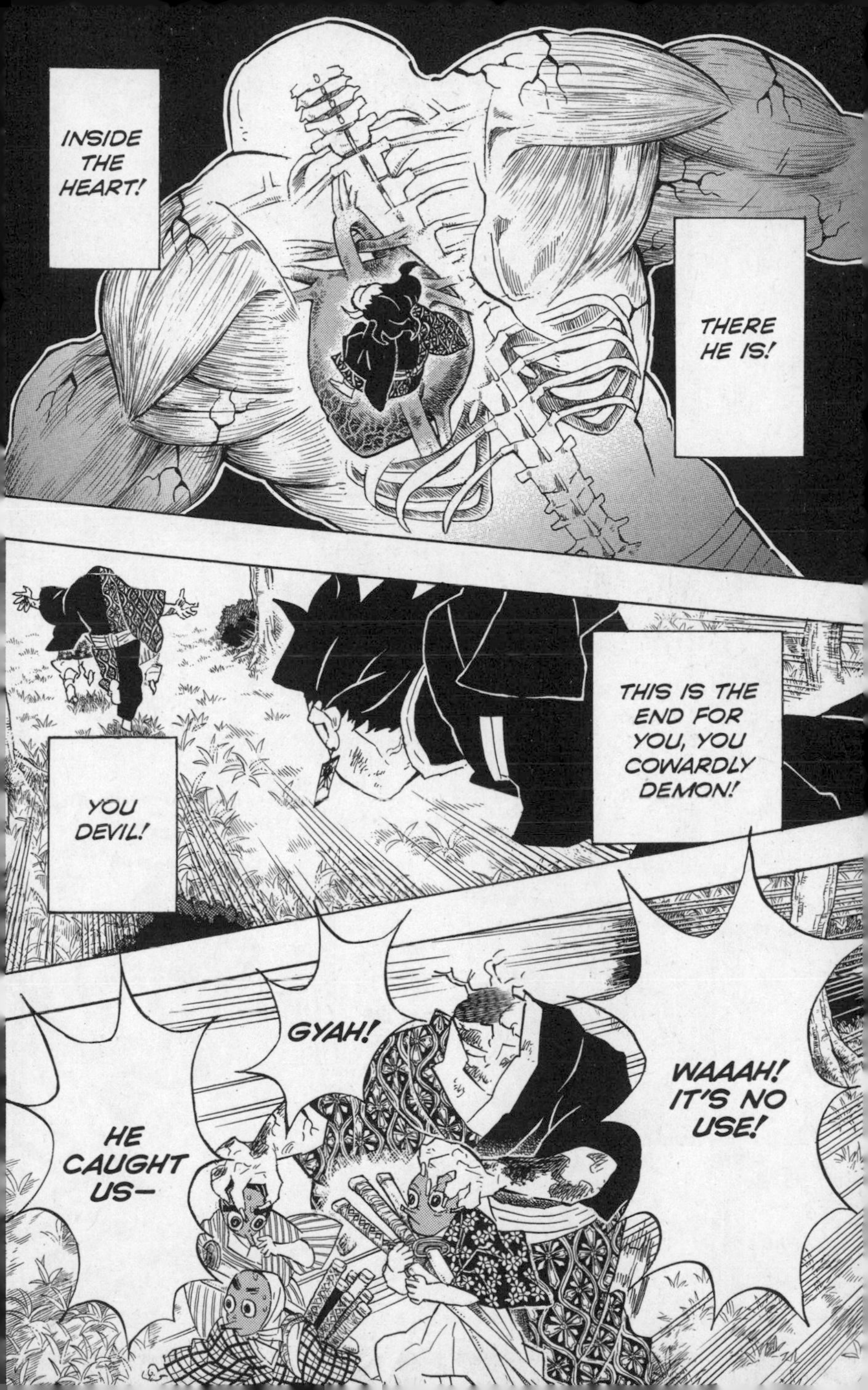
INSIDE THE HEART!
THERE HE IS!
THIS IS THE END FOR YOU, YOU COWARDLY DEMON!
YOU DEVIL!
WAAAH! IT'S NO USE!
GYAH!
HE CAUGHT US—

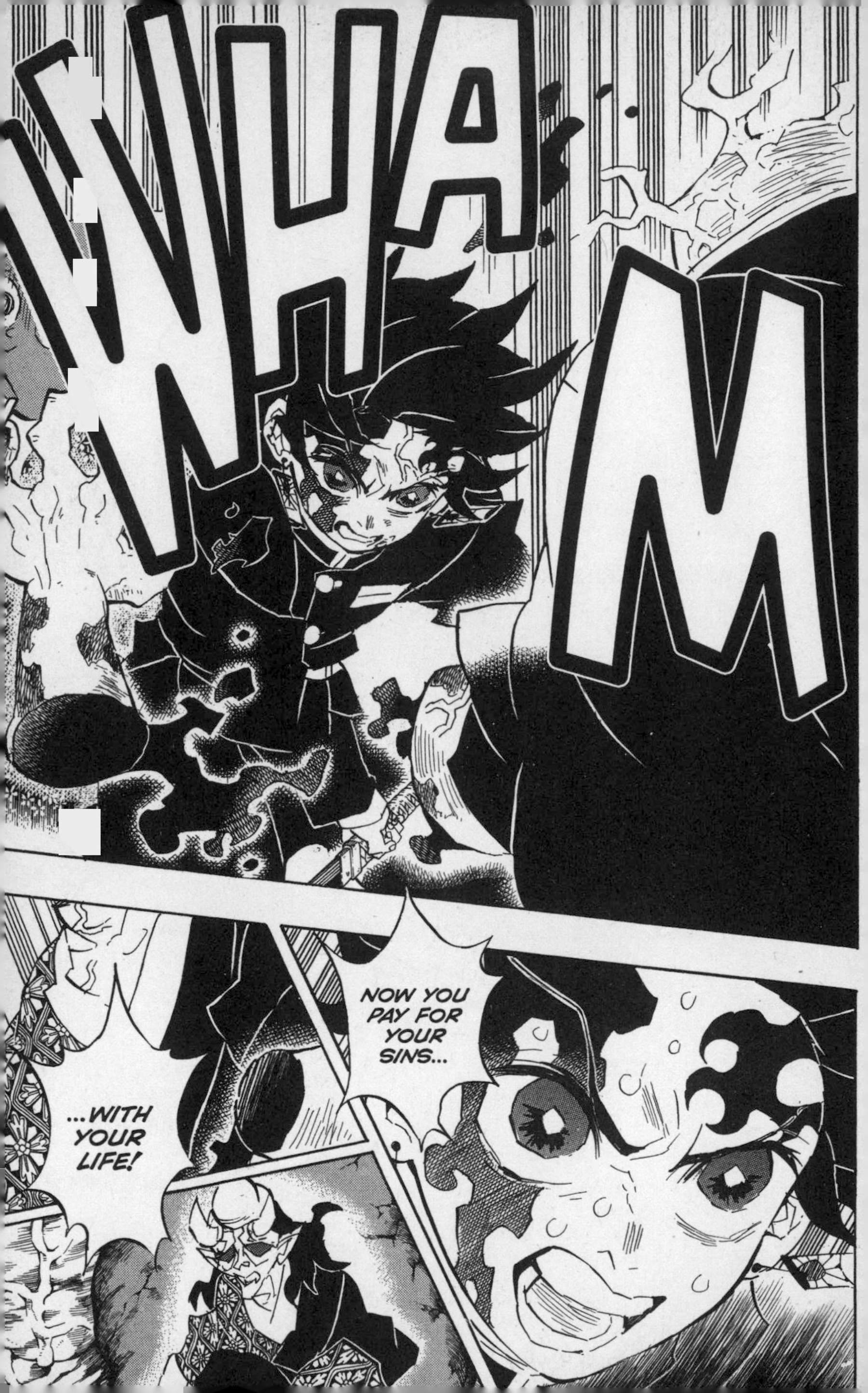
WHAM
NOW YOU PAY FOR YOUR SINS...
...WITH YOUR LIFE!

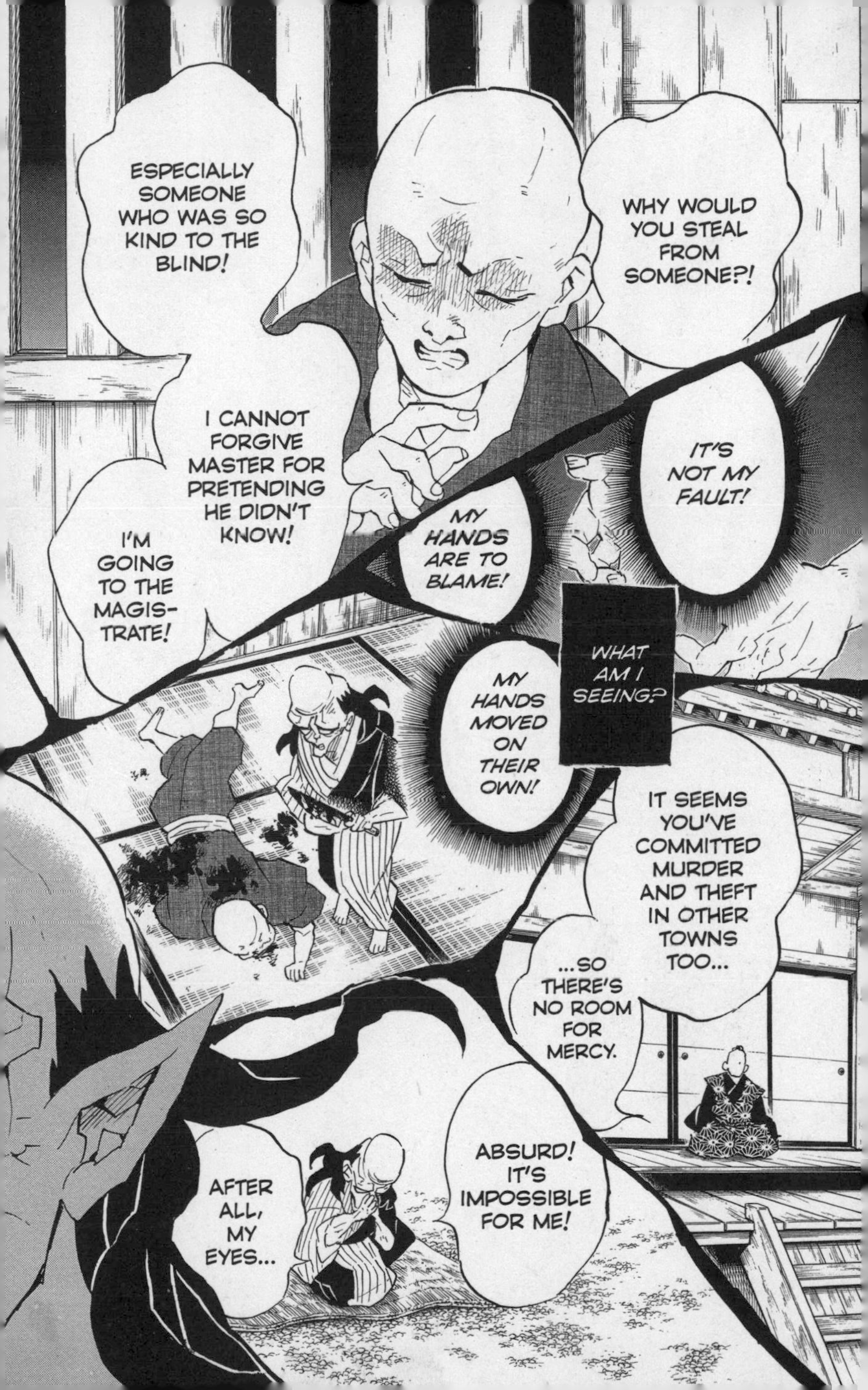
WHY WOULD YOU STEAL FROM SOMEONE?!
ESPECIALLY SOMEONE WHO WAS SO KIND TO THE BLIND!
I CANNOT FORGIVE MASTER FOR PRETENDING HE DIDN'T KNOW!
I'M GOING TO THE MAGISTRATE!
IT'S NOT MY FAULT!
MY HANDS ARE TO BLAME!
WHAT AM I SEEING?
MY HANDS MOVED ON THEIR OWN!
IT SEEMS YOU'VE COMMITTED MURDER AND THEFT IN OTHER TOWNS TOO...
...SO THERE'S NO ROOM FOR MERCY.
ABSURD! IT'S IMPOSSIBLE FOR ME!
AFTER ALL, MY EYES...

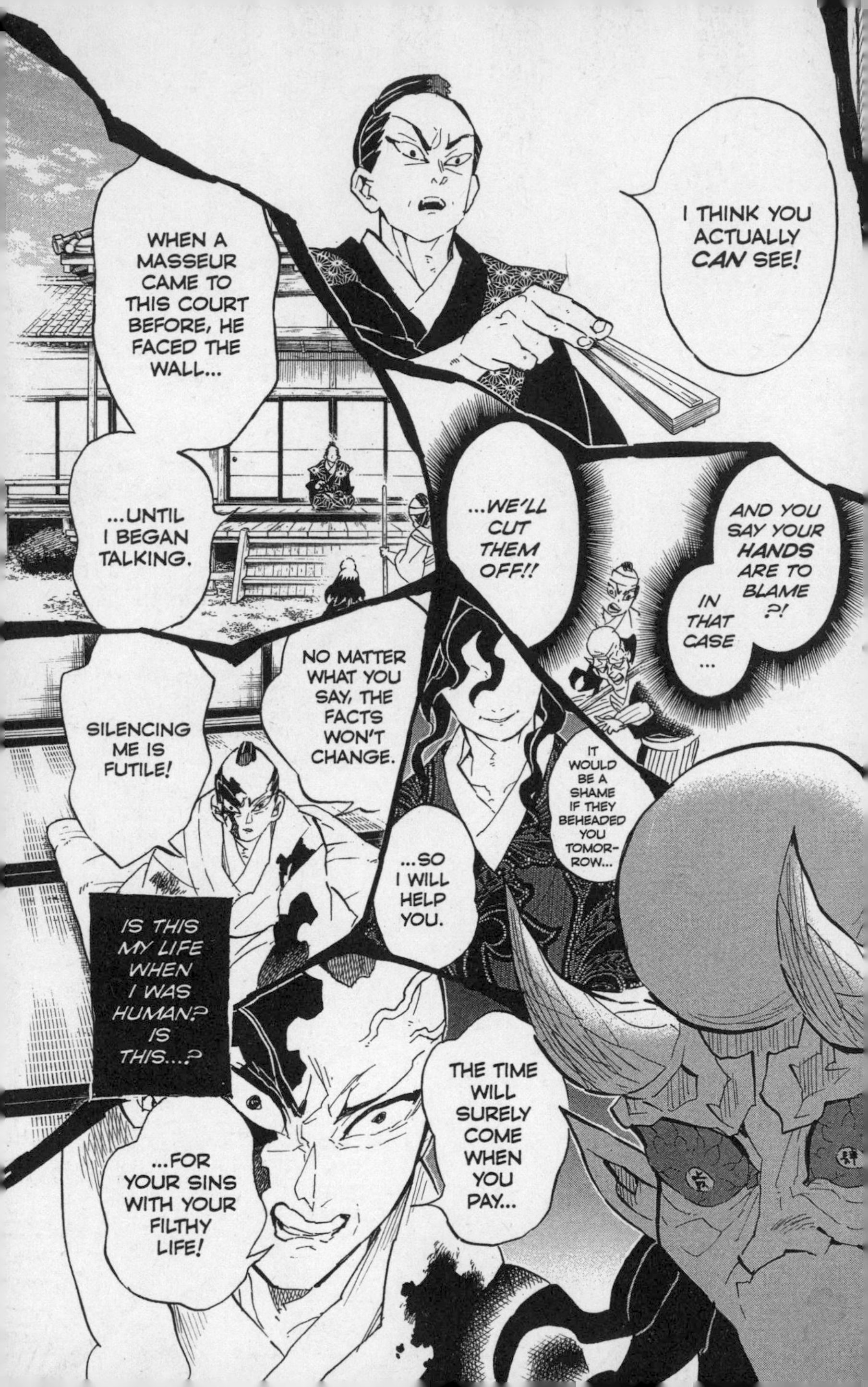
I THINK YOU ACTUALLY CAN SEE!
WHEN A MASSEUR CAME TO THIS COURT BEFORE, HE FACED THE WALL...
...UNTIL I BEGAN TALKING.
AND YOU SAY YOUR HANDS ARE TO BLAME ?!
IN THAT CASE ...
...WE'LL CUT THEM OFF!!
IT WOULD BE A SHAME IF THEY BEHEADED YOU TOMORROW...
...SO I WILL HELP YOU.
NO MATTER WHAT YOU SAY, THE FACTS WON'T CHANGE.
SILENCING ME IS FUTILE!
IS THIS MY LIFE WHEN I WAS HUMAN? IS THIS...?
THE TIME WILL SURELY COME WHEN YOU PAY...
...FOR YOUR SINS WITH YOUR FILTHY LIFE!

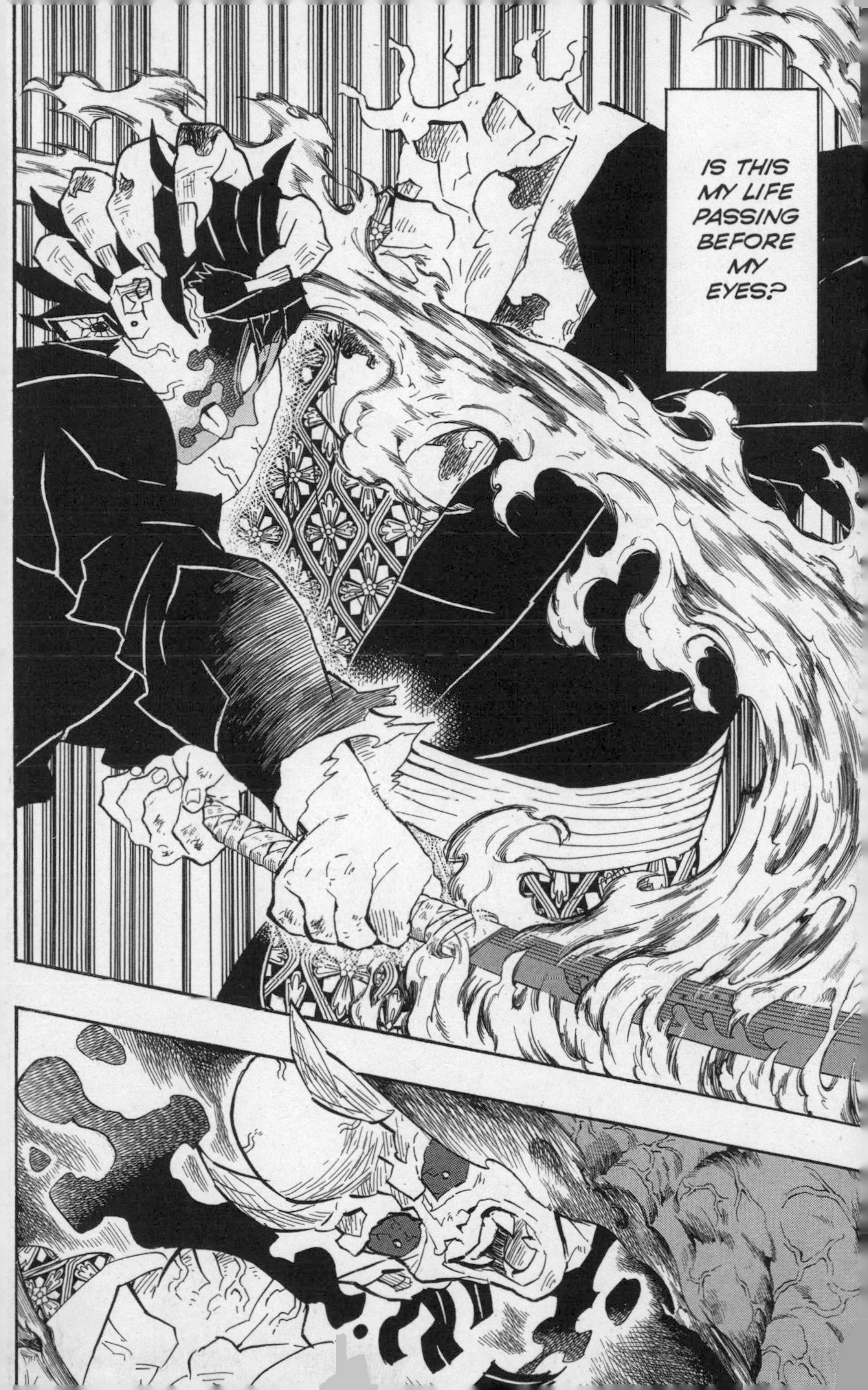
IS THIS MY LIFE PASSING BEFORE MY EYES?

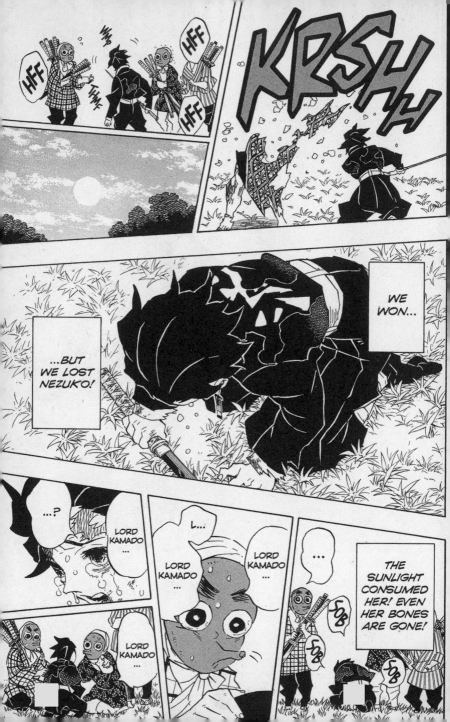

HFF
HFF
THME
HFF
HFF

KRSHH

WE WON...

...BUT WE LOST NEZUKO!

....?

LORD KAMADO...

L...

LORD KAMADO...

LORD KAMADO...

...

THE SUNLIGHT CONSUMED HER! EVEN HER BONES ARE GONE!

LORD KAMADO...

SOB

SOB

SOB

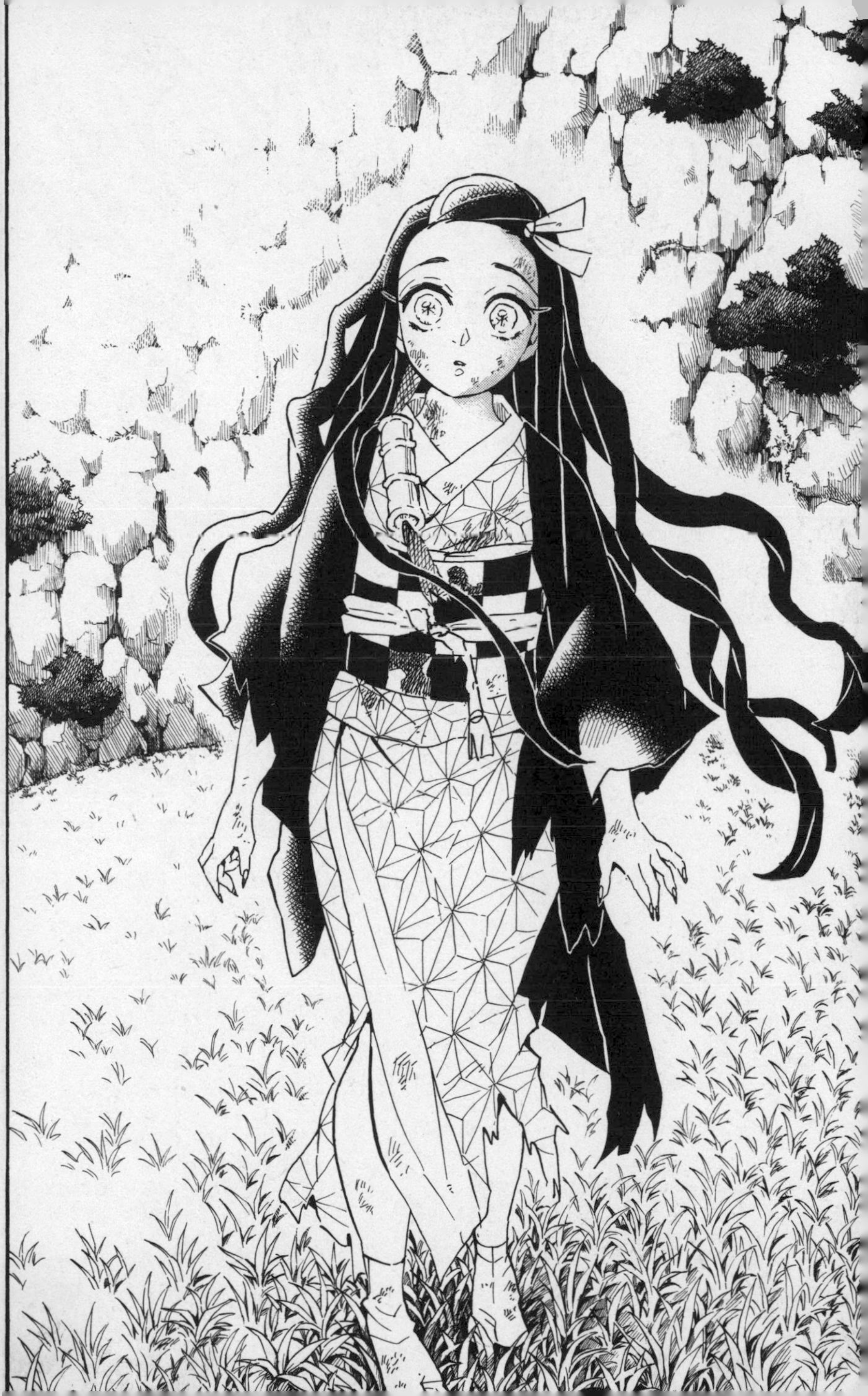

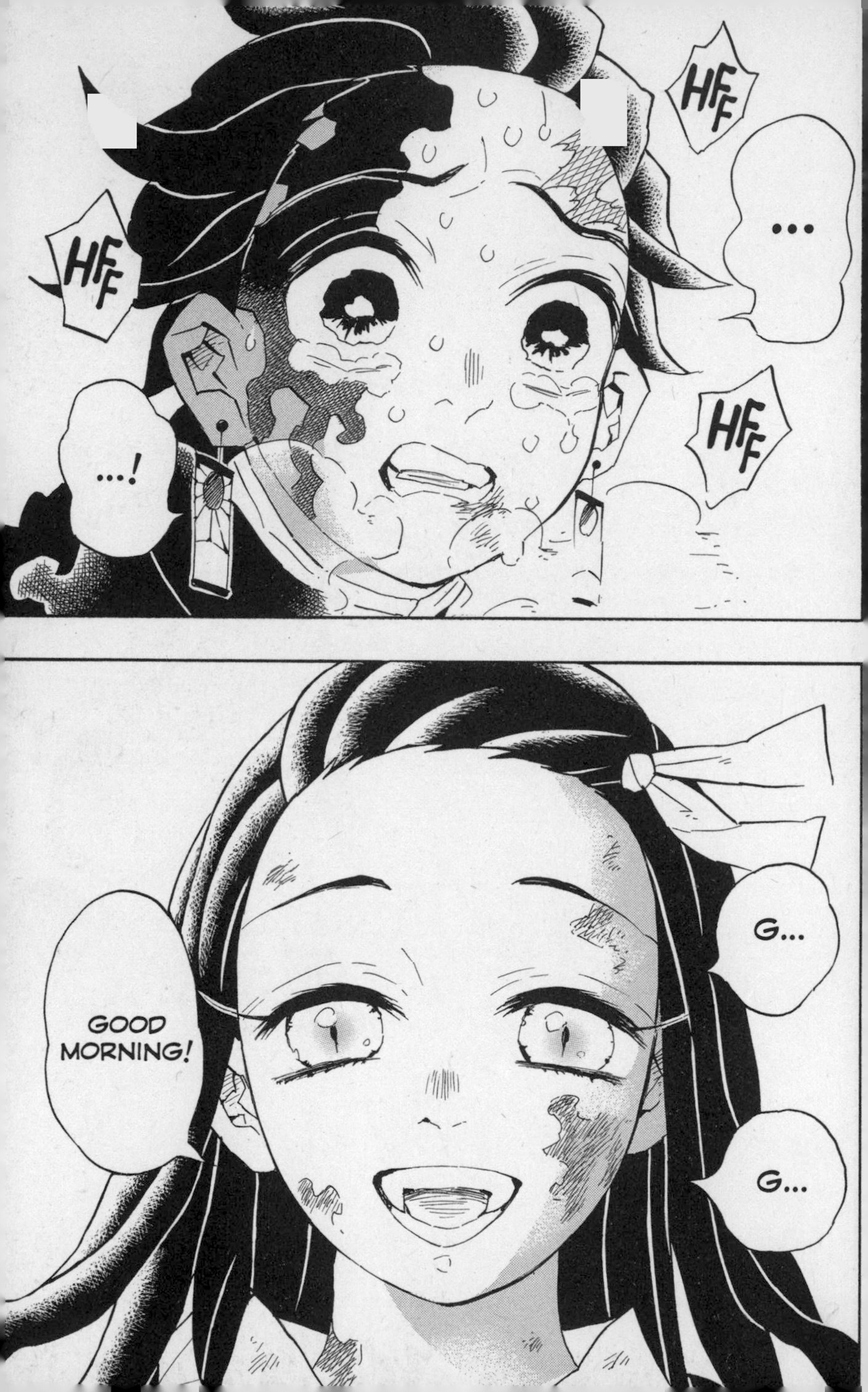
HFF
...
HFF
HFF
...!
G...
G...
GOOD MORNING!

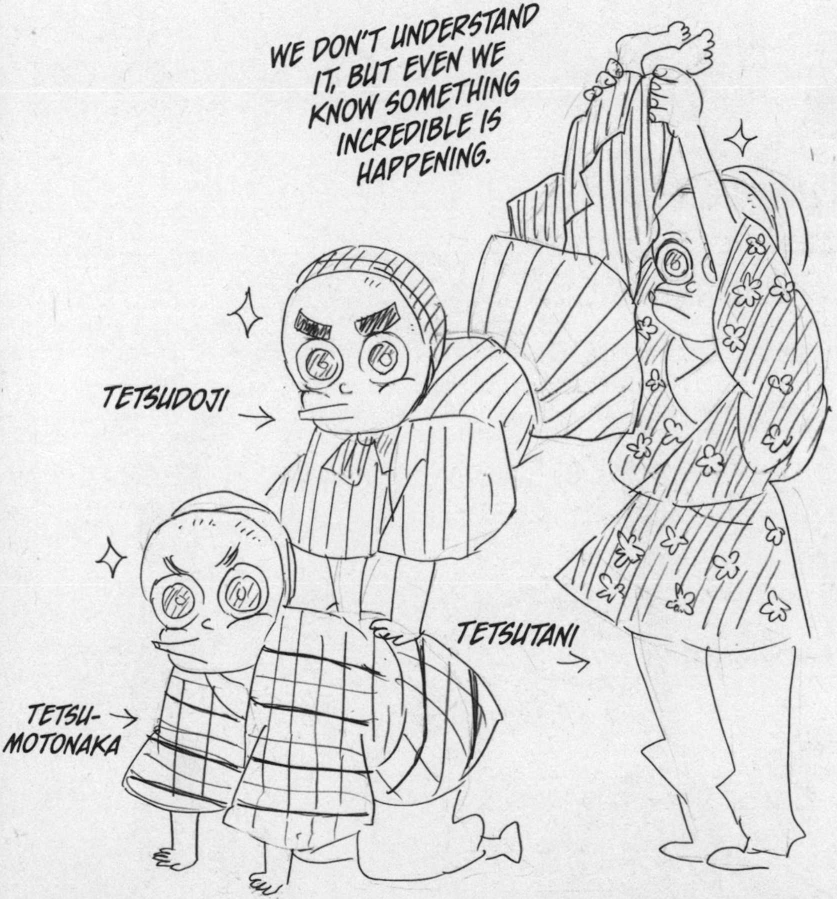
WE DON'T UNDERSTAND IT, BUT EVEN WE KNOW SOMETHING INCREDIBLE IS HAPPENING.
TETSUDOJI
TETSUTANI
TETSU-MOTONAKA

CHAPTER 127: THE RUMBLE OF VICTORY

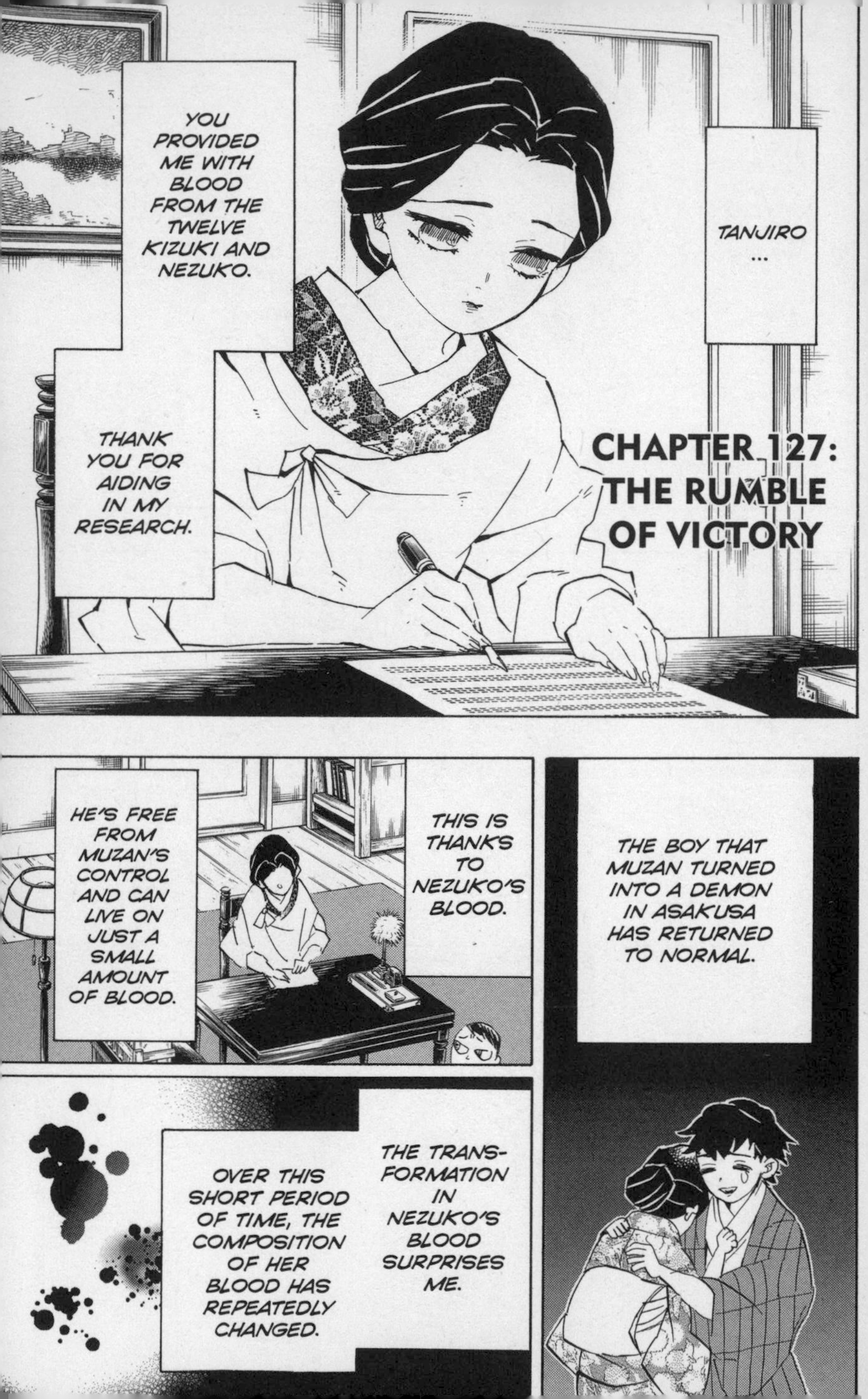
TANJIRO ...
YOU PROVIDED ME WITH BLOOD FROM THE TWELVE KIZUKI AND NEZUKO.
THANK YOU FOR AIDING IN MY RESEARCH.
THE BOY THAT MUZAN TURNED INTO A DEMON IN ASAKUSA HAS RETURNED TO NORMAL.
THIS IS THANKS TO NEZUKO'S BLOOD.
HE'S FREE FROM MUZAN'S CONTROL AND CAN LIVE ON JUST A SMALL AMOUNT OF BLOOD.
THE TRANS-FORMATION IN NEZUKO'S BLOOD SURPRISES ME.
OVER THIS SHORT PERIOD OF TIME, THE COMPOSITION OF HER BLOOD HAS REPEATEDLY CHANGED.

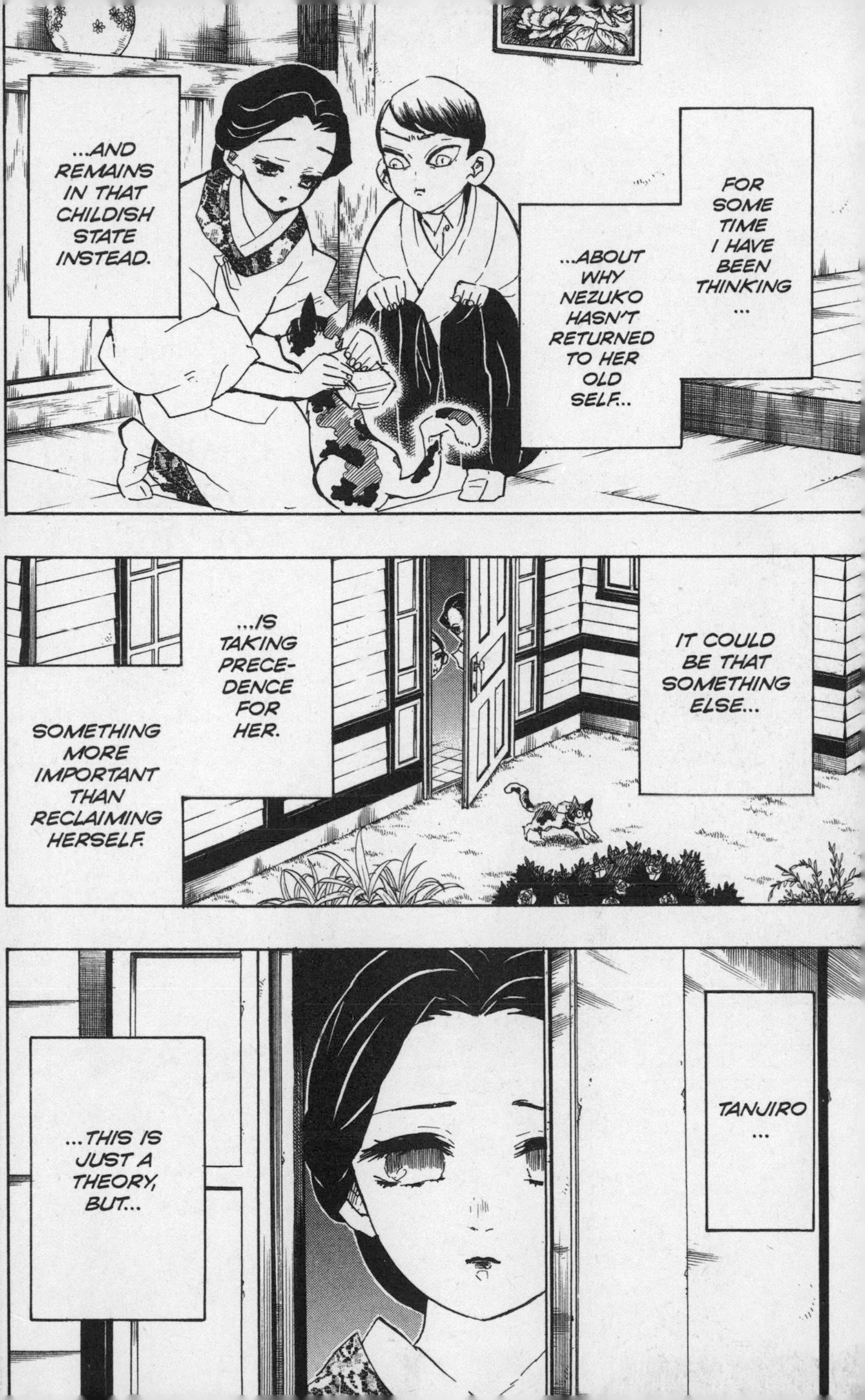
FOR SOME TIME I HAVE BEEN THINKING...
...ABOUT WHY NEZUKO HASN'T RETURNED TO HER OLD SELF...
...AND REMAINS IN THAT CHILDISH STATE INSTEAD.
IT COULD BE THAT SOMETHING ELSE...
...IS TAKING PRECE-DENCE FOR HER.
SOMETHING MORE IMPORTANT THAN RECLAIMING HERSELF.
TANJIRO...
...THIS IS JUST A THEORY, BUT...

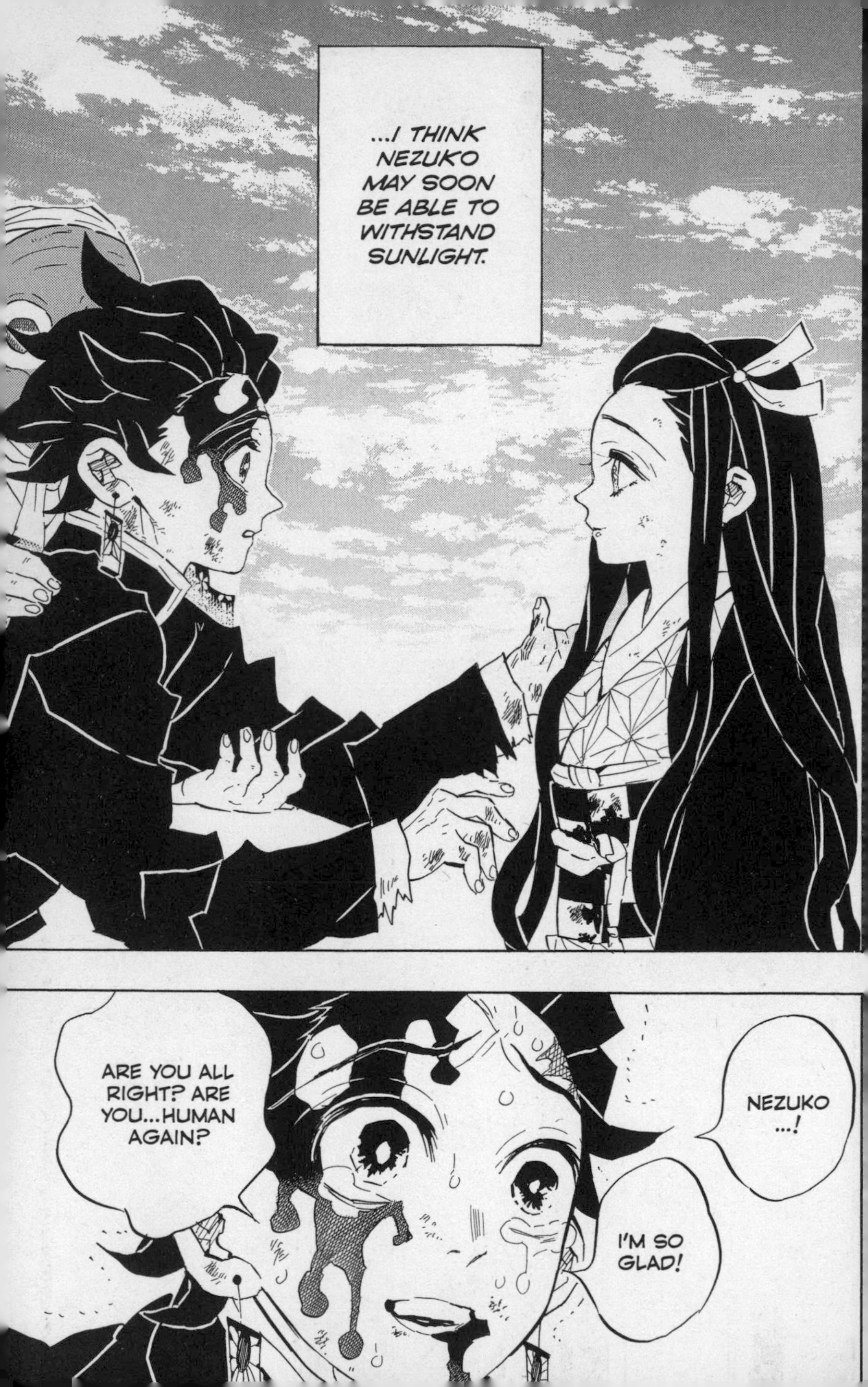
...I THINK NEZUKO MAY SOON BE ABLE TO WITHSTAND SUNLIGHT.
NEZUKO ...!
I'M SO GLAD!
ARE YOU ALL RIGHT? ARE YOU...HUMAN AGAIN?

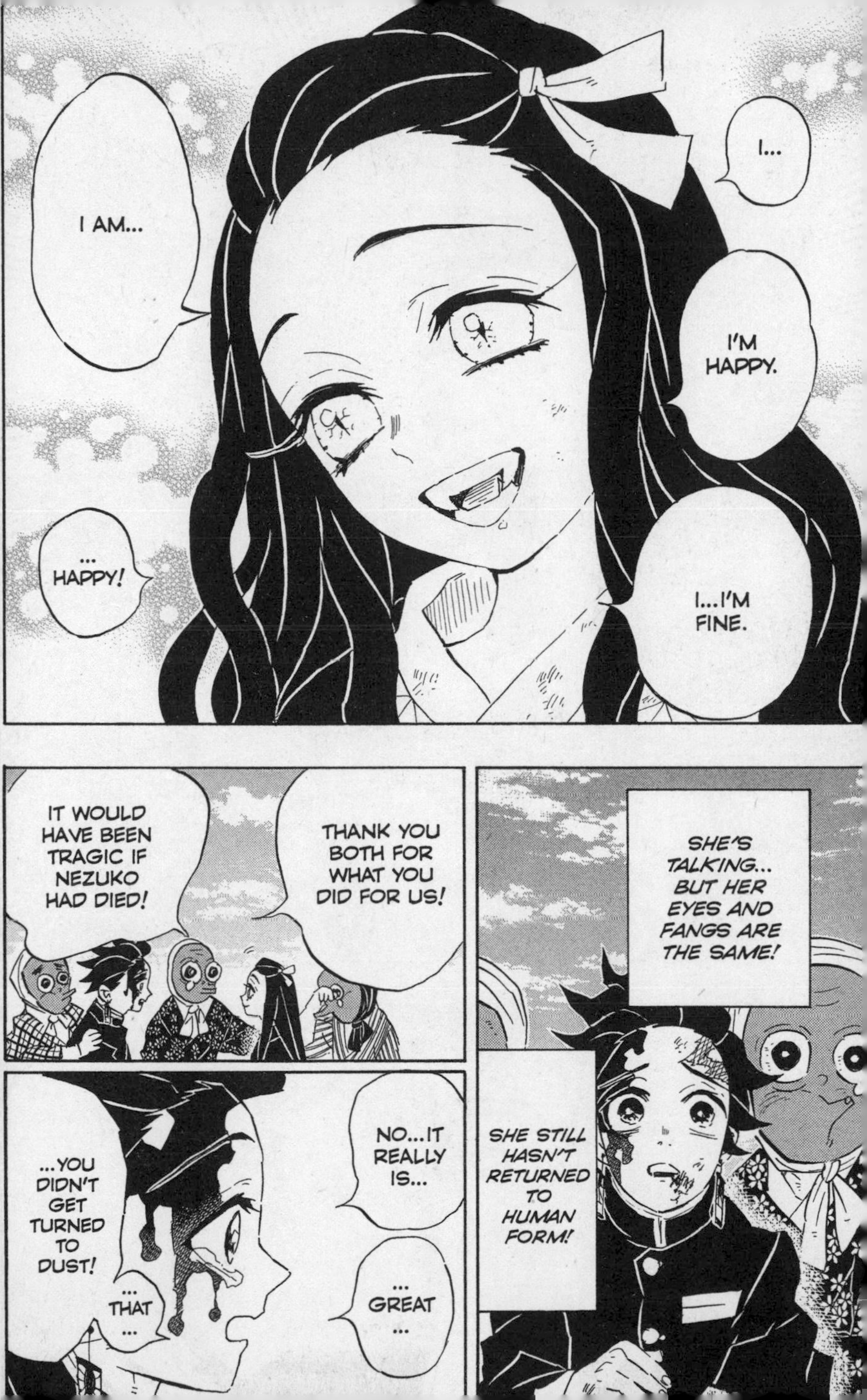
I...
I'M HAPPY.
I...I'M FINE.
I AM...
...HAPPY!
SHE'S TALKING... BUT HER EYES AND FANGS ARE THE SAME!
SHE STILL HASN'T RETURNED TO HUMAN FORM!
THANK YOU BOTH FOR WHAT YOU DID FOR US!
IT WOULD HAVE BEEN TRAGIC IF NEZUKO HAD DIED!
NO...IT REALLY IS...
...GREAT...
...YOU DIDN'T GET TURNED TO DUST!
...THAT...

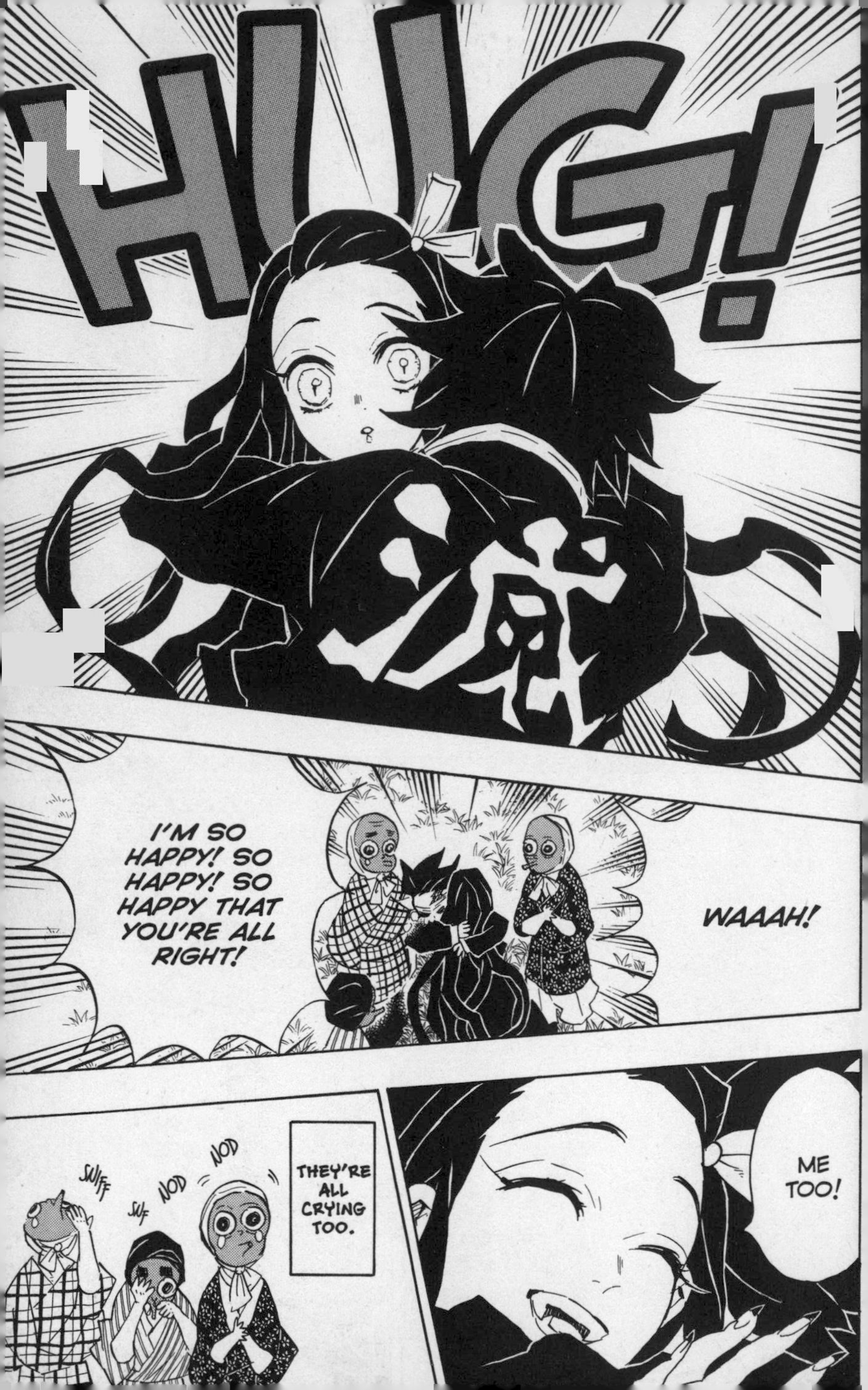
HUG!
WAAAH!
I'M SO HAPPY! SO HAPPY! SO HAPPY THAT YOU'RE ALL RIGHT!
ME TOO!
THEY'RE ALL CRYING TOO.
NOD
NOD
SNIF
SNIFF

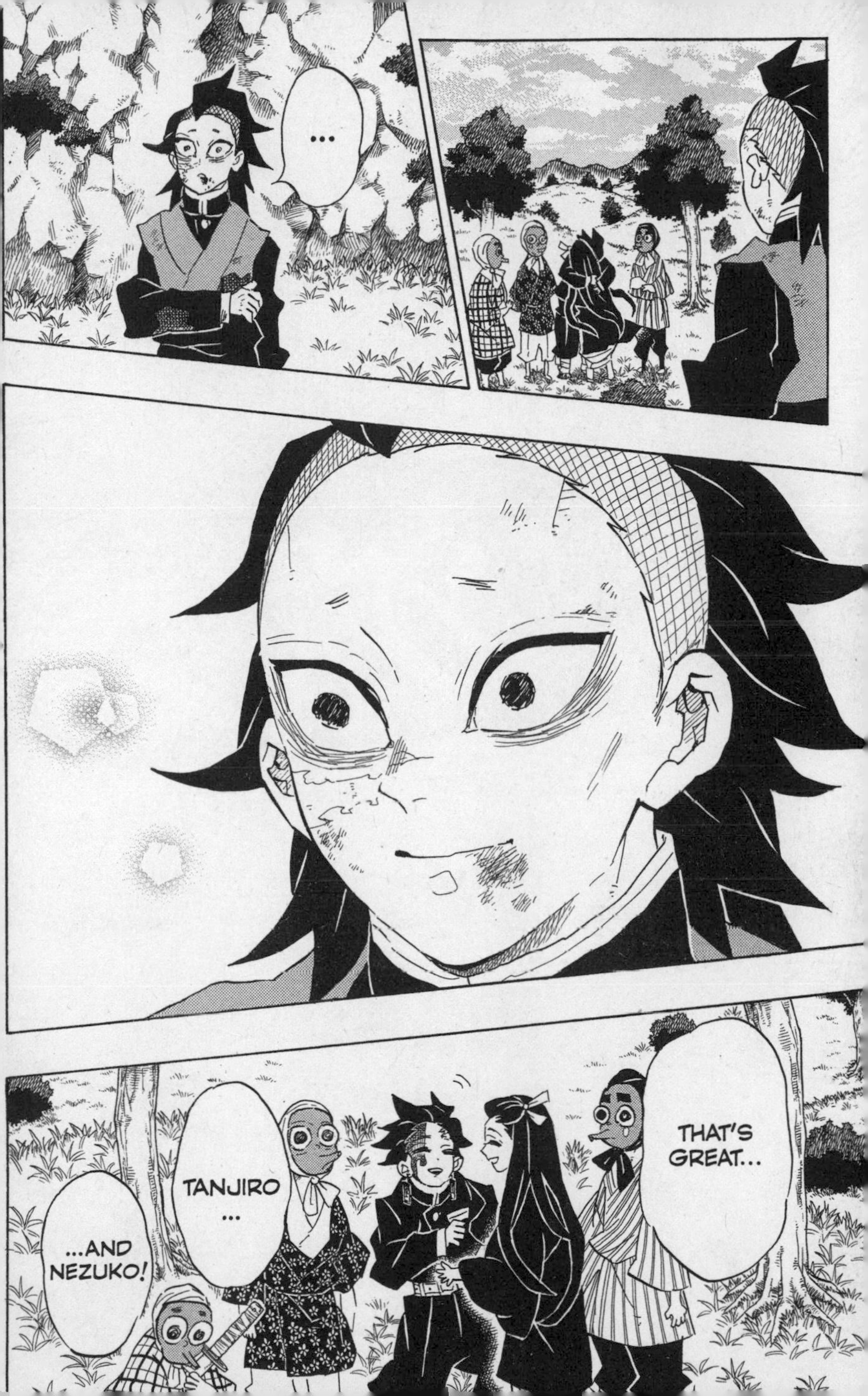
...
THAT'S GREAT...
TANJIRO ...
...AND NEZUKO!

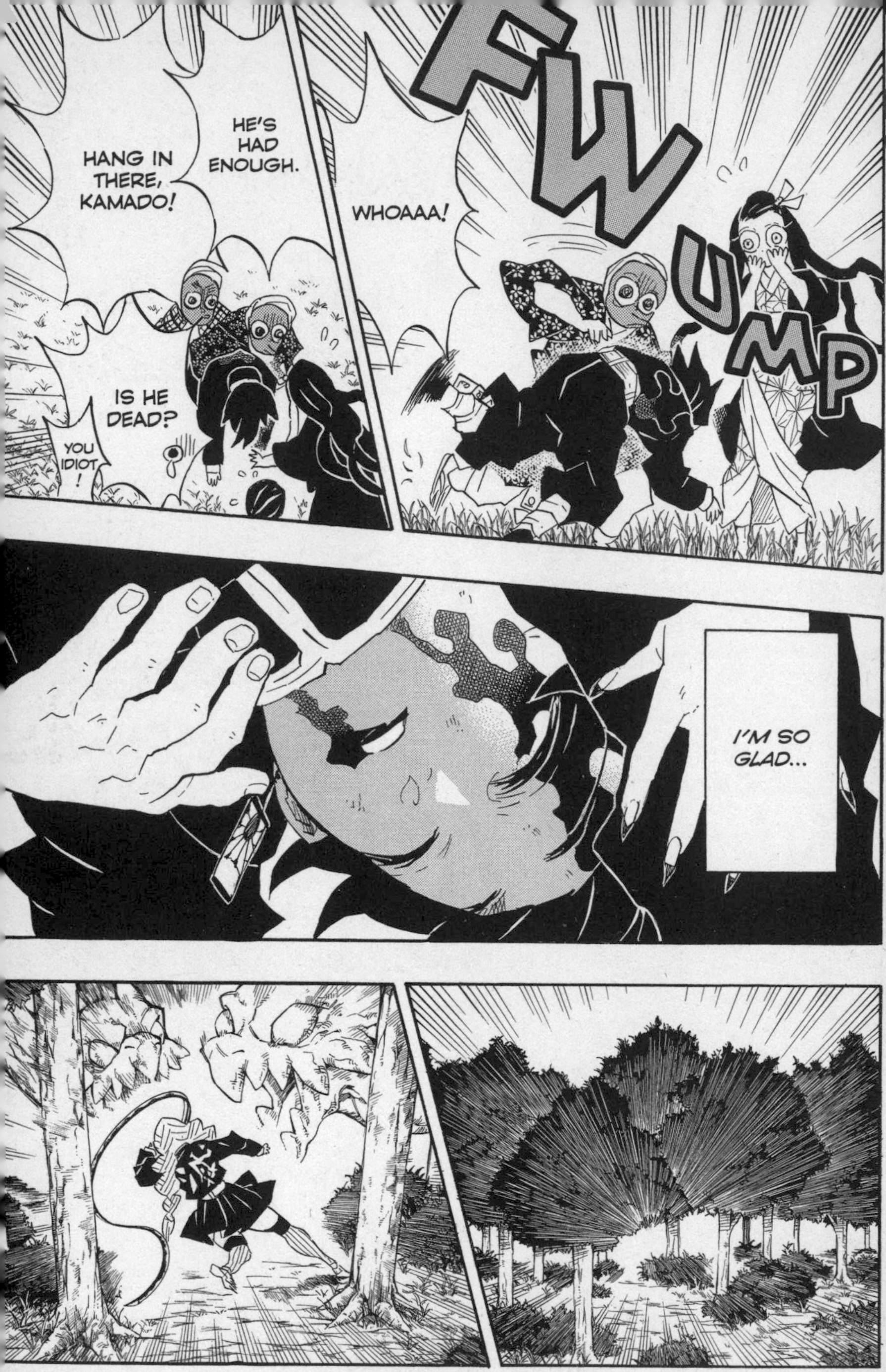
FWUMP
WHOAAA!
HE'S HAD ENOUGH.
HANG IN THERE, KAMADO!
IS HE DEAD?
YOU IDIOT!
I'M SO GLAD...

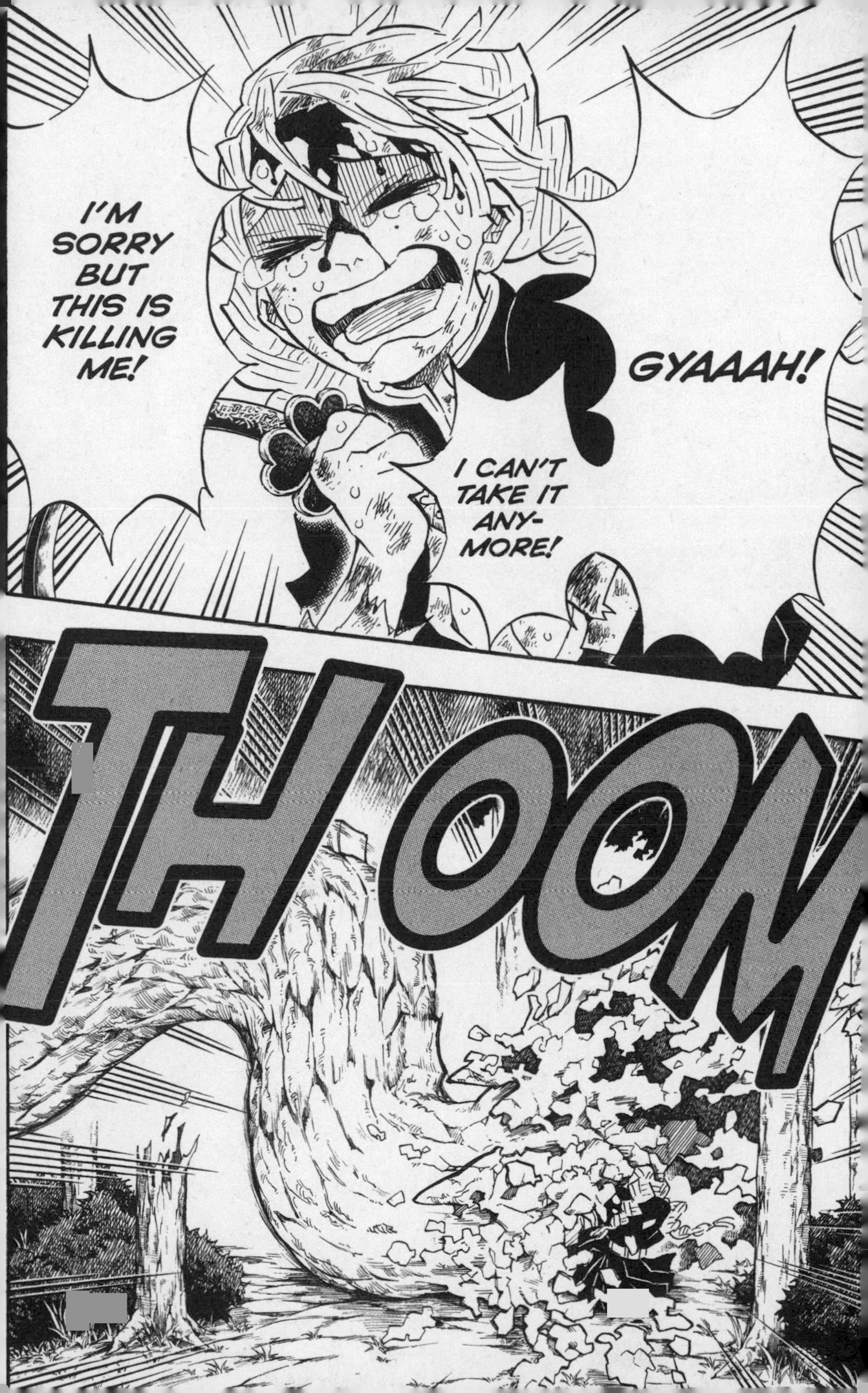
I'M SORRY BUT THIS IS KILLING ME!
GYAAAH!
I CAN'T TAKE IT ANY-MORE!
THOOM

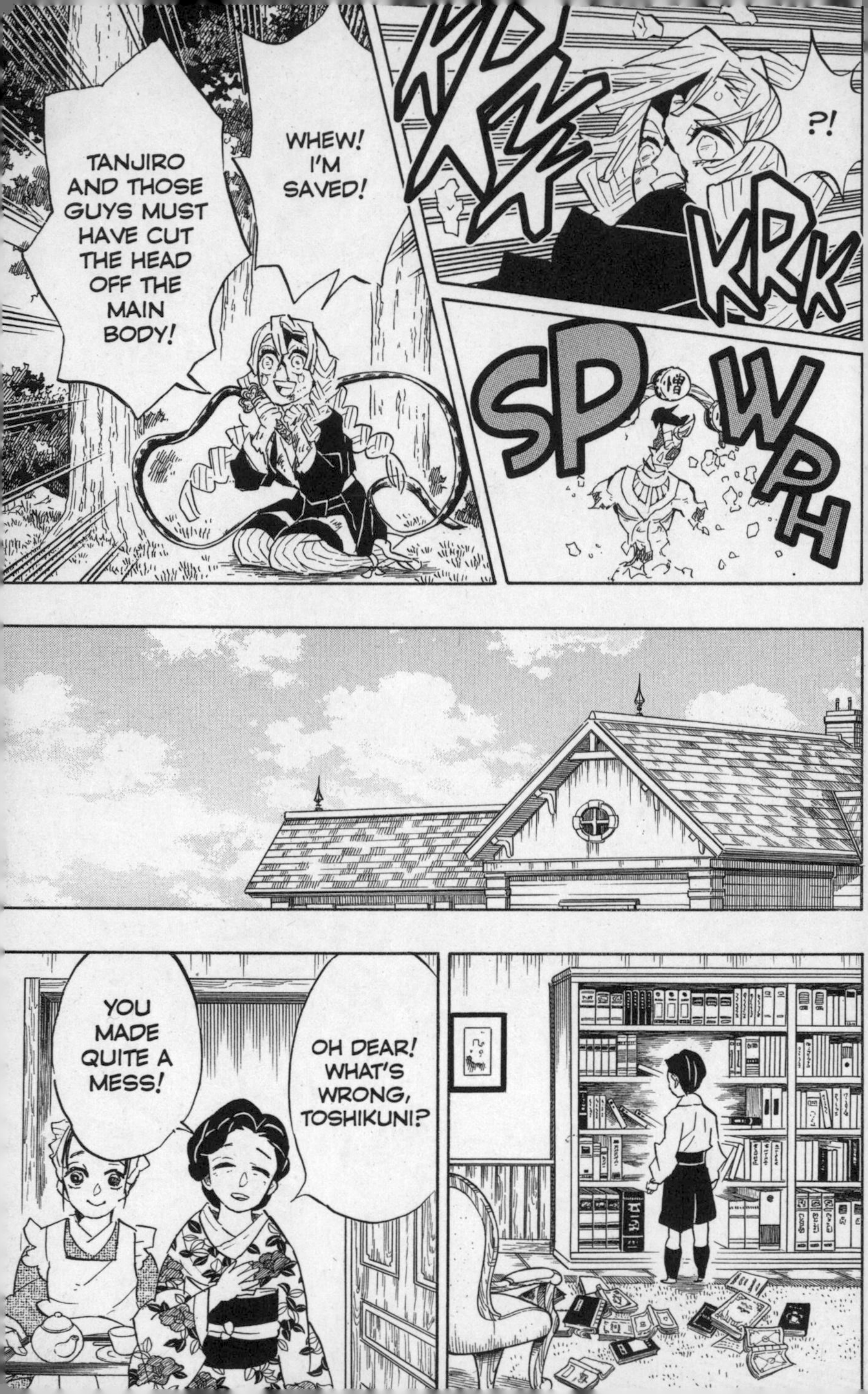
KRK
?!
KRK
SP
WPH
WHEW! I'M SAVED!
TANJIRO AND THOSE GUYS MUST HAVE CUT THE HEAD OFF THE MAIN BODY!
OH DEAR! WHAT'S WRONG, TOSHIKUNI?
YOU MADE QUITE A MESS!

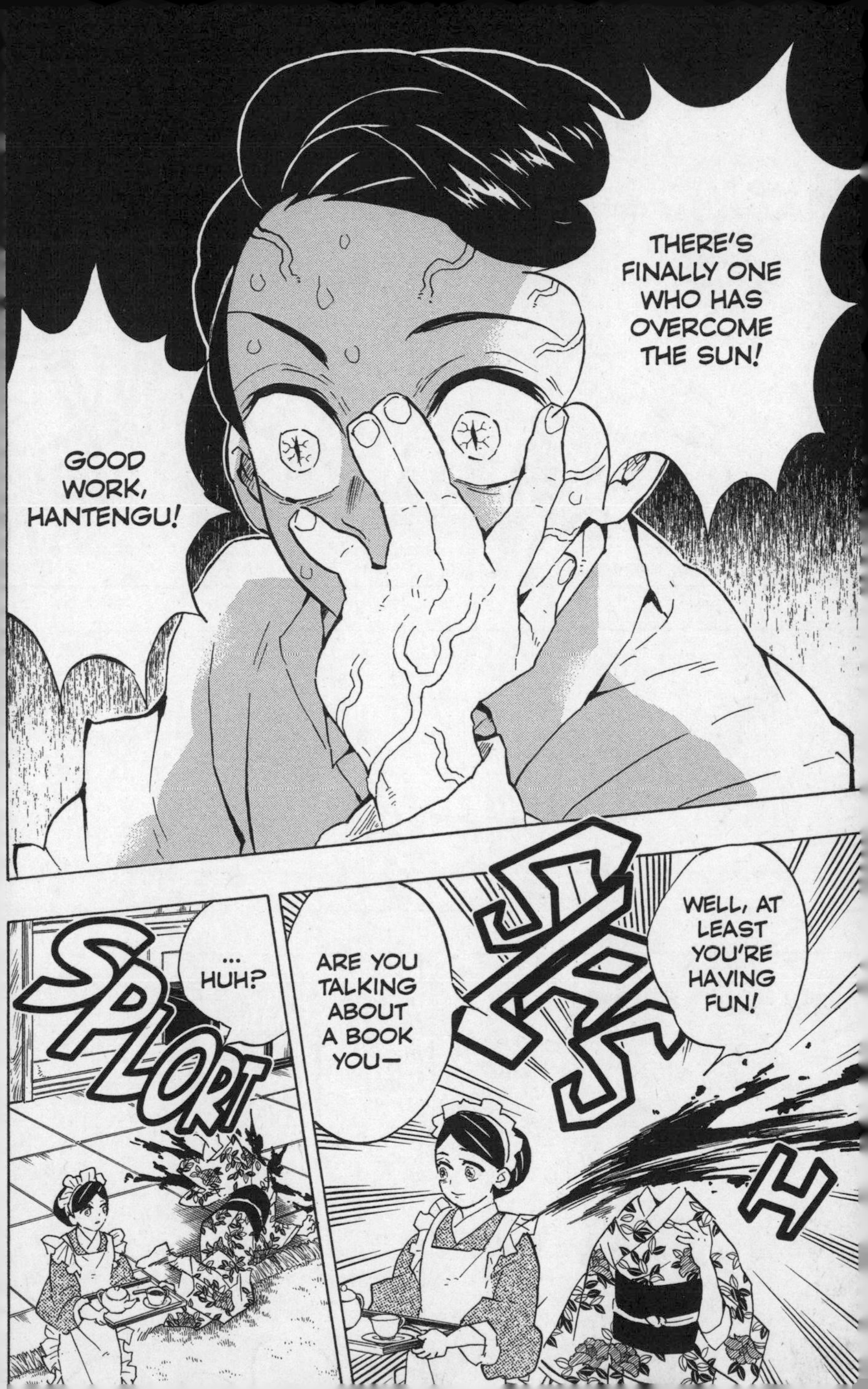
THERE'S FINALLY ONE WHO HAS OVERCOME THE SUN!
GOOD WORK, HANTENGU!
WELL, AT LEAST YOU'RE HAVING FUN!
ARE YOU TALKING ABOUT A BOOK YOU—
... HUH?
SPLORT

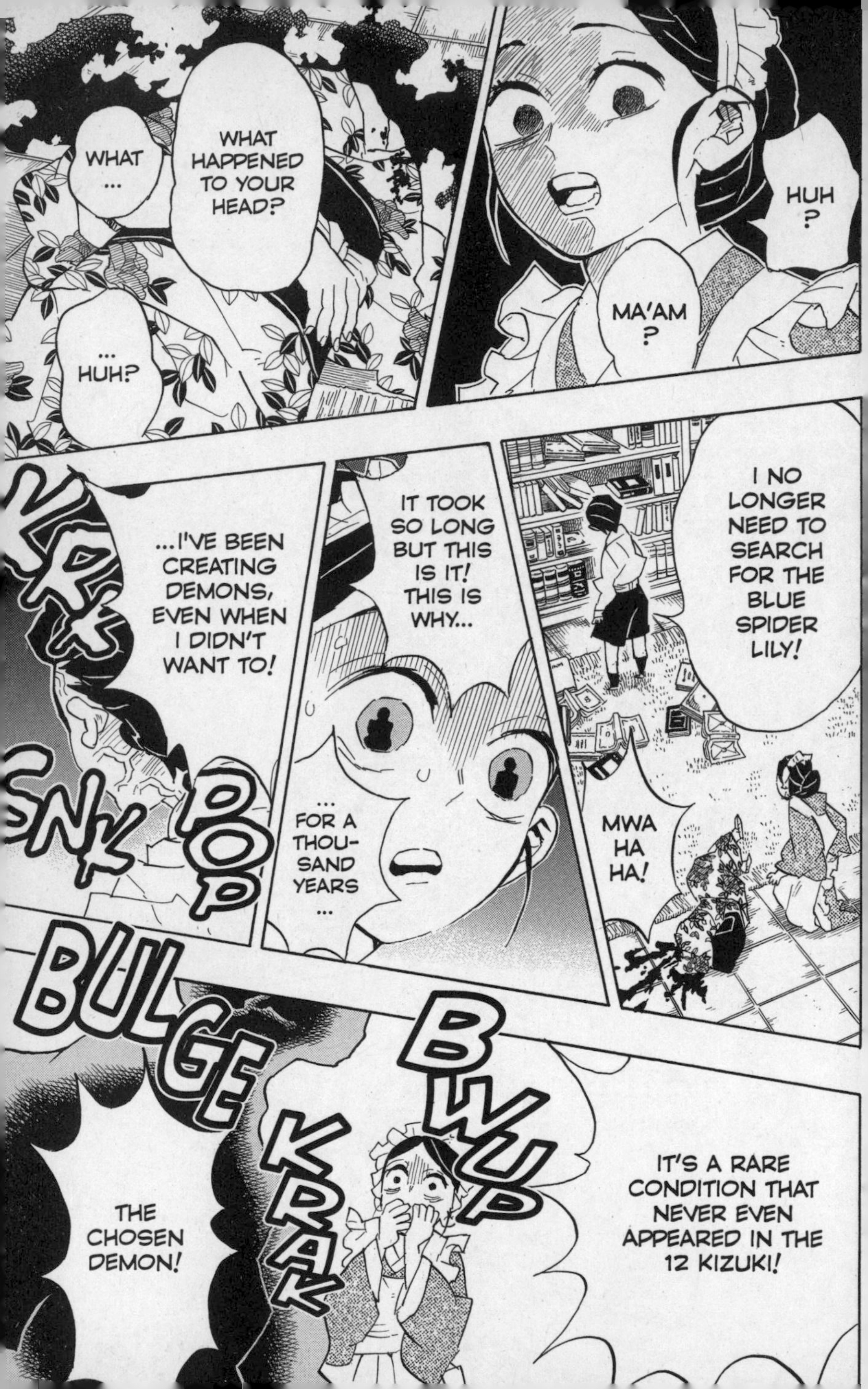
HUH ?
MA'AM ?
WHAT ...
WHAT HAPPENED TO YOUR HEAD?
... HUH?
I NO LONGER NEED TO SEARCH FOR THE BLUE SPIDER LILY!
MWA HA HA!
IT TOOK SO LONG BUT THIS IS IT! THIS IS WHY...
... FOR A THOUSAND YEARS ...
...I'VE BEEN CREATING DEMONS, EVEN WHEN I DIDN'T WANT TO!
POP
SNK
BWUP
KRAK
BULGE
IT'S A RARE CONDITION THAT NEVER EVEN APPEARED IN THE 12 KIZUKI!
THE CHOSEN DEMON!

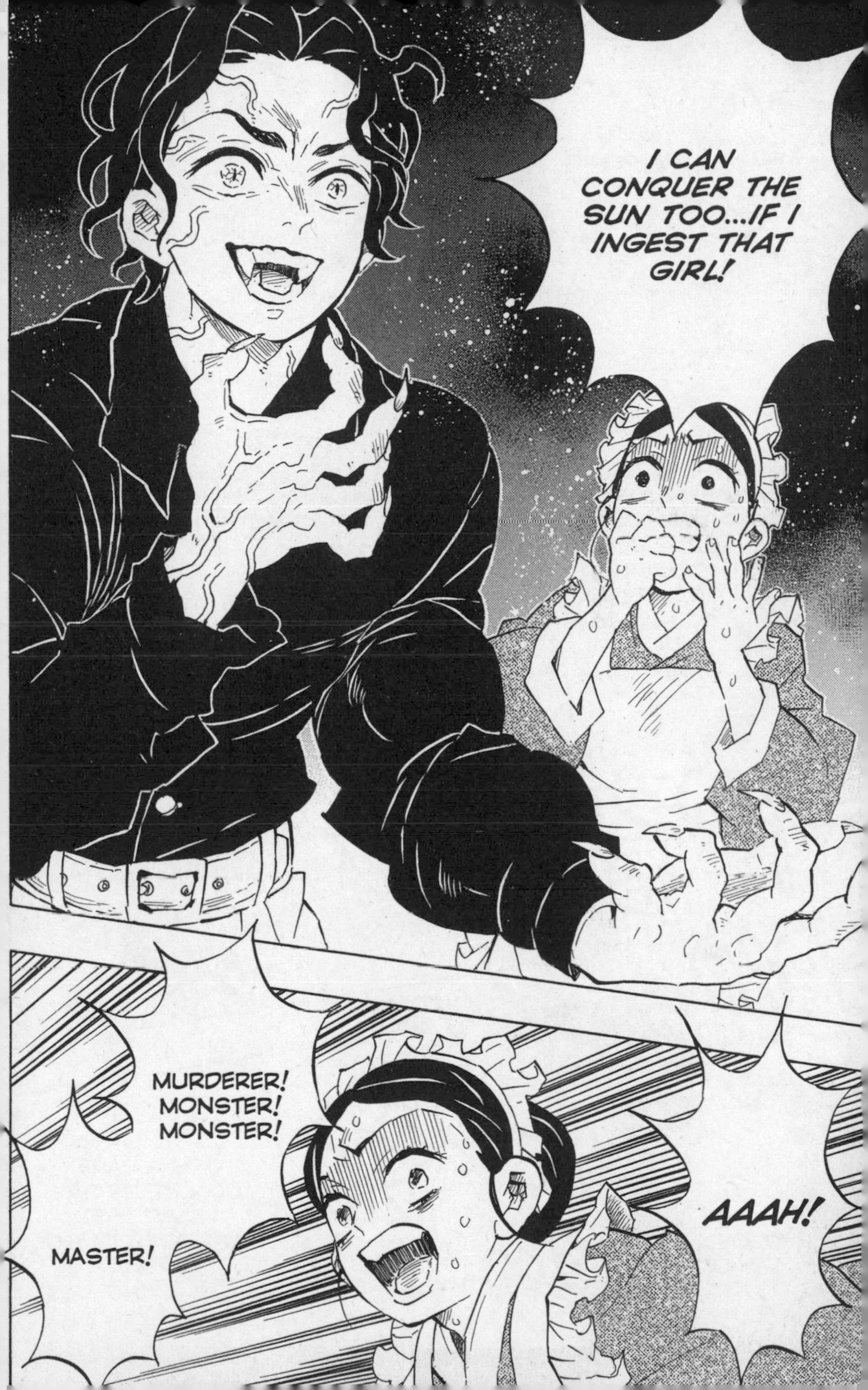
I CAN CONQUER THE SUN TOO...IF I INGEST THAT GIRL!
AAAH!
MURDERER! MONSTER! MONSTER!
MASTER!

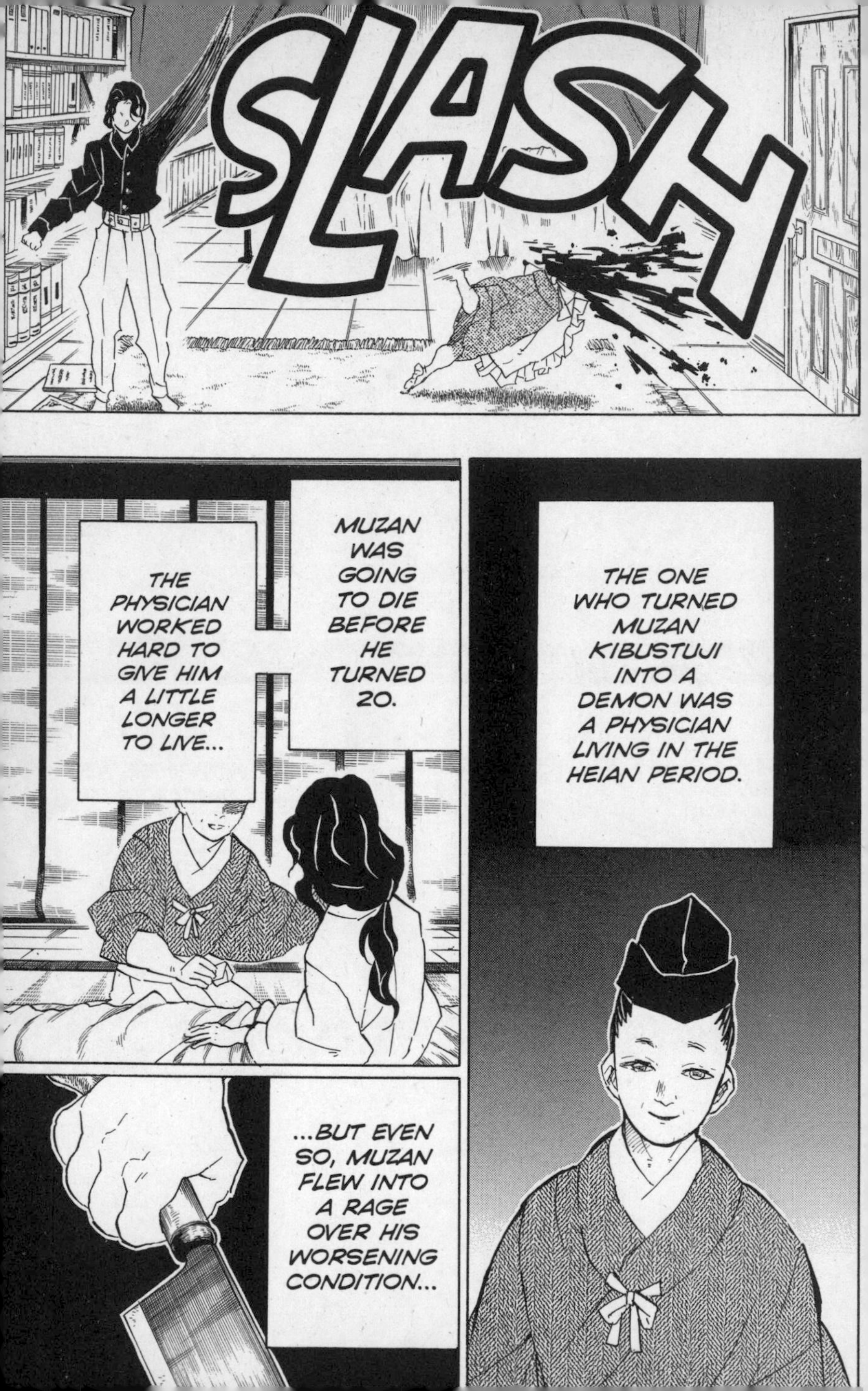
SLASH
THE ONE WHO TURNED MUZAN KIBUSTUJI INTO A DEMON WAS A PHYSICIAN LIVING IN THE HEIAN PERIOD.
MUZAN WAS GOING TO DIE BEFORE HE TURNED 20.
THE PHYSICIAN WORKED HARD TO GIVE HIM A LITTLE LONGER TO LIVE...
...BUT EVEN SO, MUZAN FLEW INTO A RAGE OVER HIS WORSENING CONDITION...

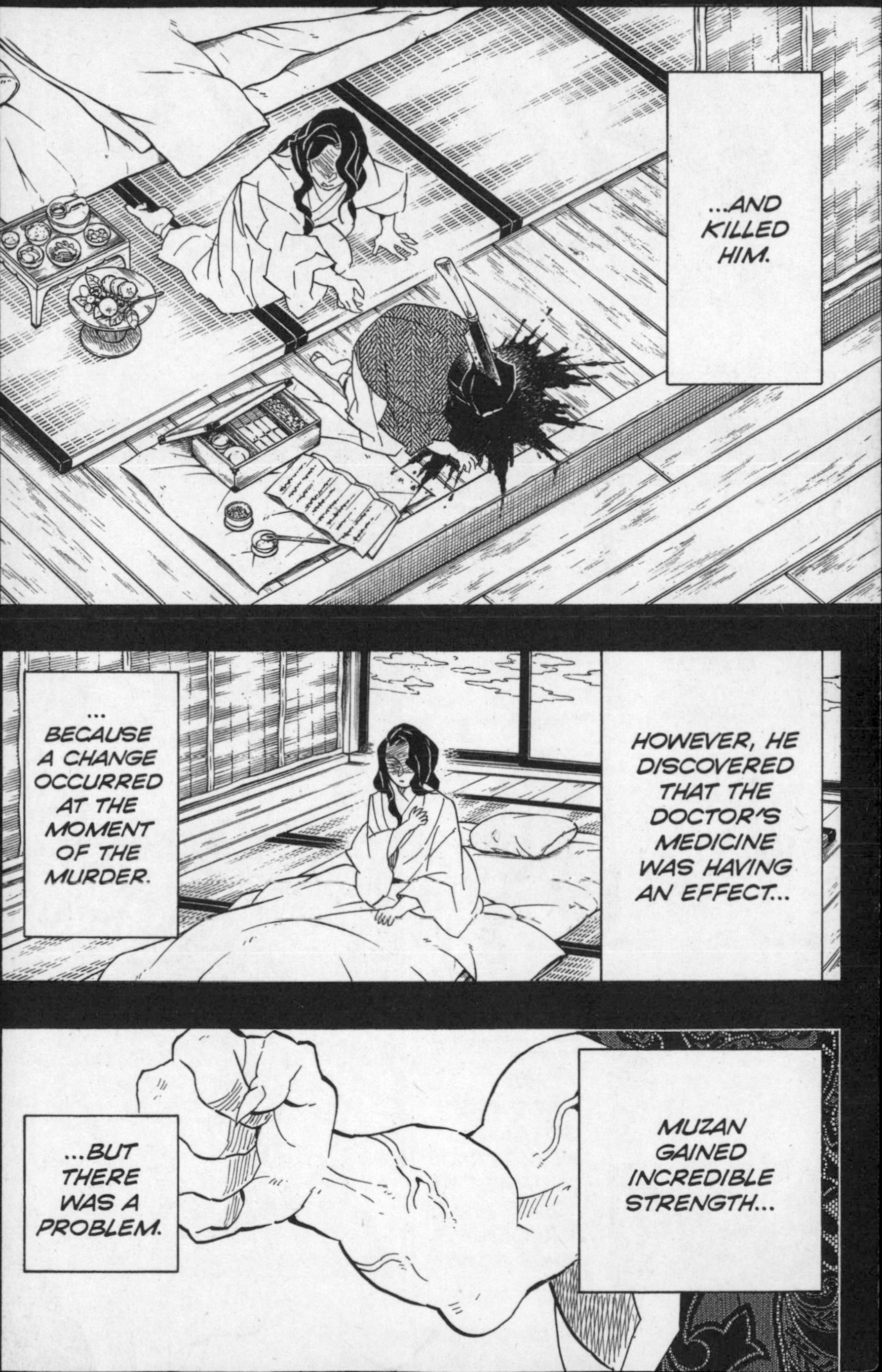
...AND KILLED HIM.
HOWEVER, HE DISCOVERED THAT THE DOCTOR'S MEDICINE WAS HAVING AN EFFECT...
... BECAUSE A CHANGE OCCURRED AT THE MOMENT OF THE MURDER.
MUZAN GAINED INCREDIBLE STRENGTH...
...BUT THERE WAS A PROBLEM.

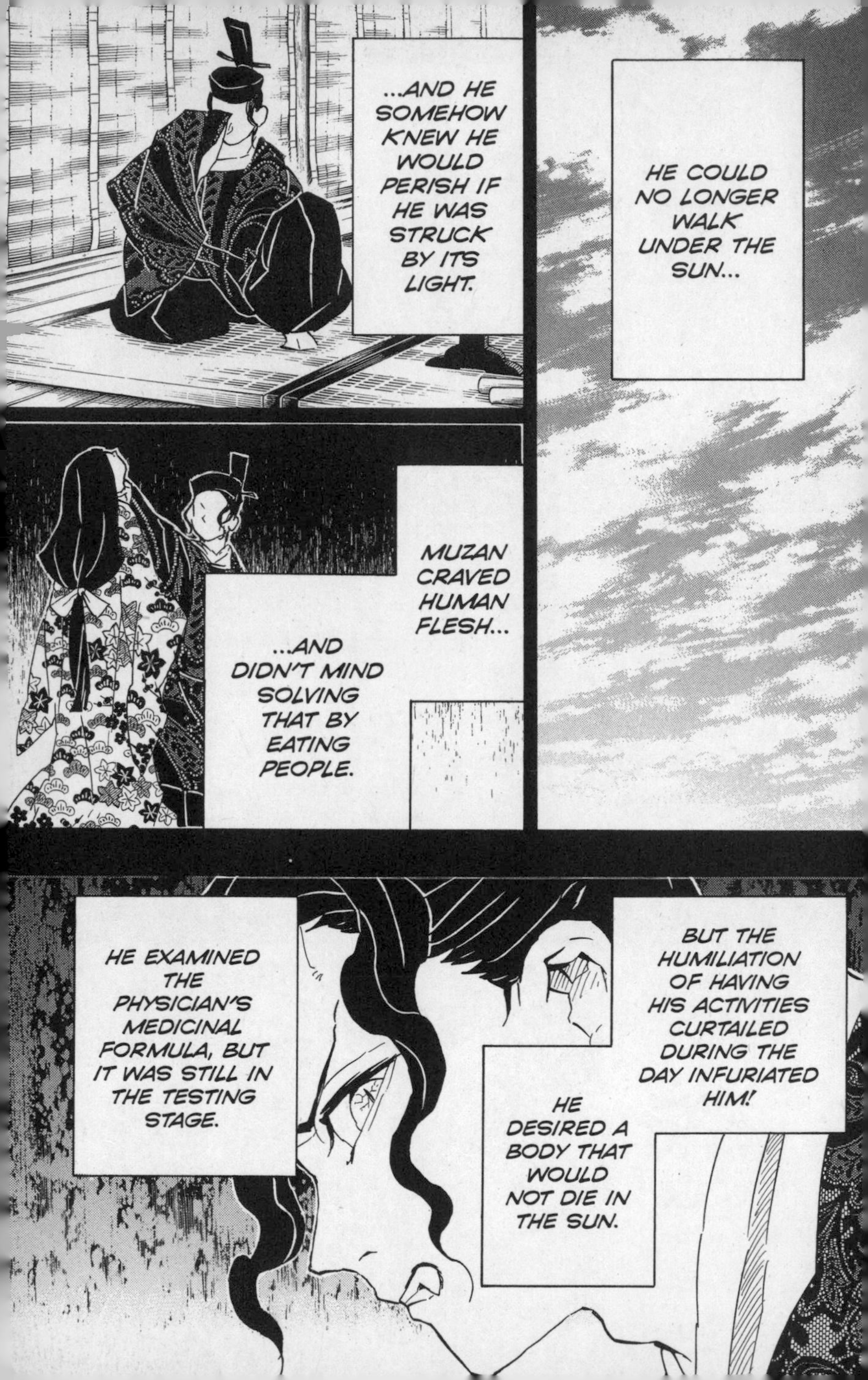
HE COULD NO LONGER WALK UNDER THE SUN...
...AND HE SOMEHOW KNEW HE WOULD PERISH IF HE WAS STRUCK BY ITS LIGHT.
MUZAN CRAVED HUMAN FLESH...
...AND DIDN'T MIND SOLVING THAT BY EATING PEOPLE.
BUT THE HUMILIATION OF HAVING HIS ACTIVITIES CURTAILED DURING THE DAY INFURIATED HIM!
HE DESIRED A BODY THAT WOULD NOT DIE IN THE SUN.
HE EXAMINED THE PHYSICIAN'S MEDICINAL FORMULA, BUT IT WAS STILL IN THE TESTING STAGE.

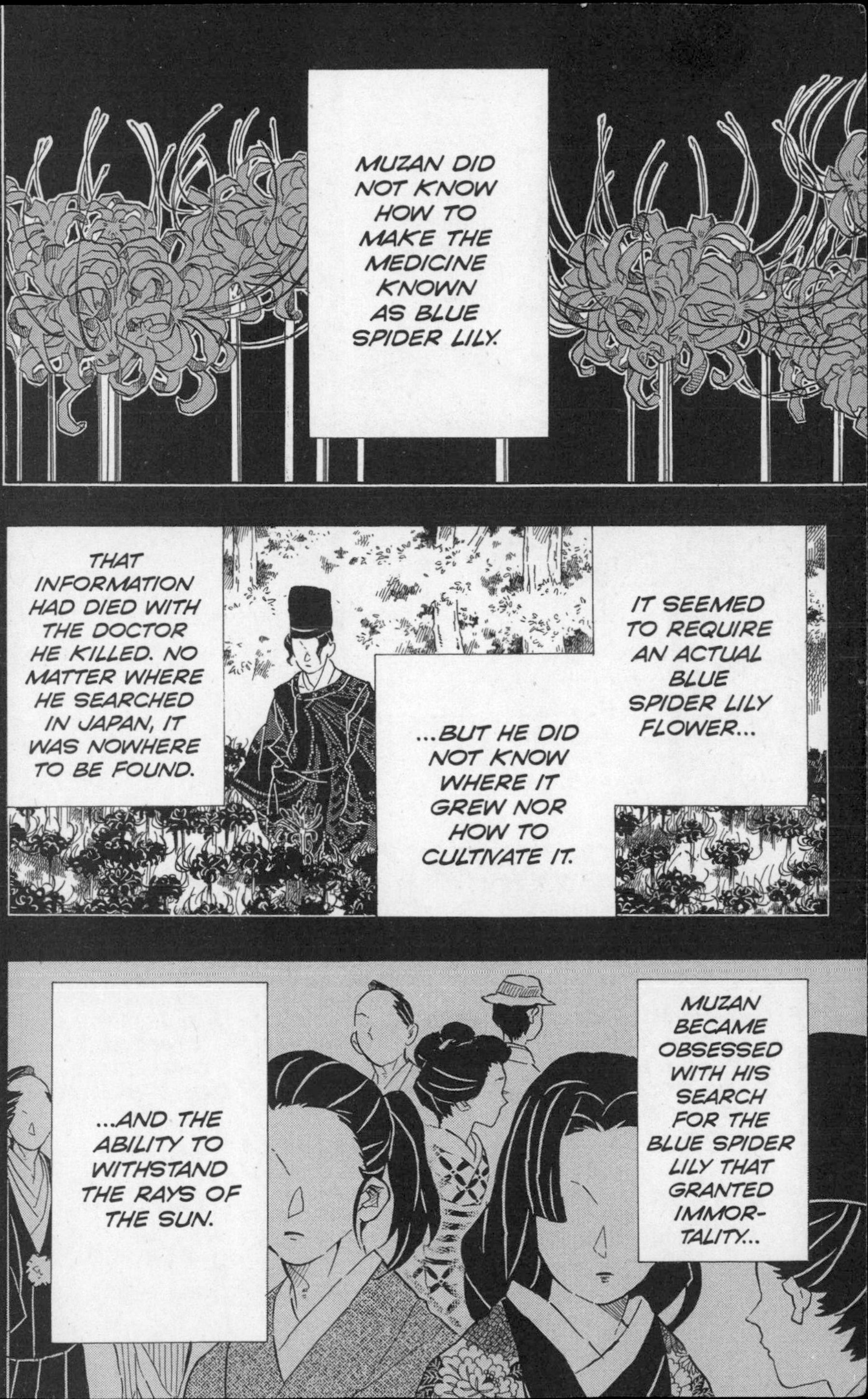
MUZAN DID NOT KNOW HOW TO MAKE THE MEDICINE KNOWN AS BLUE SPIDER LILY.
IT SEEMED TO REQUIRE AN ACTUAL BLUE SPIDER LILY FLOWER...
...BUT HE DID NOT KNOW WHERE IT GREW NOR HOW TO CULTIVATE IT.
THAT INFORMATION HAD DIED WITH THE DOCTOR HE KILLED. NO MATTER WHERE HE SEARCHED IN JAPAN, IT WAS NOWHERE TO BE FOUND.
MUZAN BECAME OBSESSED WITH HIS SEARCH FOR THE BLUE SPIDER LILY THAT GRANTED IMMOR-TALITY...
...AND THE ABILITY TO WITHSTAND THE RAYS OF THE SUN.

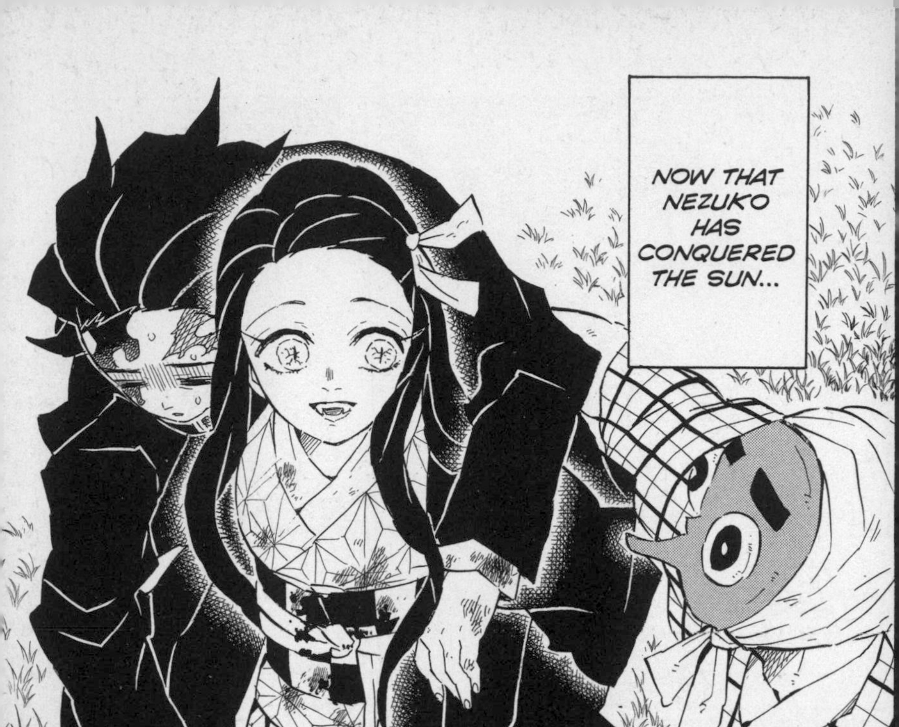
NOW THAT NEZUKO HAS CONQUERED THE SUN...
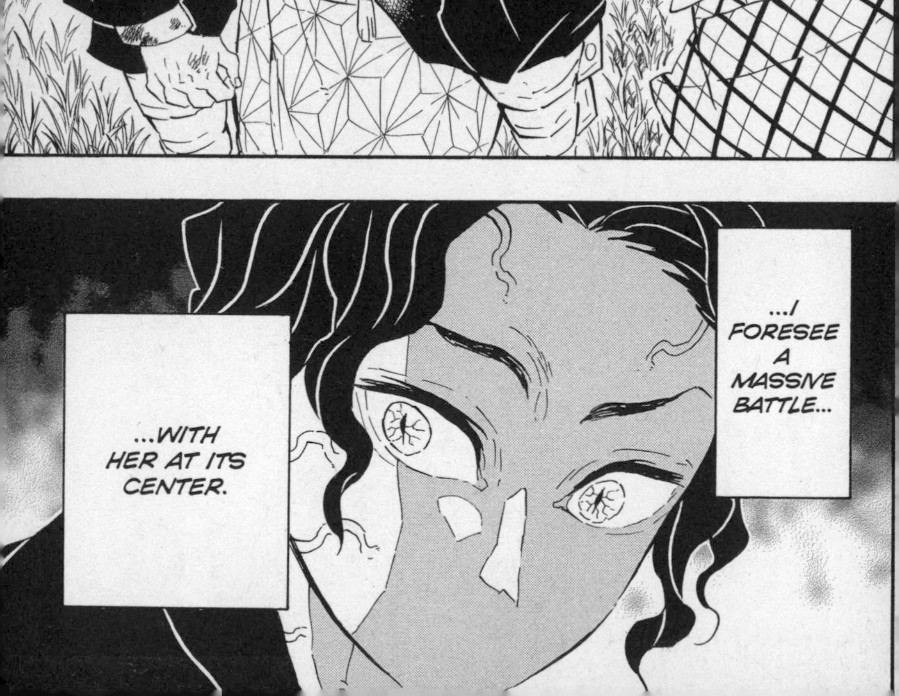
...I FORESEE A MASSIVE BATTLE...
...WITH HER AT ITS CENTER.

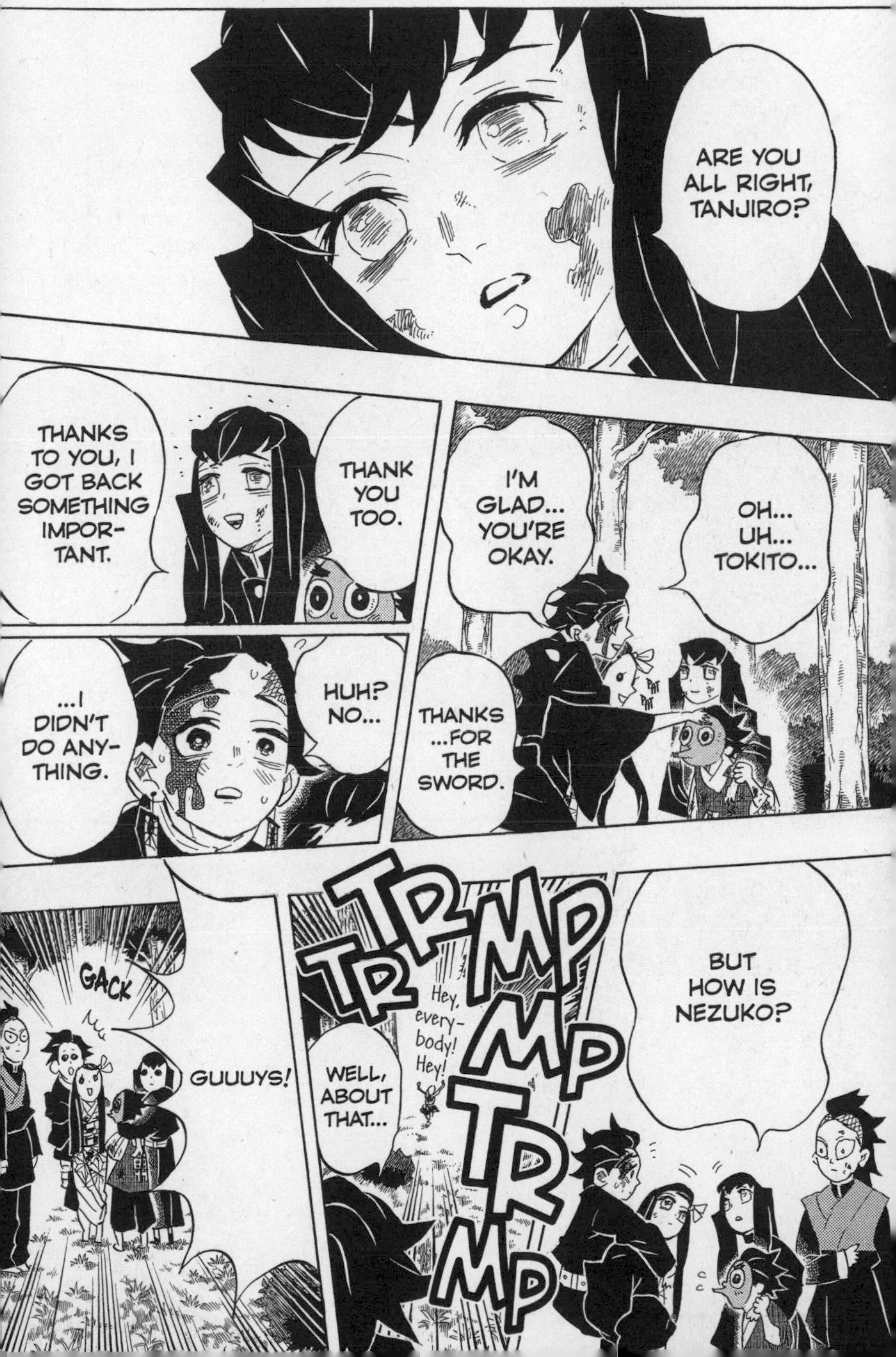
ARE YOU ALL RIGHT, TANJIRO?
OH... UH... TOKITO...
I'M GLAD... YOU'RE OKAY.
THANKS ...FOR THE SWORD.
PAT PAT
THANK YOU TOO.
THANKS TO YOU, I GOT BACK SOMETHING IMPOR-TANT.
HUH? NO...
...I DIDN'T DO ANY-THING.
BUT HOW IS NEZUKO?
WELL, ABOUT THAT...
TRMP TRMP TRMP TRMP
Hey, every-body! Hey!
GUUUYS!
GACK

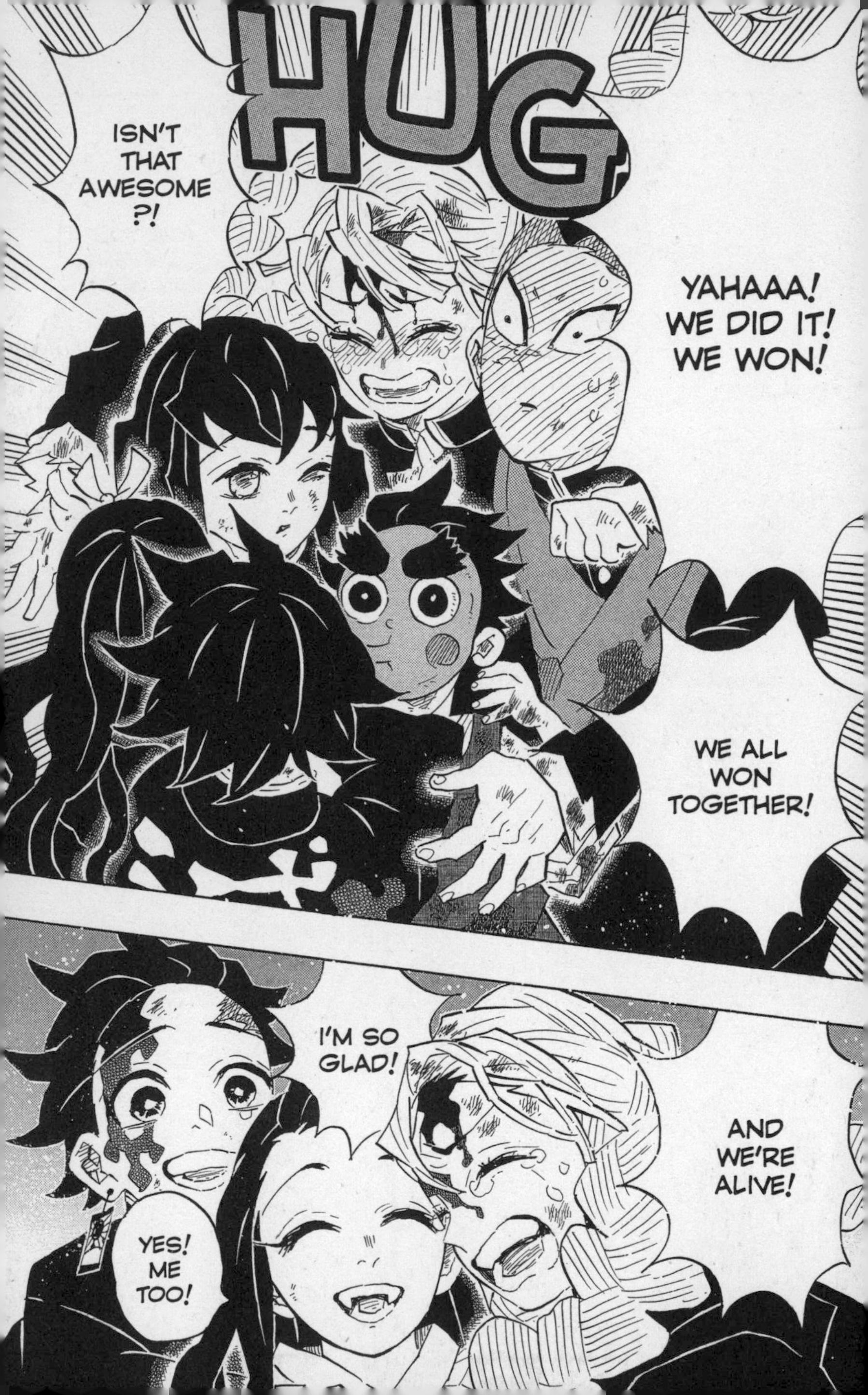
HUG
YAHAAA! WE DID IT! WE WON!
ISN'T THAT AWESOME?!
WE ALL WON TOGETHER!
AND WE'RE ALIVE!
I'M SO GLAD!
YES! ME TOO!

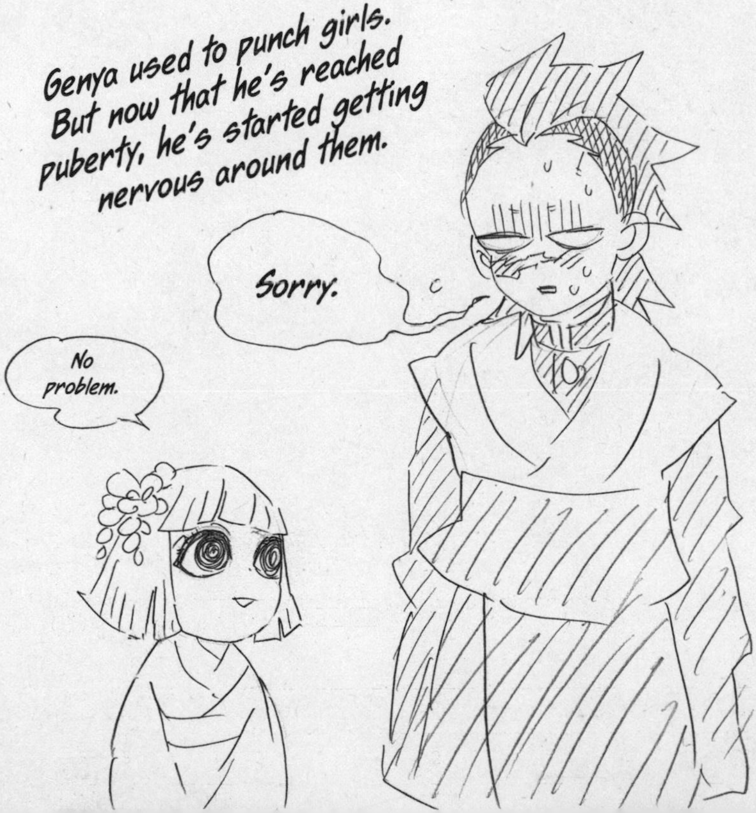
Genya used to punch girls. But now that he's reached puberty, he's started getting nervous around them.
Sorry.
No problem.

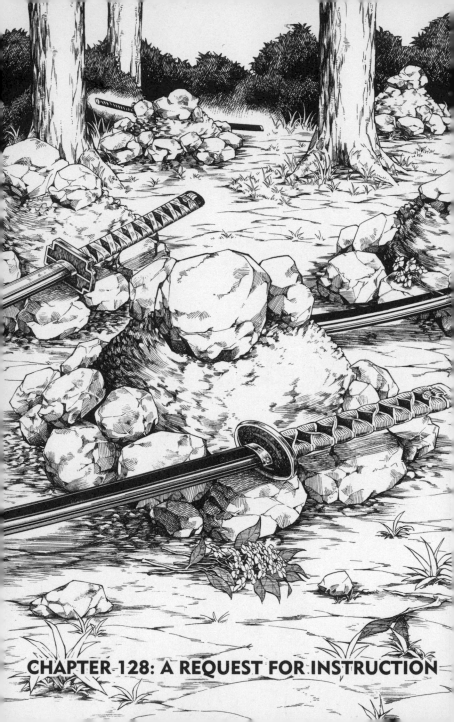

CHAPTER 128: A REQUEST FOR INSTRUCTION

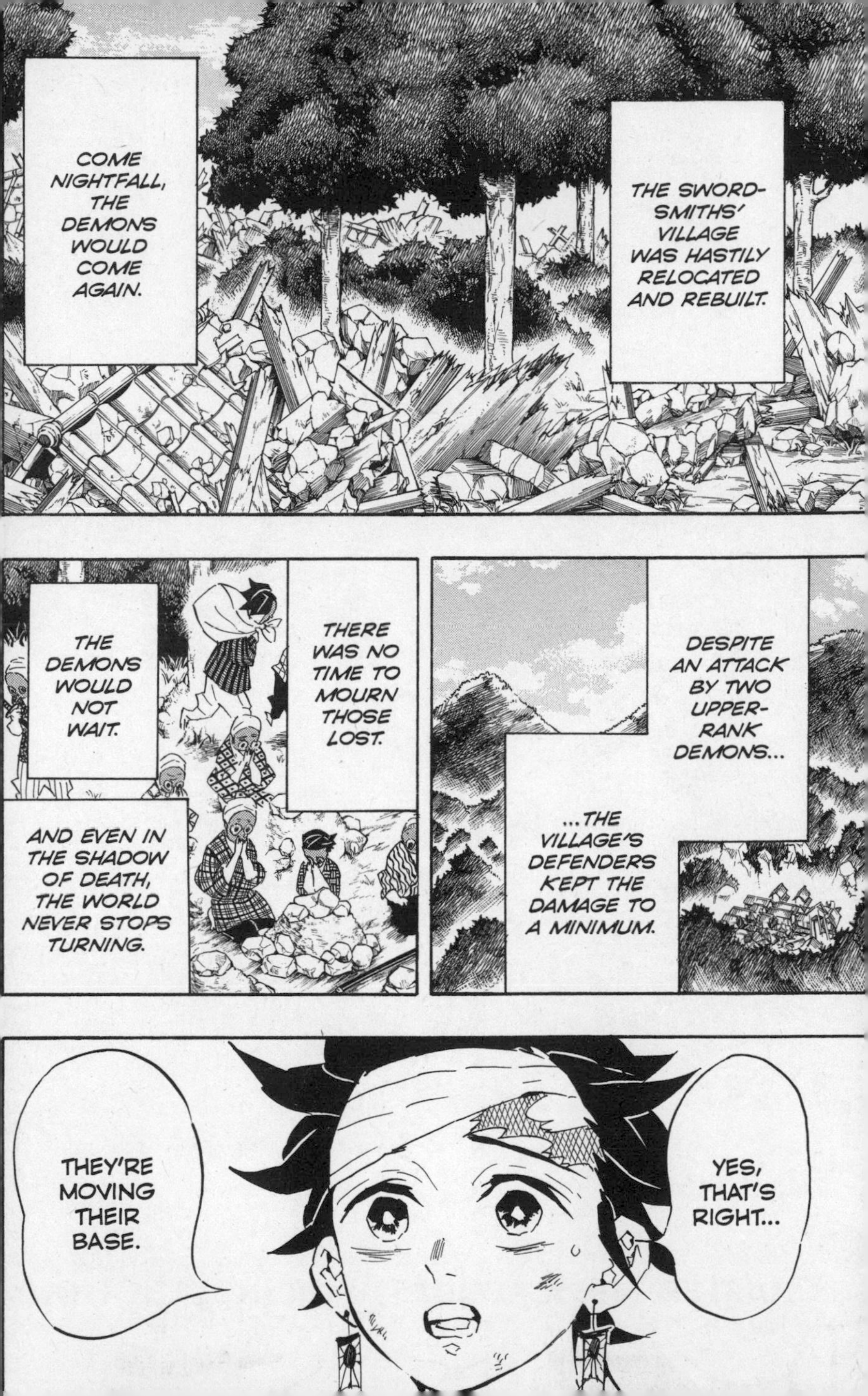
THE SWORD-SMITHS' VILLAGE WAS HASTILY RELOCATED AND REBUILT.
COME NIGHTFALL, THE DEMONS WOULD COME AGAIN.
DESPITE AN ATTACK BY TWO UPPER-RANK DEMONS...
...THE VILLAGE'S DEFENDERS KEPT THE DAMAGE TO A MINIMUM.
THERE WAS NO TIME TO MOURN THOSE LOST.
THE DEMONS WOULD NOT WAIT.
AND EVEN IN THE SHADOW OF DEATH, THE WORLD NEVER STOPS TURNING.
YES, THAT'S RIGHT...
THEY'RE MOVING THEIR BASE.

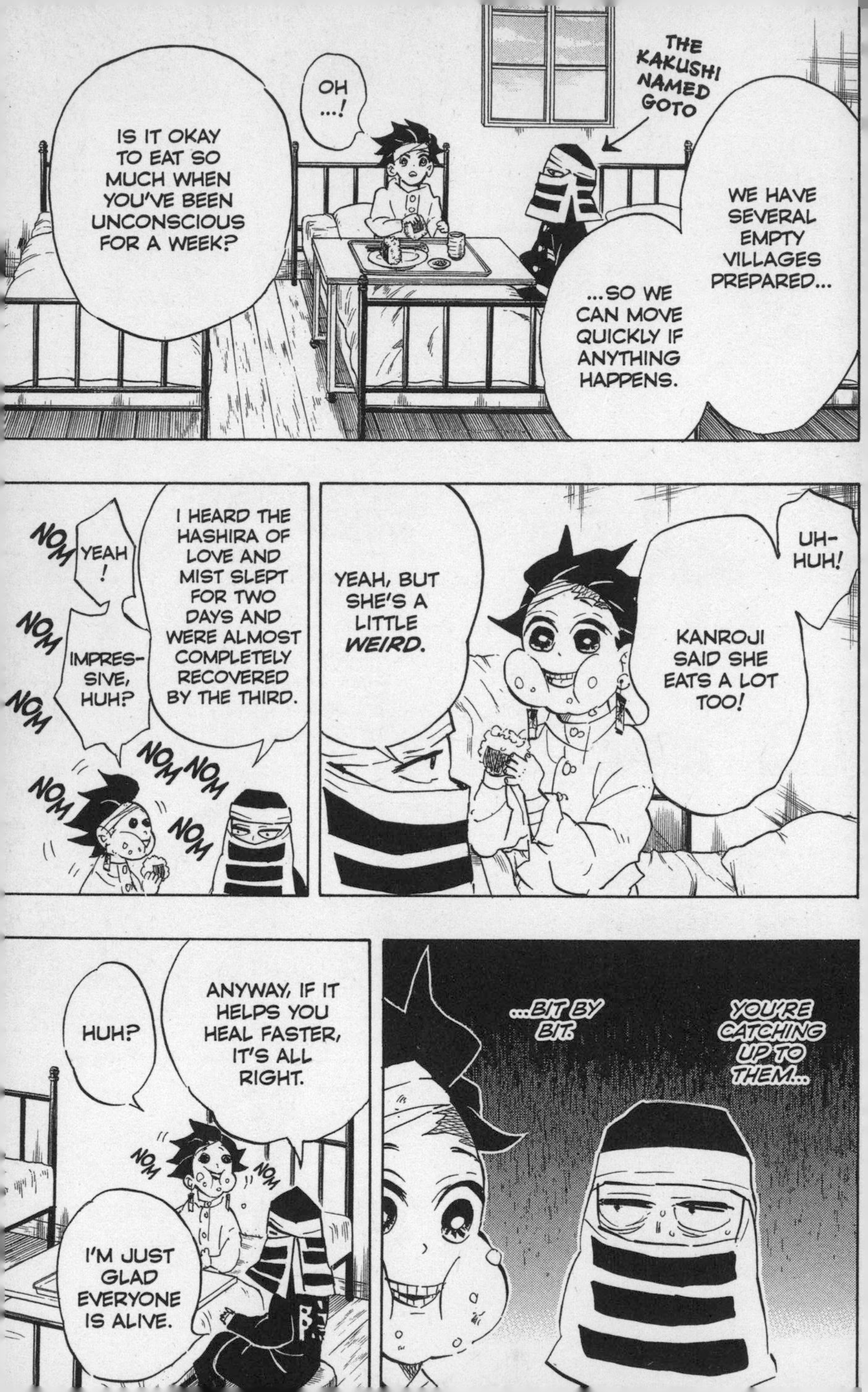
THE KAKUSHI NAMED GOTO
WE HAVE SEVERAL EMPTY VILLAGES PREPARED...
...SO WE CAN MOVE QUICKLY IF ANYTHING HAPPENS.
OH ...!
IS IT OKAY TO EAT SO MUCH WHEN YOU'VE BEEN UNCONSCIOUS FOR A WEEK?
UH-HUH!
KANROJI SAID SHE EATS A LOT TOO!
YEAH, BUT SHE'S A LITTLE *WEIRD.*
I HEARD THE HASHIRA OF LOVE AND MIST SLEPT FOR TWO DAYS AND WERE ALMOST COMPLETELY RECOVERED BY THE THIRD.
YEAH!
IMPRESSIVE, HUH?
NOM NOM NOM
NOM NOM NOM NOM
YOU'RE CATCHING UP TO THEM...
...BIT BY BIT.
ANYWAY, IF IT HELPS YOU HEAL FASTER, IT'S ALL RIGHT.
HUH?
NOM NOM
I'M JUST GLAD EVERYONE IS ALIVE.

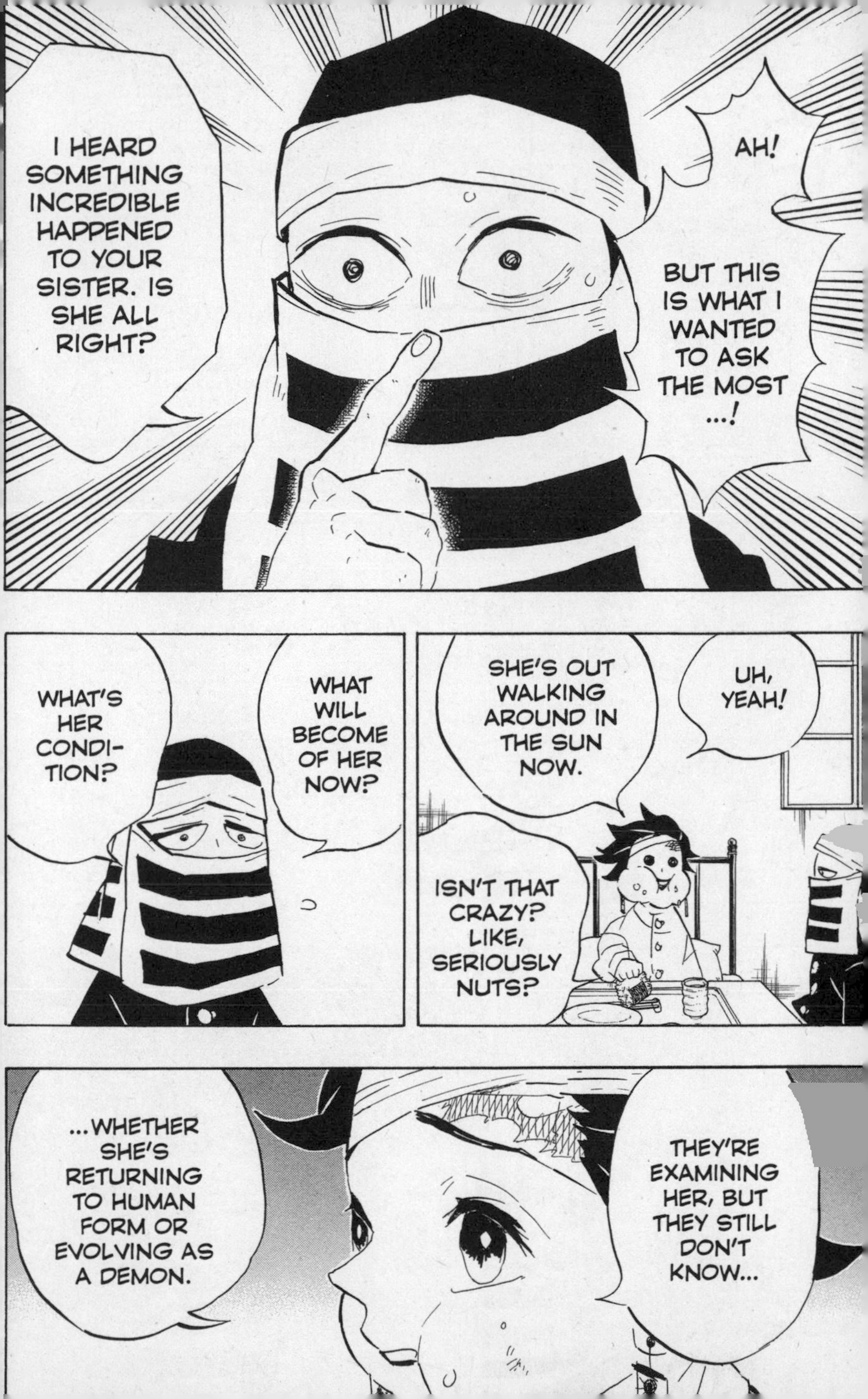
AH! BUT THIS IS WHAT I WANTED TO ASK THE MOST ...!
I HEARD SOMETHING INCREDIBLE HAPPENED TO YOUR SISTER. IS SHE ALL RIGHT?
UH, YEAH!
SHE'S OUT WALKING AROUND IN THE SUN NOW.
ISN'T THAT CRAZY? LIKE, SERIOUSLY NUTS?
WHAT WILL BECOME OF HER NOW?
WHAT'S HER CONDITION?
THEY'RE EXAMINING HER, BUT THEY STILL DON'T KNOW...
...WHETHER SHE'S RETURNING TO HUMAN FORM OR EVOLVING AS A DEMON.

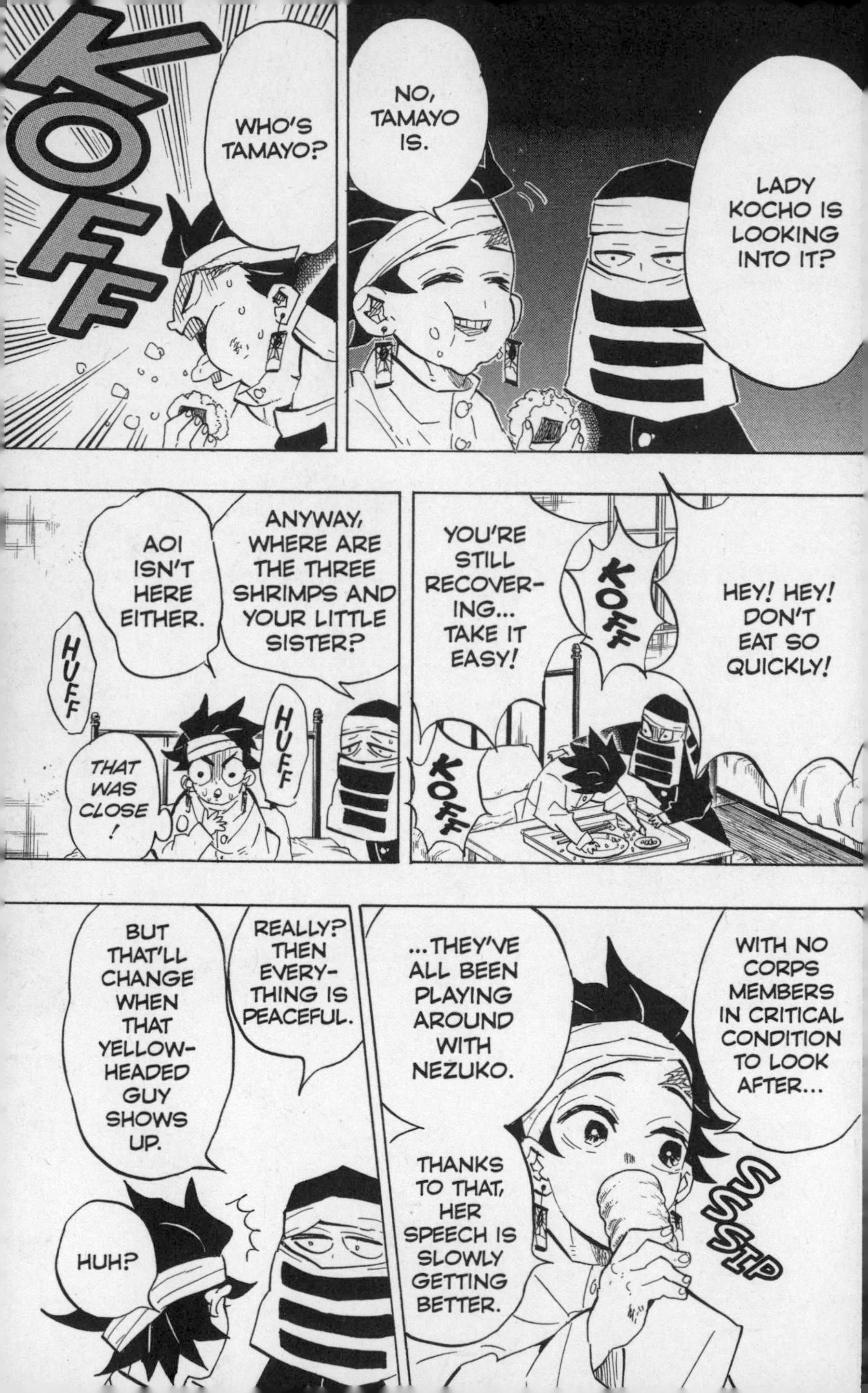
LADY KOCHO IS LOOKING INTO IT?
NO, TAMAYO IS.
WHO'S TAMAYO?
KOFF
HEY! HEY! DON'T EAT SO QUICKLY!
KOFF
YOU'RE STILL RECOVER-ING... TAKE IT EASY!
KOFF
ANYWAY, WHERE ARE THE THREE SHRIMPS AND YOUR LITTLE SISTER?
AOI ISN'T HERE EITHER.
HUFF
HUFF
THAT WAS CLOSE!
WITH NO CORPS MEMBERS IN CRITICAL CONDITION TO LOOK AFTER...
SSSIP
...THEY'VE ALL BEEN PLAYING AROUND WITH NEZUKO.
THANKS TO THAT, HER SPEECH IS SLOWLY GETTING BETTER.
REALLY? THEN EVERY-THING IS PEACEFUL.
BUT THAT'LL CHANGE WHEN THAT YELLOW-HEADED GUY SHOWS UP.
HUH?

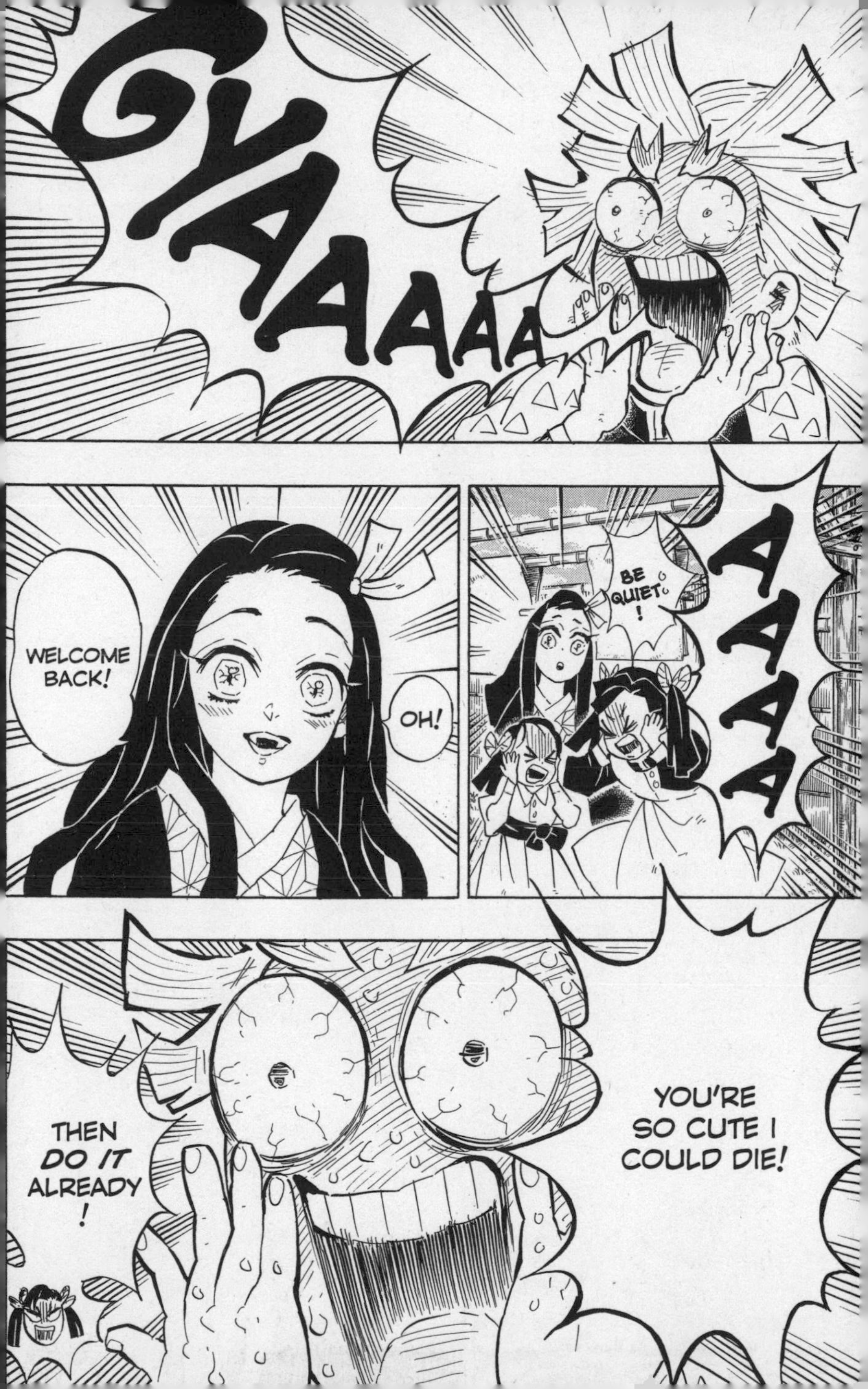
GYAAAAA
AAAA
BE QUIET!
OH!
WELCOME BACK!
YOU'RE SO CUTE I COULD DIE!
THEN *DO IT* ALREADY!

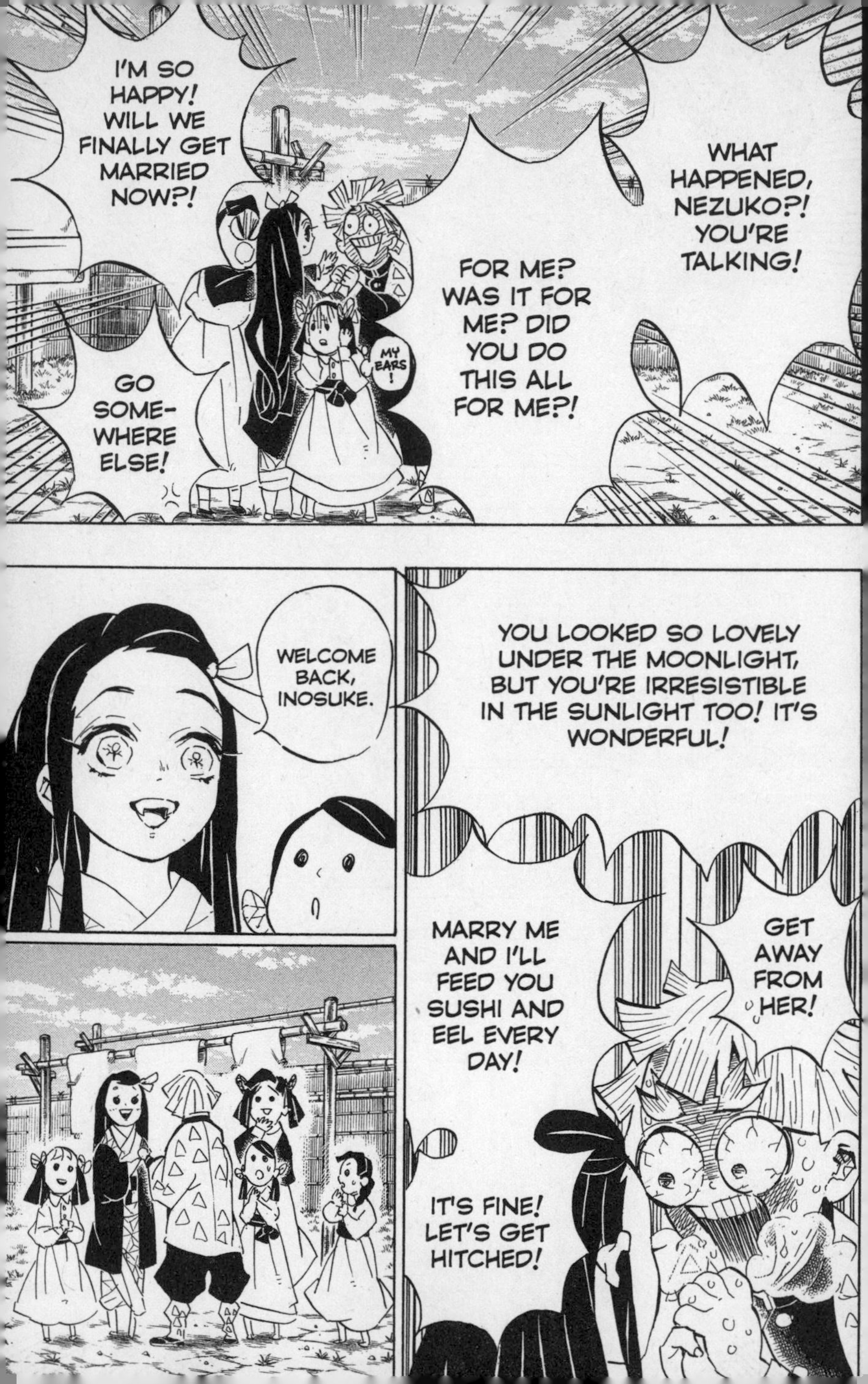
WHAT HAPPENED, NEZUKO?! YOU'RE TALKING!
FOR ME? WAS IT FOR ME? DID YOU DO THIS ALL FOR ME?!
I'M SO HAPPY! WILL WE FINALLY GET MARRIED NOW?!
MY EARS!
GO SOME-WHERE ELSE!
YOU LOOKED SO LOVELY UNDER THE MOONLIGHT, BUT YOU'RE IRRESISTIBLE IN THE SUNLIGHT TOO! IT'S WONDERFUL!
GET AWAY FROM HER!
MARRY ME AND I'LL FEED YOU SUSHI AND EEL EVERY DAY!
IT'S FINE! LET'S GET HITCHED!
WELCOME BACK, INOSUKE.

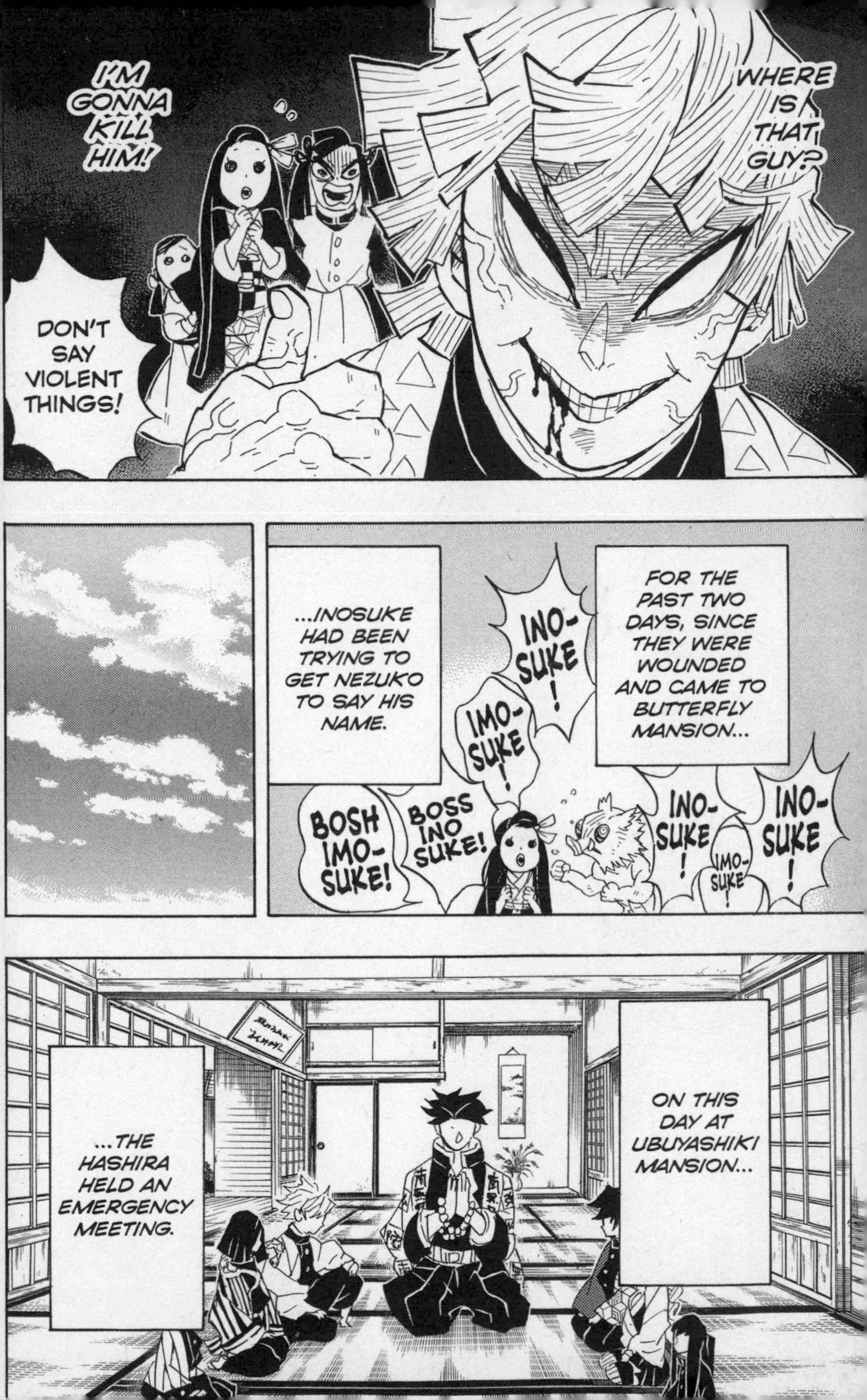
WHERE IS THAT GUY?
I'M GONNA KILL HIM!
DON'T SAY VIOLENT THINGS!
FOR THE PAST TWO DAYS, SINCE THEY WERE WOUNDED AND CAME TO BUTTERFLY MANSION...
INO-SUKE!
...INOSUKE HAD BEEN TRYING TO GET NEZUKO TO SAY HIS NAME.
IMO-SUKE!
INO-SUKE!
INO-SUKE!
IMO-SUKE
BOSS INO SUKE!
BOSH IMO-SUKE!
ON THIS DAY AT UBUYASHIKI MANSION...
...THE HASHIRA HELD AN EMERGENCY MEETING.

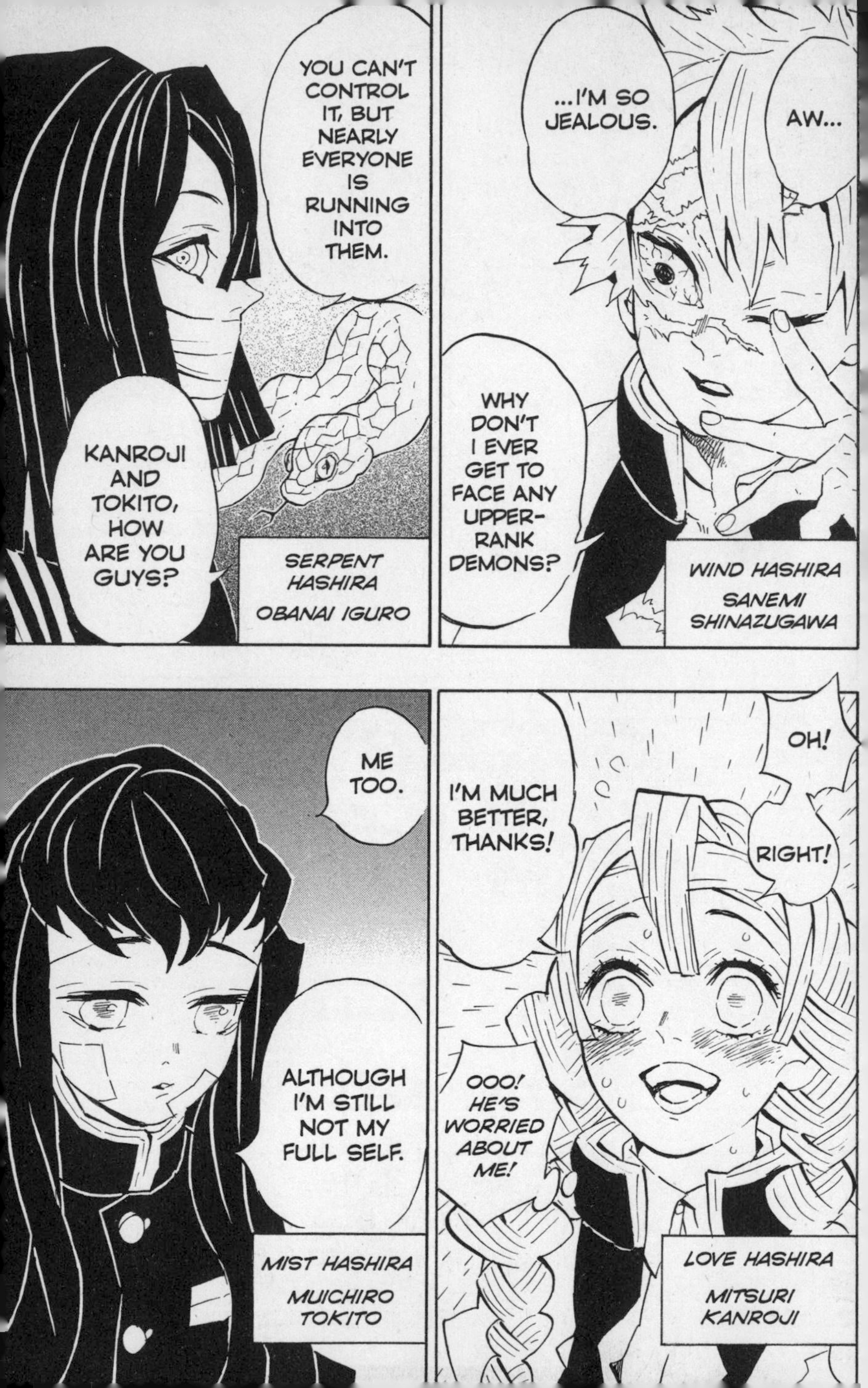
AW...
...I'M SO JEALOUS.
WHY DON'T I EVER GET TO FACE ANY UPPER-RANK DEMONS?
WIND HASHIRA SANEMI SHINAZUGAWA
YOU CAN'T CONTROL IT, BUT NEARLY EVERYONE IS RUNNING INTO THEM.
KANROJI AND TOKITO, HOW ARE YOU GUYS?
SERPENT HASHIRA OBANAI IGURO
OH!
RIGHT!
I'M MUCH BETTER, THANKS!
OOO! HE'S WORRIED ABOUT ME!
LOVE HASHIRA MITSURI KANROJI
ME TOO.
ALTHOUGH I'M STILL NOT MY FULL SELF.
MIST HASHIRA MUICHIRO TOKITO

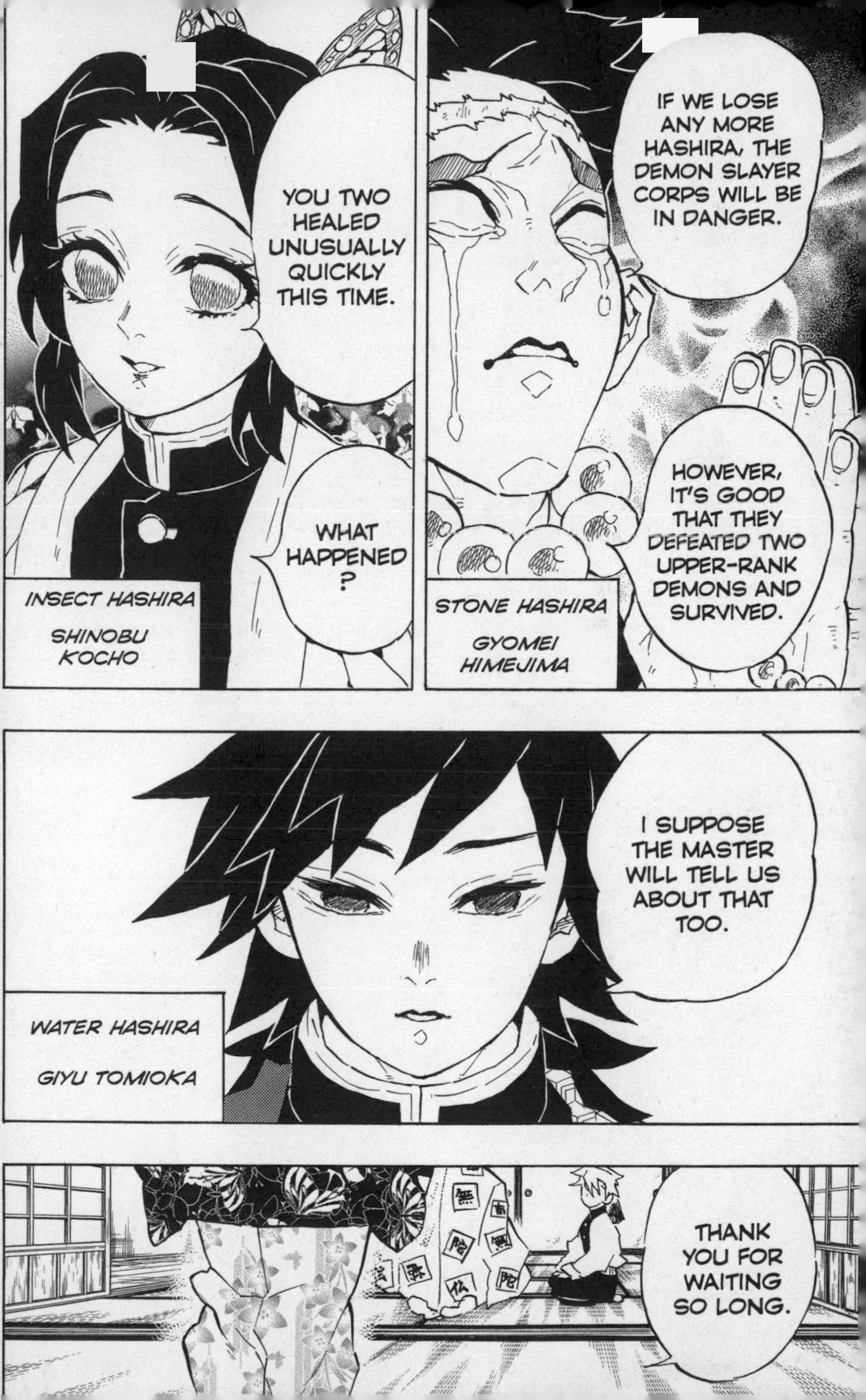
STONE HASHIRA GYOMEI HIMEJIMA
IF WE LOSE ANY MORE HASHIRA, THE DEMON SLAYER CORPS WILL BE IN DANGER.
HOWEVER, IT'S GOOD THAT THEY DEFEATED TWO UPPER-RANK DEMONS AND SURVIVED.
INSECT HASHIRA SHINOBU KOCHO
YOU TWO HEALED UNUSUALLY QUICKLY THIS TIME.
WHAT HAPPENED?
I SUPPOSE THE MASTER WILL TELL US ABOUT THAT TOO.
WATER HASHIRA GIYU TOMIOKA
THANK YOU FOR WAITING SO LONG.

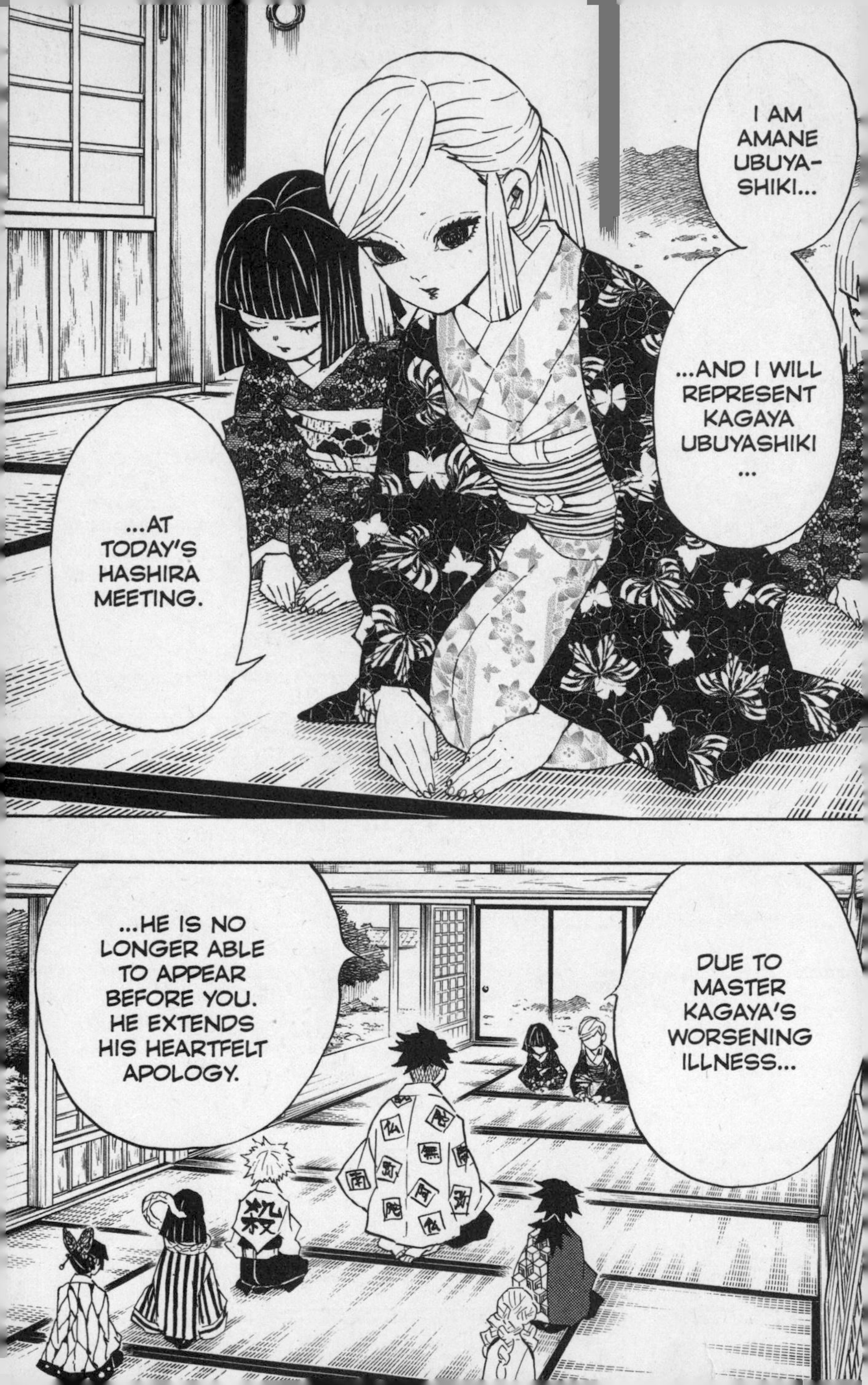
I AM AMANE UBUYASHIKI...
...AND I WILL REPRESENT KAGAYA UBUYASHIKI ...
...AT TODAY'S HASHIRA MEETING.
DUE TO MASTER KAGAYA'S WORSENING ILLNESS...
...HE IS NO LONGER ABLE TO APPEAR BEFORE YOU. HE EXTENDS HIS HEARTFELT APOLOGY.

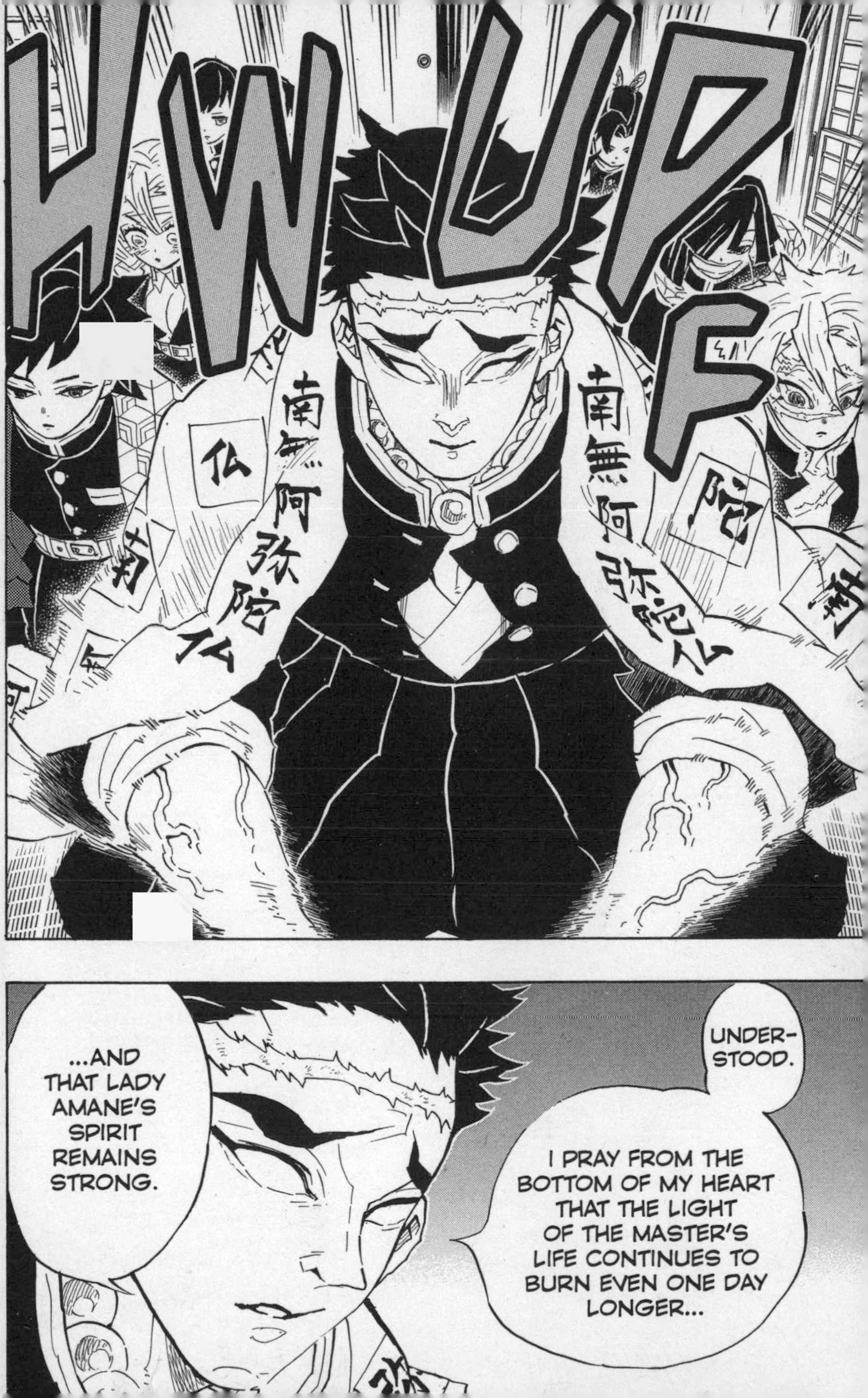
HWUPF
南無阿弥陀仏
南無阿弥陀仏
UNDER-STOOD.
I PRAY FROM THE BOTTOM OF MY HEART THAT THE LIGHT OF THE MASTER'S LIFE CONTINUES TO BURN EVEN ONE DAY LONGER...
...AND THAT LADY AMANE'S SPIRIT REMAINS STRONG.

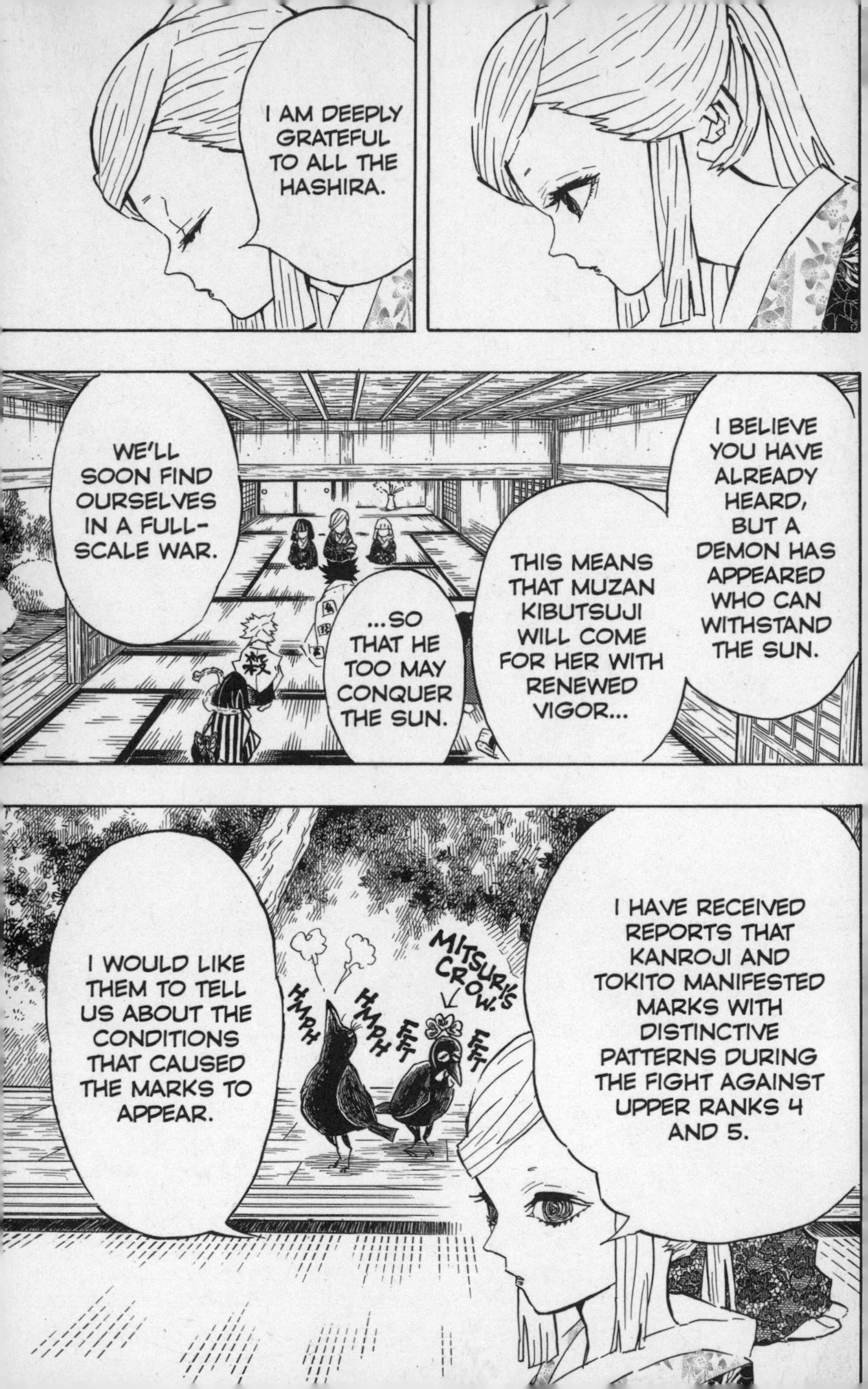
I AM DEEPLY GRATEFUL TO ALL THE HASHIRA.
I BELIEVE YOU HAVE ALREADY HEARD, BUT A DEMON HAS APPEARED WHO CAN WITHSTAND THE SUN.
THIS MEANS THAT MUZAN KIBUTSUJI WILL COME FOR HER WITH RENEWED VIGOR...
...SO THAT HE TOO MAY CONQUER THE SUN.
WE'LL SOON FIND OURSELVES IN A FULL-SCALE WAR.
I HAVE RECEIVED REPORTS THAT KANROJI AND TOKITO MANIFESTED MARKS WITH DISTINCTIVE PATTERNS DURING THE FIGHT AGAINST UPPER RANKS 4 AND 5.
MITSURI'S CROW.
EEK
EEK
HMPH
HMPH
I WOULD LIKE THEM TO TELL US ABOUT THE CONDITIONS THAT CAUSED THE MARKS TO APPEAR.

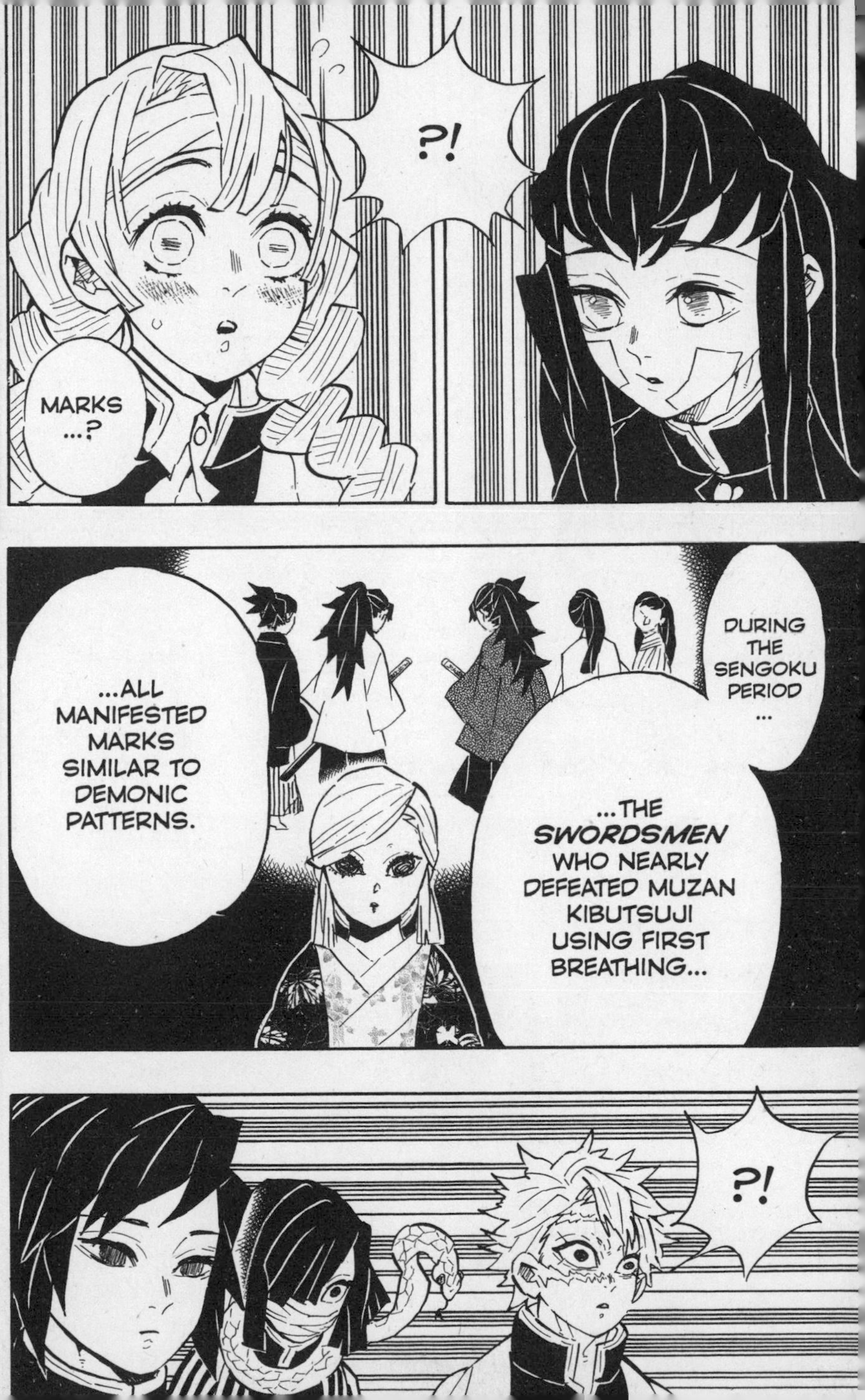
?!
MARKS ...?
DURING THE SENGOKU PERIOD ...
...THE *SWORDSMEN* WHO NEARLY DEFEATED MUZAN KIBUTSUJI USING FIRST BREATHING...
...ALL MANIFESTED MARKS SIMILAR TO DEMONIC PATTERNS.
?!

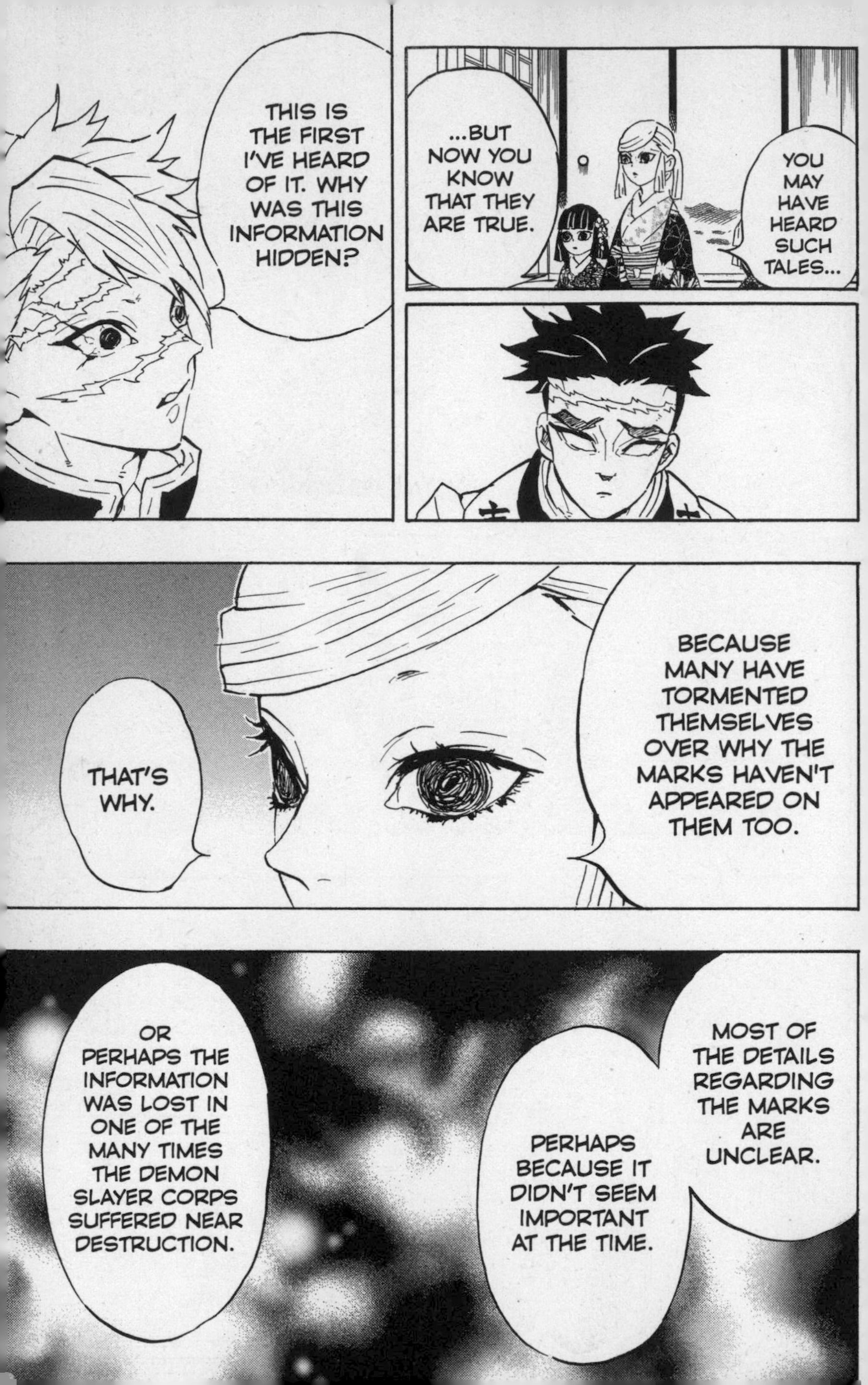
YOU MAY HAVE HEARD SUCH TALES...
...BUT NOW YOU KNOW THAT THEY ARE TRUE.
THIS IS THE FIRST I'VE HEARD OF IT. WHY WAS THIS INFORMATION HIDDEN?
BECAUSE MANY HAVE TORMENTED THEMSELVES OVER WHY THE MARKS HAVEN'T APPEARED ON THEM TOO.
THAT'S WHY.
MOST OF THE DETAILS REGARDING THE MARKS ARE UNCLEAR.
PERHAPS BECAUSE IT DIDN'T SEEM IMPORTANT AT THE TIME.
OR PERHAPS THE INFORMATION WAS LOST IN ONE OF THE MANY TIMES THE DEMON SLAYER CORPS SUFFERED NEAR DESTRUCTION.

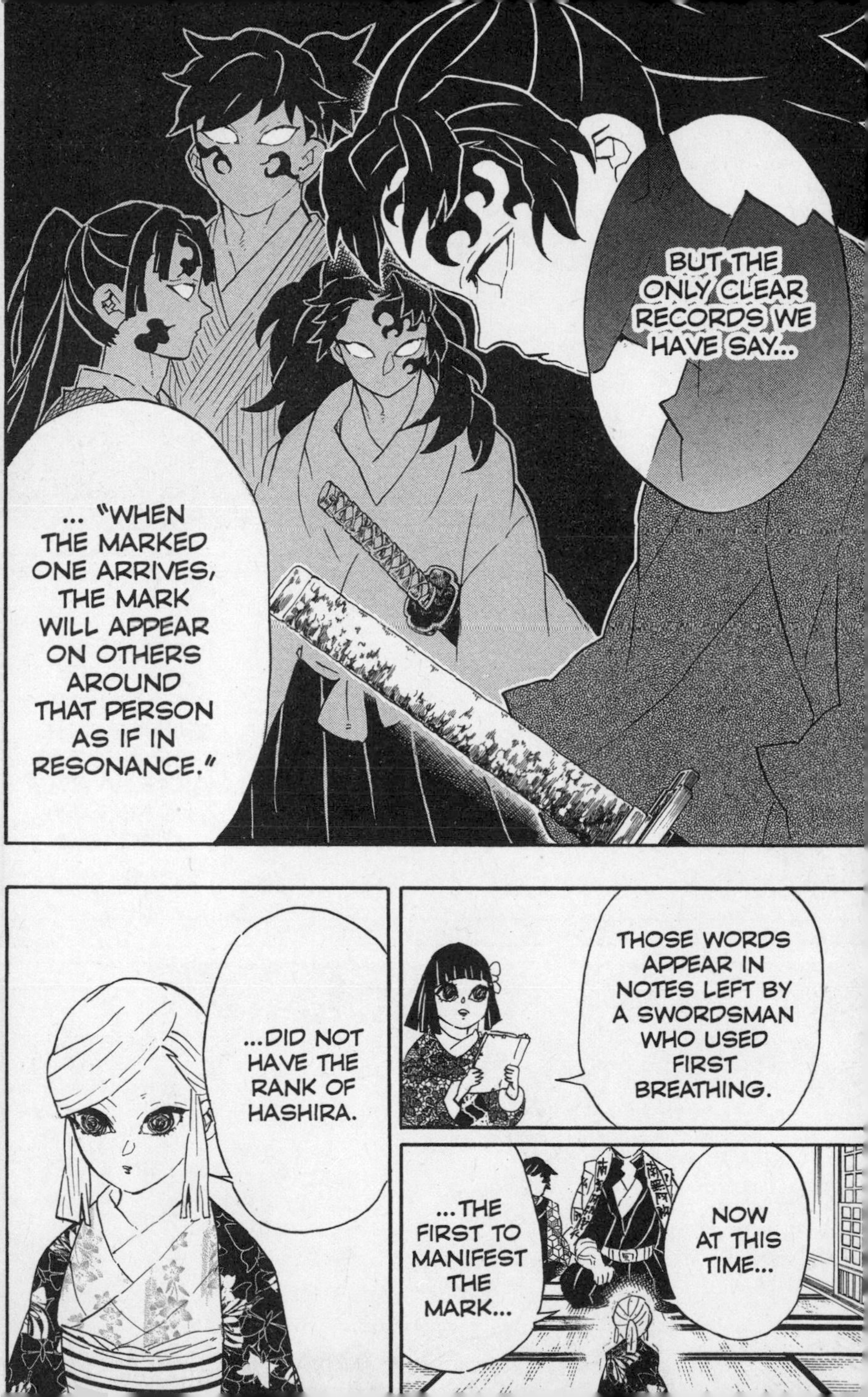
BUT THE ONLY CLEAR RECORDS WE HAVE SAY...
... "WHEN THE MARKED ONE ARRIVES, THE MARK WILL APPEAR ON OTHERS AROUND THAT PERSON AS IF IN RESONANCE."
THOSE WORDS APPEAR IN NOTES LEFT BY A SWORDSMAN WHO USED FIRST BREATHING.
NOW AT THIS TIME...
...THE FIRST TO MANIFEST THE MARK...
...DID NOT HAVE THE RANK OF HASHIRA.

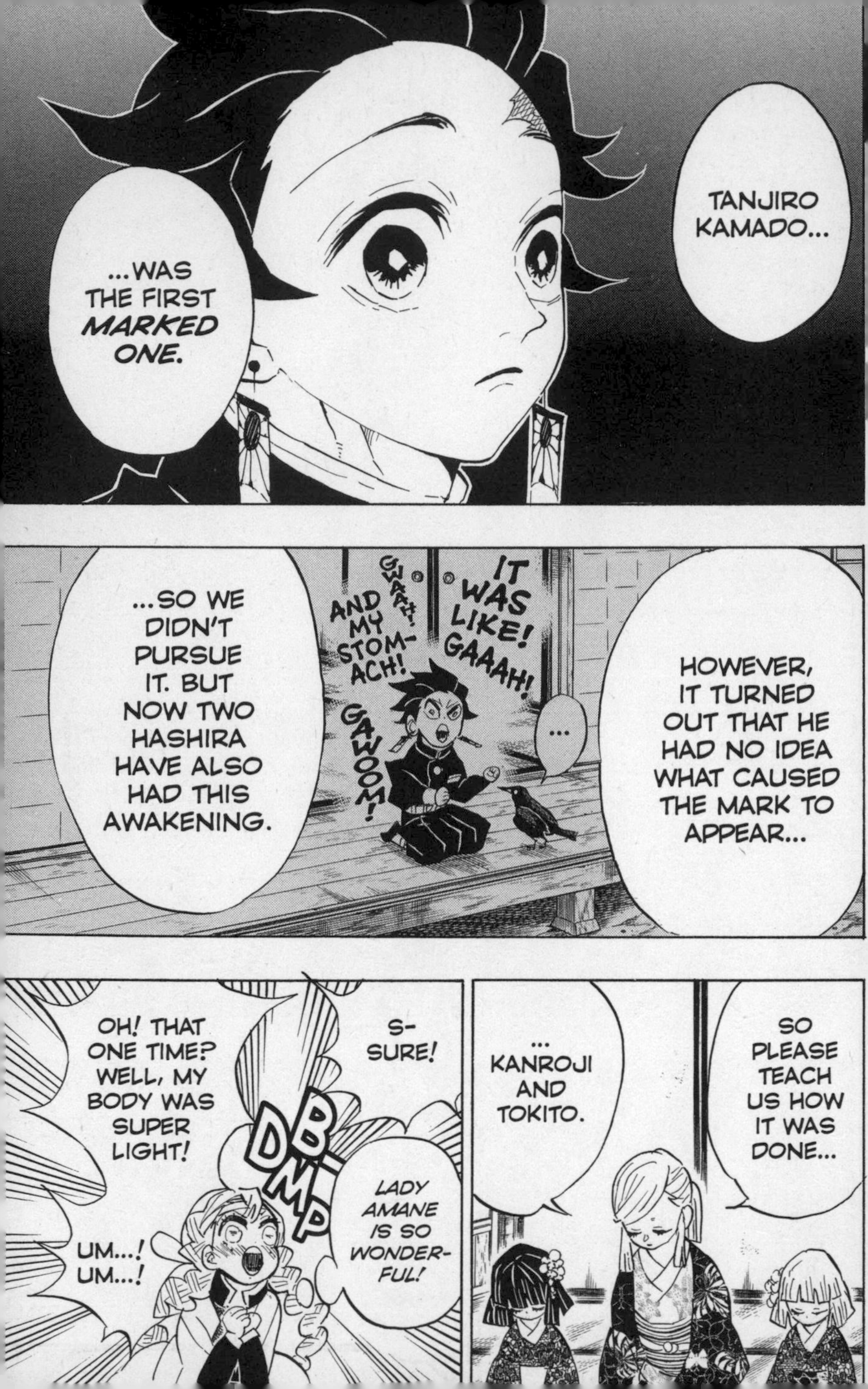
TANJIRO KAMADO...
...WAS THE FIRST *MARKED* ONE.
HOWEVER, IT TURNED OUT THAT HE HAD NO IDEA WHAT CAUSED THE MARK TO APPEAR...
...
IT WAS LIKE! GAAAH!
GWAAH! AND MY STOMACH!
GAWOOM!
...SO WE DIDN'T PURSUE IT. BUT NOW TWO HASHIRA HAVE ALSO HAD THIS AWAKENING.
SO PLEASE TEACH US HOW IT WAS DONE...
... KANROJI AND TOKITO.
S-SURE!
BDMP
LADY AMANE IS SO WONDERFUL!
OH! THAT ONE TIME? WELL, MY BODY WAS SUPER LIGHT!
UM...! UM...!

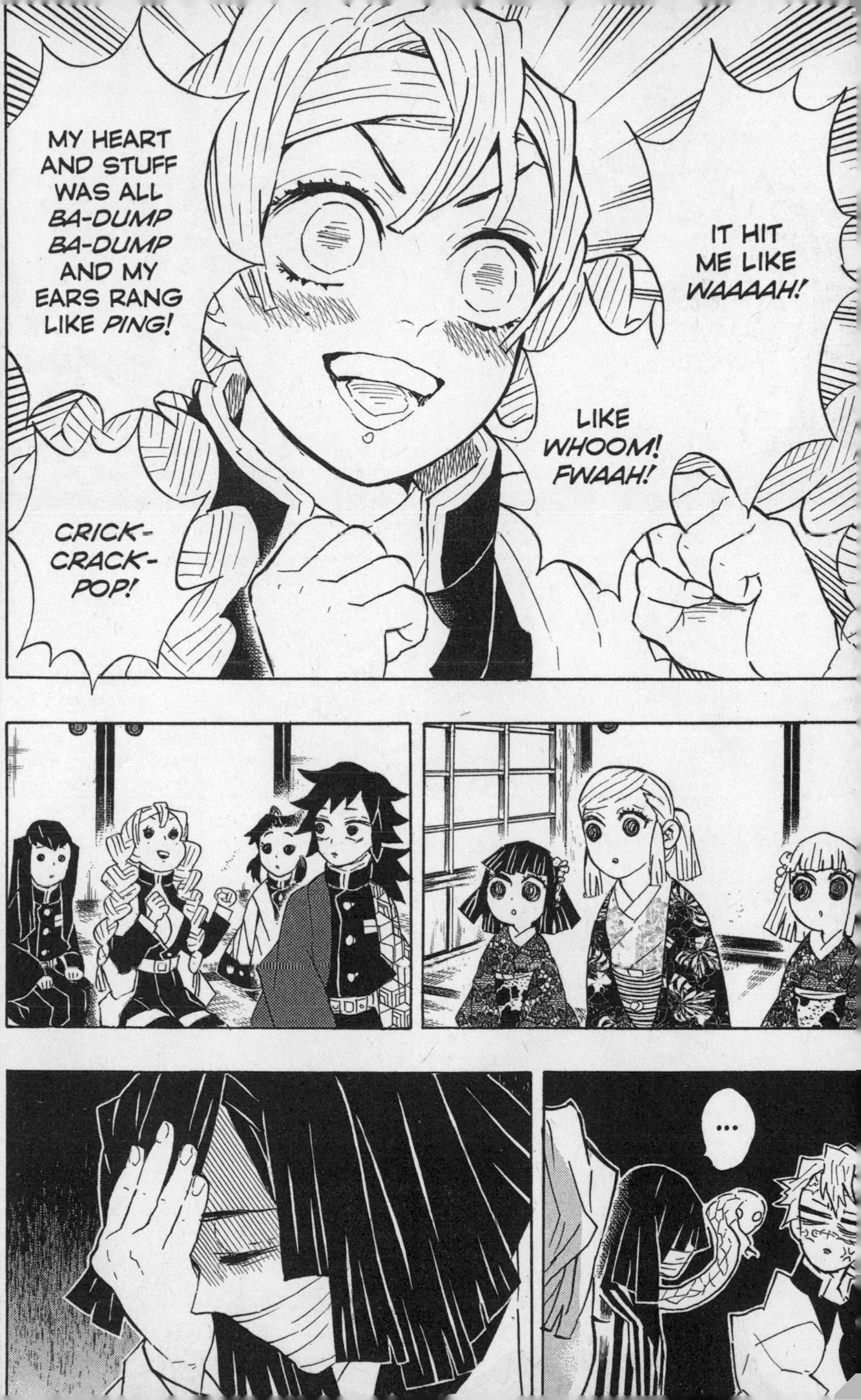
IT HIT ME LIKE *WAAAAH!*
LIKE *WHOOM! FWAAH!*
MY HEART AND STUFF WAS ALL *BA-DUMP BA-DUMP* AND MY EARS RANG LIKE *PING!*
CRICK-CRACK-POP!
...

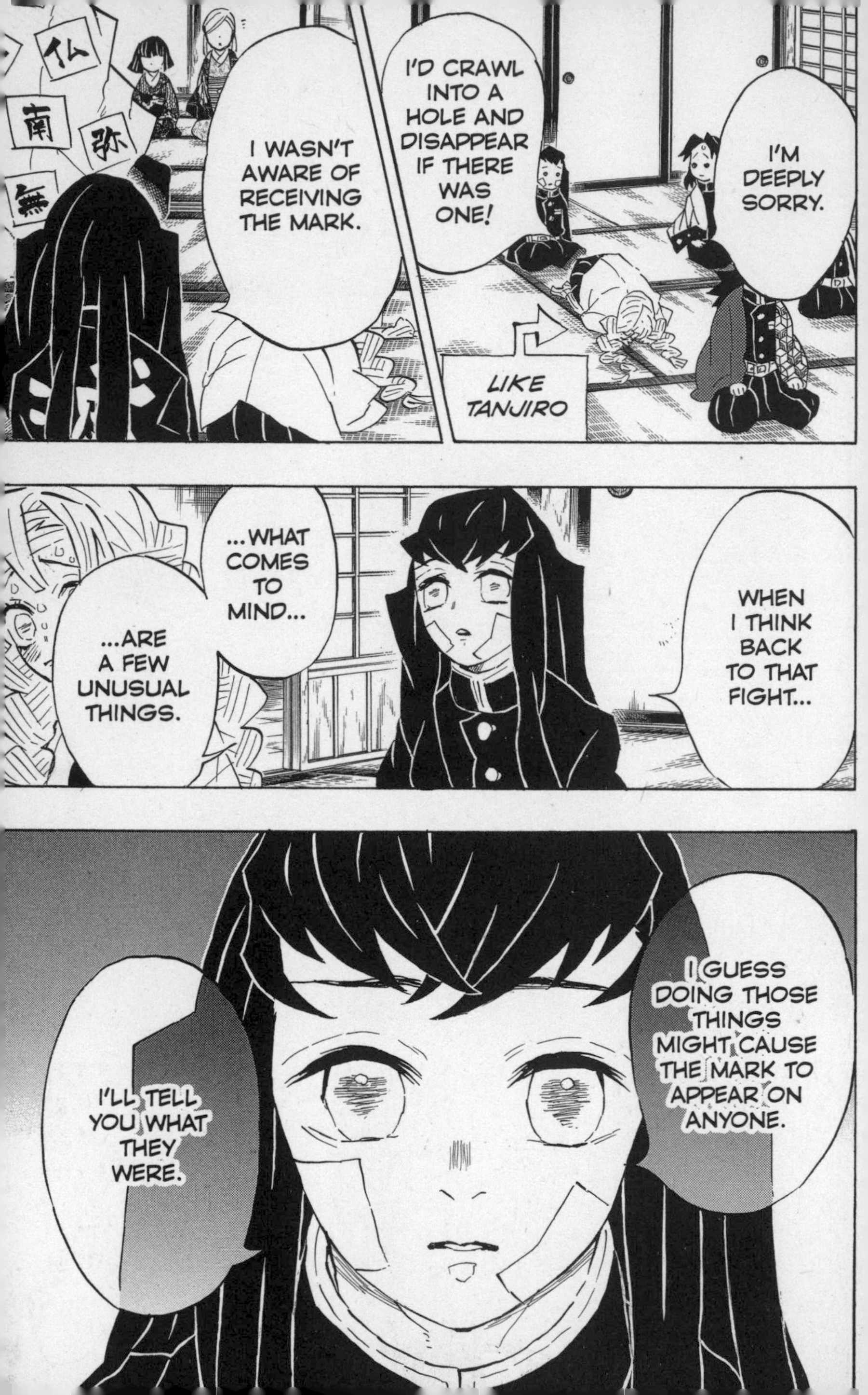
I'M DEEPLY SORRY.
I'D CRAWL INTO A HOLE AND DISAPPEAR IF THERE WAS ONE!
LIKE TANJIRO
I WASN'T AWARE OF RECEIVING THE MARK.
WHEN I THINK BACK TO THAT FIGHT...
...WHAT COMES TO MIND...
...ARE A FEW UNUSUAL THINGS.
I GUESS DOING THOSE THINGS MIGHT CAUSE THE MARK TO APPEAR ON ANYONE.
I'LL TELL YOU WHAT THEY WERE.

Shinobu hands Mitsuri a handkerchief because she is too embarrassed and can't stop sweating.

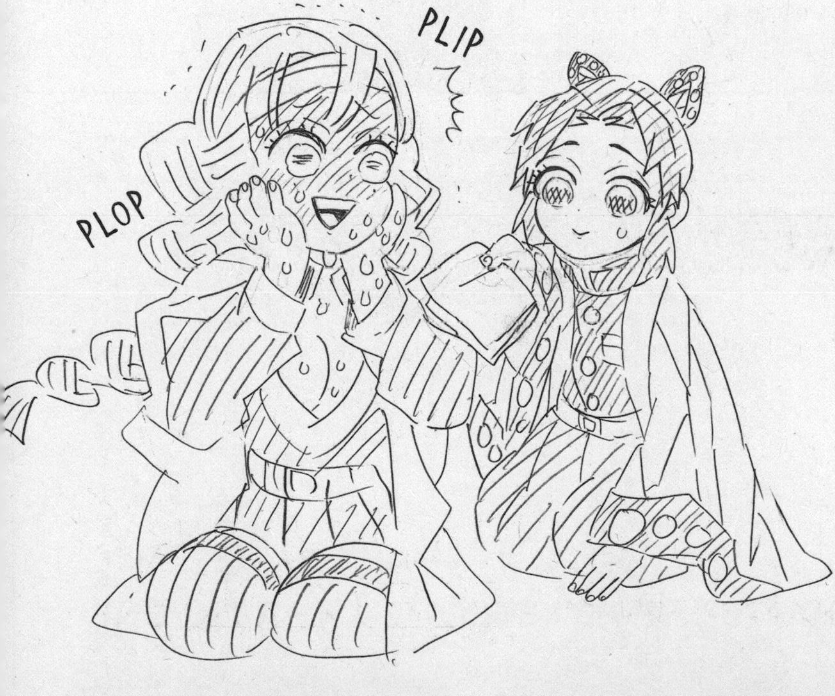
PLIP
PLOP

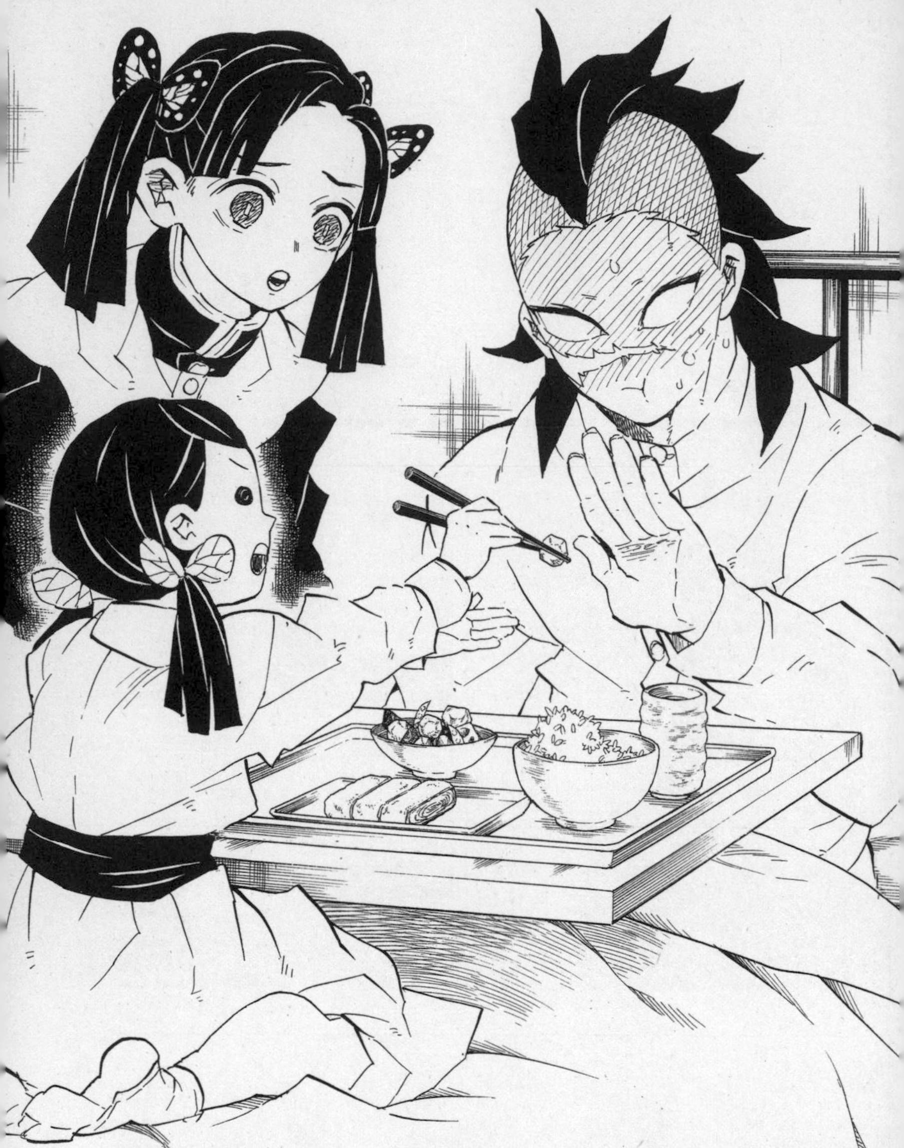

CHAPTER 129: TO BECOME A MARKED ONE

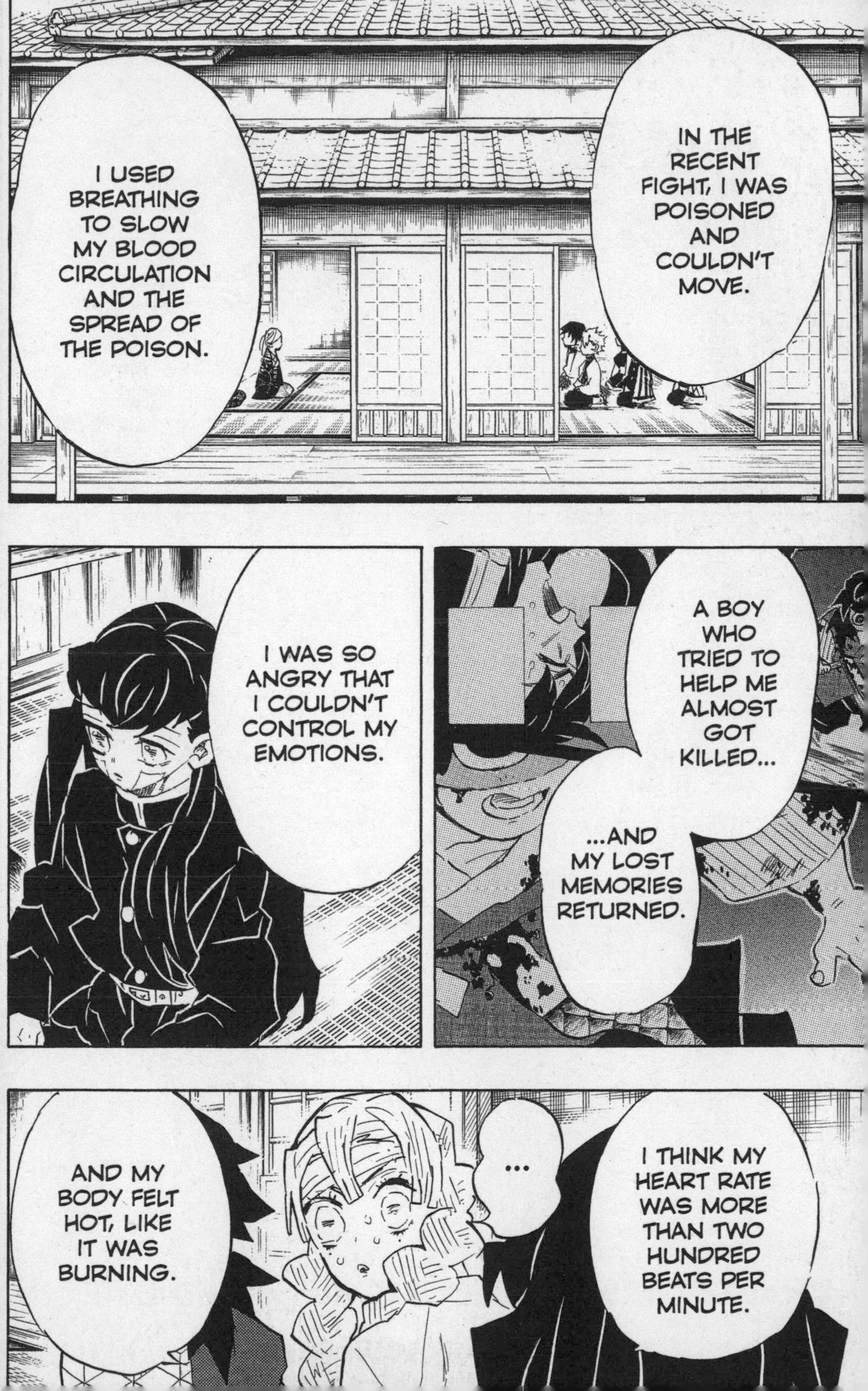
IN THE RECENT FIGHT, I WAS POISONED AND COULDN'T MOVE.
I USED BREATHING TO SLOW MY BLOOD CIRCULATION AND THE SPREAD OF THE POISON.
A BOY WHO TRIED TO HELP ME ALMOST GOT KILLED...
...AND MY LOST MEMORIES RETURNED.
I WAS SO ANGRY THAT I COULDN'T CONTROL MY EMOTIONS.
I THINK MY HEART RATE WAS MORE THAN TWO HUNDRED BEATS PER MINUTE.
...
AND MY BODY FELT HOT, LIKE IT WAS BURNING.

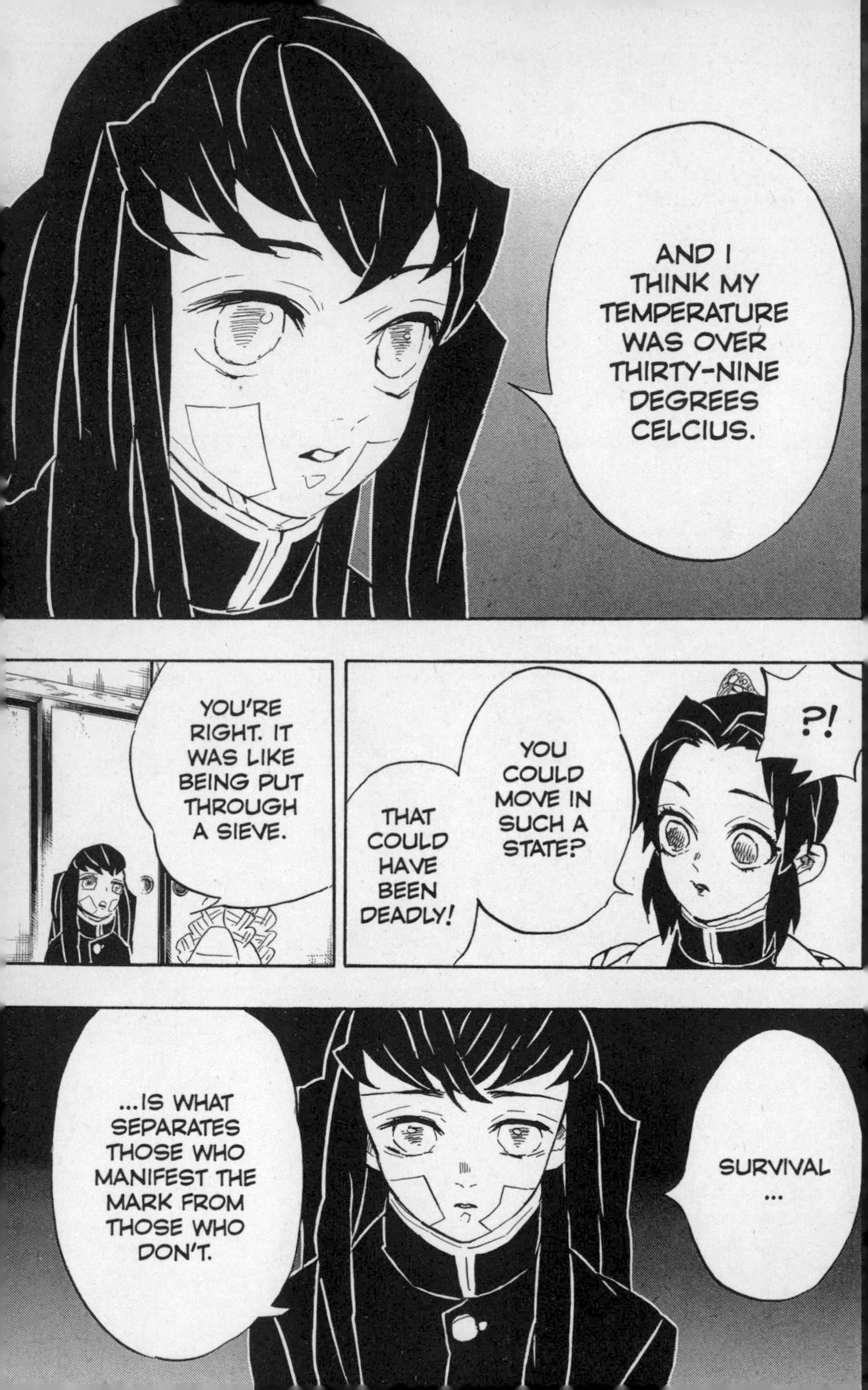
AND I THINK MY TEMPERATURE WAS OVER THIRTY-NINE DEGREES CELCIUS.
?!
YOU COULD MOVE IN SUCH A STATE?
THAT COULD HAVE BEEN DEADLY!
YOU'RE RIGHT. IT WAS LIKE BEING PUT THROUGH A SIEVE.
SURVIVAL...
...IS WHAT SEPARATES THOSE WHO MANIFEST THE MARK FROM THOSE WHO DON'T.

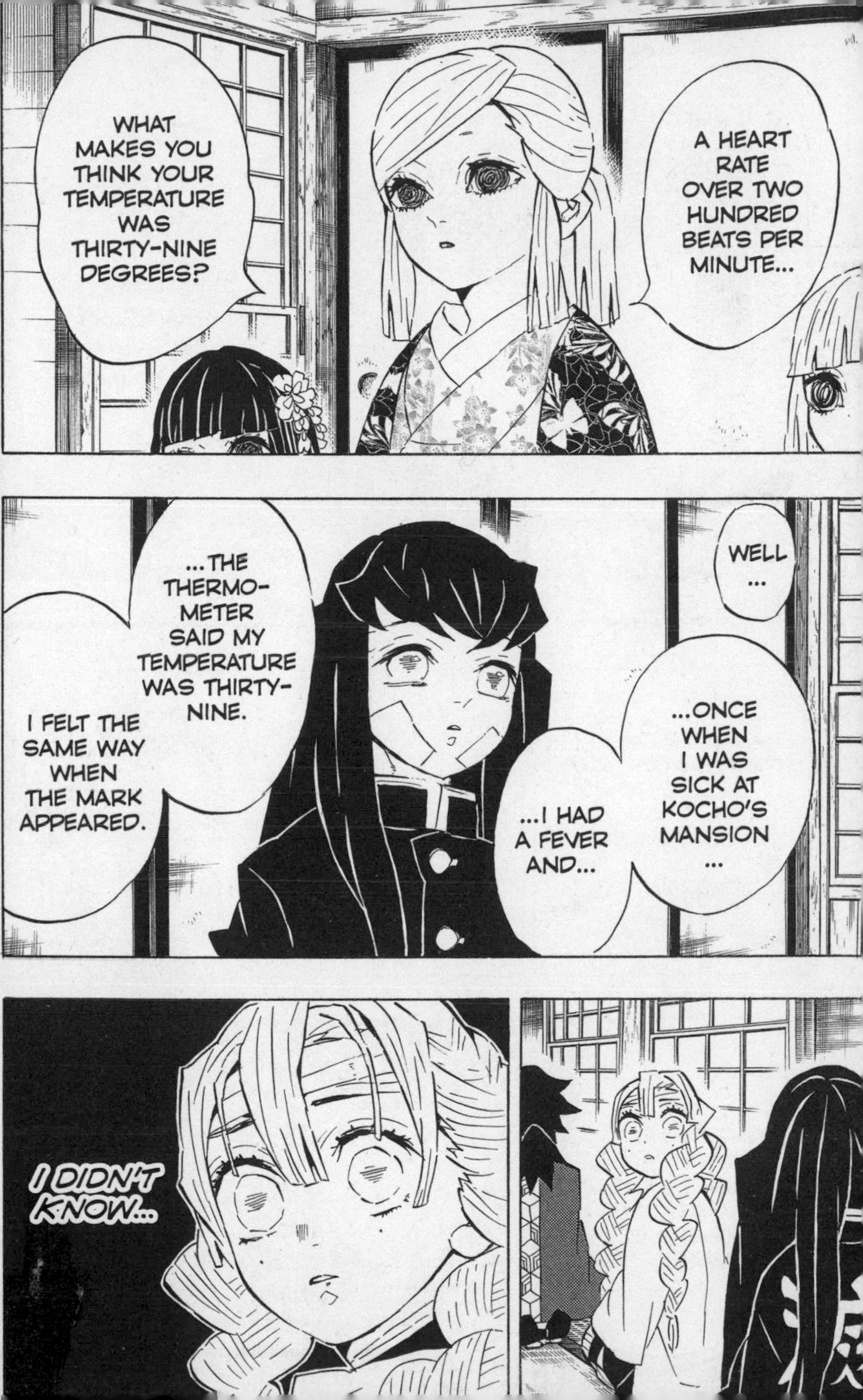
A HEART RATE OVER TWO HUNDRED BEATS PER MINUTE...
WHAT MAKES YOU THINK YOUR TEMPERATURE WAS THIRTY-NINE DEGREES?
WELL ...
...ONCE WHEN I WAS SICK AT KOCHO'S MANSION ...
...I HAD A FEVER AND...
...THE THERMOMETER SAID MY TEMPERATURE WAS THIRTY-NINE.
I FELT THE SAME WAY WHEN THE MARK APPEARED.
I DIDN'T KNOW...

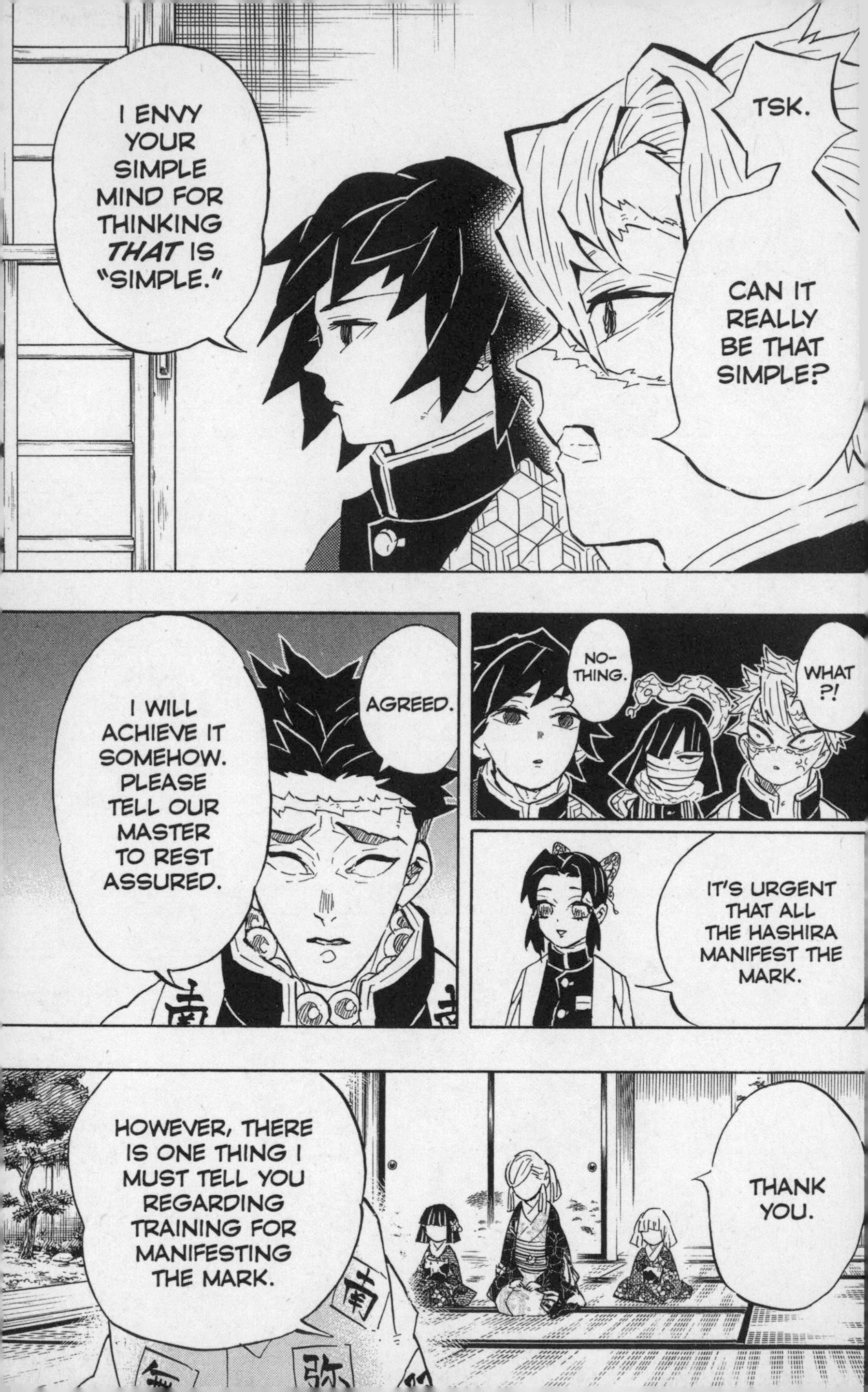
TSK.
CAN IT REALLY BE THAT SIMPLE?
I ENVY YOUR SIMPLE MIND FOR THINKING *THAT* IS "SIMPLE."
WHAT?!
NO-THING.
IT'S URGENT THAT ALL THE HASHIRA MANIFEST THE MARK.
AGREED.
I WILL ACHIEVE IT SOMEHOW. PLEASE TELL OUR MASTER TO REST ASSURED.
THANK YOU.
HOWEVER, THERE IS ONE THING I MUST TELL YOU REGARDING TRAINING FOR MANIFESTING THE MARK.

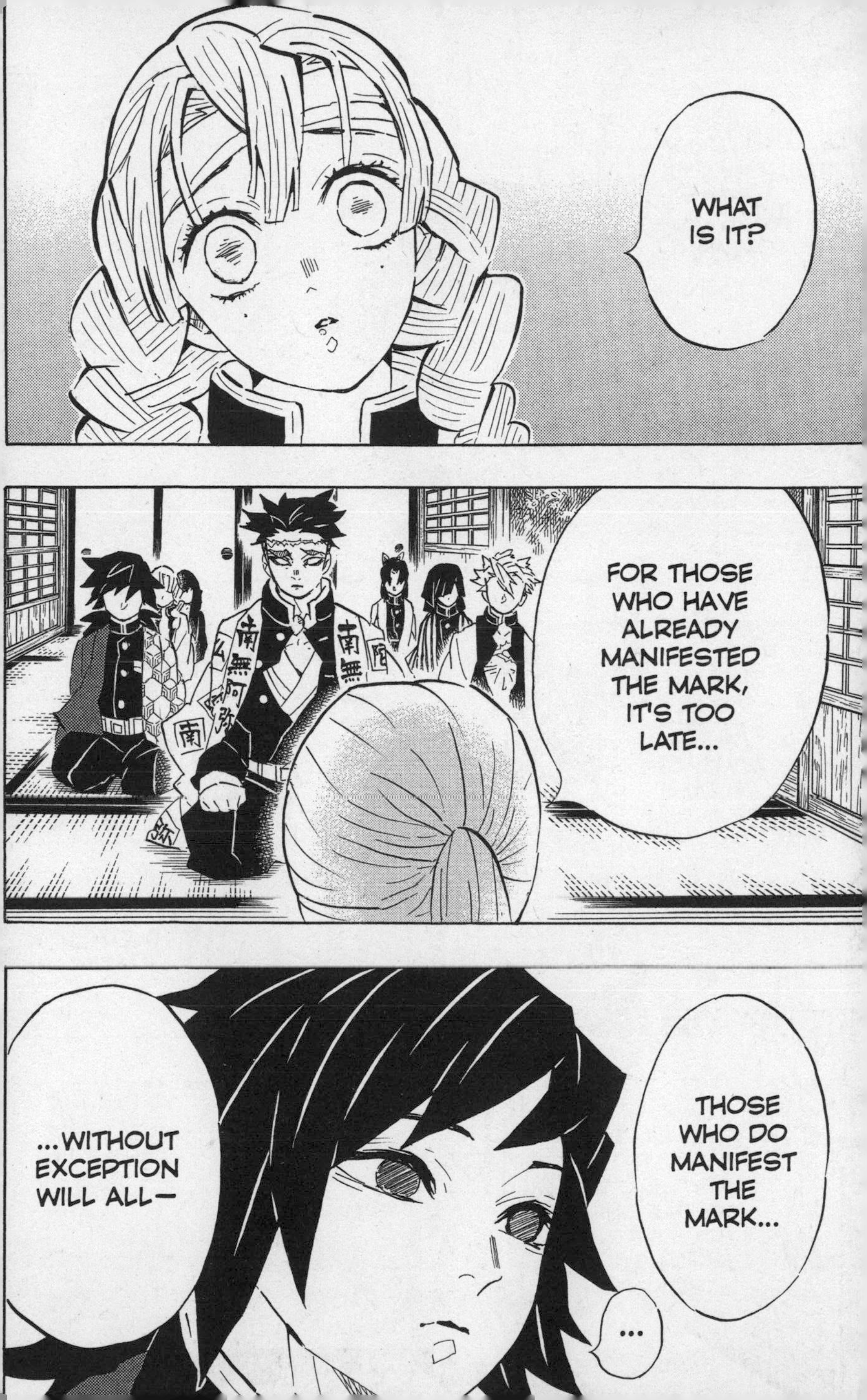
WHAT IS IT?
FOR THOSE WHO HAVE ALREADY MANIFESTED THE MARK, IT'S TOO LATE...
THOSE WHO DO MANIFEST THE MARK...
...WITHOUT EXCEPTION WILL ALL—
...

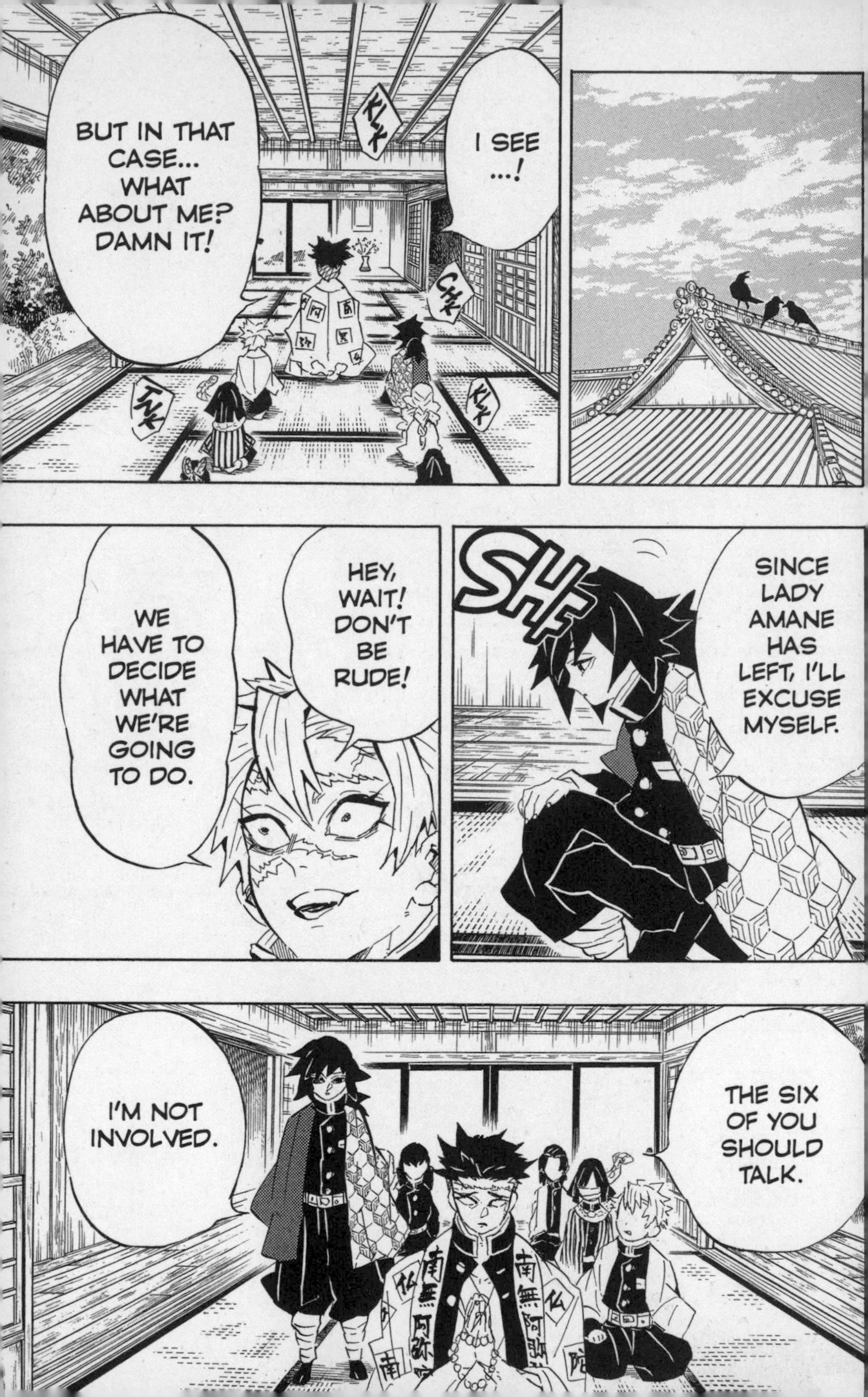
I SEE ...!
KLK
CHK
KLK
BUT IN THAT CASE... WHAT ABOUT ME? DAMN IT!
TNK
SINCE LADY AMANE HAS LEFT, I'LL EXCUSE MYSELF.
SHF
HEY, WAIT! DON'T BE RUDE!
WE HAVE TO DECIDE WHAT WE'RE GOING TO DO.
THE SIX OF YOU SHOULD TALK.
I'M NOT INVOLVED.

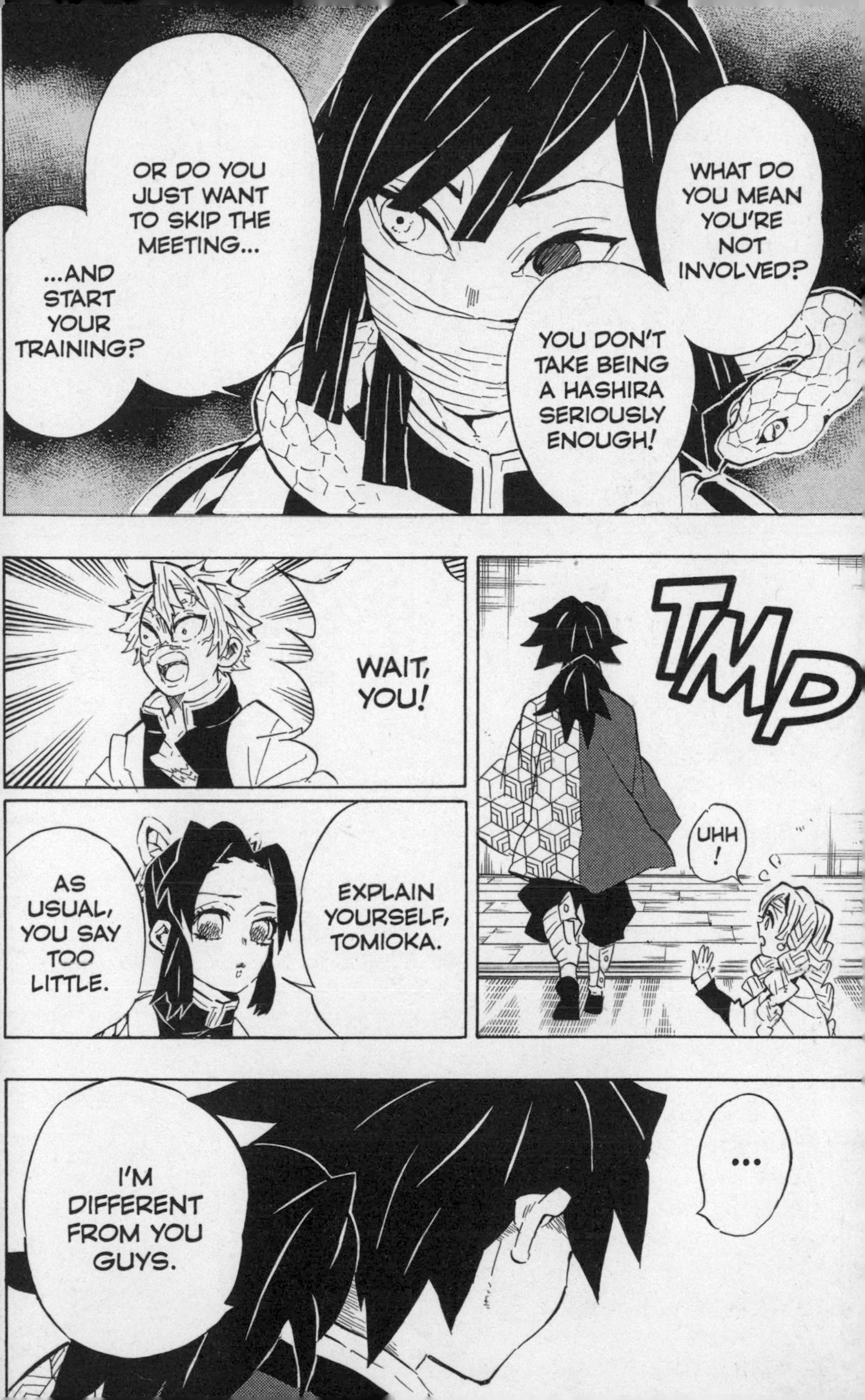
WHAT DO YOU MEAN YOU'RE NOT INVOLVED?
YOU DON'T TAKE BEING A HASHIRA SERIOUSLY ENOUGH!
OR DO YOU JUST WANT TO SKIP THE MEETING...
...AND START YOUR TRAINING?
TMP
UHH!
WAIT, YOU!
EXPLAIN YOURSELF, TOMIOKA.
AS USUAL, YOU SAY TOO LITTLE.
...
I'M DIFFERENT FROM YOU GUYS.

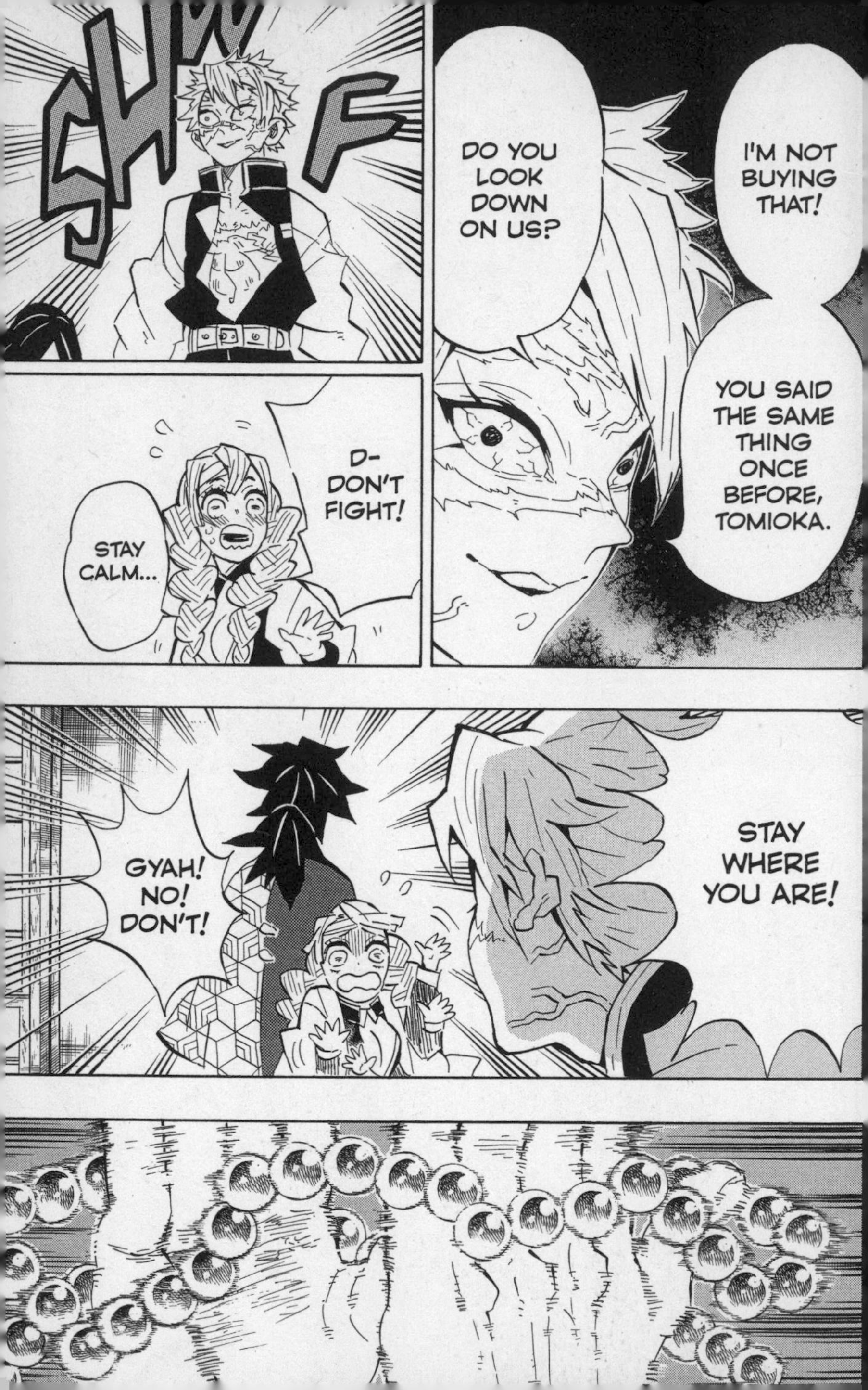
I'M NOT BUYING THAT!
DO YOU LOOK DOWN ON US?
YOU SAID THE SAME THING ONCE BEFORE, TOMIOKA.
SHFF
D-DON'T FIGHT!
STAY CALM...
STAY WHERE YOU ARE!
GYAH! NO! DON'T!

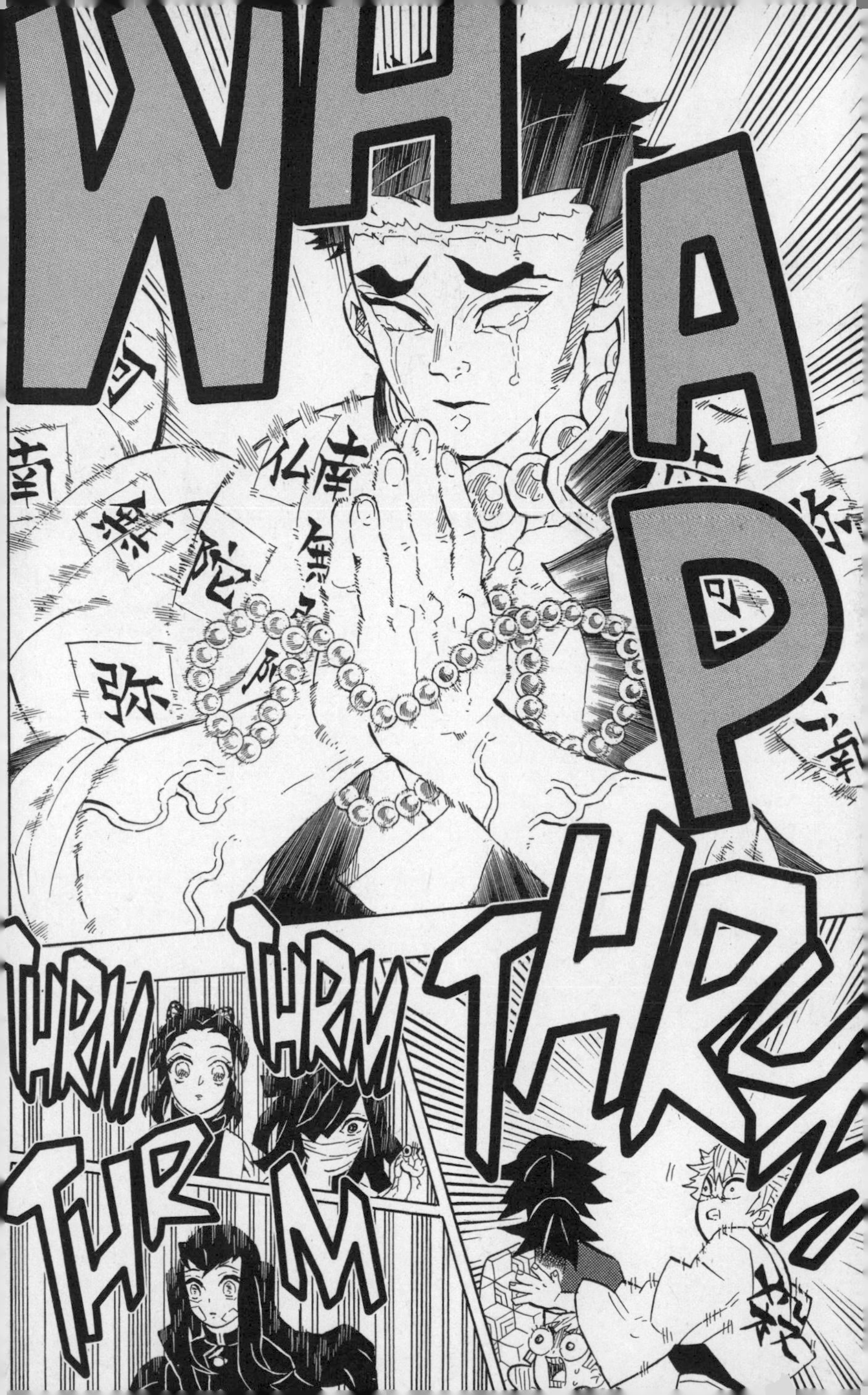
WHAP
THRM
THRM
THRM
THRM

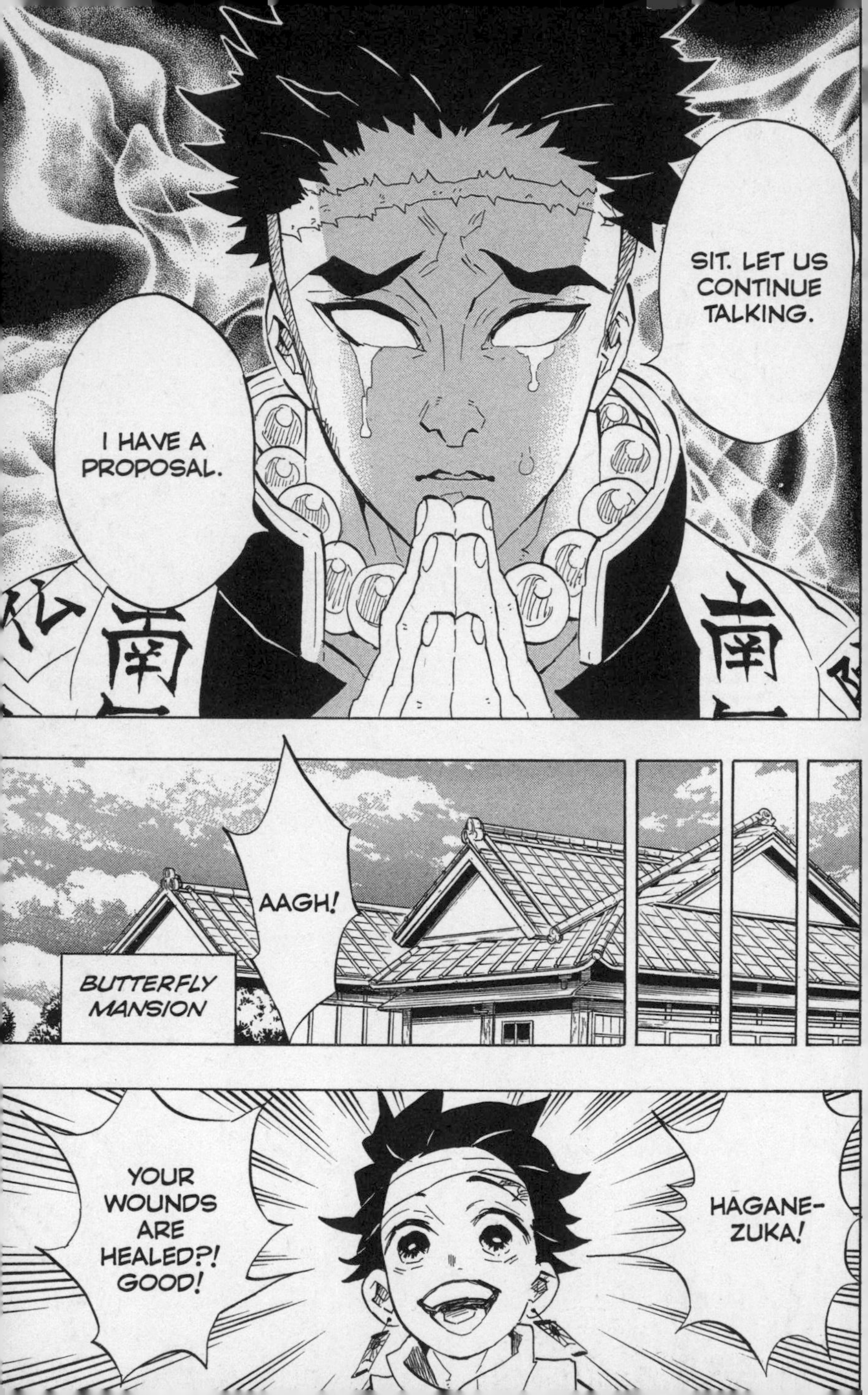
SIT. LET US CONTINUE TALKING.
I HAVE A PROPOSAL.
AAGH!
BUTTERFLY MANSION
HAGANE-ZUKA!
YOUR WOUNDS ARE HEALED?! GOOD!

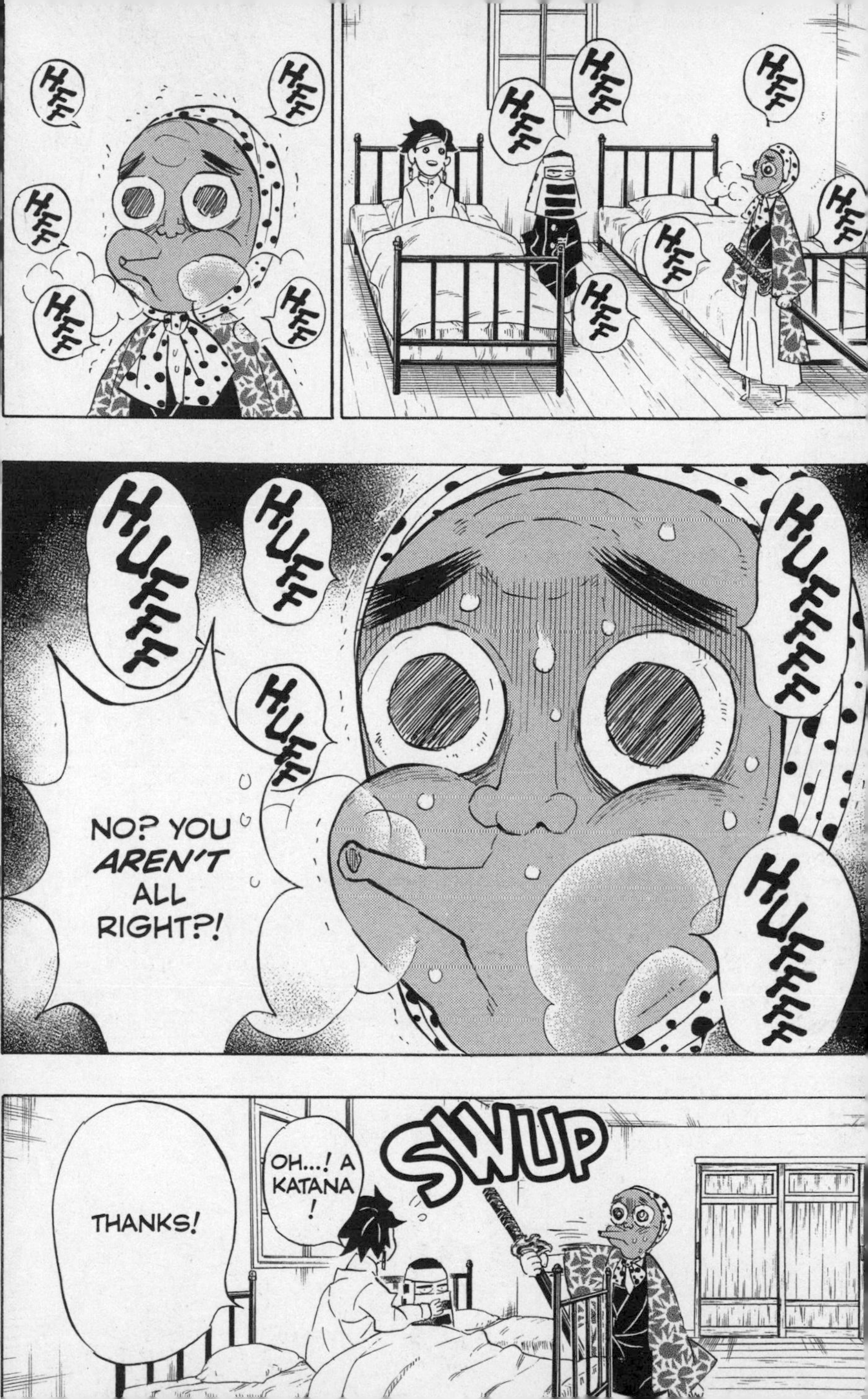
HFFF
HFFF
HFFF
HFFF
HFFF
HFFF
HFFF
HFFF
HFFF
HFFF
HUFFFFF
HUFFFFF
HUFF
HUFF
HUFFFF
NO? YOU *AREN'T* ALL RIGHT?!
SWUP
OH...! A KATANA !
THANKS!

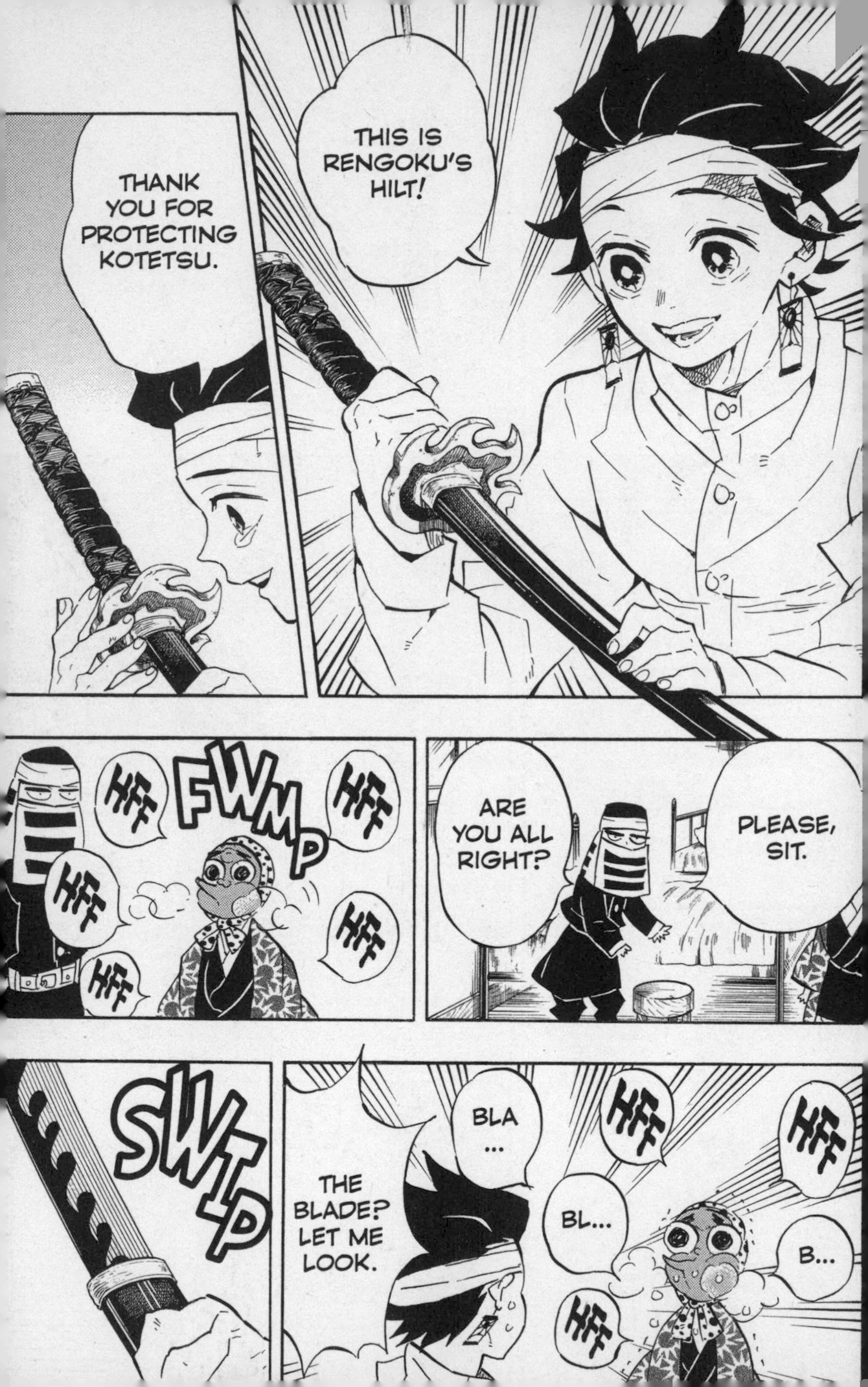
THIS IS RENGOKU'S HILT!
THANK YOU FOR PROTECTING KOTETSU.
PLEASE, SIT.
ARE YOU ALL RIGHT?
HFF
HFF
FWMP
HFF
HFF
HFF
HFF
HFF
B...
BL...
BLA ...
HFF
THE BLADE? LET ME LOOK.
SWIP

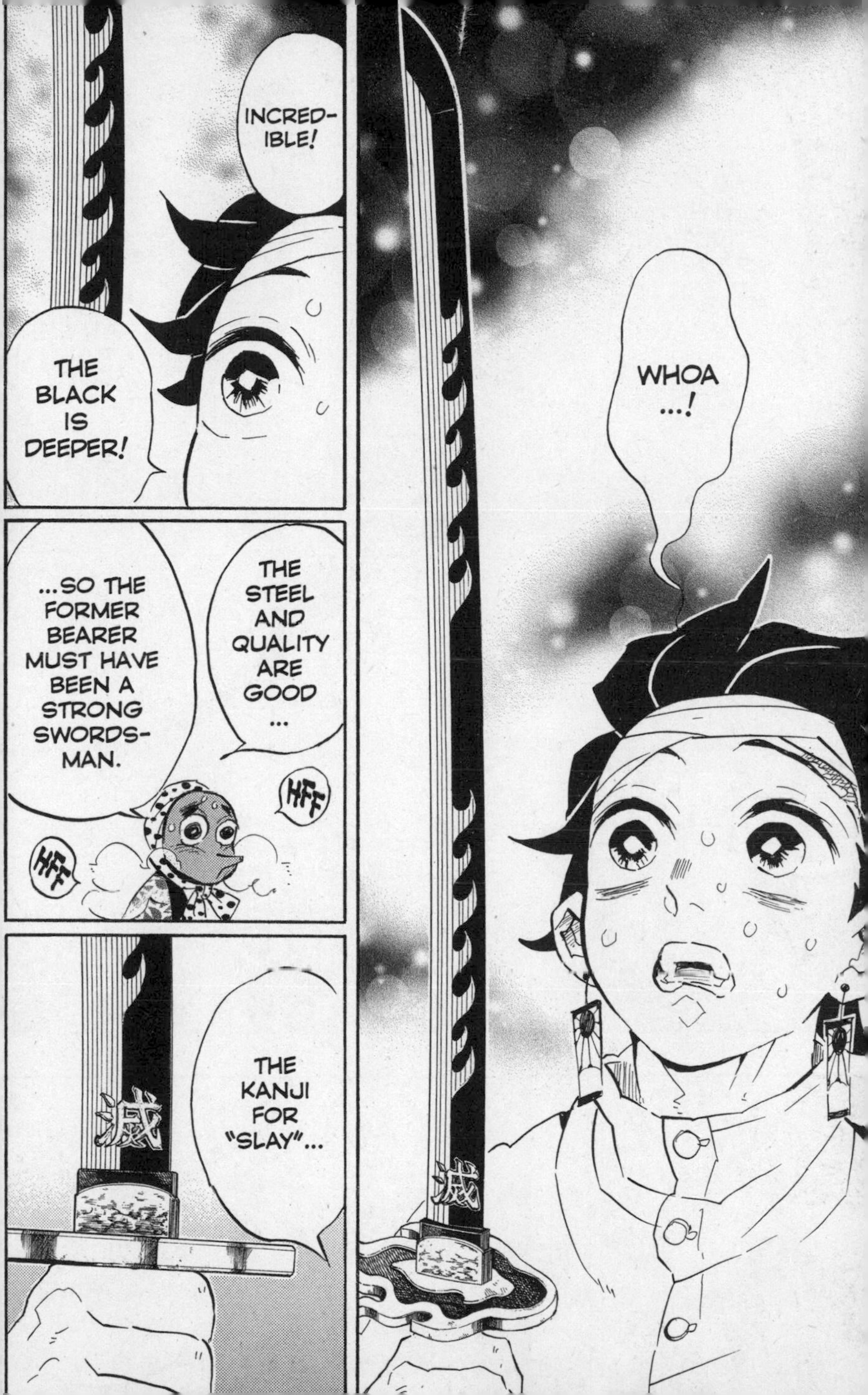
WHOA ...!
滅
INCREDIBLE!
THE BLACK IS DEEPER!
THE STEEL AND QUALITY ARE GOOD ...
...SO THE FORMER BEARER MUST HAVE BEEN A STRONG SWORDSMAN.
HFF
HFF
THE KANJI FOR "SLAY"...
滅

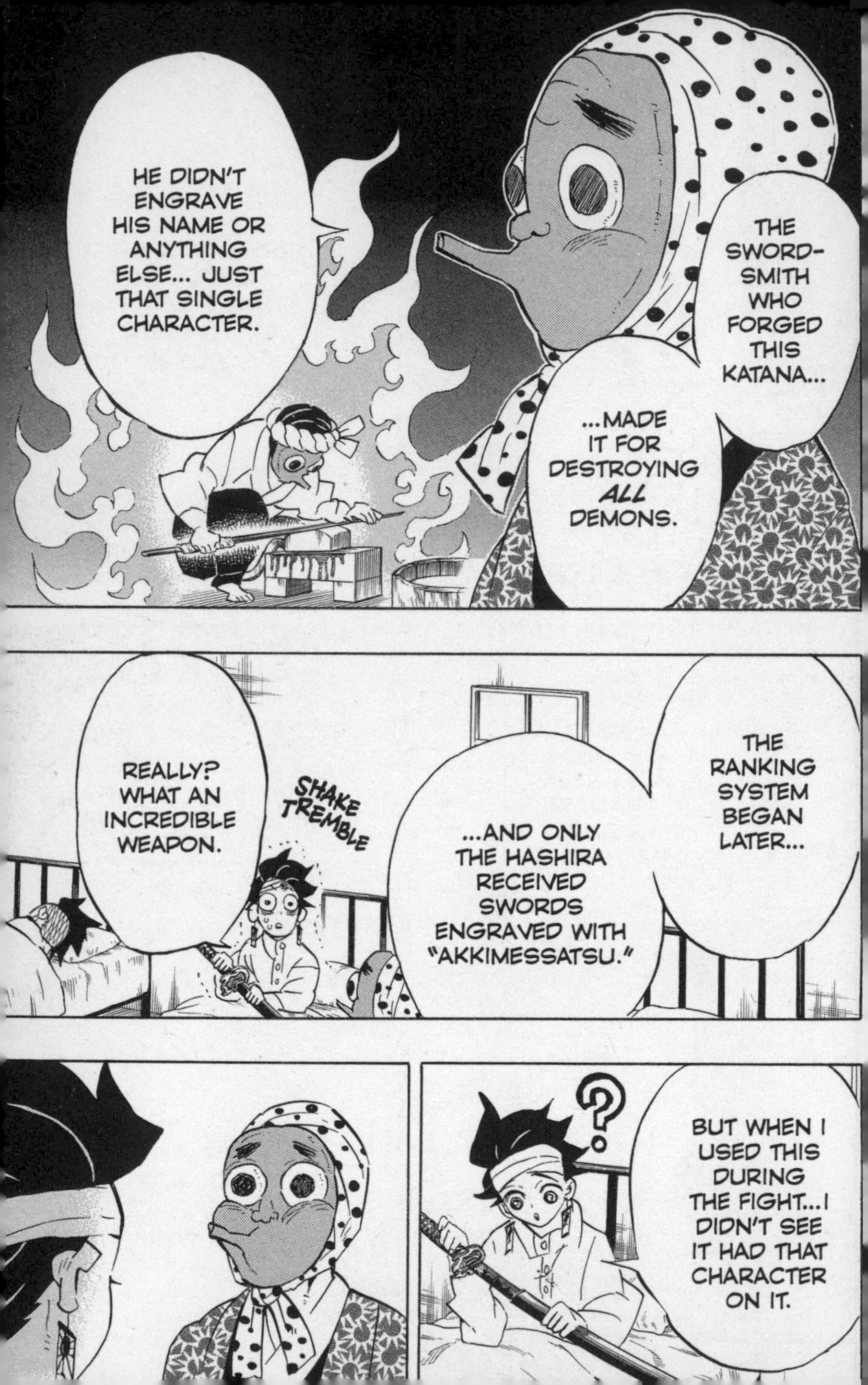
THE SWORD-SMITH WHO FORGED THIS KATANA...
...MADE IT FOR DESTROYING *ALL* DEMONS.
HE DIDN'T ENGRAVE HIS NAME OR ANYTHING ELSE... JUST THAT SINGLE CHARACTER.
THE RANKING SYSTEM BEGAN LATER...
...AND ONLY THE HASHIRA RECEIVED SWORDS ENGRAVED WITH "AKKIMESSATSU."
SHAKE TREMBLE
REALLY? WHAT AN INCREDIBLE WEAPON.
?
BUT WHEN I USED THIS DURING THE FIGHT...I DIDN'T SEE IT HAD THAT CHARACTER ON IT.

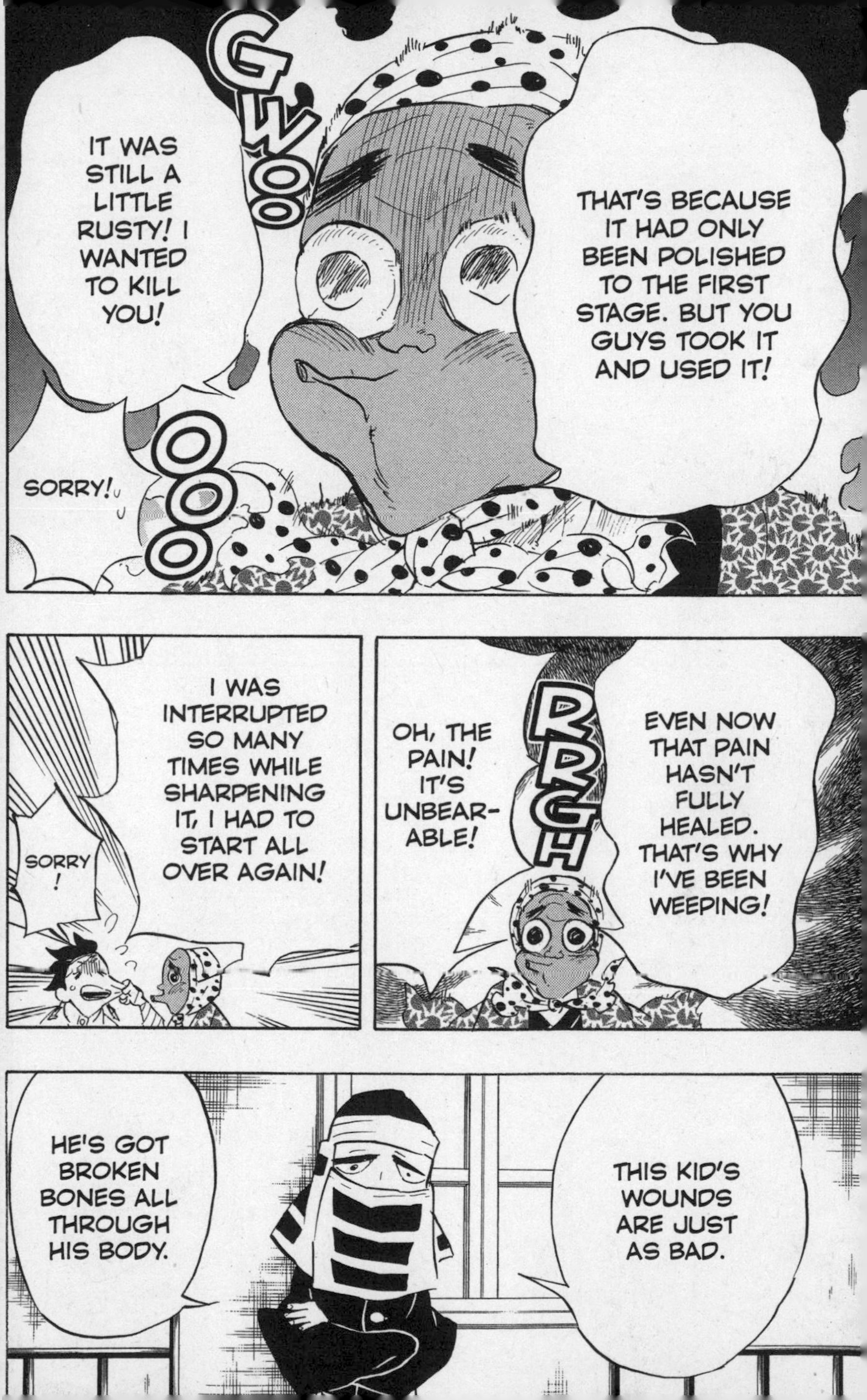
THAT'S BECAUSE IT HAD ONLY BEEN POLISHED TO THE FIRST STAGE. BUT YOU GUYS TOOK IT AND USED IT!
GWOOOOO
IT WAS STILL A LITTLE RUSTY! I WANTED TO KILL YOU!
SORRY!
RRGH
EVEN NOW THAT PAIN HASN'T FULLY HEALED. THAT'S WHY I'VE BEEN WEEPING!
OH, THE PAIN! IT'S UNBEARABLE!
I WAS INTERRUPTED SO MANY TIMES WHILE SHARPENING IT, I HAD TO START ALL OVER AGAIN!
SORRY!
THIS KID'S WOUNDS ARE JUST AS BAD.
HE'S GOT BROKEN BONES ALL THROUGH HIS BODY.

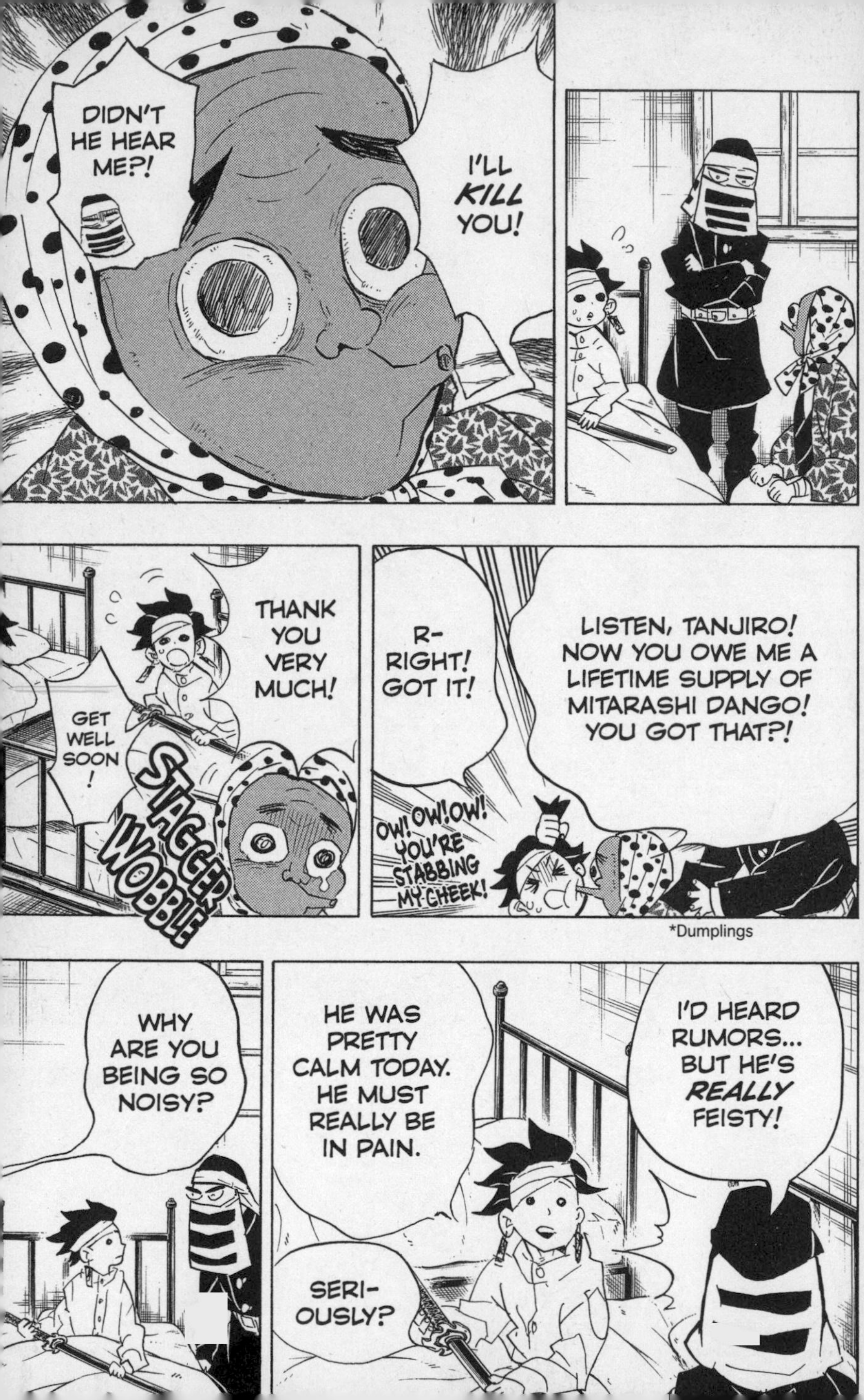
I'LL *KILL* YOU!
DIDN'T HE HEAR ME?!
LISTEN, TANJIRO! NOW YOU OWE ME A LIFETIME SUPPLY OF MITARASHI DANGO! YOU GOT THAT?!
R- RIGHT! GOT IT!
OW! OW! OW! YOU'RE STABBING MY CHEEK!
THANK YOU VERY MUCH!
GET WELL SOON!
STAGGER WOBBLE
I'D HEARD RUMORS... BUT HE'S *REALLY* FEISTY!
HE WAS PRETTY CALM TODAY. HE MUST REALLY BE IN PAIN.
SERIOUSLY?
WHY ARE YOU BEING SO NOISY?
*Dumplings

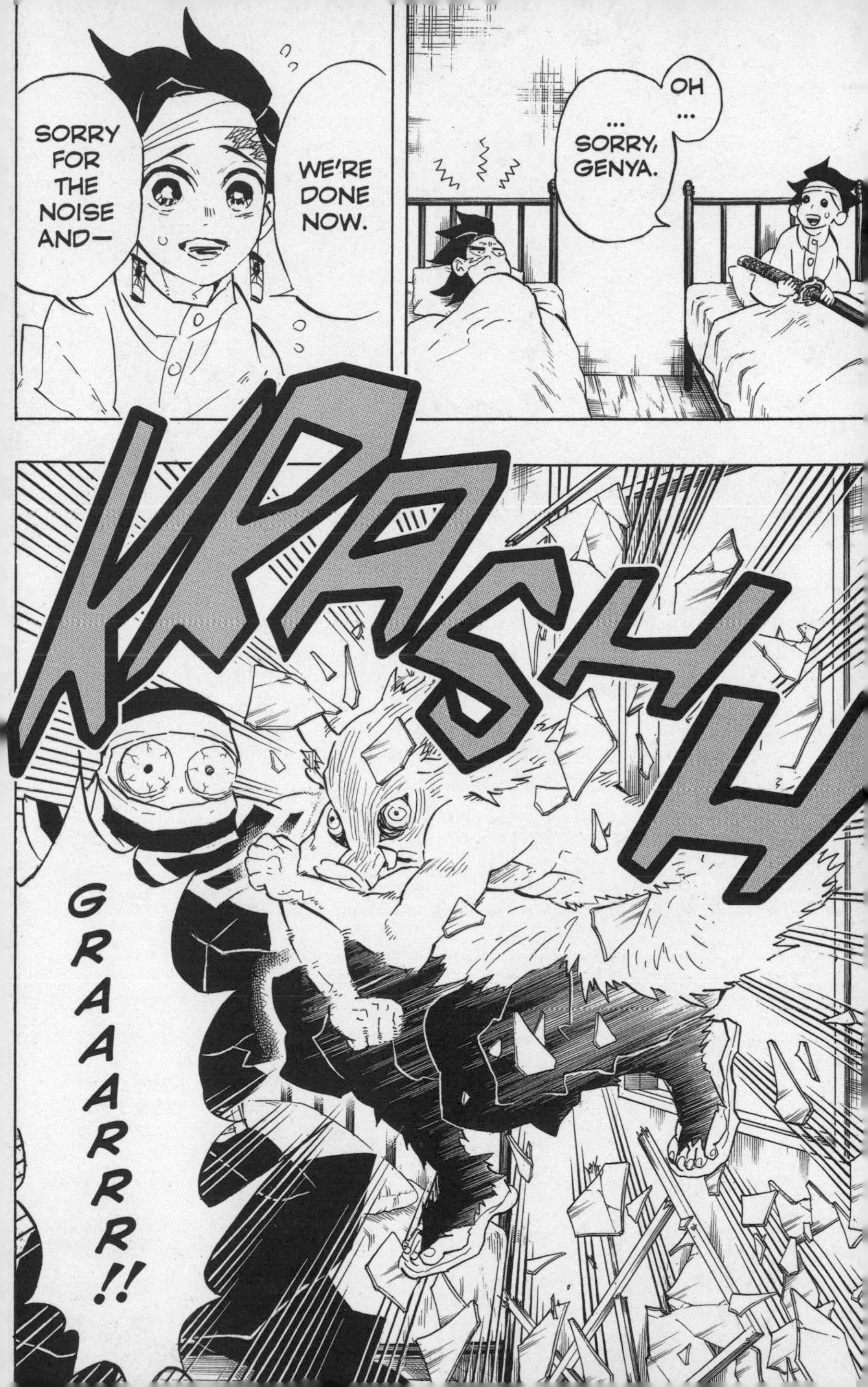
OH ...
... SORRY, GENYA.
SORRY FOR THE NOISE AND—
WE'RE DONE NOW.
KRASHH
GRAAARRR!!

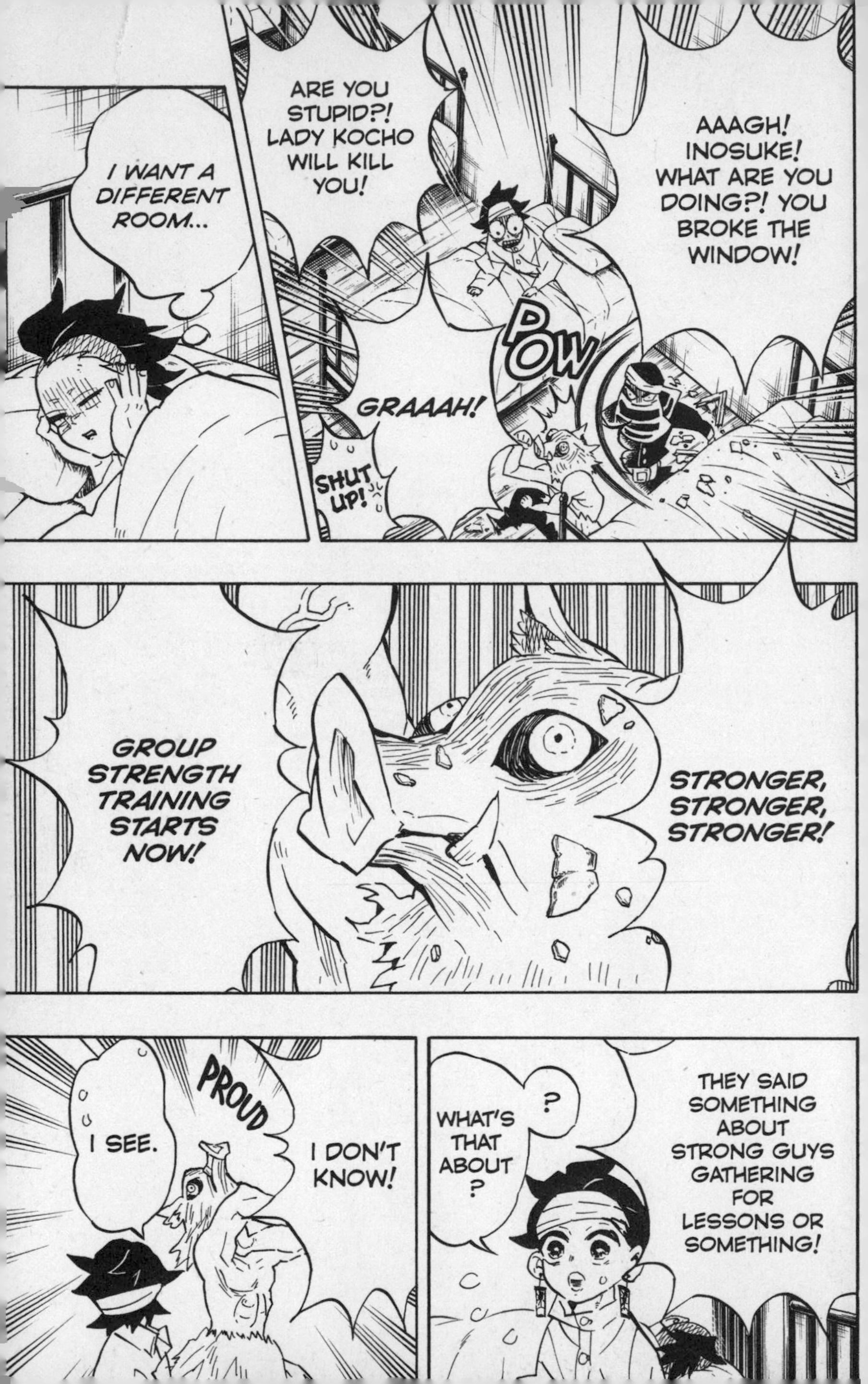
AAAGH! INOSUKE! WHAT ARE YOU DOING?! YOU BROKE THE WINDOW!
POW
ARE YOU STUPID?! LADY KOCHO WILL KILL YOU!
GRAAAH!
SHUT UP!
I WANT A DIFFERENT ROOM...
STRONGER, STRONGER, STRONGER!
GROUP STRENGTH TRAINING STARTS NOW!
THEY SAID SOMETHING ABOUT STRONG GUYS GATHERING FOR LESSONS OR SOMETHING!
?
WHAT'S THAT ABOUT?
I DON'T KNOW!
PROUD
I SEE.

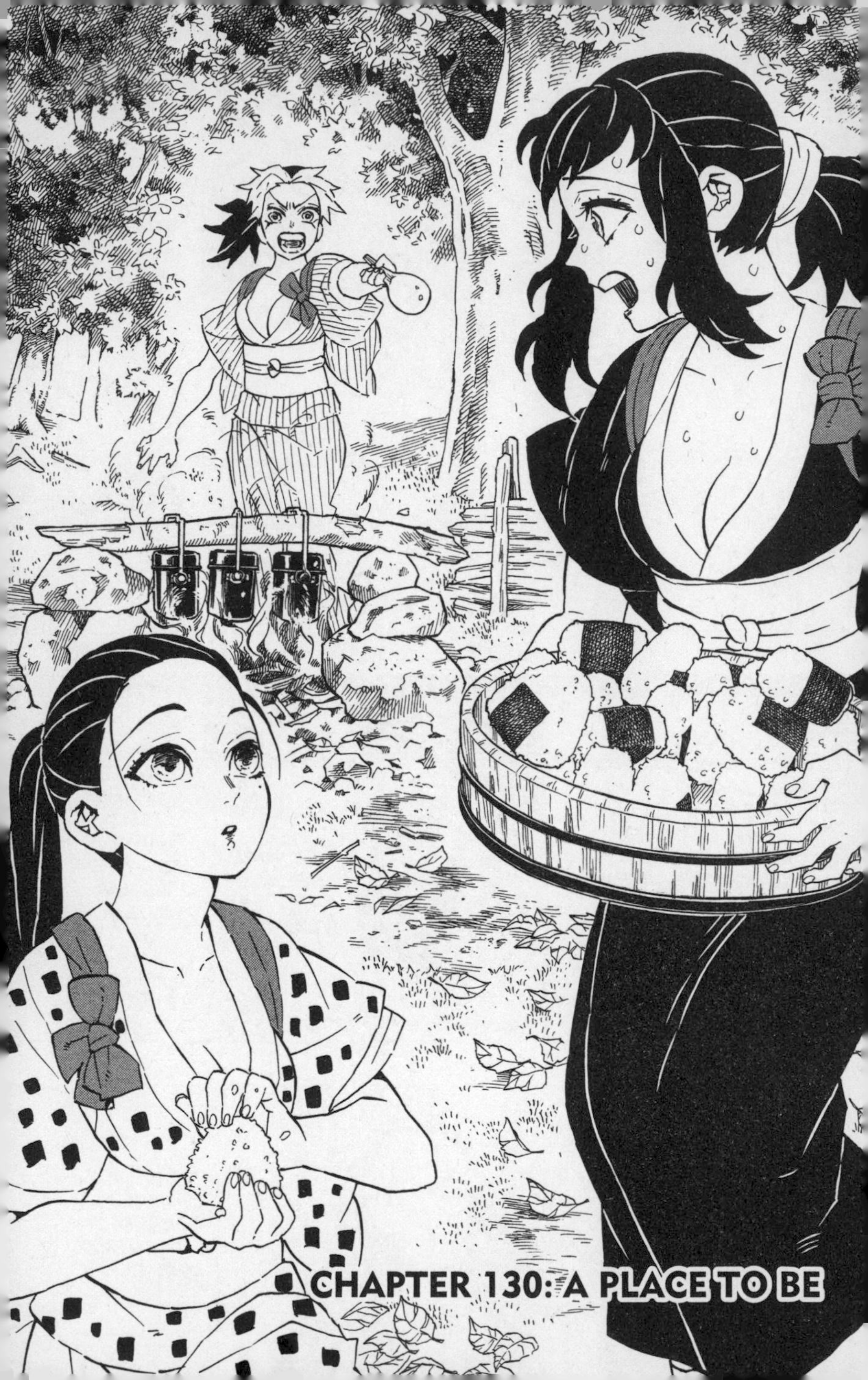
CHAPTER 130: A PLACE TO BE

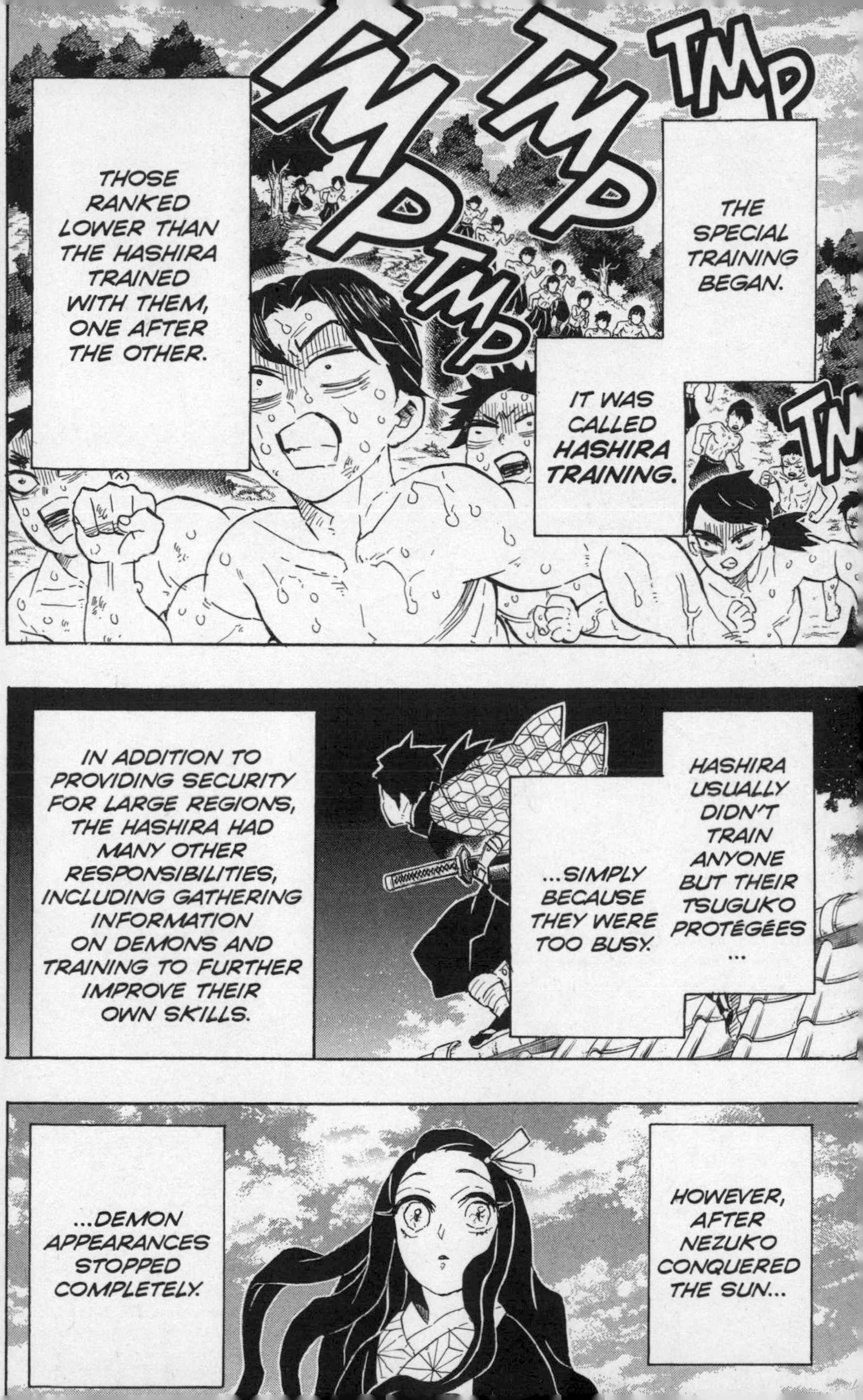
TMP
THE SPECIAL TRAINING BEGAN.
IT WAS CALLED HASHIRA TRAINING.
TMP TMP
TMP TMP
THOSE RANKED LOWER THAN THE HASHIRA TRAINED WITH THEM, ONE AFTER THE OTHER.
HASHIRA USUALLY DIDN'T TRAIN ANYONE BUT THEIR TSUGUKO PROTÉGÉES ...
...SIMPLY BECAUSE THEY WERE TOO BUSY.
IN ADDITION TO PROVIDING SECURITY FOR LARGE REGIONS, THE HASHIRA HAD MANY OTHER RESPONSIBILITIES, INCLUDING GATHERING INFORMATION ON DEMONS AND TRAINING TO FURTHER IMPROVE THEIR OWN SKILLS.
HOWEVER, AFTER NEZUKO CONQUERED THE SUN...
...DEMON APPEARANCES STOPPED COMPLETELY.

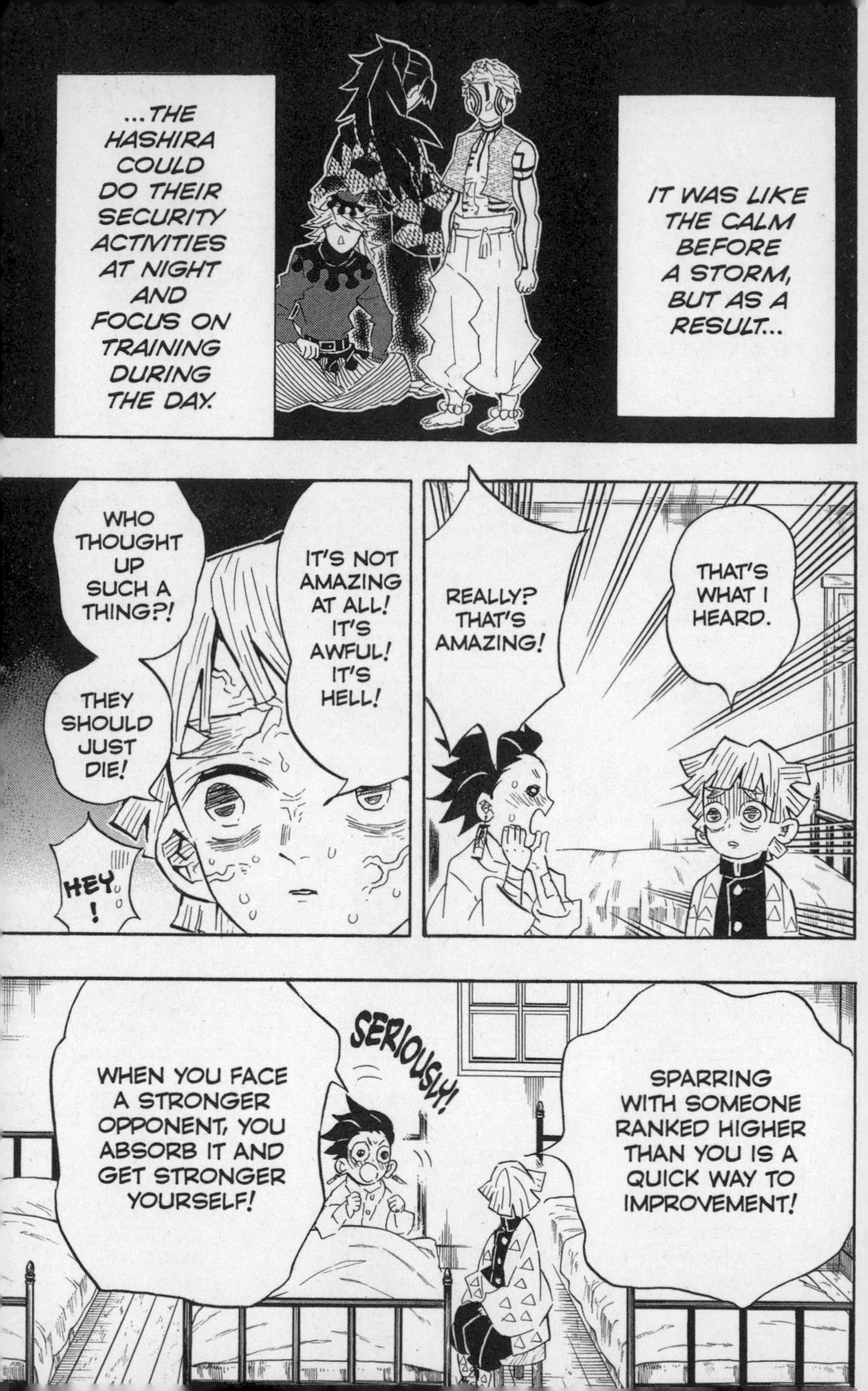
IT WAS LIKE THE CALM BEFORE A STORM, BUT AS A RESULT...
...THE HASHIRA COULD DO THEIR SECURITY ACTIVITIES AT NIGHT AND FOCUS ON TRAINING DURING THE DAY.
THAT'S WHAT I HEARD.
REALLY? THAT'S AMAZING!
IT'S NOT AMAZING AT ALL! IT'S AWFUL! IT'S HELL!
WHO THOUGHT UP SUCH A THING?!
THEY SHOULD JUST DIE!
HEY!
SPARRING WITH SOMEONE RANKED HIGHER THAN YOU IS A QUICK WAY TO IMPROVEMENT!
SERIOUSLY!
WHEN YOU FACE A STRONGER OPPONENT, YOU ABSORB IT AND GET STRONGER YOURSELF!

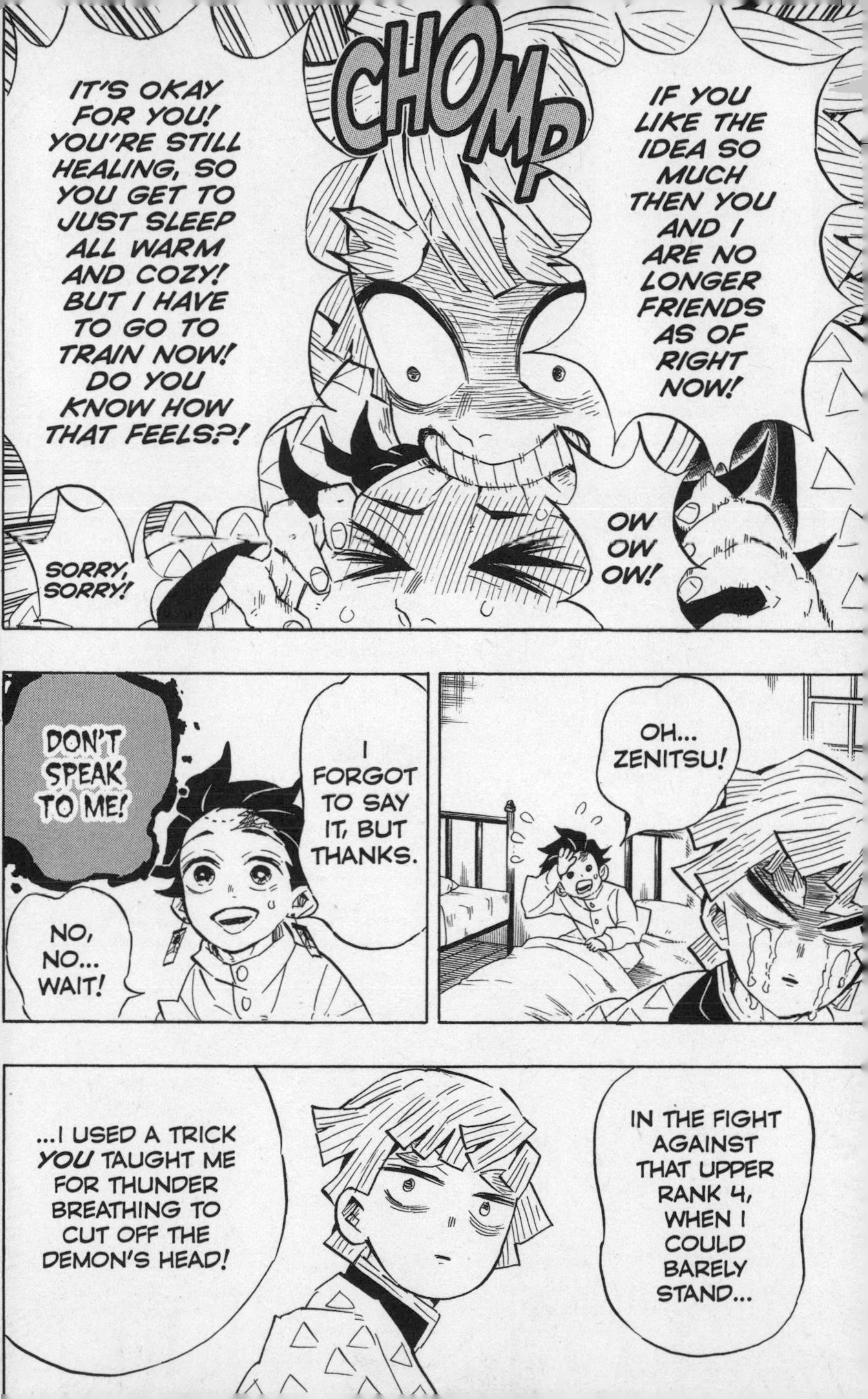
IF YOU LIKE THE IDEA SO MUCH THEN YOU AND I ARE NO LONGER FRIENDS AS OF RIGHT NOW!
CHOMP
IT'S OKAY FOR YOU! YOU'RE STILL HEALING, SO YOU GET TO JUST SLEEP ALL WARM AND COZY! BUT I HAVE TO GO TO TRAIN NOW! DO YOU KNOW HOW THAT FEELS?!
OW OW OW!
SORRY, SORRY!
OH... ZENITSU!
I FORGOT TO SAY IT, BUT THANKS.
DON'T SPEAK TO ME!
NO, NO... WAIT!
IN THE FIGHT AGAINST THAT UPPER RANK 4, WHEN I COULD BARELY STAND...
...I USED A TRICK *YOU* TAUGHT ME FOR THUNDER BREATHING TO CUT OFF THE DEMON'S HEAD!

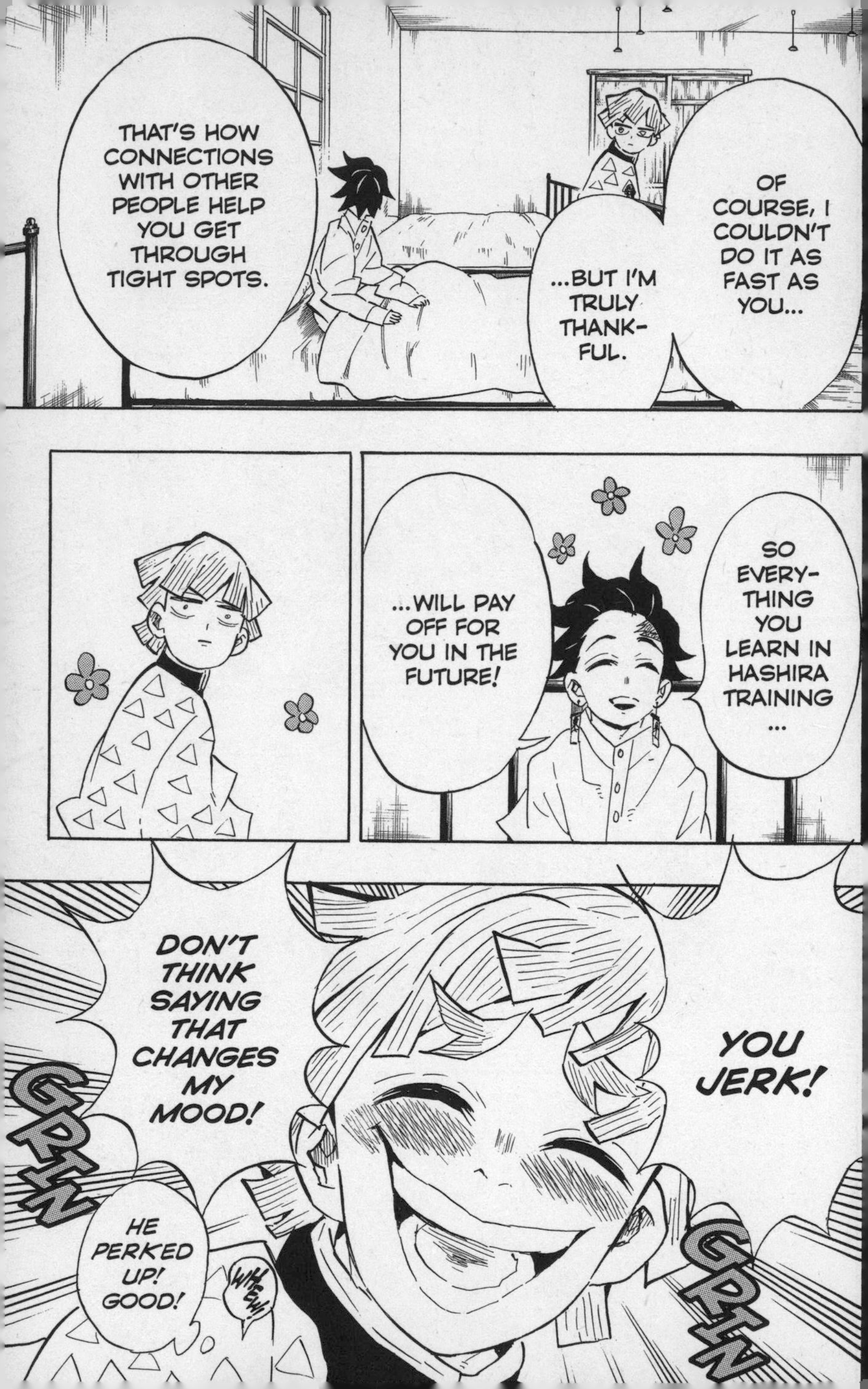
OF COURSE, I COULDN'T DO IT AS FAST AS YOU...
...BUT I'M TRULY THANK-FUL.
THAT'S HOW CONNECTIONS WITH OTHER PEOPLE HELP YOU GET THROUGH TIGHT SPOTS.
SO EVERY-THING YOU LEARN IN HASHIRA TRAINING ...
...WILL PAY OFF FOR YOU IN THE FUTURE!
YOU JERK!
GRIN
DON'T THINK SAYING THAT CHANGES MY MOOD!
GRIN
HE PERKED UP! GOOD!
WHEW!

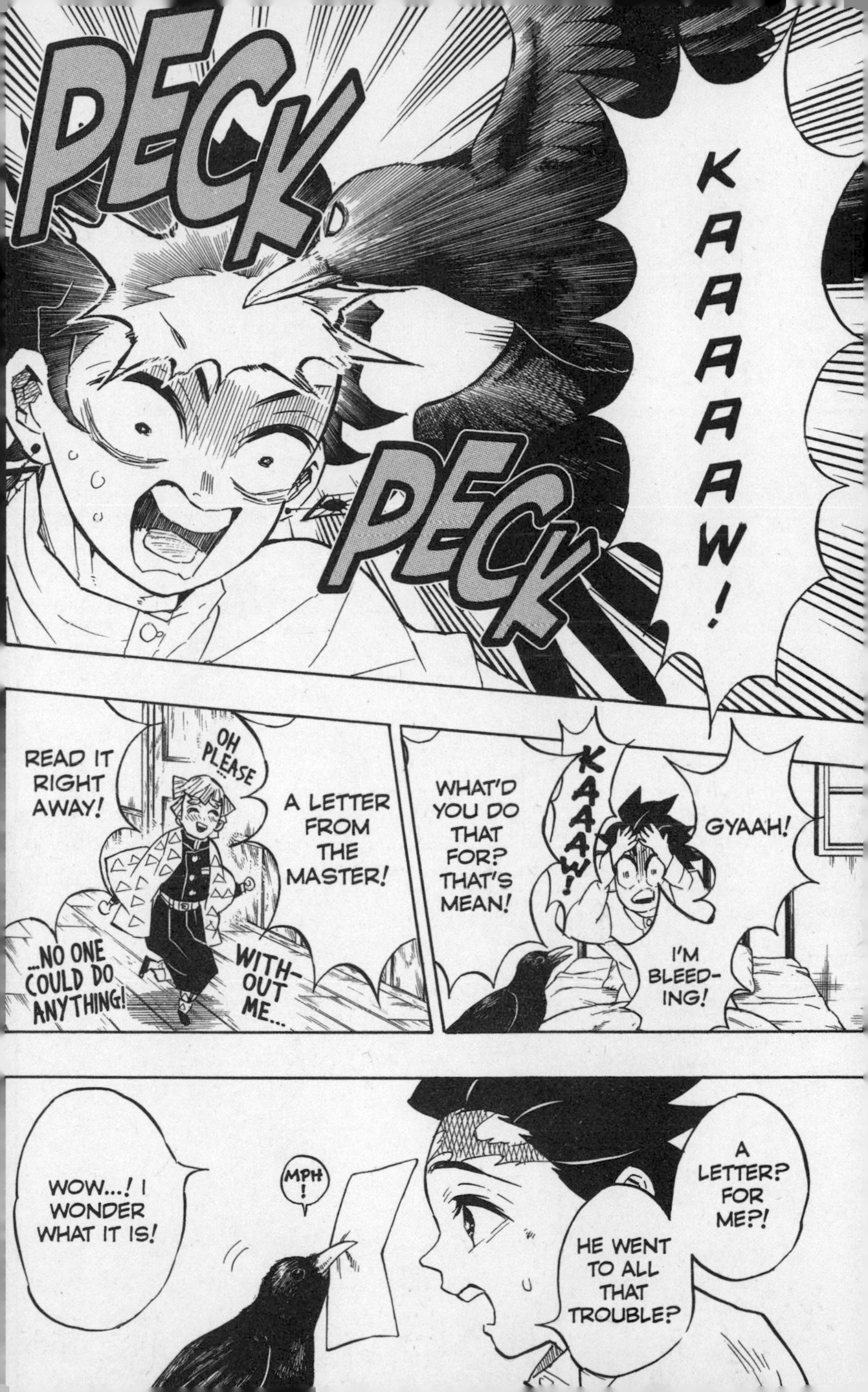
KAAAAAAW!
PECK
PECK
GYAAH!
I'M BLEEDING!
KAAAAW!
WHAT'D YOU DO THAT FOR? THAT'S MEAN!
A LETTER FROM THE MASTER!
OH PLEASE...
READ IT RIGHT AWAY!
WITHOUT ME...
...NO ONE COULD DO ANYTHING!
A LETTER? FOR ME?!
HE WENT TO ALL THAT TROUBLE?
MPH!
WOW...! I WONDER WHAT IT IS!

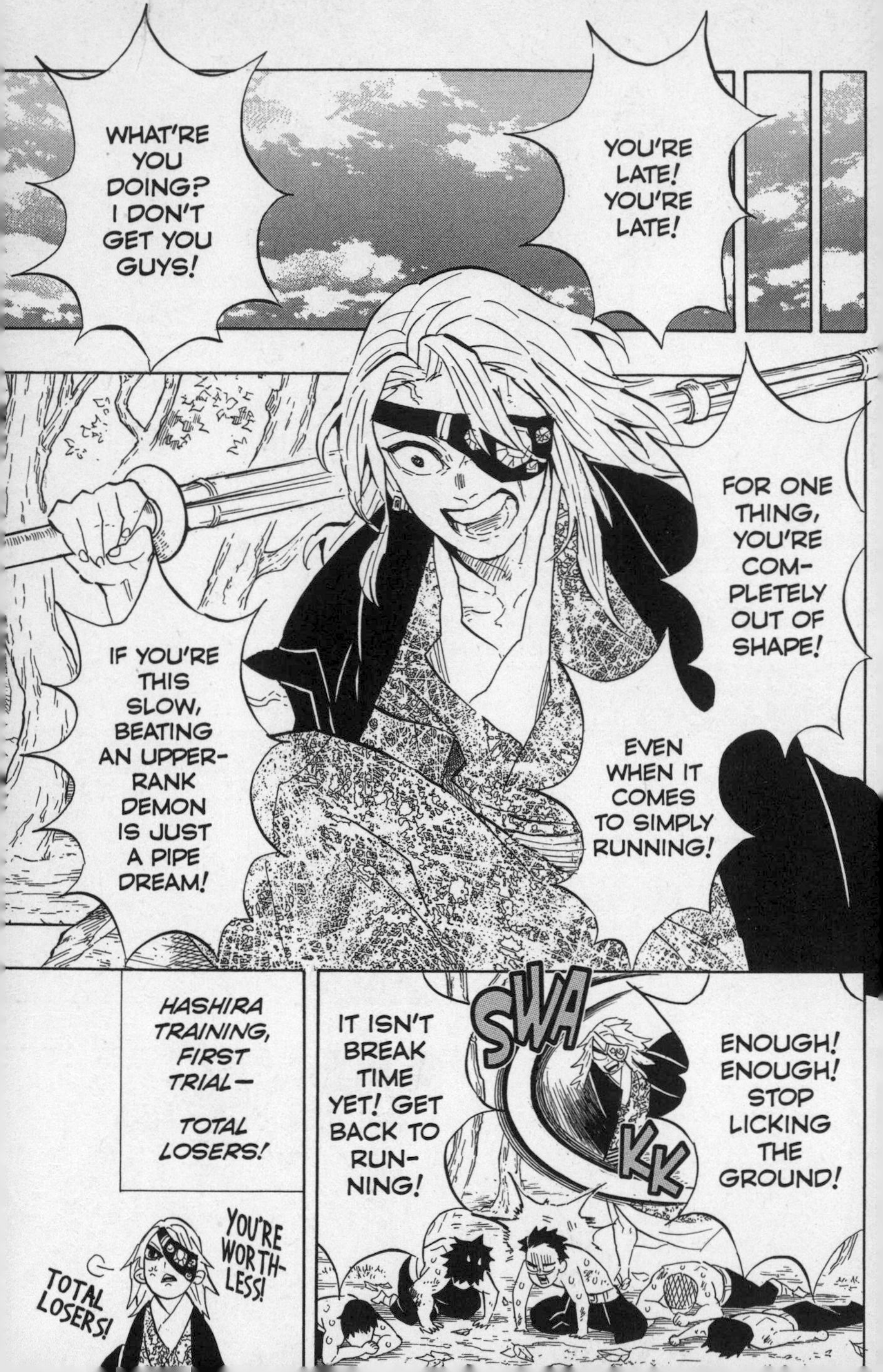
YOU'RE LATE! YOU'RE LATE!
WHAT'RE YOU DOING? I DON'T GET YOU GUYS!
FOR ONE THING, YOU'RE COM-PLETELY OUT OF SHAPE!
EVEN WHEN IT COMES TO SIMPLY RUNNING!
IF YOU'RE THIS SLOW, BEATING AN UPPER-RANK DEMON IS JUST A PIPE DREAM!
ENOUGH! ENOUGH! STOP LICKING THE GROUND!
SWAKK
IT ISN'T BREAK TIME YET! GET BACK TO RUN-NING!
HASHIRA TRAINING, FIRST TRIAL—
TOTAL LOSERS!
YOU'RE WORTH-LESS!
TOTAL LOSERS!

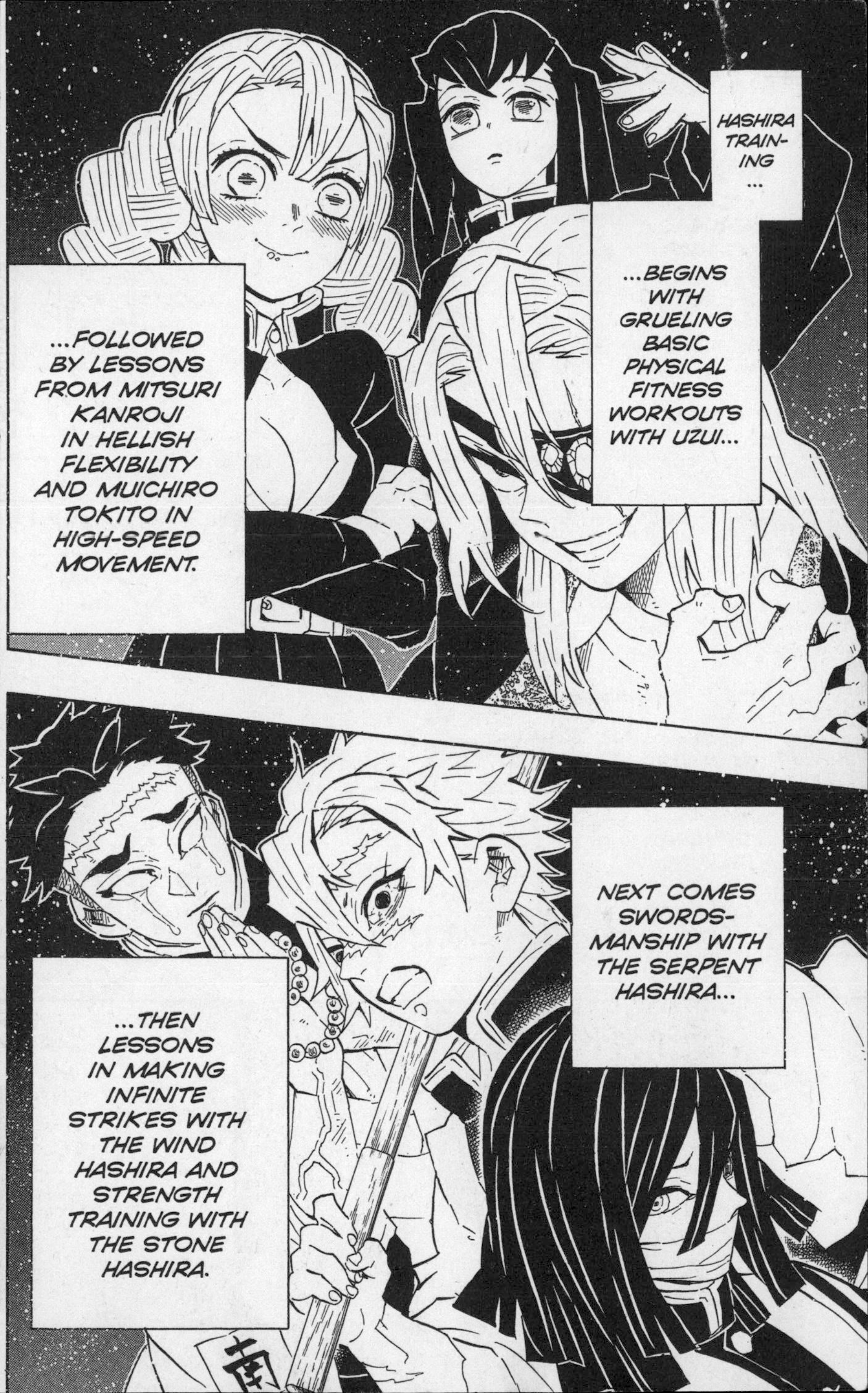
HASHIRA TRAINING...
...BEGINS WITH GRUELING BASIC PHYSICAL FITNESS WORKOUTS WITH UZUI...
...FOLLOWED BY LESSONS FROM MITSURI KANROJI IN HELLISH FLEXIBILITY AND MUICHIRO TOKITO IN HIGH-SPEED MOVEMENT.
NEXT COMES SWORDSMANSHIP WITH THE SERPENT HASHIRA...
...THEN LESSONS IN MAKING INFINITE STRIKES WITH THE WIND HASHIRA AND STRENGTH TRAINING WITH THE STONE HASHIRA.

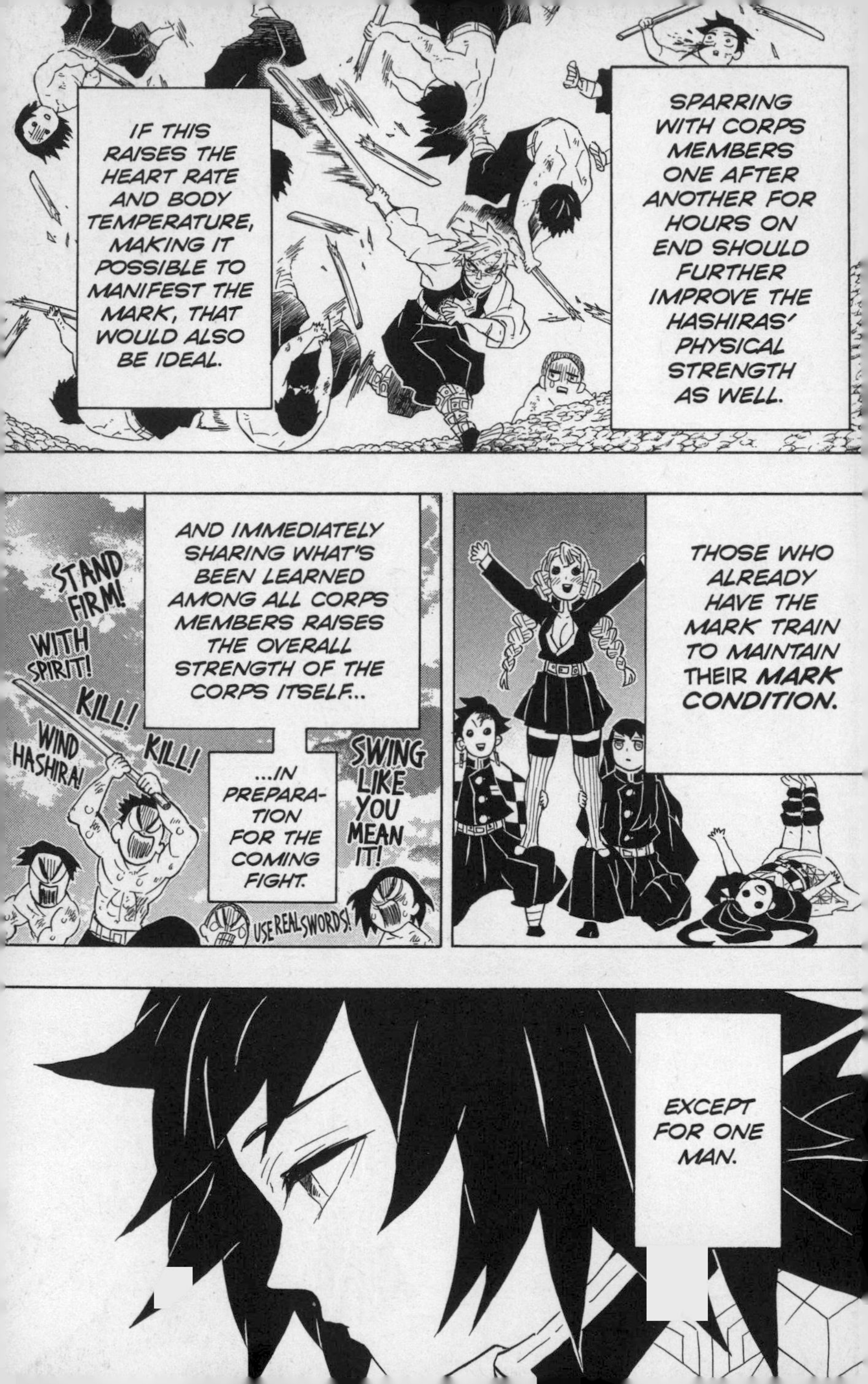
SPARRING WITH CORPS MEMBERS ONE AFTER ANOTHER FOR HOURS ON END SHOULD FURTHER IMPROVE THE HASHIRAS' PHYSICAL STRENGTH AS WELL.
IF THIS RAISES THE HEART RATE AND BODY TEMPERATURE, MAKING IT POSSIBLE TO MANIFEST THE MARK, THAT WOULD ALSO BE IDEAL.
THOSE WHO ALREADY HAVE THE MARK TRAIN TO MAINTAIN THEIR MARK CONDITION.
AND IMMEDIATELY SHARING WHAT'S BEEN LEARNED AMONG ALL CORPS MEMBERS RAISES THE OVERALL STRENGTH OF THE CORPS ITSELF...
...IN PREPARATION FOR THE COMING FIGHT.
STAND FIRM!
WITH SPIRIT!
KILL!
KILL!
WIND HASHIRA!
SWING LIKE YOU MEAN IT!
USE REAL SWORDS!
EXCEPT FOR ONE MAN.

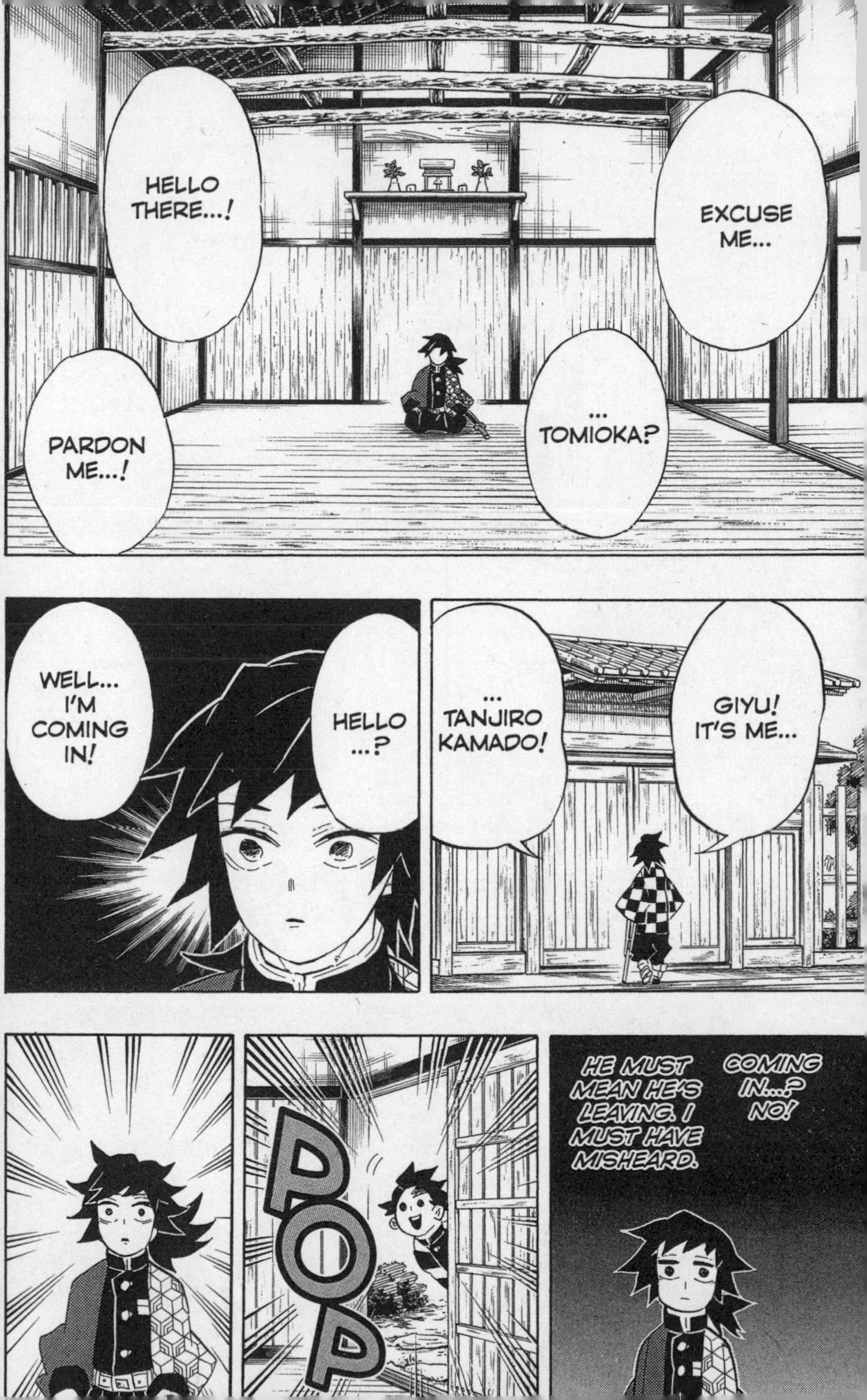
EXCUSE ME...
HELLO THERE...!
... TOMIOKA?
PARDON ME...!
GIYU! IT'S ME...
... TANJIRO KAMADO!
HELLO ...?
WELL... I'M COMING IN!
COMING IN...? NO!
HE MUST MEAN HE'S LEAVING. I MUST HAVE MISHEARD.
POP

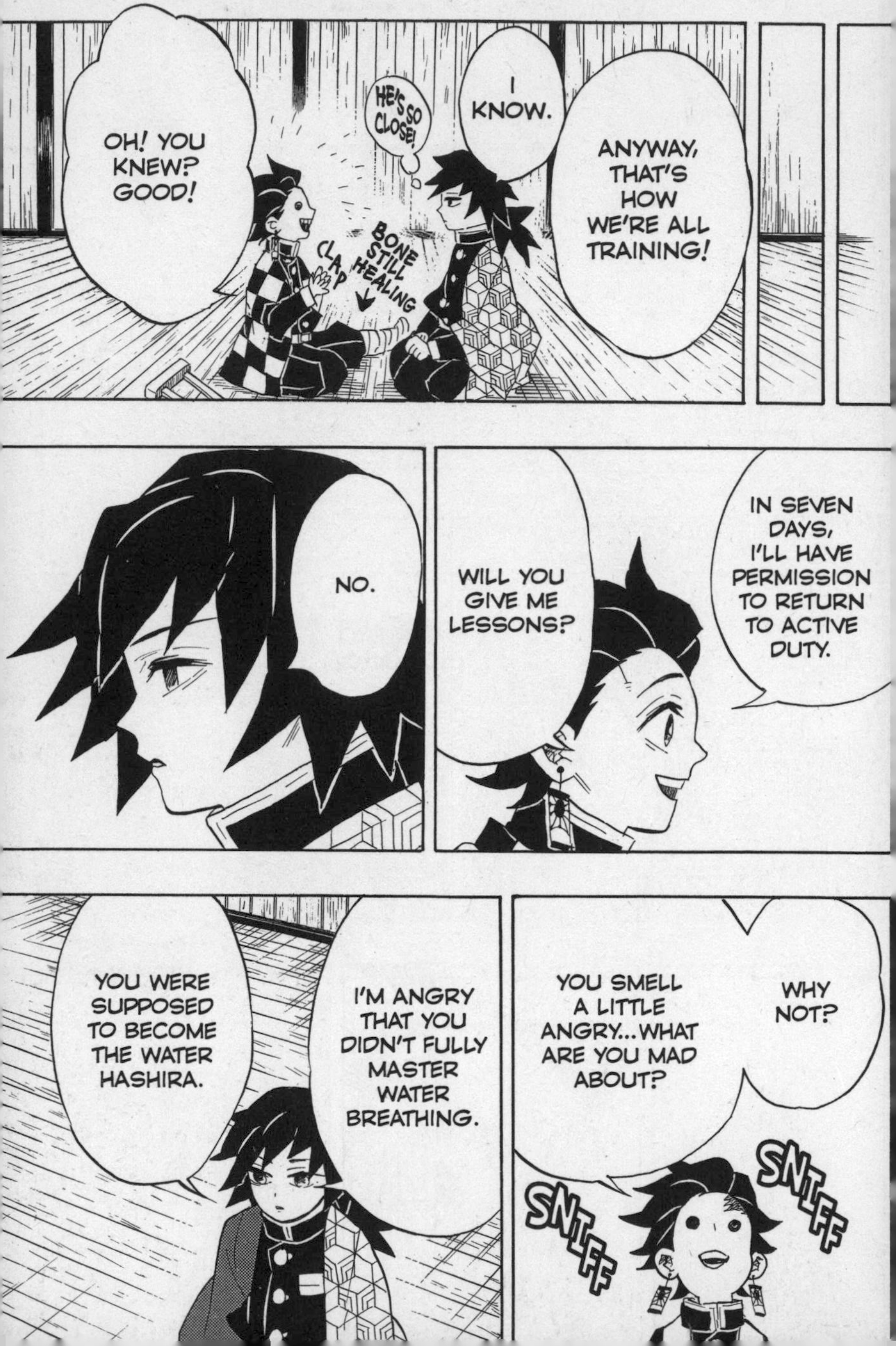
ANYWAY, THAT'S HOW WE'RE ALL TRAINING!
I KNOW.
HE'S SO CLOSE!
BONE STILL HEALING
OH! YOU KNEW? GOOD!
CLAP
IN SEVEN DAYS, I'LL HAVE PERMISSION TO RETURN TO ACTIVE DUTY.
WILL YOU GIVE ME LESSONS?
NO.
WHY NOT?
YOU SMELL A LITTLE ANGRY...WHAT ARE YOU MAD ABOUT?
SNIFF
SNIFF
I'M ANGRY THAT YOU DIDN'T FULLY MASTER WATER BREATHING.
YOU WERE SUPPOSED TO BECOME THE WATER HASHIRA.

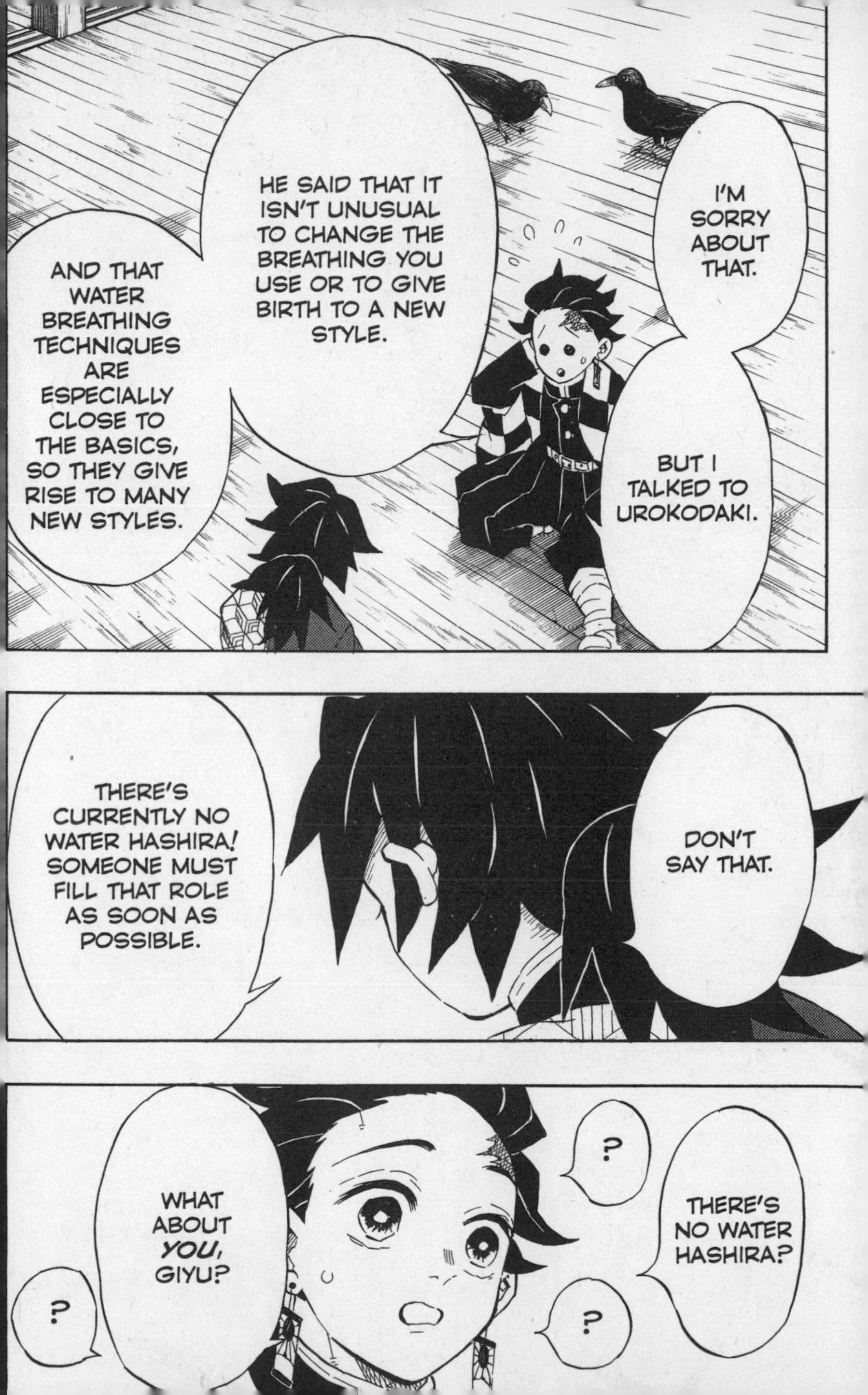
I'M SORRY ABOUT THAT.
BUT I TALKED TO UROKODAKI.
HE SAID THAT IT ISN'T UNUSUAL TO CHANGE THE BREATHING YOU USE OR TO GIVE BIRTH TO A NEW STYLE.
AND THAT WATER BREATHING TECHNIQUES ARE ESPECIALLY CLOSE TO THE BASICS, SO THEY GIVE RISE TO MANY NEW STYLES.
DON'T SAY THAT.
THERE'S CURRENTLY NO WATER HASHIRA! SOMEONE MUST FILL THAT ROLE AS SOON AS POSSIBLE.
?
THERE'S NO WATER HASHIRA?
?
WHAT ABOUT *YOU*, GIYU?
?

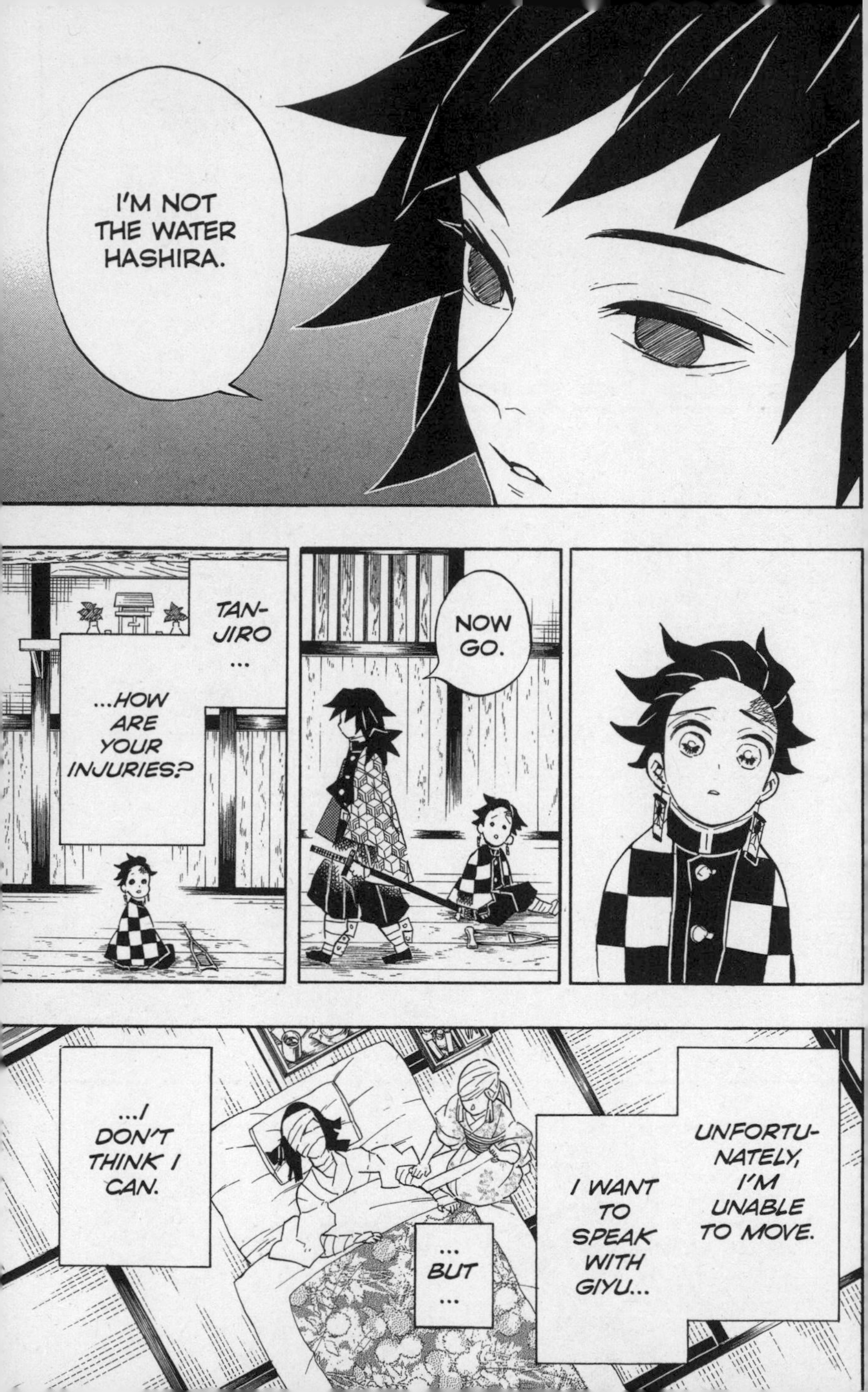
I'M NOT THE WATER HASHIRA.
NOW GO.
TAN-JIRO ...
...HOW ARE YOUR INJURIES?
UNFORTU-NATELY, I'M UNABLE TO MOVE.
I WANT TO SPEAK WITH GIYU...
... BUT ...
...I DON'T THINK I CAN.

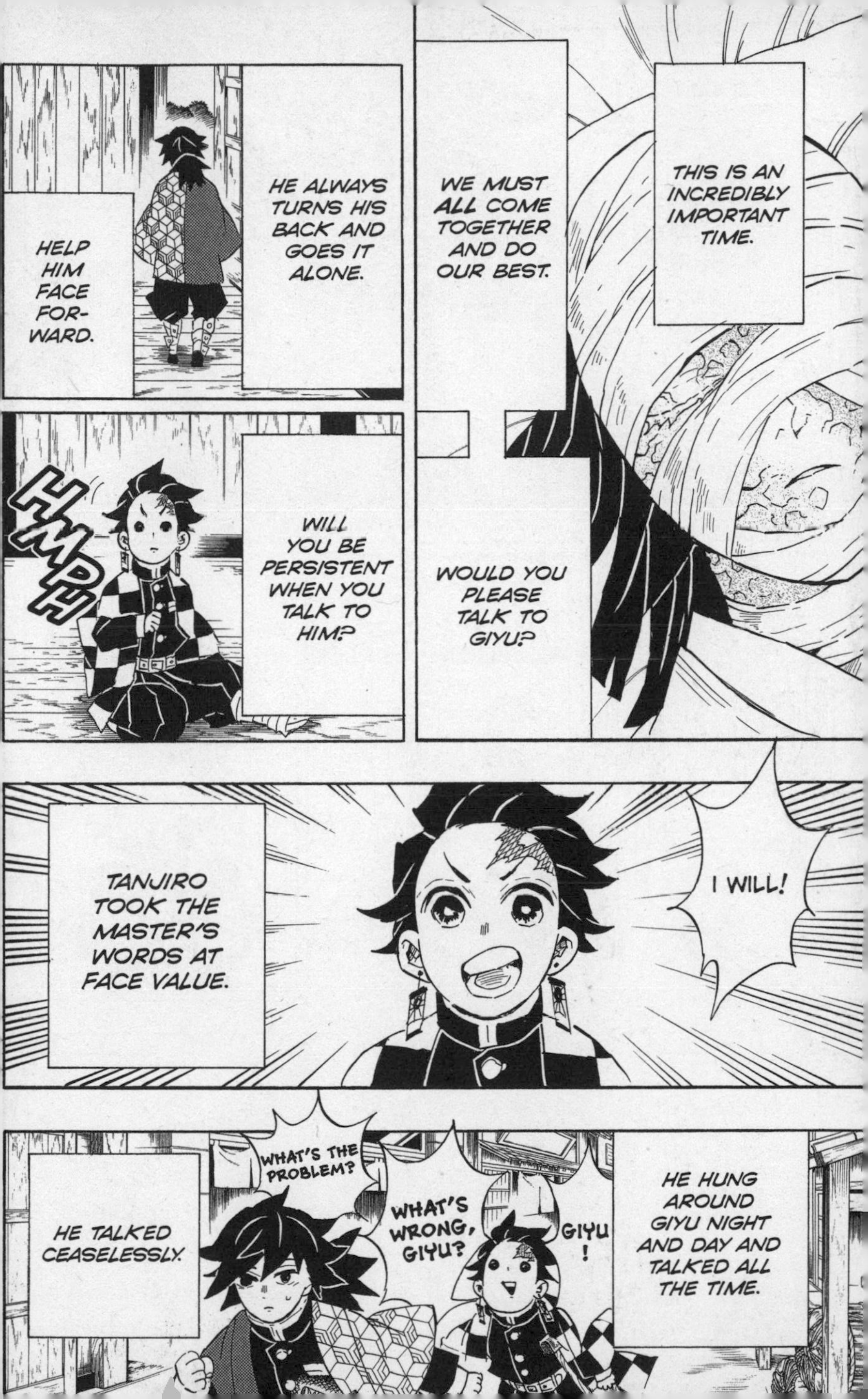

THIS IS AN INCREDIBLY IMPORTANT TIME.
WE MUST ALL COME TOGETHER AND DO OUR BEST.
WOULD YOU PLEASE TALK TO GIYU?
HE ALWAYS TURNS HIS BACK AND GOES IT ALONE.
HELP HIM FACE FOR-WARD.
WILL YOU BE PERSISTENT WHEN YOU TALK TO HIM?
HMPH
I WILL!
TANJIRO TOOK THE MASTER'S WORDS AT FACE VALUE.
HE HUNG AROUND GIYU NIGHT AND DAY AND TALKED ALL THE TIME.
GIYU!
WHAT'S WRONG, GIYU?
WHAT'S THE PROBLEM?
HE TALKED CEASELESSLY.

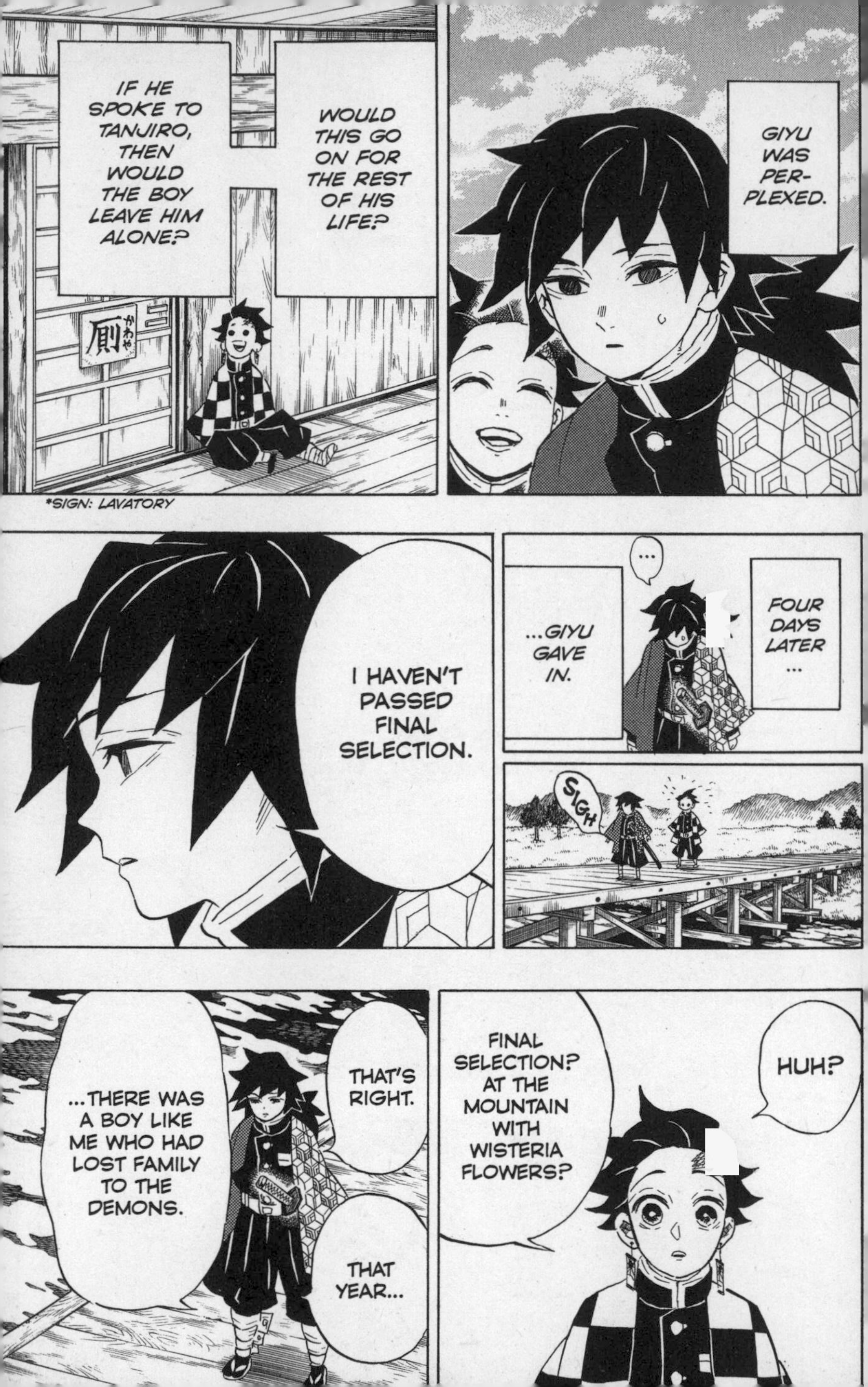
GIYU WAS PER-PLEXED.
WOULD THIS GO ON FOR THE REST OF HIS LIFE?
IF HE SPOKE TO TANJIRO, THEN WOULD THE BOY LEAVE HIM ALONE?
厠 かわや
*SIGN: LAVATORY
FOUR DAYS LATER...
...
...GIYU GAVE IN.
SIGH
I HAVEN'T PASSED FINAL SELECTION.
HUH?
FINAL SELECTION? AT THE MOUNTAIN WITH WISTERIA FLOWERS?
THAT'S RIGHT.
THAT YEAR...
...THERE WAS A BOY LIKE ME WHO HAD LOST FAMILY TO THE DEMONS.

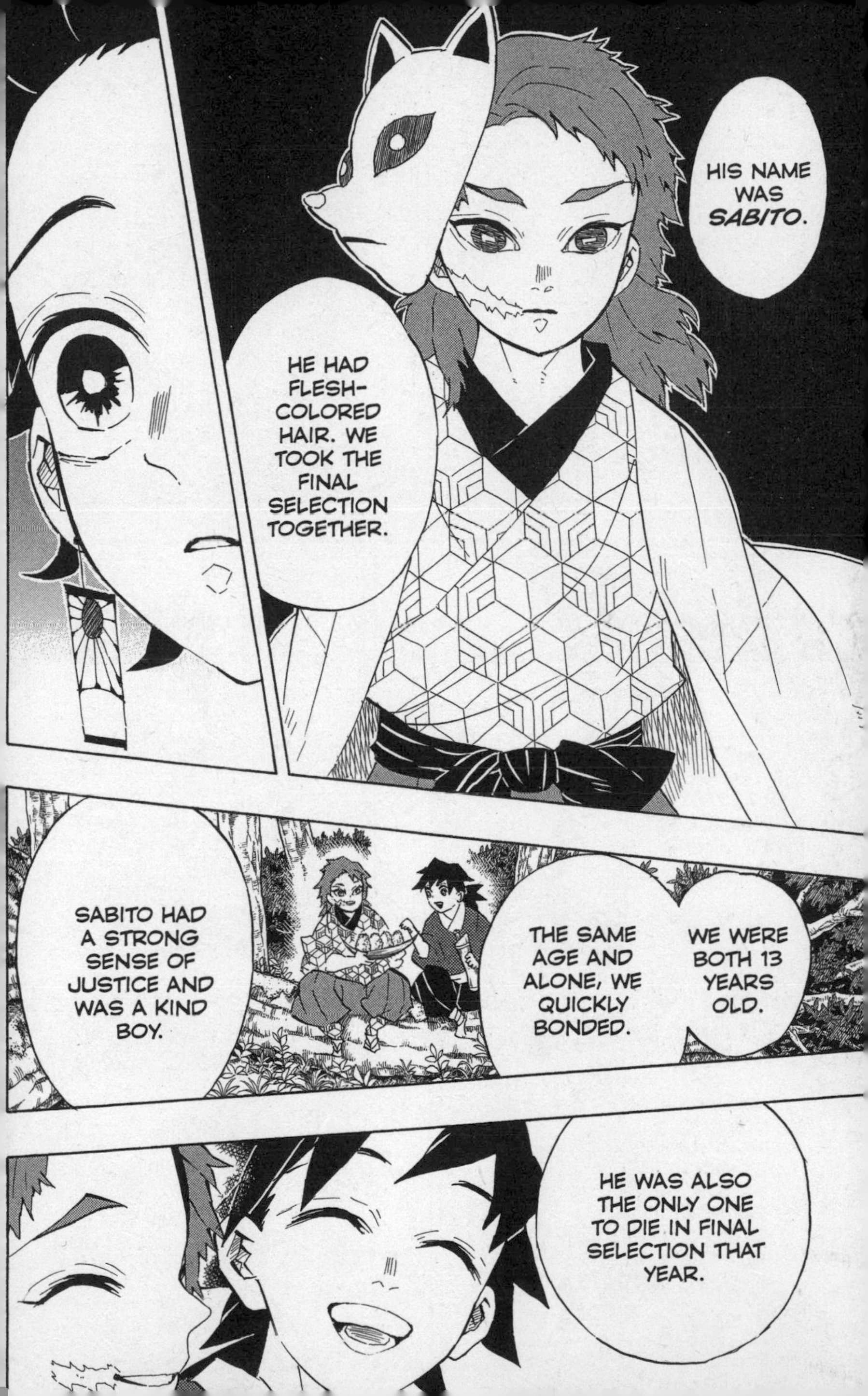
HIS NAME WAS *SABITO*.
HE HAD FLESH-COLORED HAIR. WE TOOK THE FINAL SELECTION TOGETHER.
WE WERE BOTH 13 YEARS OLD.
THE SAME AGE AND ALONE, WE QUICKLY BONDED.
SABITO HAD A STRONG SENSE OF JUSTICE AND WAS A KIND BOY.
HE WAS ALSO THE ONLY ONE TO DIE IN FINAL SELECTION THAT YEAR.

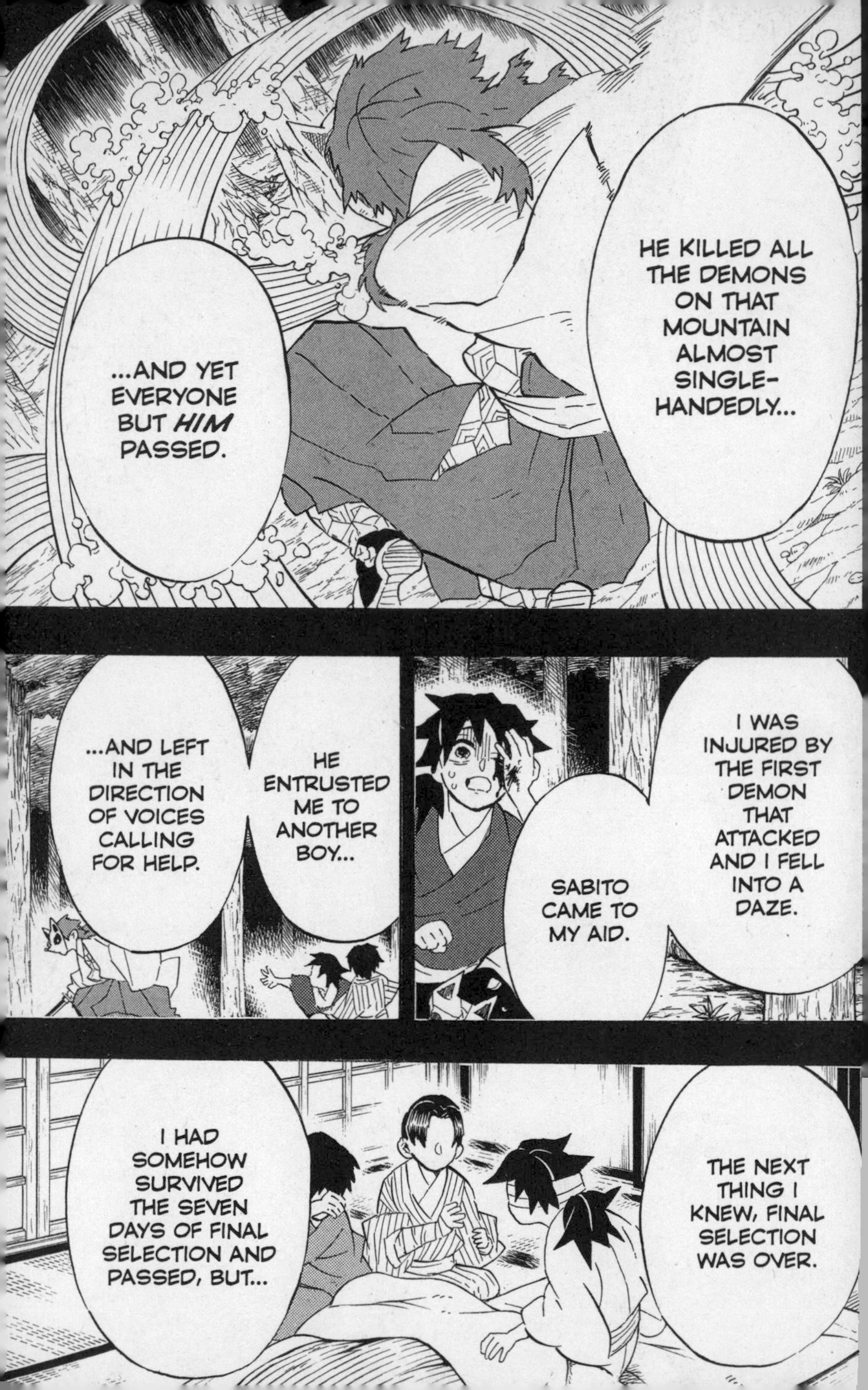
HE KILLED ALL THE DEMONS ON THAT MOUNTAIN ALMOST SINGLE-HANDEDLY...
...AND YET EVERYONE BUT *HIM* PASSED.
I WAS INJURED BY THE FIRST DEMON THAT ATTACKED AND I FELL INTO A DAZE.
SABITO CAME TO MY AID.
HE ENTRUSTED ME TO ANOTHER BOY...
...AND LEFT IN THE DIRECTION OF VOICES CALLING FOR HELP.
THE NEXT THING I KNEW, FINAL SELECTION WAS OVER.
I HAD SOMEHOW SURVIVED THE SEVEN DAYS OF FINAL SELECTION AND PASSED, BUT...

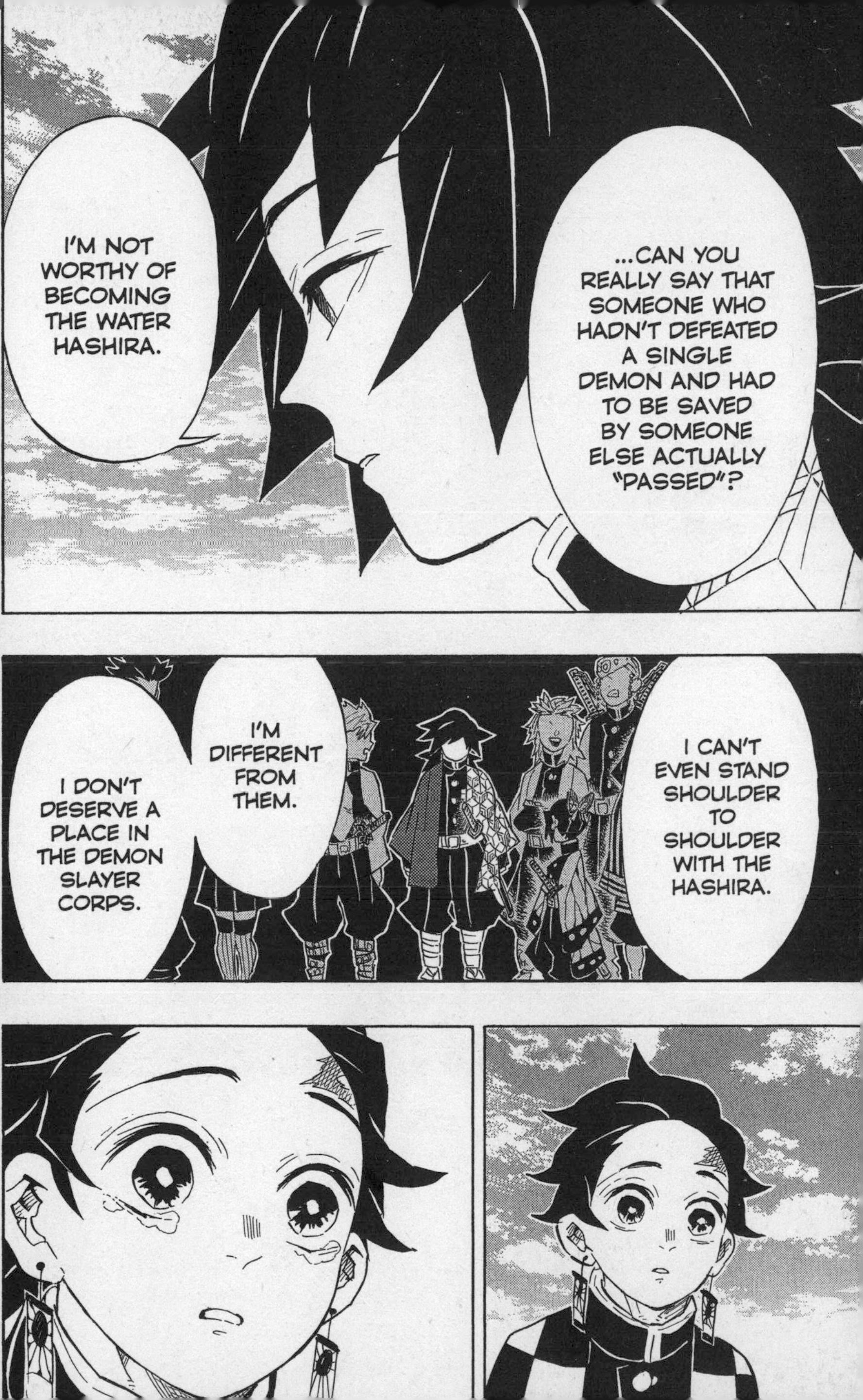
...CAN YOU REALLY SAY THAT SOMEONE WHO HADN'T DEFEATED A SINGLE DEMON AND HAD TO BE SAVED BY SOMEONE ELSE ACTUALLY "PASSED"?
I'M NOT WORTHY OF BECOMING THE WATER HASHIRA.
I CAN'T EVEN STAND SHOULDER TO SHOULDER WITH THE HASHIRA.
I'M DIFFERENT FROM THEM.
I DON'T DESERVE A PLACE IN THE DEMON SLAYER CORPS.

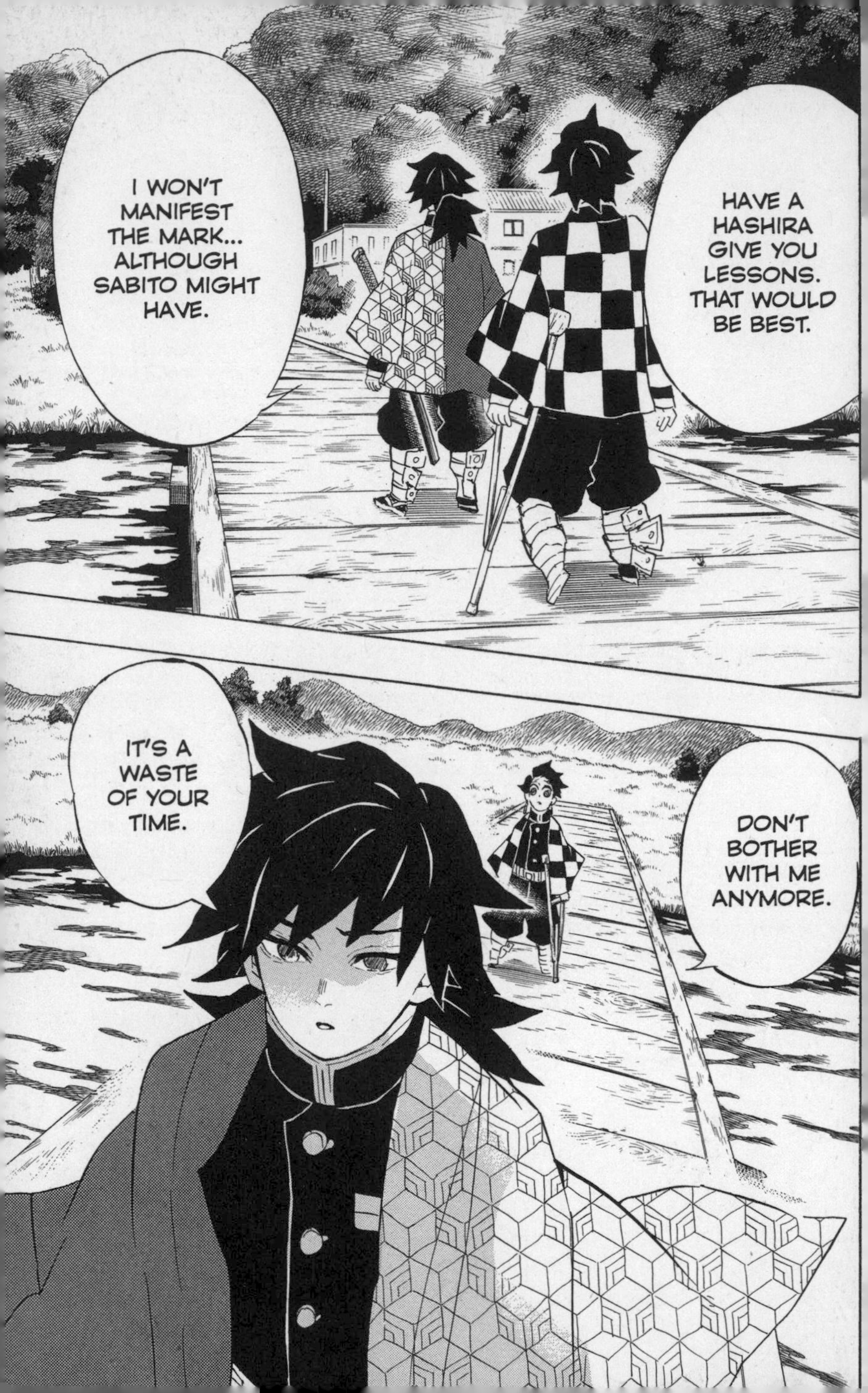
HAVE A HASHIRA GIVE YOU LESSONS. THAT WOULD BE BEST.
I WON'T MANIFEST THE MARK... ALTHOUGH SABITO MIGHT HAVE.
DON'T BOTHER WITH ME ANYMORE.
IT'S A WASTE OF YOUR TIME.

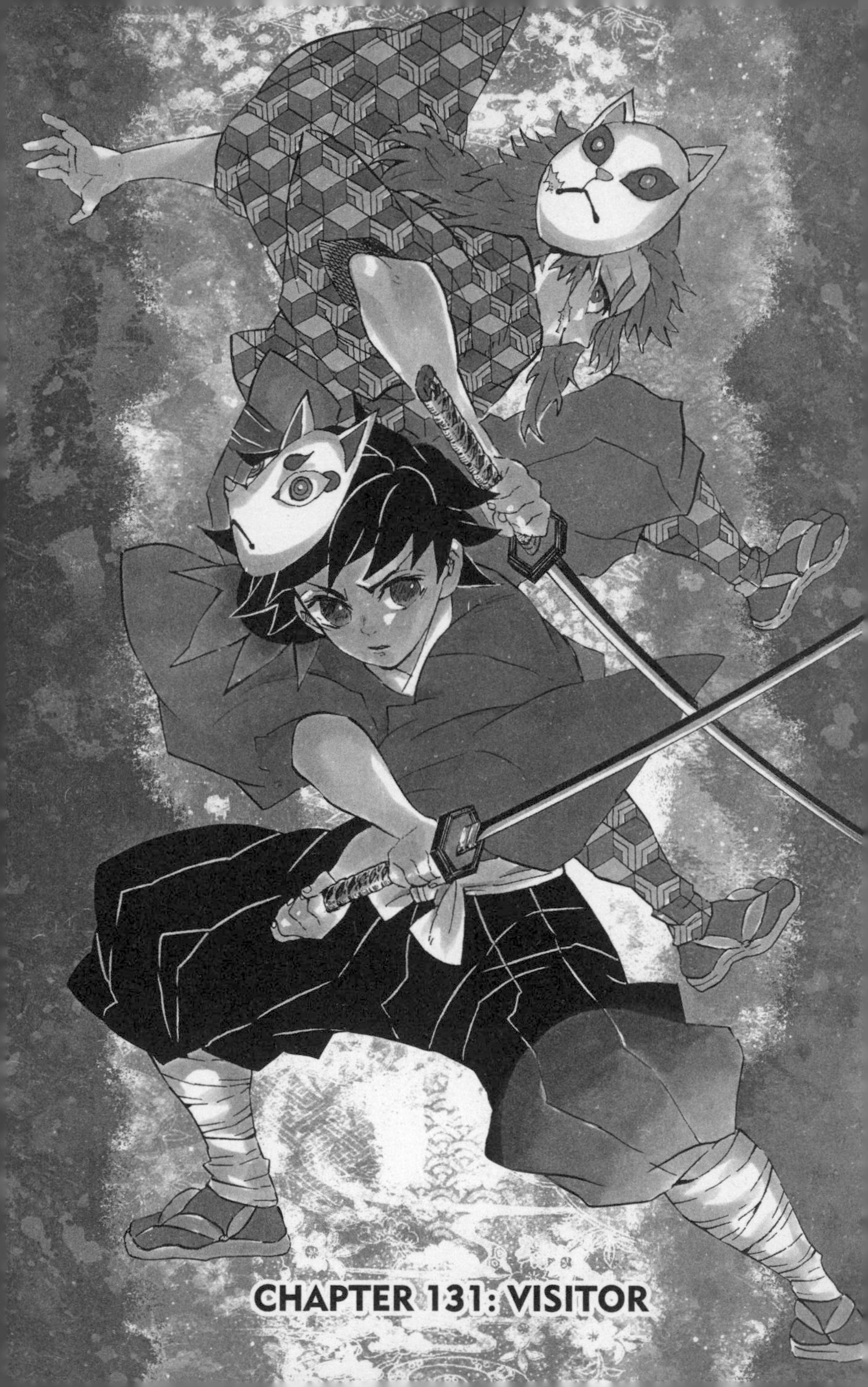

CHAPTER 131: VISITOR

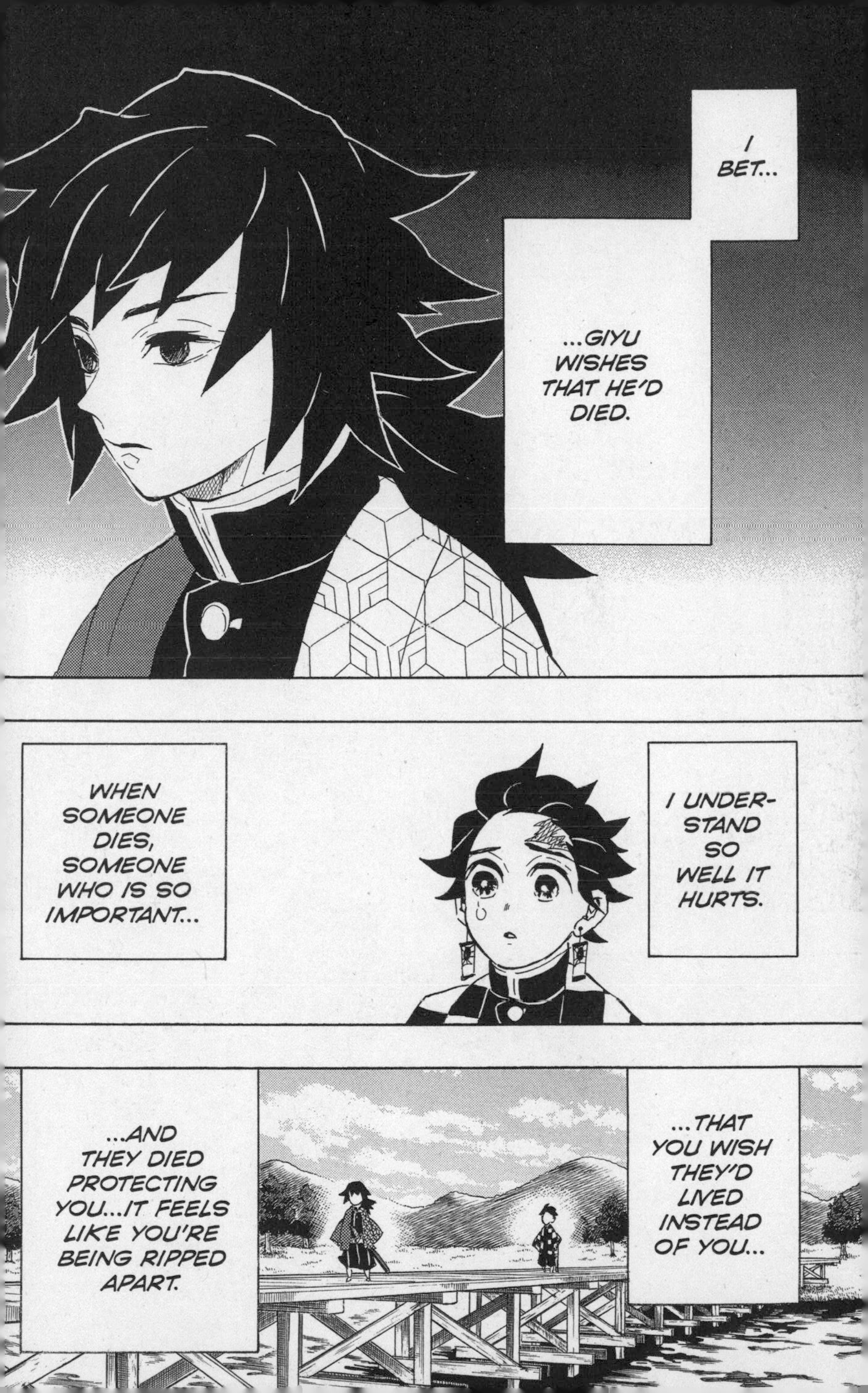
I BET...
...GIYU WISHES THAT HE'D DIED.
I UNDER-STAND SO WELL IT HURTS.
WHEN SOMEONE DIES, SOMEONE WHO IS SO IMPORTANT...
...THAT YOU WISH THEY'D LIVED INSTEAD OF YOU...
...AND THEY DIED PROTECTING YOU...IT FEELS LIKE YOU'RE BEING RIPPED APART.

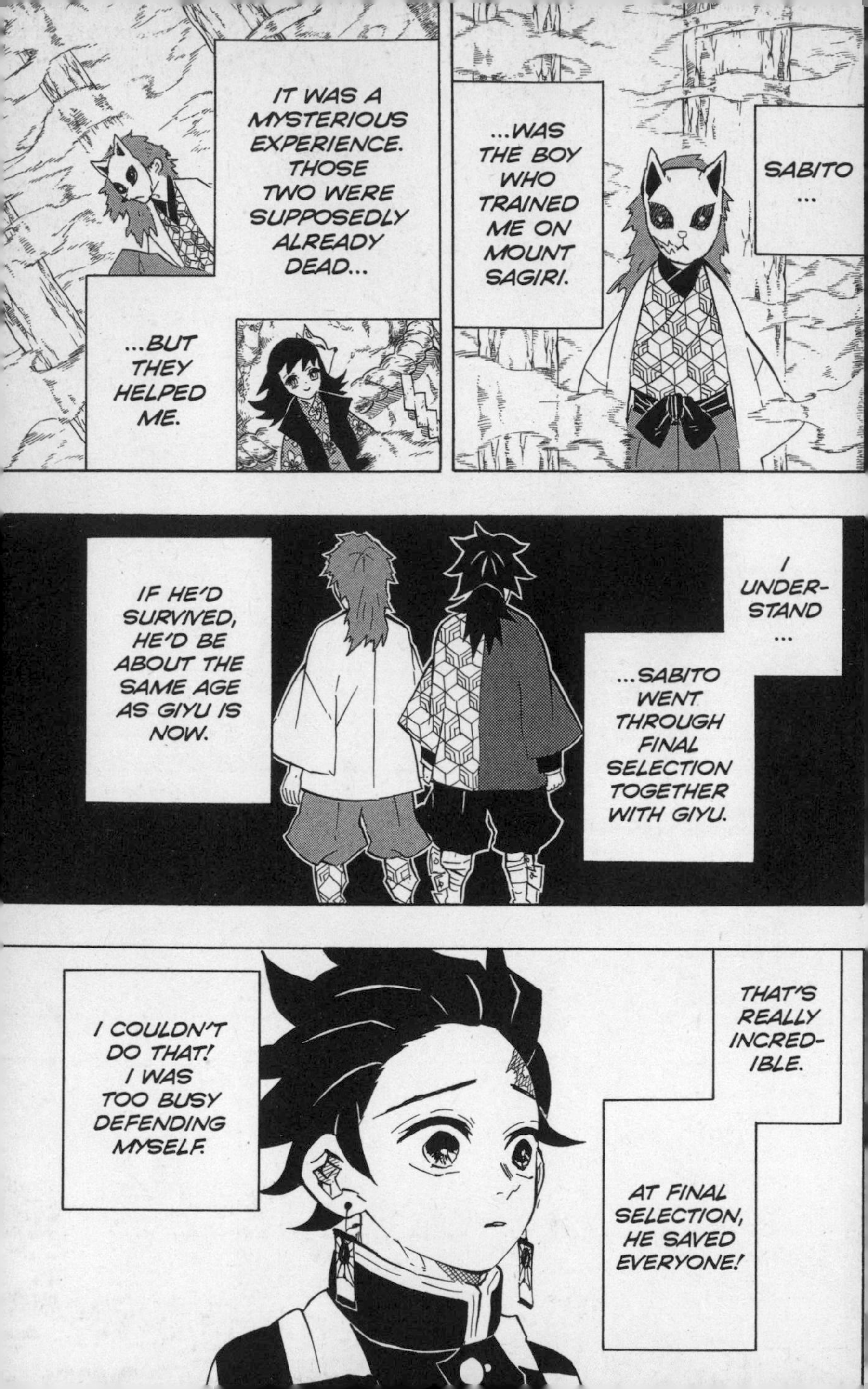
SABITO ...
...WAS THE BOY WHO TRAINED ME ON MOUNT SAGIRI.
IT WAS A MYSTERIOUS EXPERIENCE. THOSE TWO WERE SUPPOSEDLY ALREADY DEAD...
...BUT THEY HELPED ME.
I UNDER-STAND ...
...SABITO WENT THROUGH FINAL SELECTION TOGETHER WITH GIYU.
IF HE'D SURVIVED, HE'D BE ABOUT THE SAME AGE AS GIYU IS NOW.
THAT'S REALLY INCRED-IBLE.
AT FINAL SELECTION, HE SAVED EVERYONE!
I COULDN'T DO THAT! I WAS TOO BUSY DEFENDING MYSELF.

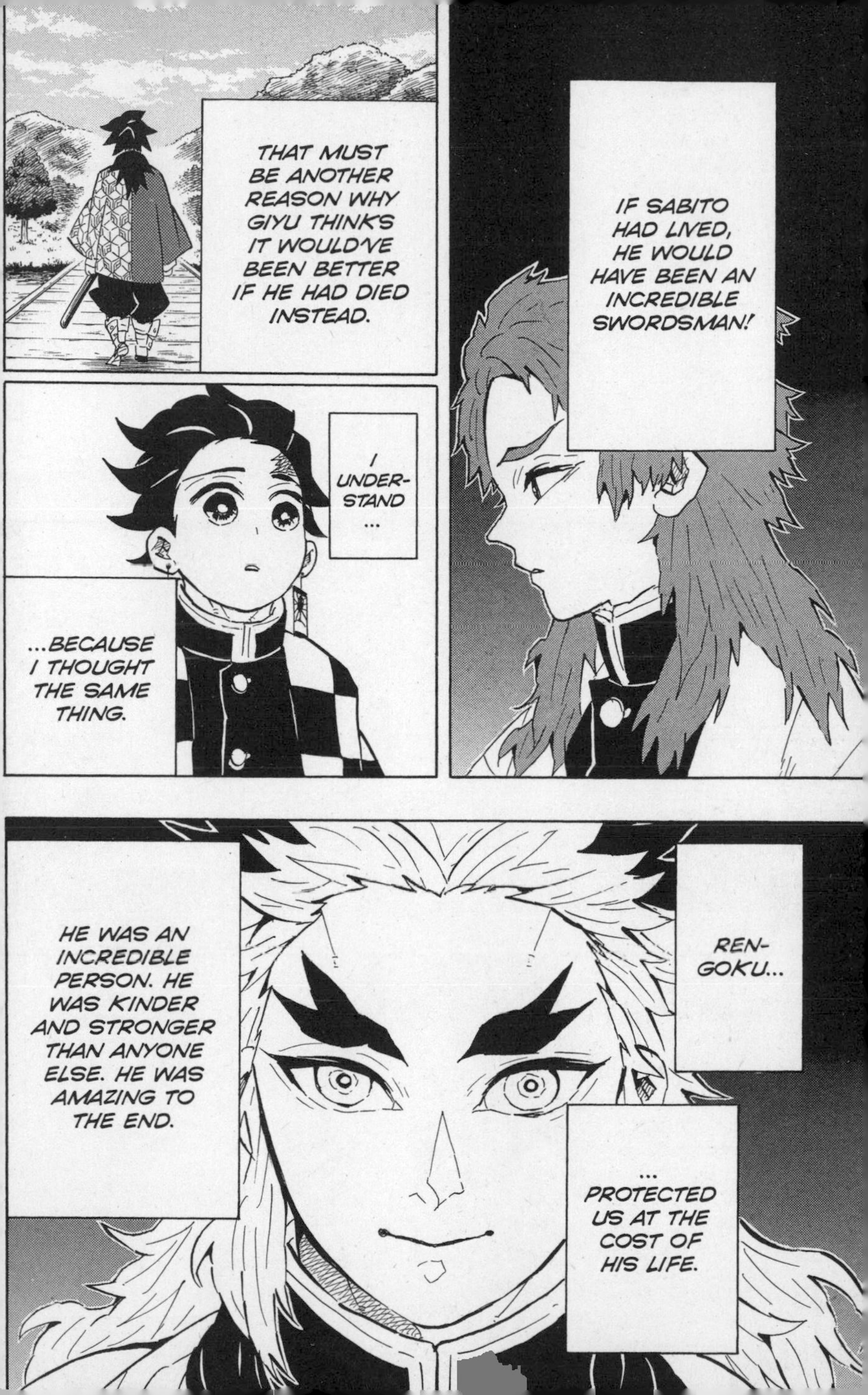
IF SABITO HAD LIVED, HE WOULD HAVE BEEN AN INCREDIBLE SWORDSMAN!
THAT MUST BE ANOTHER REASON WHY GIYU THINKS IT WOULD'VE BEEN BETTER IF HE HAD DIED INSTEAD.
I UNDER-STAND...
...BECAUSE I THOUGHT THE SAME THING.
REN-GOKU...
...PROTECTED US AT THE COST OF HIS LIFE.
HE WAS AN INCREDIBLE PERSON. HE WAS KINDER AND STRONGER THAN ANYONE ELSE. HE WAS AMAZING TO THE END.

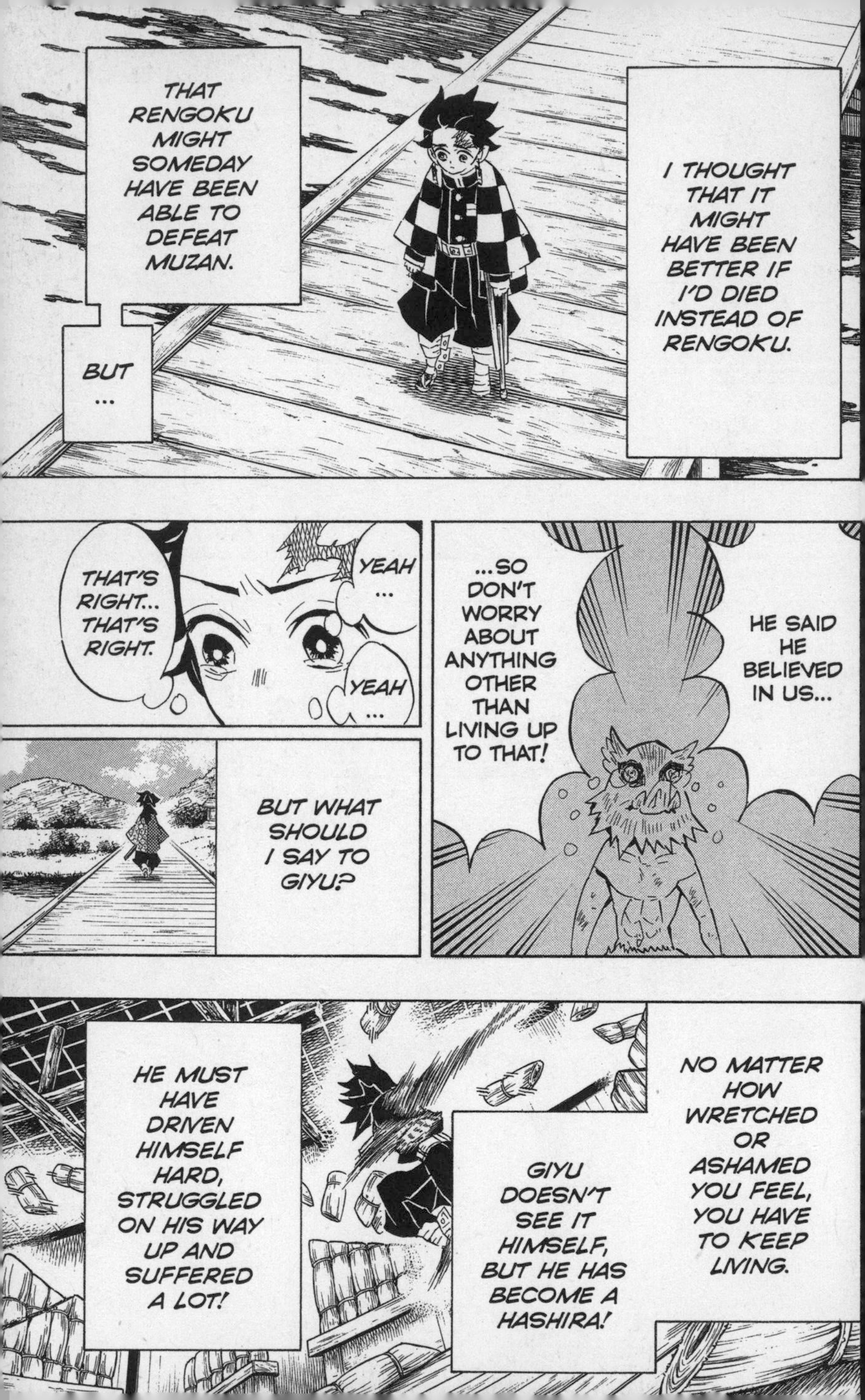
I THOUGHT THAT IT MIGHT HAVE BEEN BETTER IF I'D DIED INSTEAD OF RENGOKU.
THAT RENGOKU MIGHT SOMEDAY HAVE BEEN ABLE TO DEFEAT MUZAN.
BUT ...
HE SAID HE BELIEVED IN US...
...SO DON'T WORRY ABOUT ANYTHING OTHER THAN LIVING UP TO THAT!
YEAH ...
YEAH ...
THAT'S RIGHT... THAT'S RIGHT.
BUT WHAT SHOULD I SAY TO GIYU?
NO MATTER HOW WRETCHED OR ASHAMED YOU FEEL, YOU HAVE TO KEEP LIVING.
GIYU DOESN'T SEE IT HIMSELF, BUT HE HAS BECOME A HASHIRA!
HE MUST HAVE DRIVEN HIMSELF HARD, STRUGGLED ON HIS WAY UP AND SUFFERED A LOT!

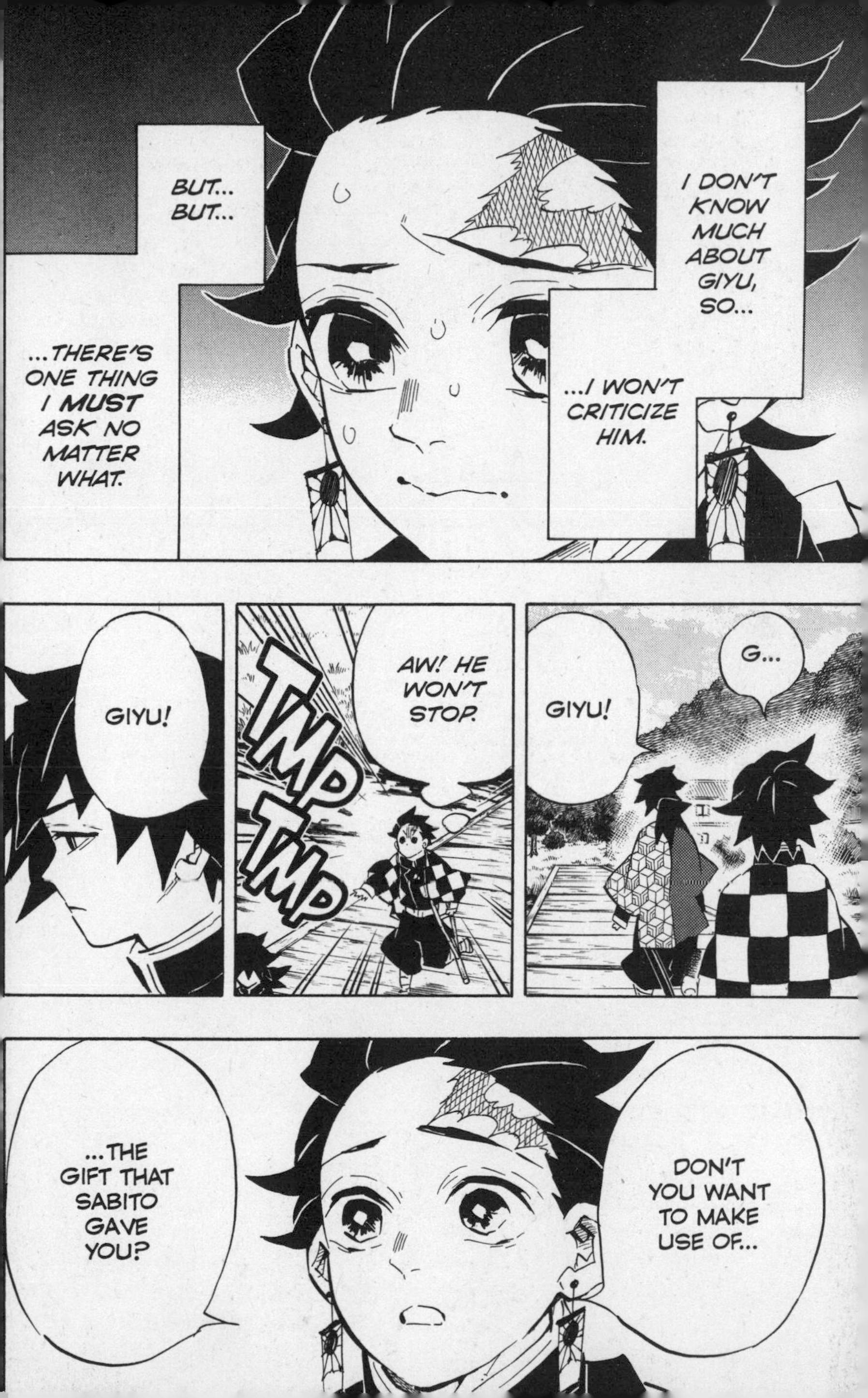
I DON'T KNOW MUCH ABOUT GIYU, SO...
...I WON'T CRITICIZE HIM.
BUT... BUT...
...THERE'S ONE THING I **MUST** ASK NO MATTER WHAT.
G...
GIYU!
AW! HE WON'T STOP.
TMP TMP
GIYU!
DON'T YOU WANT TO MAKE USE OF...
...THE GIFT THAT SABITO GAVE YOU?

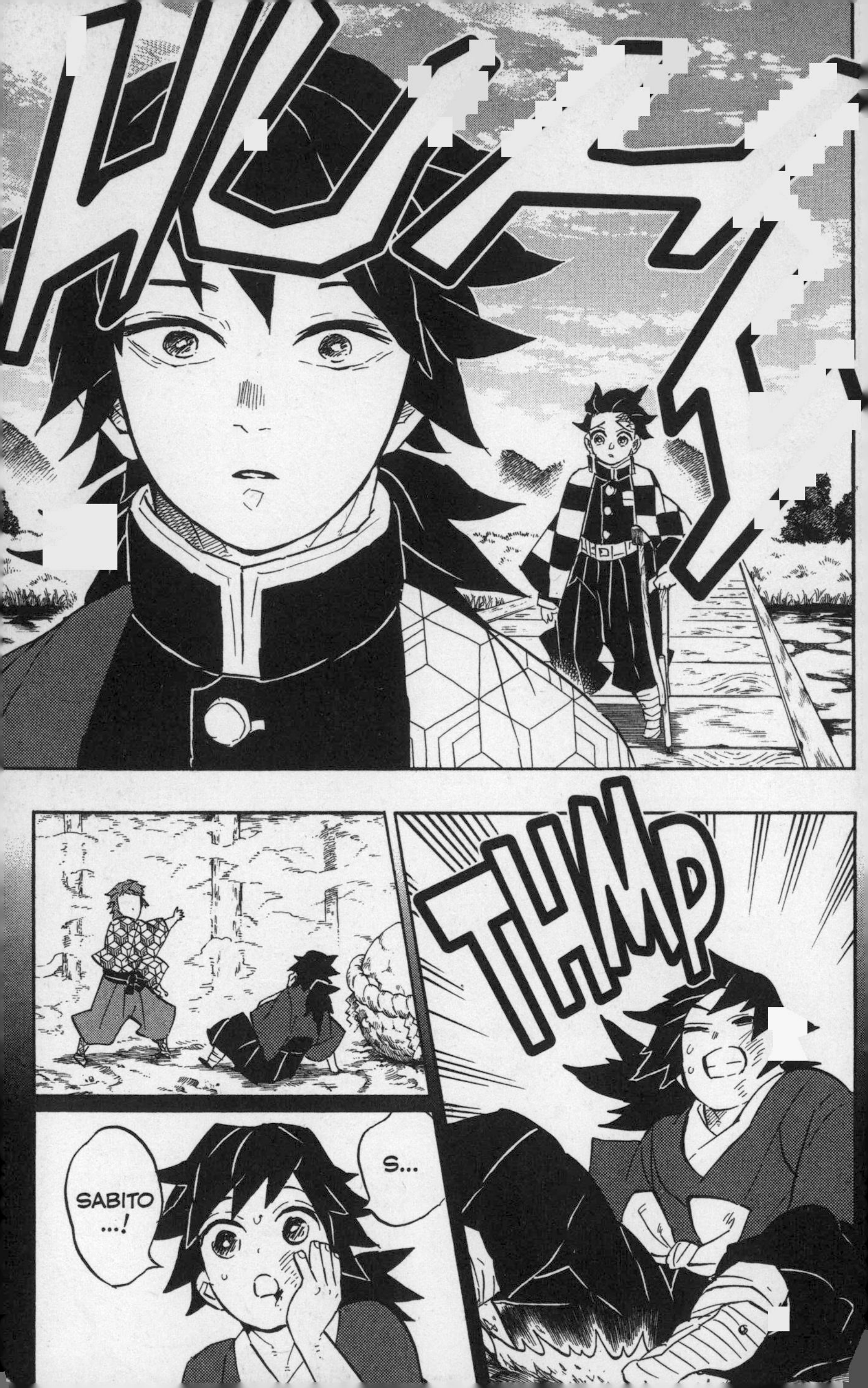
THUMP
S...
SABITO ...!

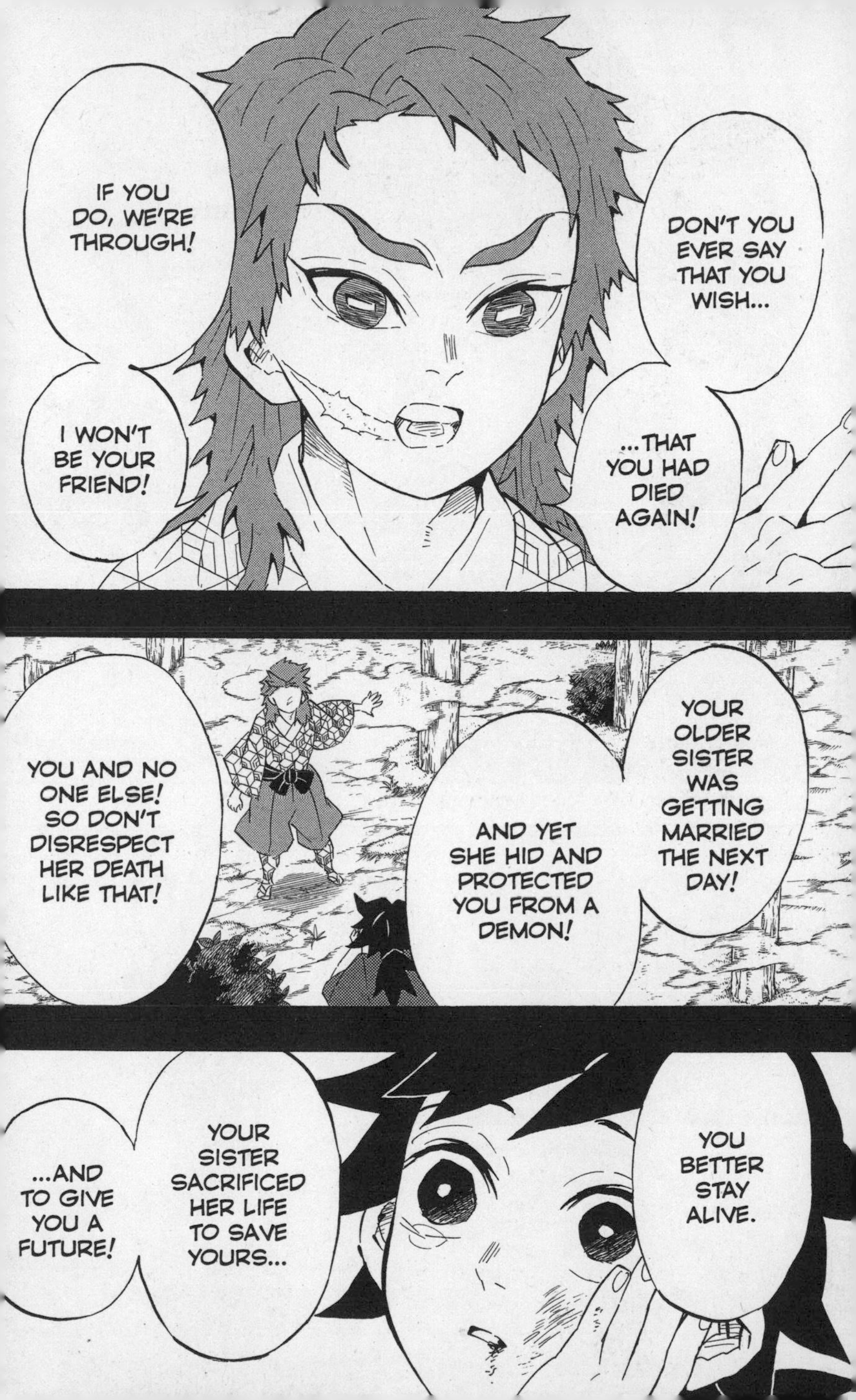
DON'T YOU EVER SAY THAT YOU WISH...
...THAT YOU HAD DIED AGAIN!
IF YOU DO, WE'RE THROUGH!
I WON'T BE YOUR FRIEND!
YOUR OLDER SISTER WAS GETTING MARRIED THE NEXT DAY!
AND YET SHE HID AND PROTECTED YOU FROM A DEMON!
YOU AND NO ONE ELSE! SO DON'T DISRESPECT HER DEATH LIKE THAT!
YOU BETTER STAY ALIVE.
YOUR SISTER SACRIFICED HER LIFE TO SAVE YOURS...
...AND TO GIVE YOU A FUTURE!

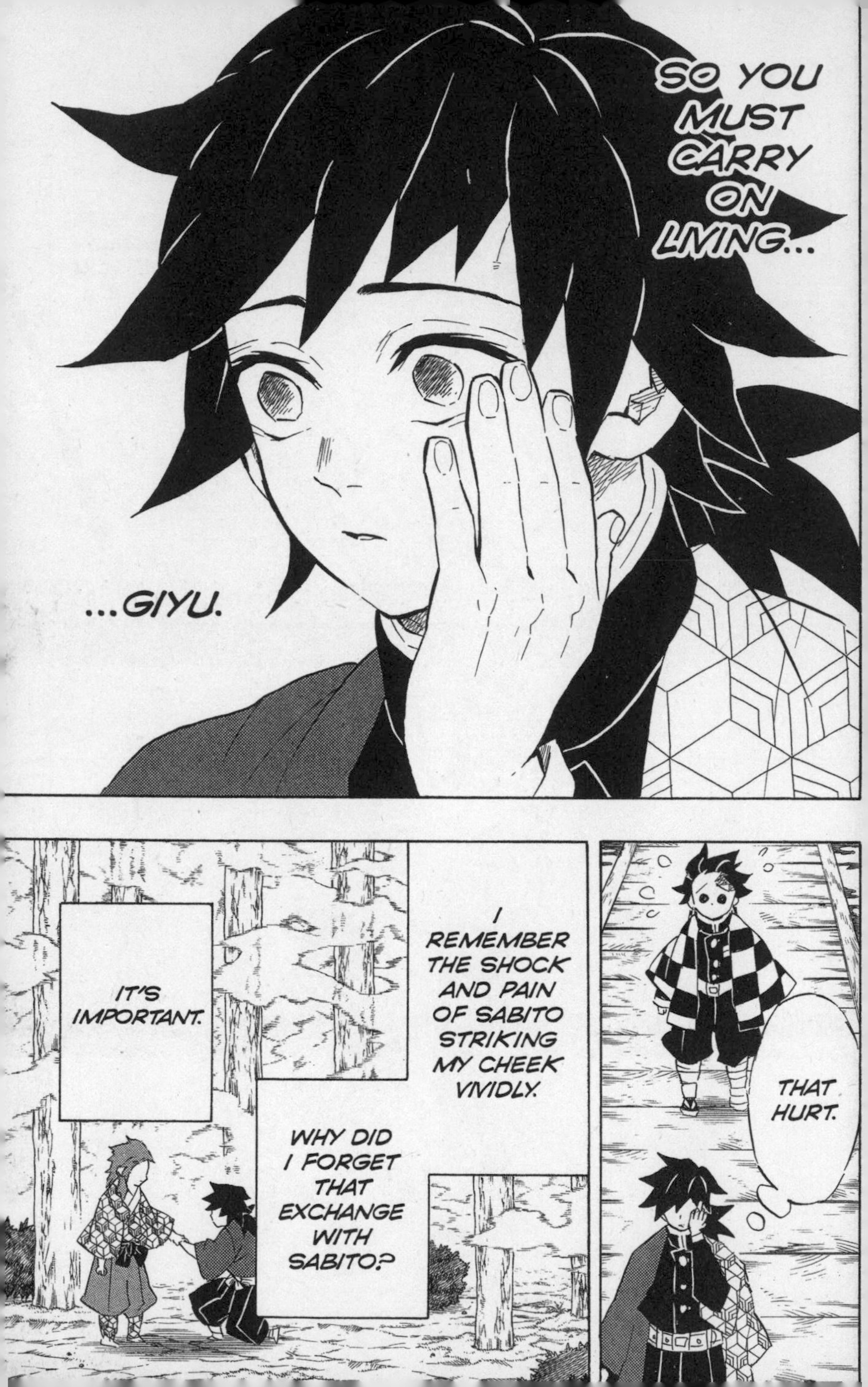
SO YOU MUST CARRY ON LIVING...
...GIYU.
THAT HURT.
I REMEMBER THE SHOCK AND PAIN OF SABITO STRIKING MY CHEEK VIVIDLY.
IT'S IMPORTANT.
WHY DID I FORGET THAT EXCHANGE WITH SABITO?

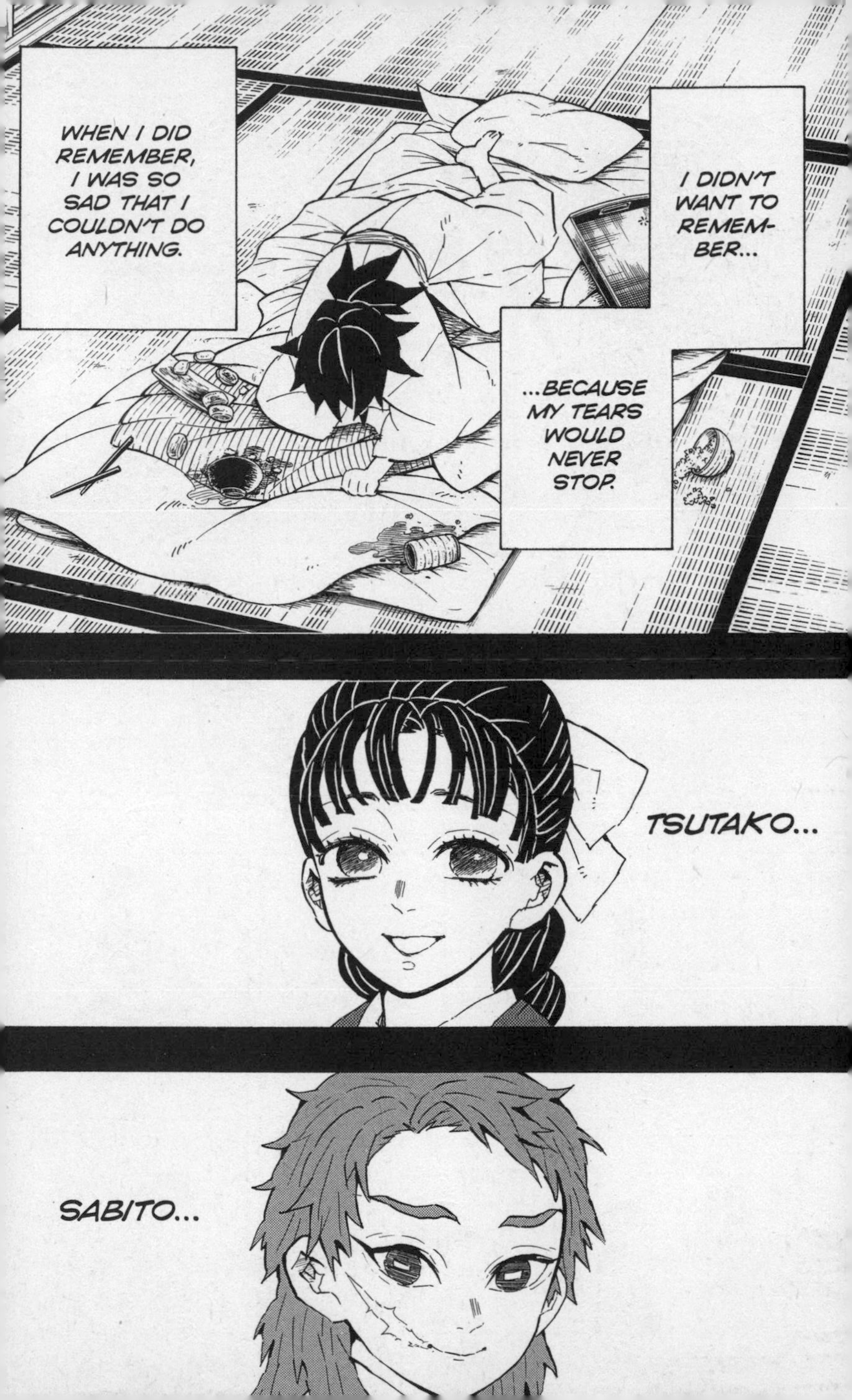
I DIDN'T WANT TO REMEMBER...
...BECAUSE MY TEARS WOULD NEVER STOP.
WHEN I DID REMEMBER, I WAS SO SAD THAT I COULDN'T DO ANYTHING.
TSUTAKO...
SABITO...

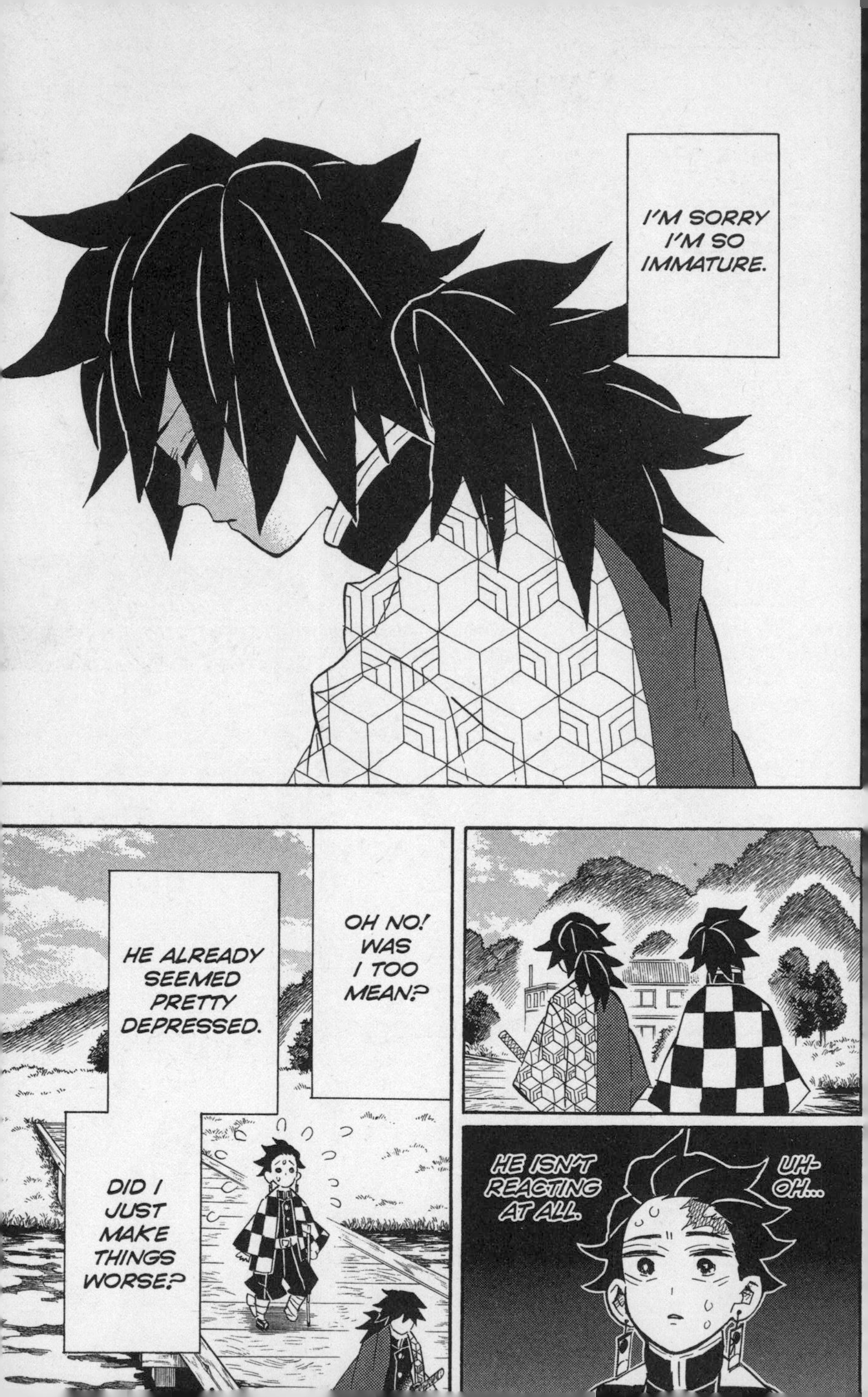
I'M SORRY I'M SO IMMATURE.
UH-OH...
HE ISN'T REACTING AT ALL.
OH NO! WAS I TOO MEAN?
HE ALREADY SEEMED PRETTY DEPRESSED.
DID I JUST MAKE THINGS WORSE?

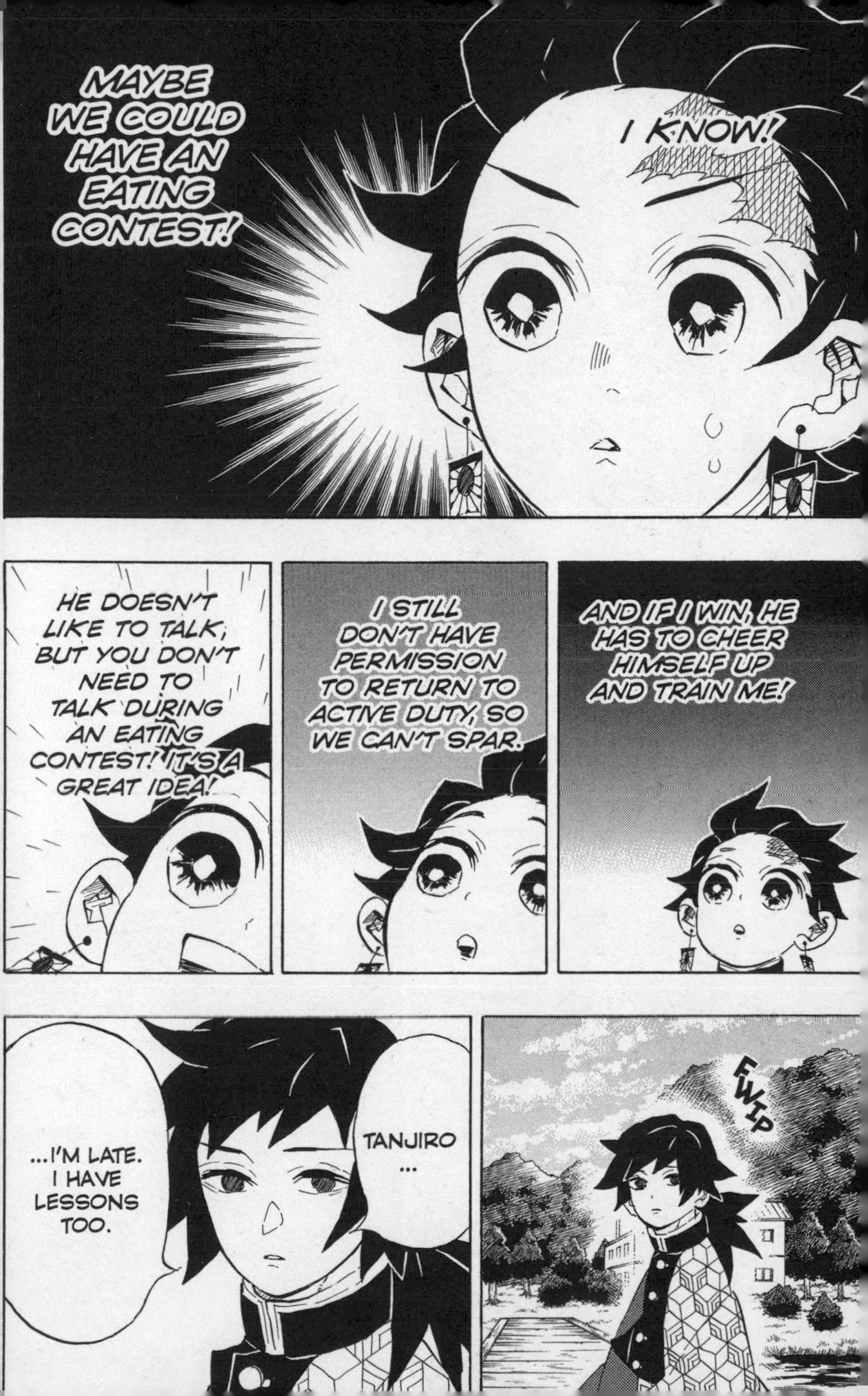
I KNOW!
MAYBE WE COULD HAVE AN EATING CONTEST!
AND IF I WIN, HE HAS TO CHEER HIMSELF UP AND TRAIN ME!
I STILL DON'T HAVE PERMISSION TO RETURN TO ACTIVE DUTY, SO WE CAN'T SPAR.
HE DOESN'T LIKE TO TALK, BUT YOU DON'T NEED TO TALK DURING AN EATING CONTEST! IT'S A GREAT IDEA!
FWIP
TANJIRO ...
...I'M LATE. I HAVE LESSONS TOO.

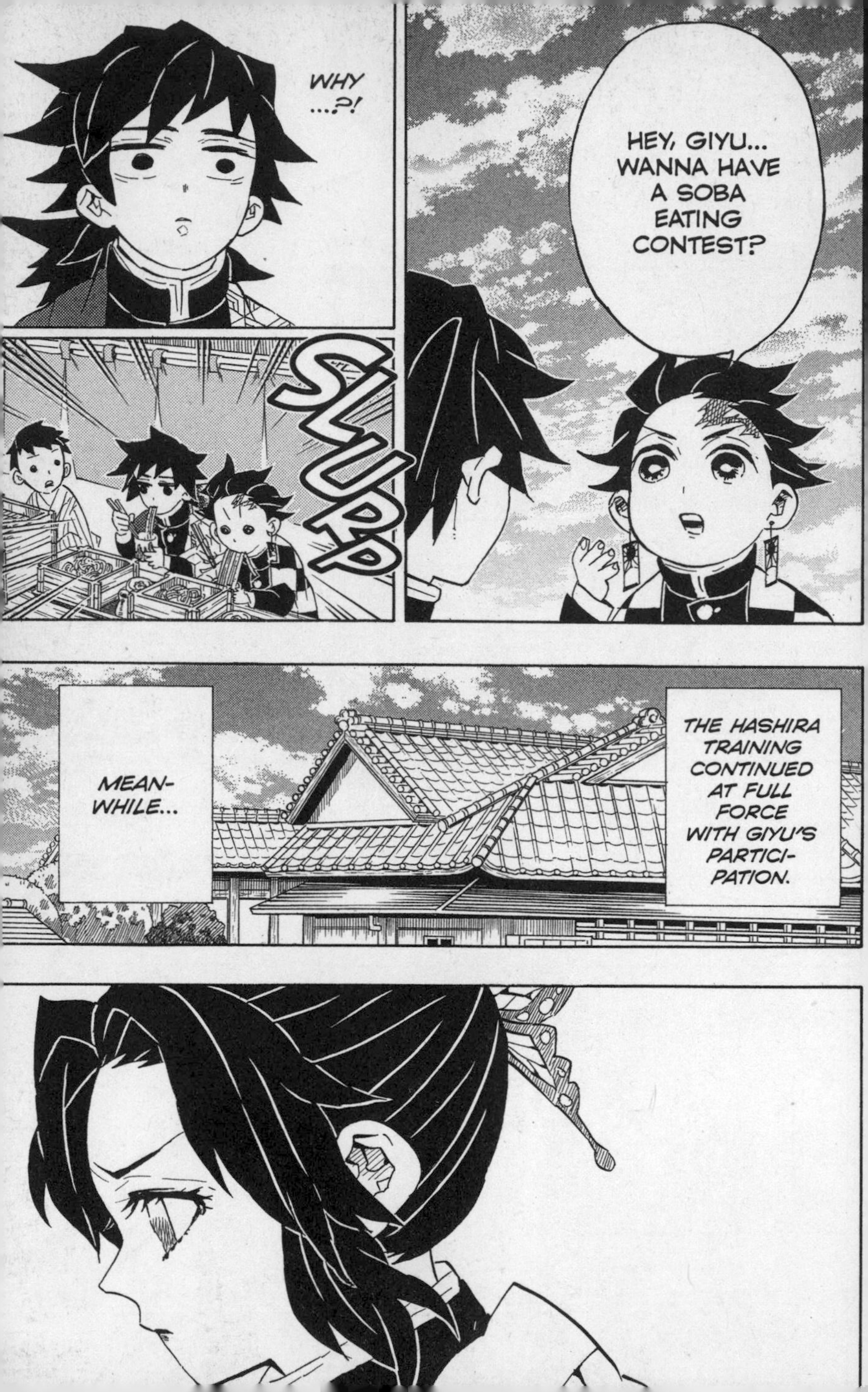
HEY, GIYU... WANNA HAVE A SOBA EATING CONTEST?
WHY ...?!
SLURP
THE HASHIRA TRAINING CONTINUED AT FULL FORCE WITH GIYU'S PARTICI-PATION.
MEAN-WHILE...

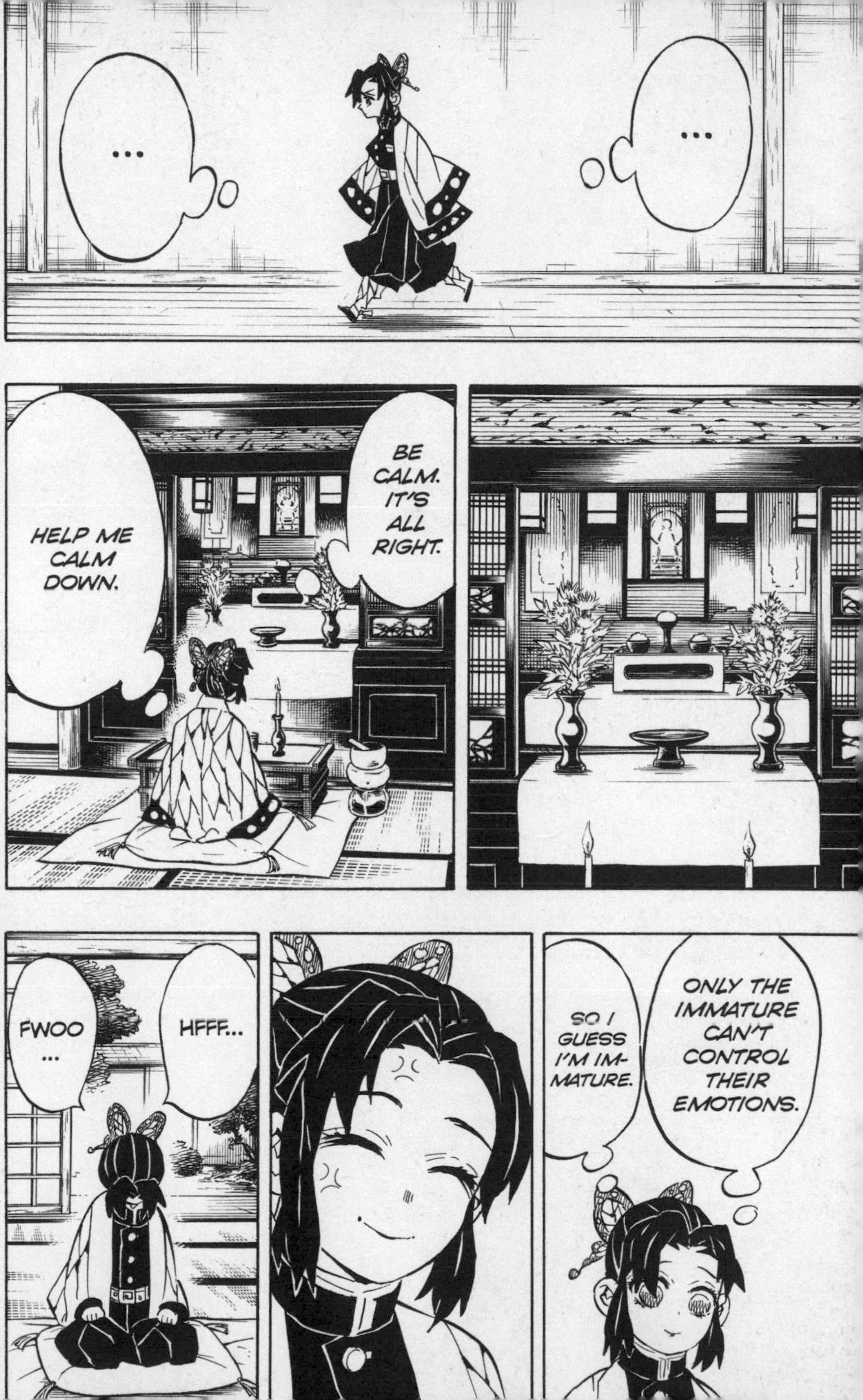
...
...
BE CALM. IT'S ALL RIGHT.
HELP ME CALM DOWN.
ONLY THE IMMATURE CAN'T CONTROL THEIR EMOTIONS.
SO I GUESS I'M IMMATURE.
HFFF...
FWOO ...

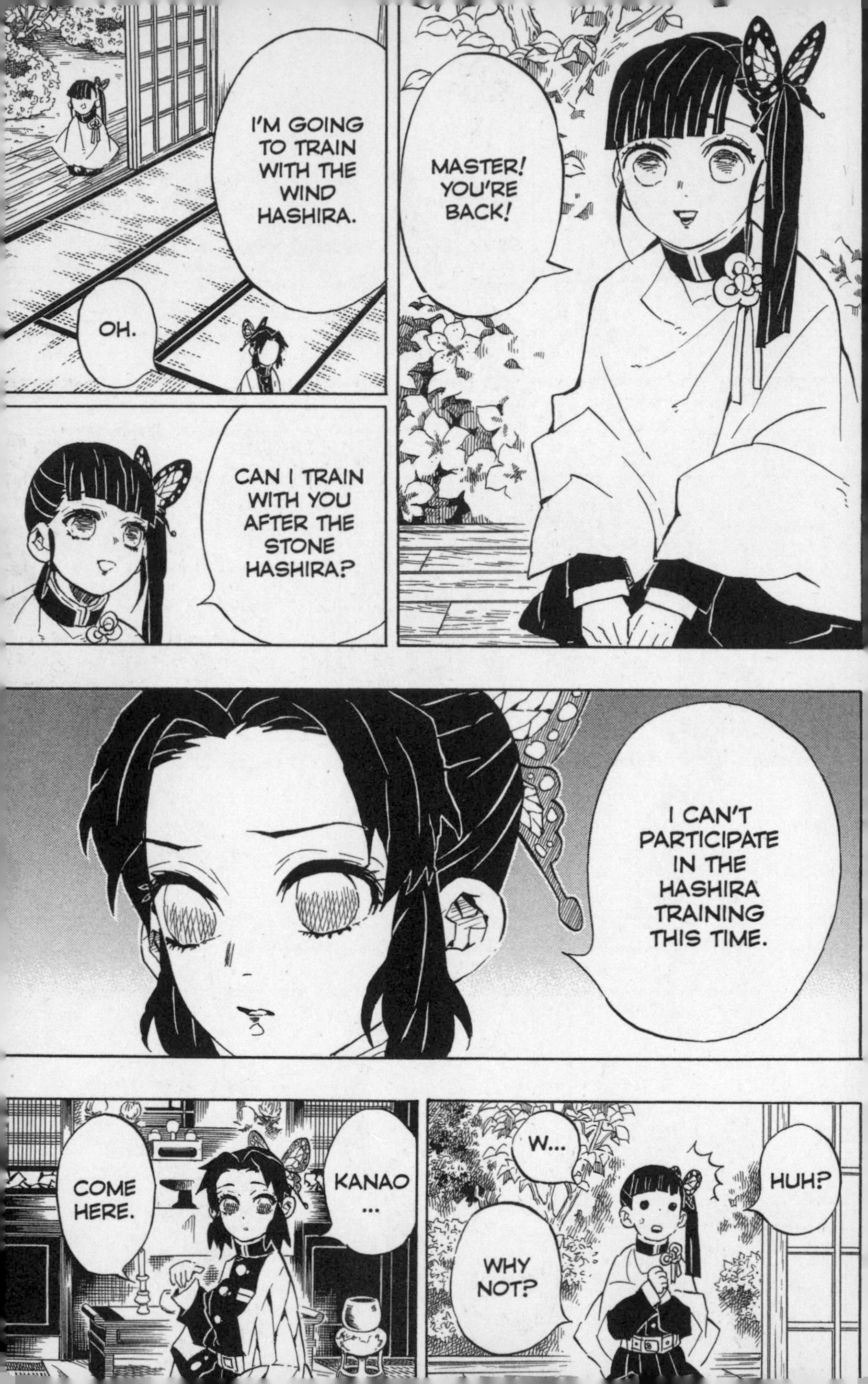
MASTER! YOU'RE BACK!
I'M GOING TO TRAIN WITH THE WIND HASHIRA.
OH.
CAN I TRAIN WITH YOU AFTER THE STONE HASHIRA?
I CAN'T PARTICIPATE IN THE HASHIRA TRAINING THIS TIME.
HUH?
W...
WHY NOT?
KANAO...
COME HERE.

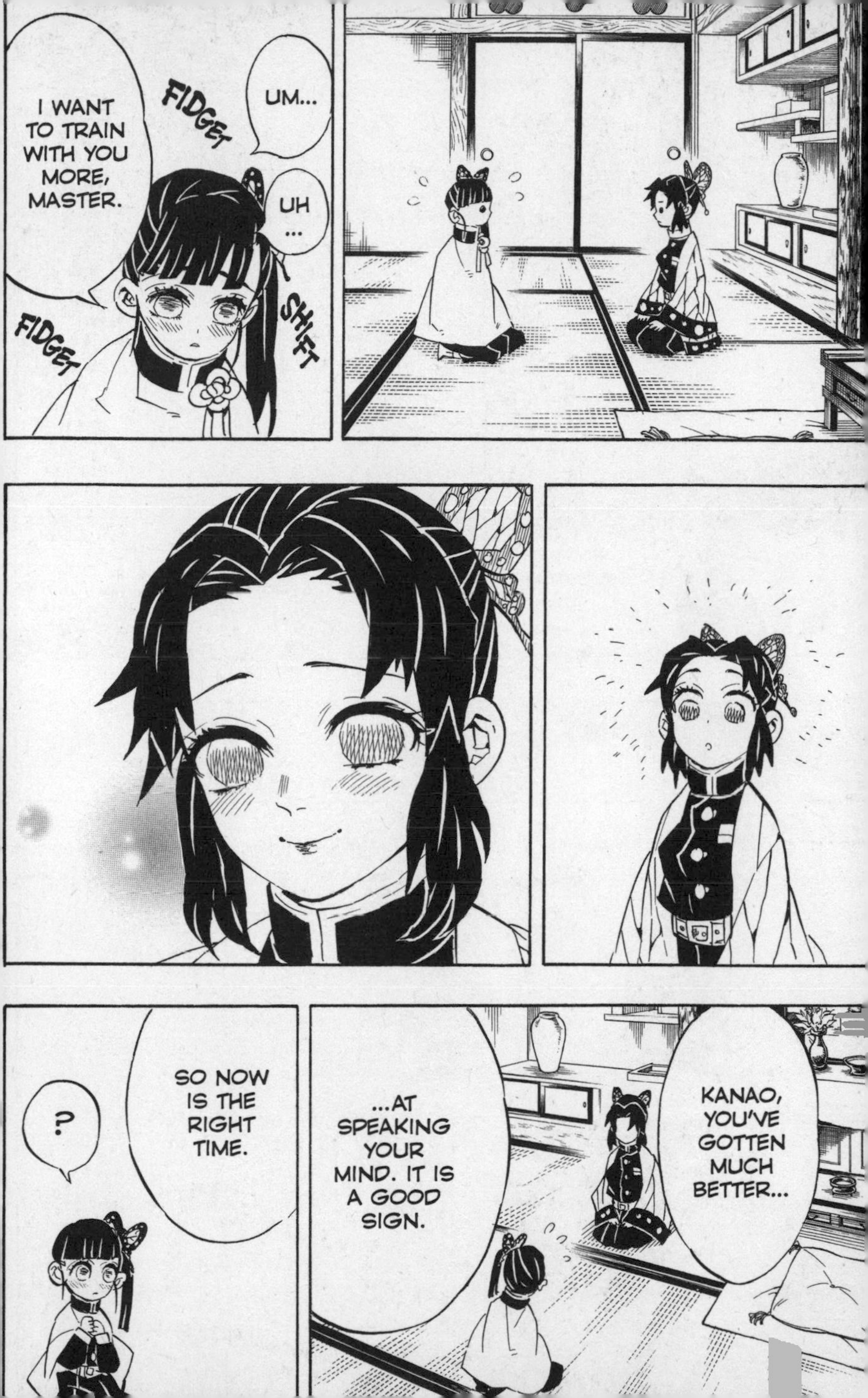
UM...
FIDGET
UH ...
I WANT TO TRAIN WITH YOU MORE, MASTER.
SHIFT
FIDGET
KANAO, YOU'VE GOTTEN MUCH BETTER...
...AT SPEAKING YOUR MIND. IT IS A GOOD SIGN.
SO NOW IS THE RIGHT TIME.
?

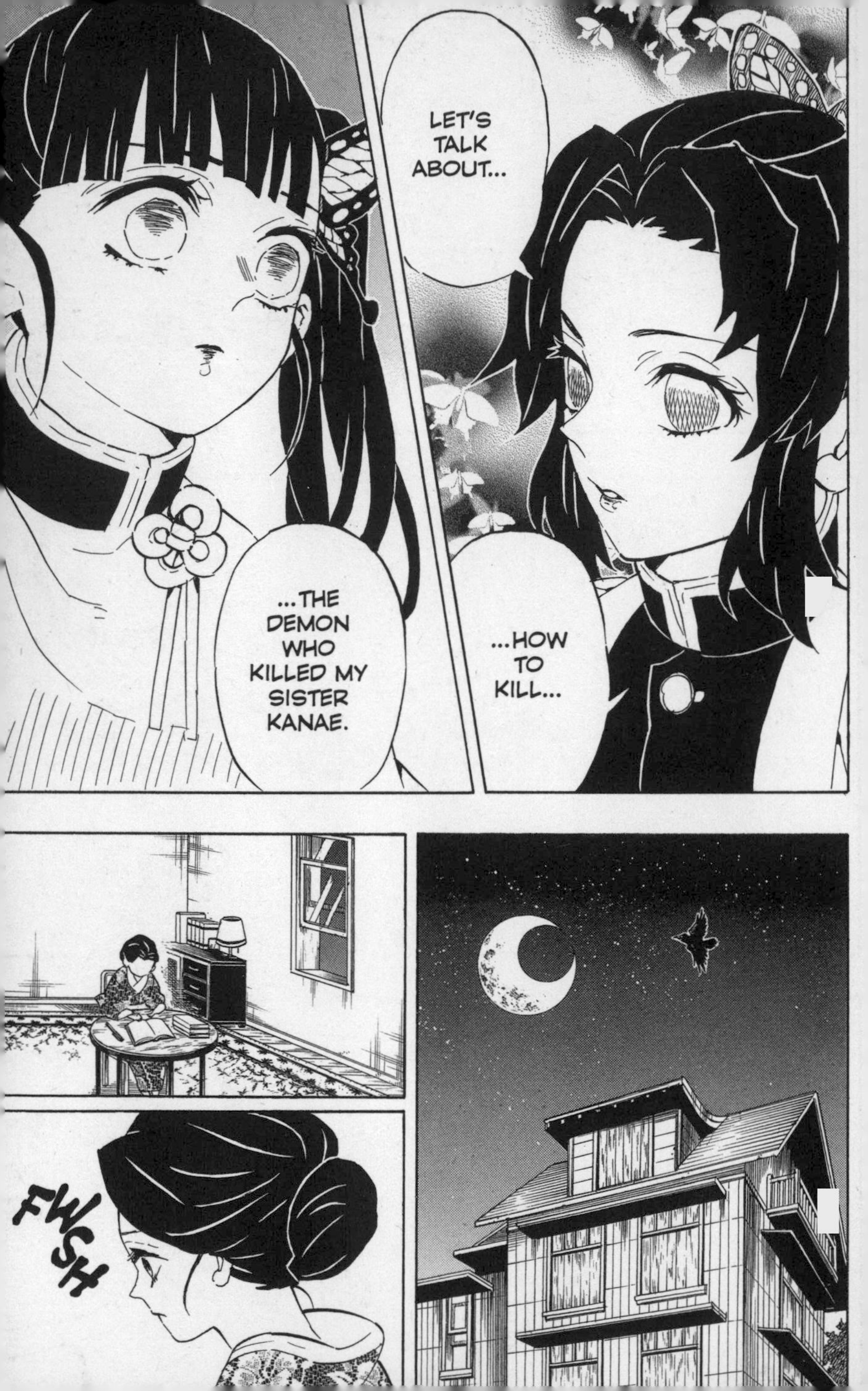
LET'S TALK ABOUT...
...HOW TO KILL...
...THE DEMON WHO KILLED MY SISTER KANAE.
FWSH

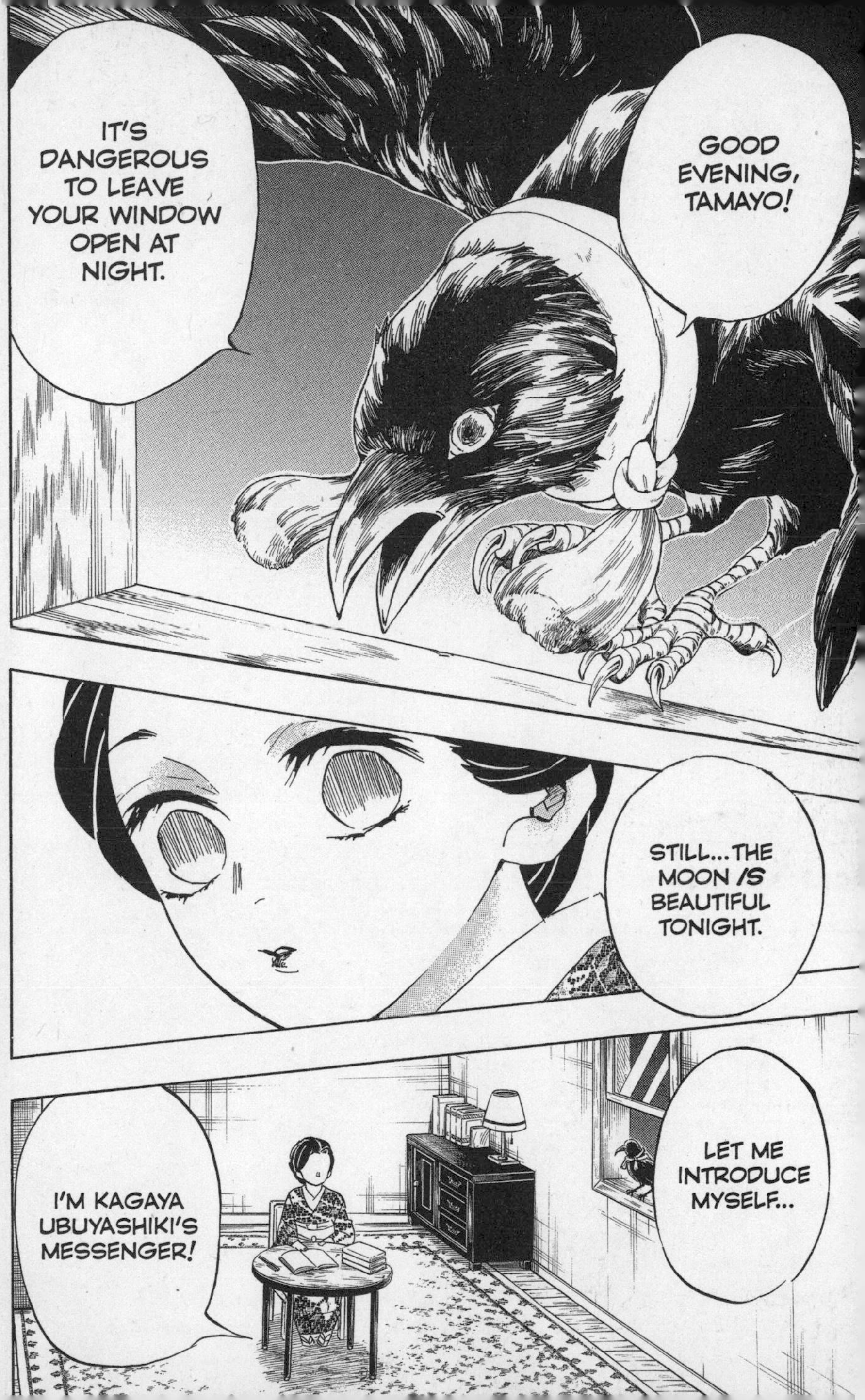
GOOD EVENING, TAMAYO!
IT'S DANGEROUS TO LEAVE YOUR WINDOW OPEN AT NIGHT.
STILL... THE MOON *IS* BEAUTIFUL TONIGHT.
LET ME INTRODUCE MYSELF...
I'M KAGAYA UBUYASHIKI'S MESSENGER!

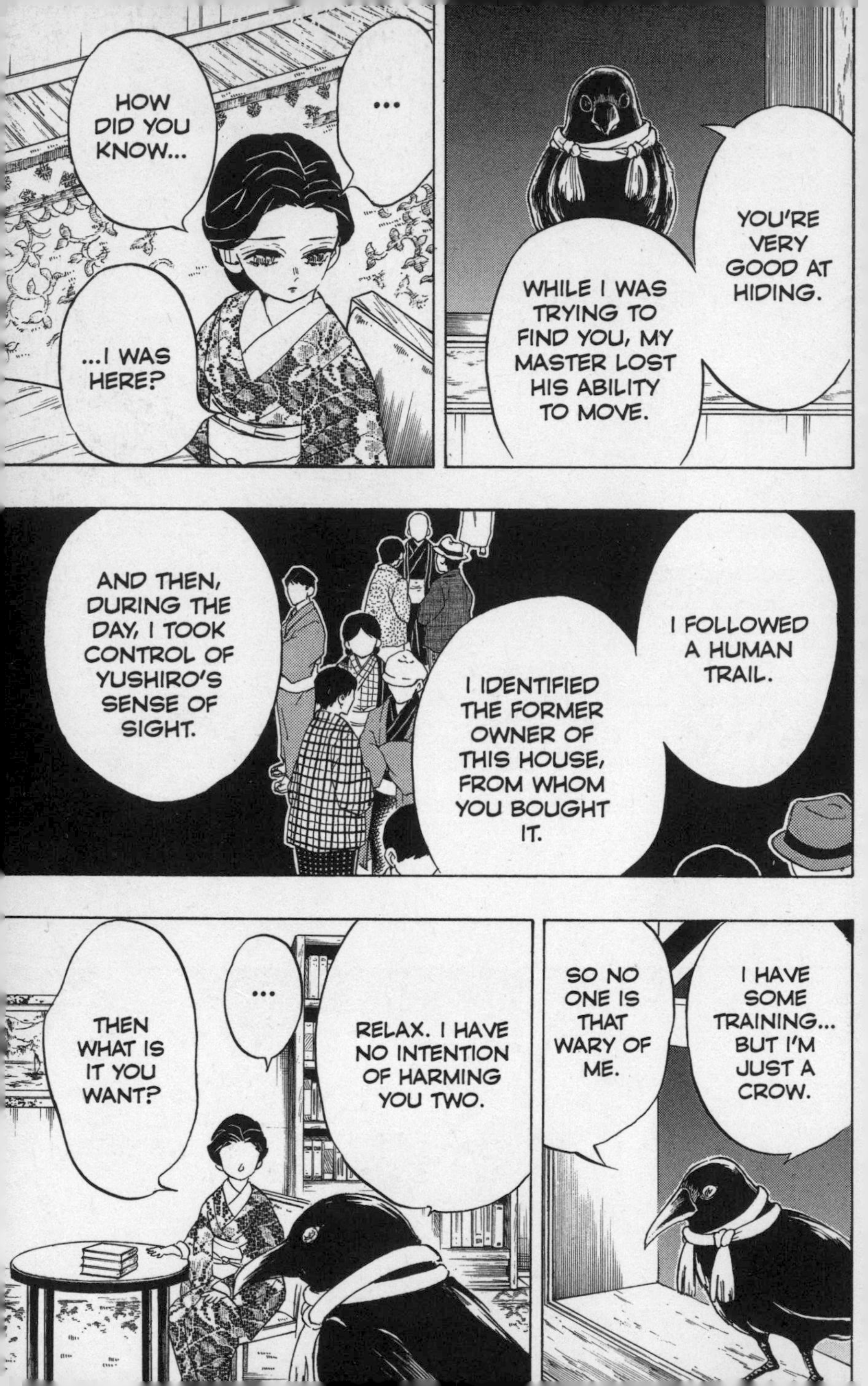
YOU'RE VERY GOOD AT HIDING.
WHILE I WAS TRYING TO FIND YOU, MY MASTER LOST HIS ABILITY TO MOVE.
...
HOW DID YOU KNOW...
...I WAS HERE?
I FOLLOWED A HUMAN TRAIL.
I IDENTIFIED THE FORMER OWNER OF THIS HOUSE, FROM WHOM YOU BOUGHT IT.
AND THEN, DURING THE DAY, I TOOK CONTROL OF YUSHIRO'S SENSE OF SIGHT.
I HAVE SOME TRAINING... BUT I'M JUST A CROW.
SO NO ONE IS THAT WARY OF ME.
RELAX. I HAVE NO INTENTION OF HARMING YOU TWO.
...
THEN WHAT IS IT YOU WANT?

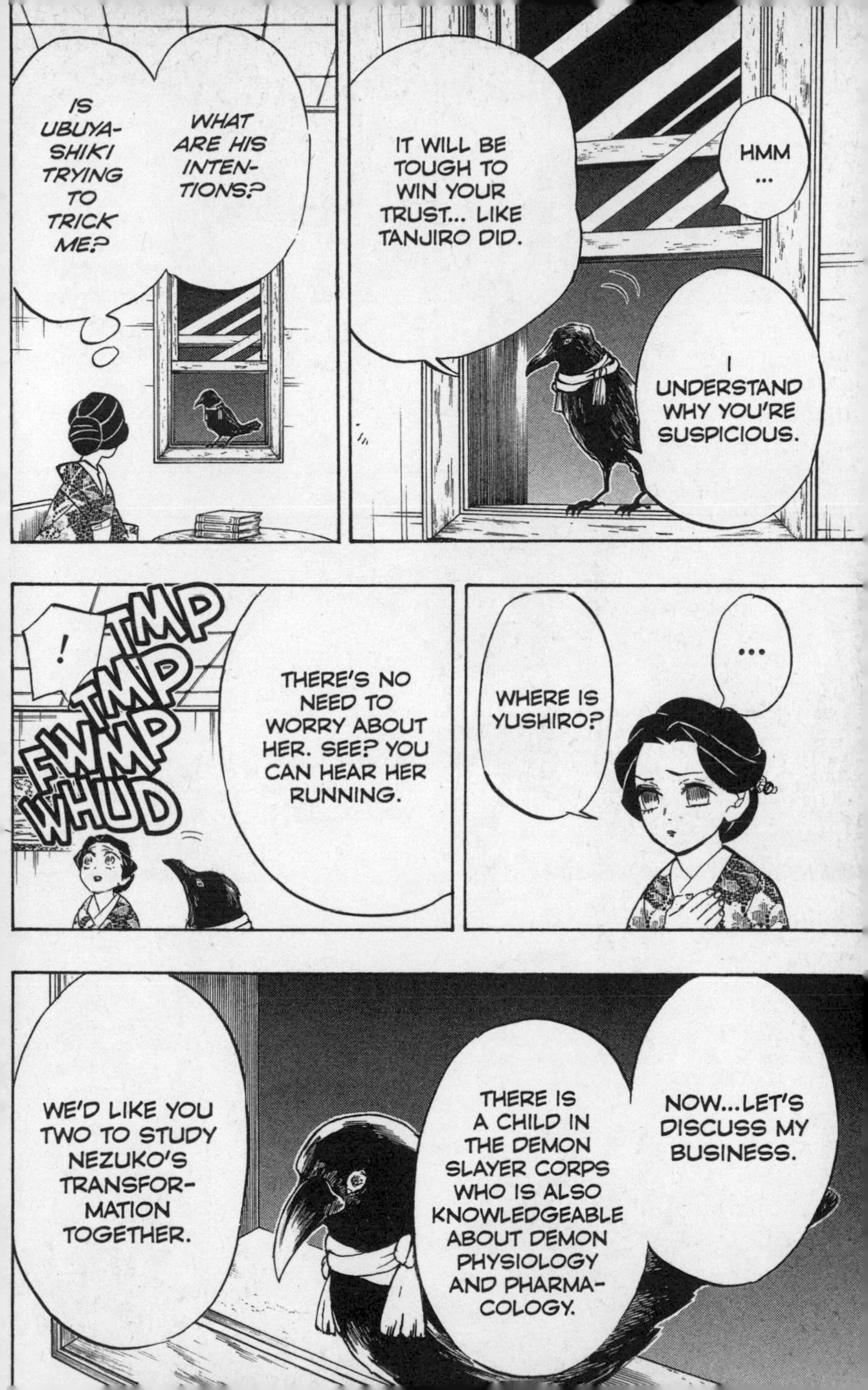
HMM ...
I UNDERSTAND WHY YOU'RE SUSPICIOUS.
IT WILL BE TOUGH TO WIN YOUR TRUST... LIKE TANJIRO DID.
WHAT ARE HIS INTENTIONS?
IS UBUYASHIKI TRYING TO TRICK ME?
...
WHERE IS YUSHIRO?
TMP TMP FWMP WHUD
!
THERE'S NO NEED TO WORRY ABOUT HER. SEE? YOU CAN HEAR HER RUNNING.
NOW...LET'S DISCUSS MY BUSINESS.
THERE IS A CHILD IN THE DEMON SLAYER CORPS WHO IS ALSO KNOWLEDGEABLE ABOUT DEMON PHYSIOLOGY AND PHARMACOLOGY.
WE'D LIKE YOU TWO TO STUDY NEZUKO'S TRANSFORMATION TOGETHER.

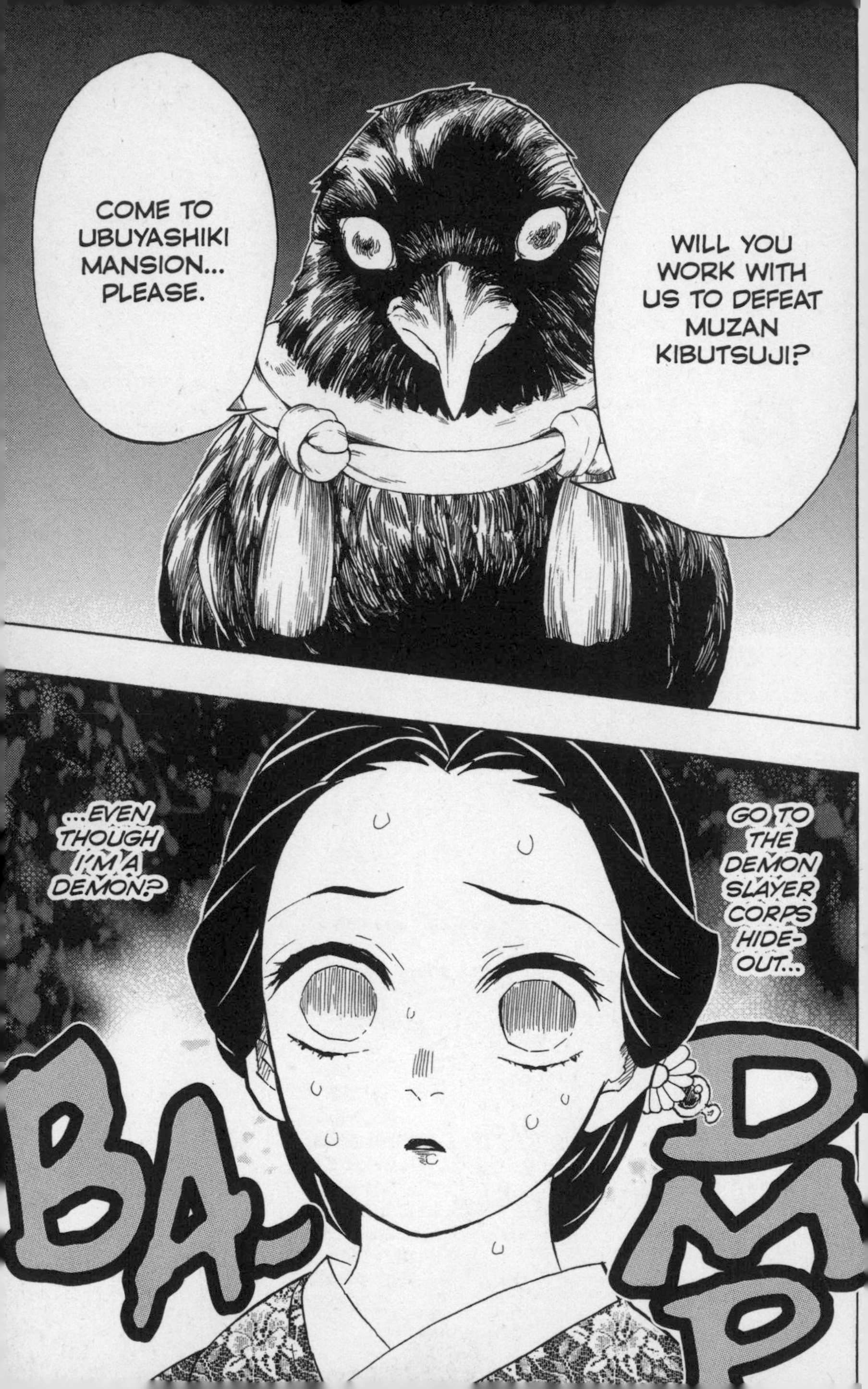
WILL YOU WORK WITH US TO DEFEAT MUZAN KIBUTSUJI?
COME TO UBUYASHIKI MANSION... PLEASE.
GO TO THE DEMON SLAYER CORPS HIDE-OUT...
...EVEN THOUGH I'M A DEMON?
BA-DMP

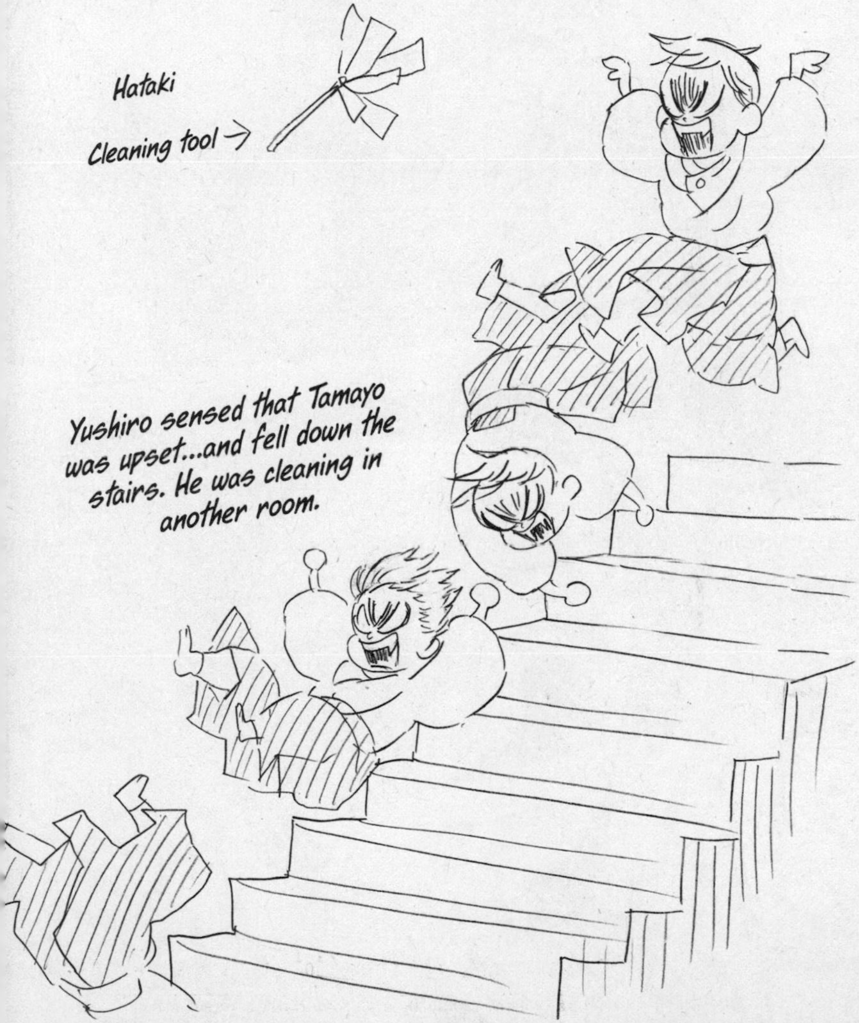
Hataki
Cleaning tool →
Yushiro sensed that Tamayo was upset...and fell down the stairs. He was cleaning in another room.

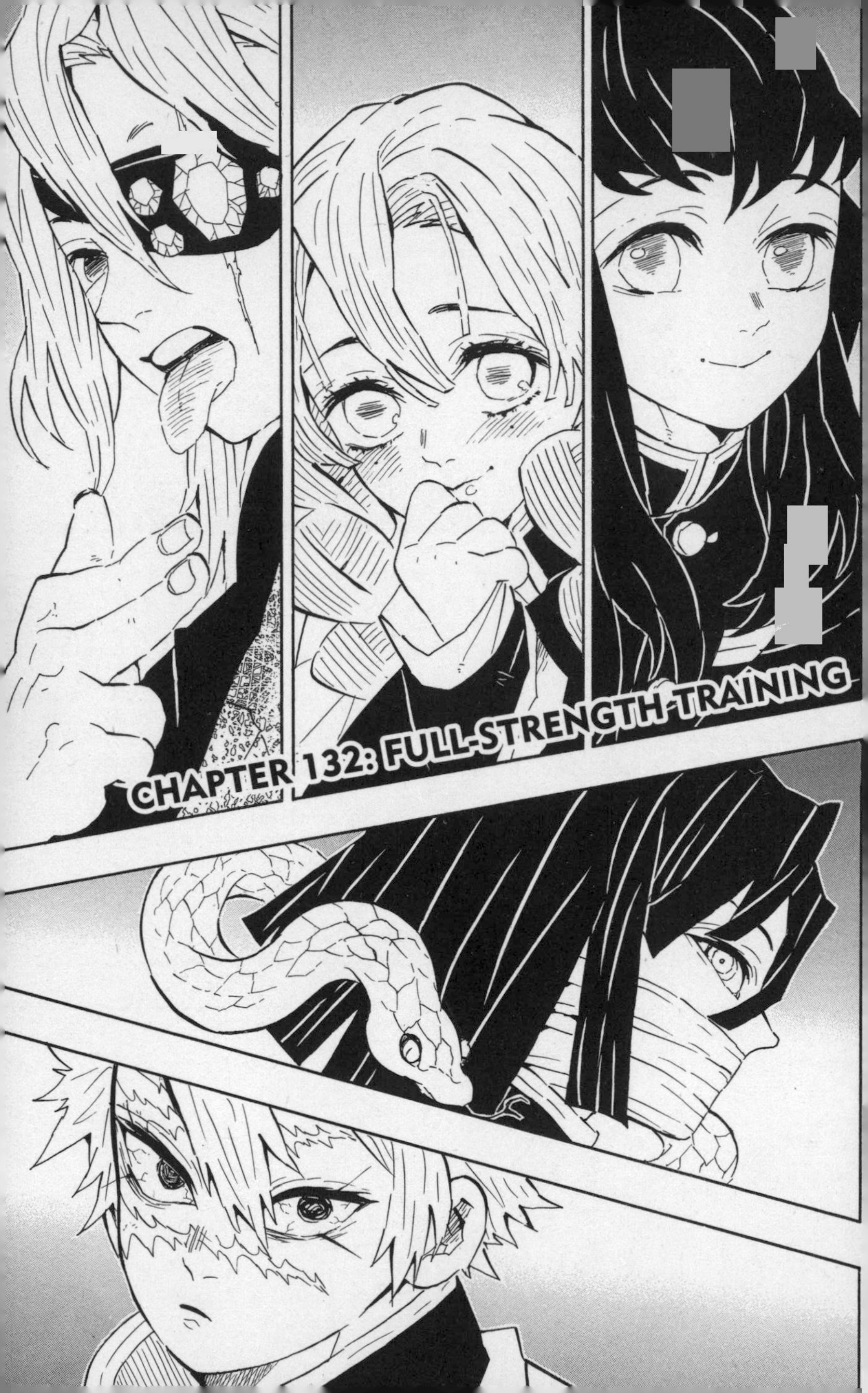
CHAPTER 132: FULL-STRENGTH TRAINING

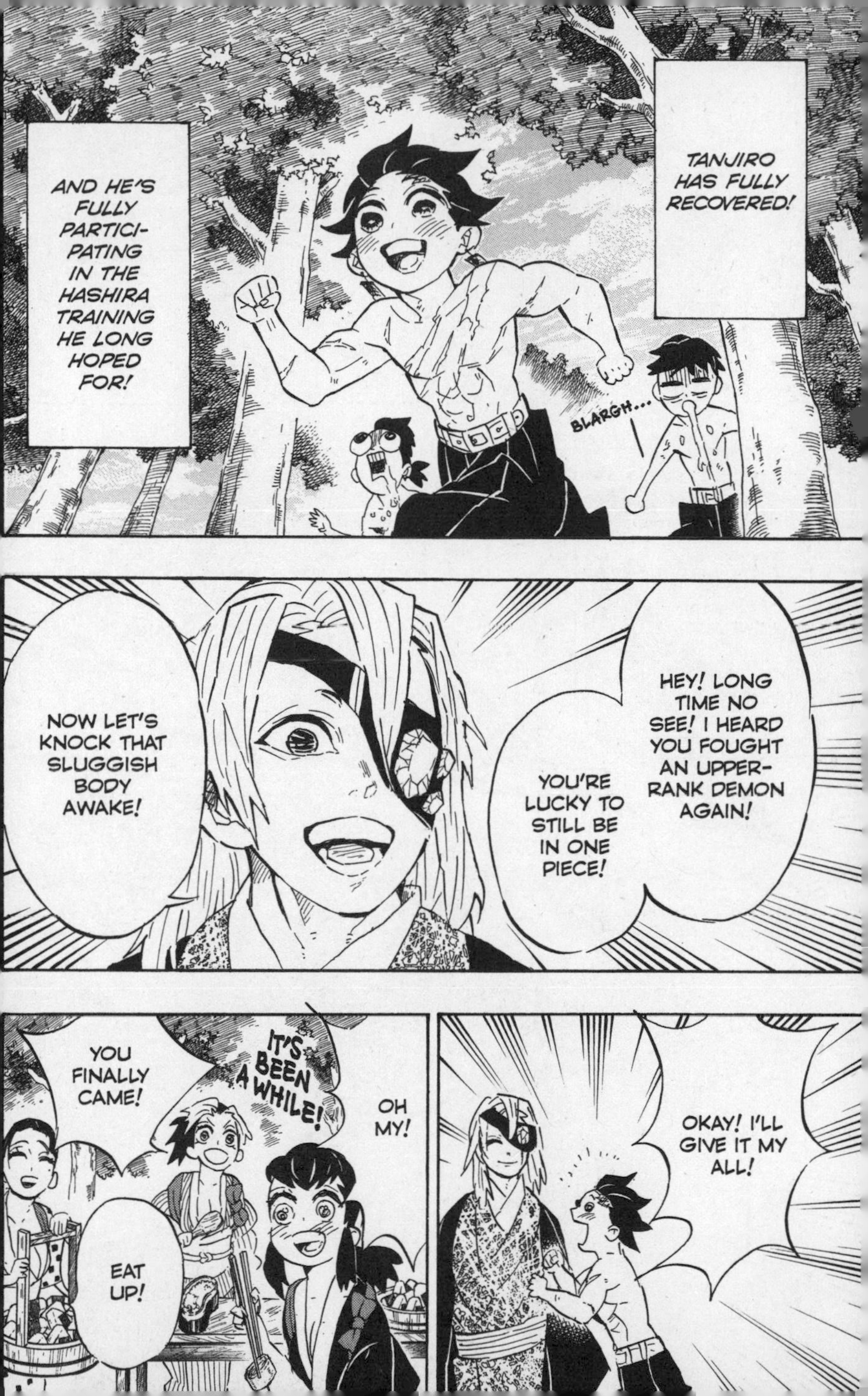
TANJIRO HAS FULLY RECOVERED!
AND HE'S FULLY PARTICI-PATING IN THE HASHIRA TRAINING HE LONG HOPED FOR!
BLARGH...
HEY! LONG TIME NO SEE! I HEARD YOU FOUGHT AN UPPER-RANK DEMON AGAIN!
YOU'RE LUCKY TO STILL BE IN ONE PIECE!
NOW LET'S KNOCK THAT SLUGGISH BODY AWAKE!
OKAY! I'LL GIVE IT MY ALL!
OH MY!
IT'S BEEN A WHILE!
YOU FINALLY CAME!
EAT UP!

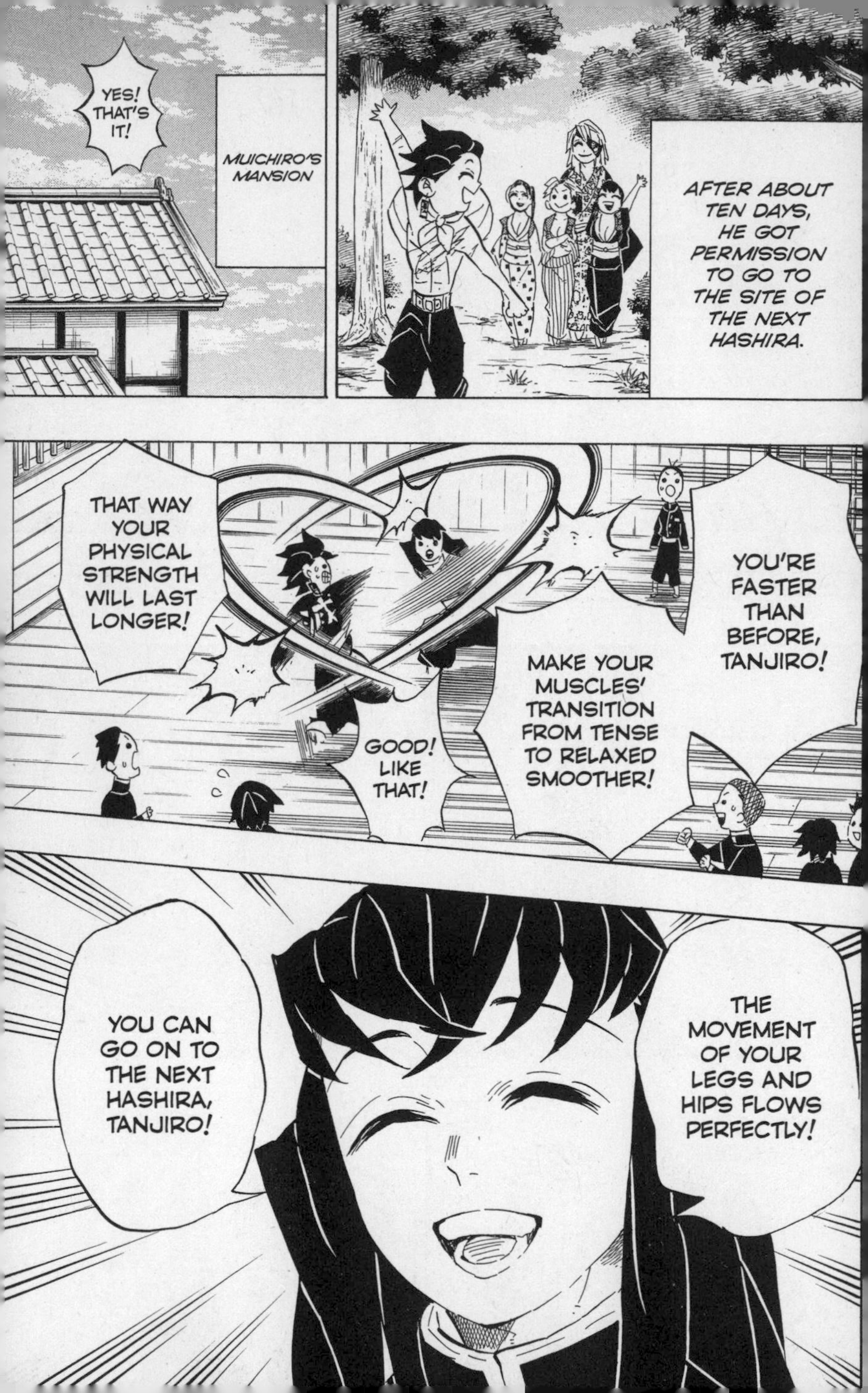
AFTER ABOUT TEN DAYS, HE GOT PERMISSION TO GO TO THE SITE OF THE NEXT HASHIRA.
MUICHIRO'S MANSION
YES! THAT'S IT!
YOU'RE FASTER THAN BEFORE, TANJIRO!
MAKE YOUR MUSCLES' TRANSITION FROM TENSE TO RELAXED SMOOTHER!
THAT WAY YOUR PHYSICAL STRENGTH WILL LAST LONGER!
GOOD! LIKE THAT!
THE MOVEMENT OF YOUR LEGS AND HIPS FLOWS PERFECTLY!
YOU CAN GO ON TO THE NEXT HASHIRA, TANJIRO!

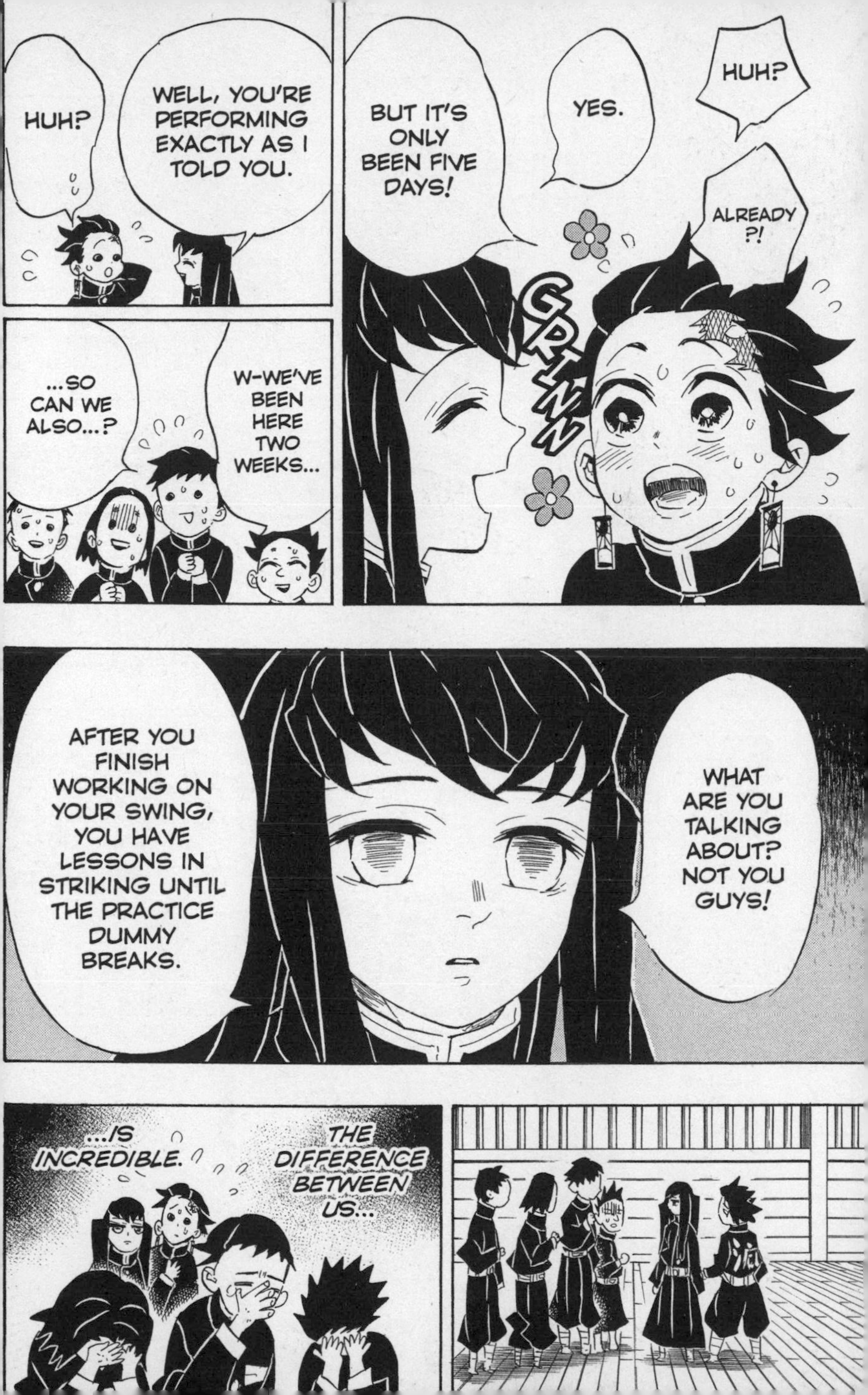
HUH?
ALREADY ?!
YES.
BUT IT'S ONLY BEEN FIVE DAYS!
GRINN
WELL, YOU'RE PERFORMING EXACTLY AS I TOLD YOU.
HUH?
W-WE'VE BEEN HERE TWO WEEKS...
...SO CAN WE ALSO...?
WHAT ARE YOU TALKING ABOUT? NOT YOU GUYS!
AFTER YOU FINISH WORKING ON YOUR SWING, YOU HAVE LESSONS IN STRIKING UNTIL THE PRACTICE DUMMY BREAKS.
THE DIFFERENCE BETWEEN US...
...IS INCREDIBLE.

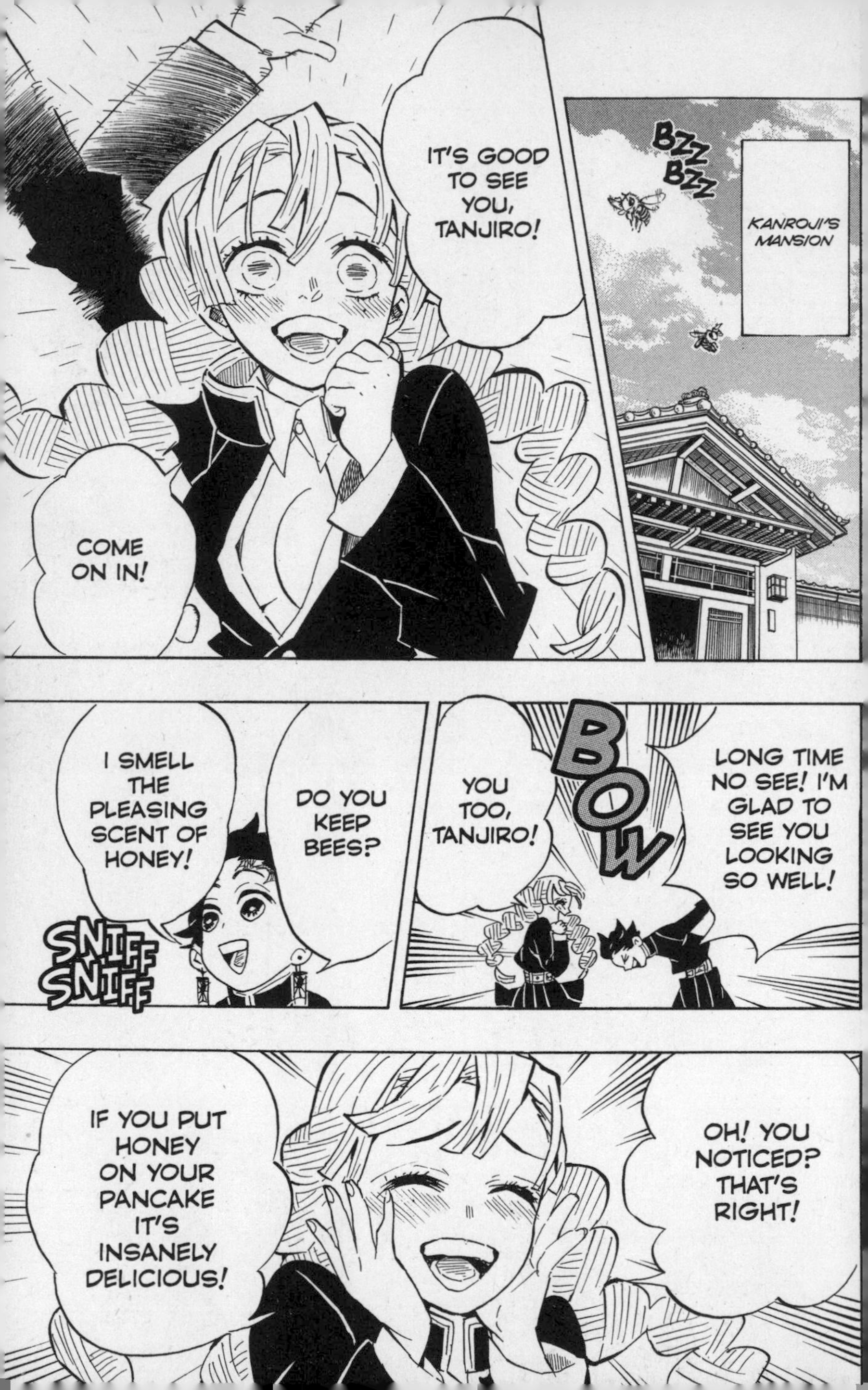
BZZ BZZ
KANROJI'S MANSION
IT'S GOOD TO SEE YOU, TANJIRO!
COME ON IN!
LONG TIME NO SEE! I'M GLAD TO SEE YOU LOOKING SO WELL!
BOW
YOU TOO, TANJIRO!
DO YOU KEEP BEES?
I SMELL THE PLEASING SCENT OF HONEY!
SNIFF SNIFF
OH! YOU NOTICED? THAT'S RIGHT!
IF YOU PUT HONEY ON YOUR PANCAKE IT'S INSANELY DELICIOUS!

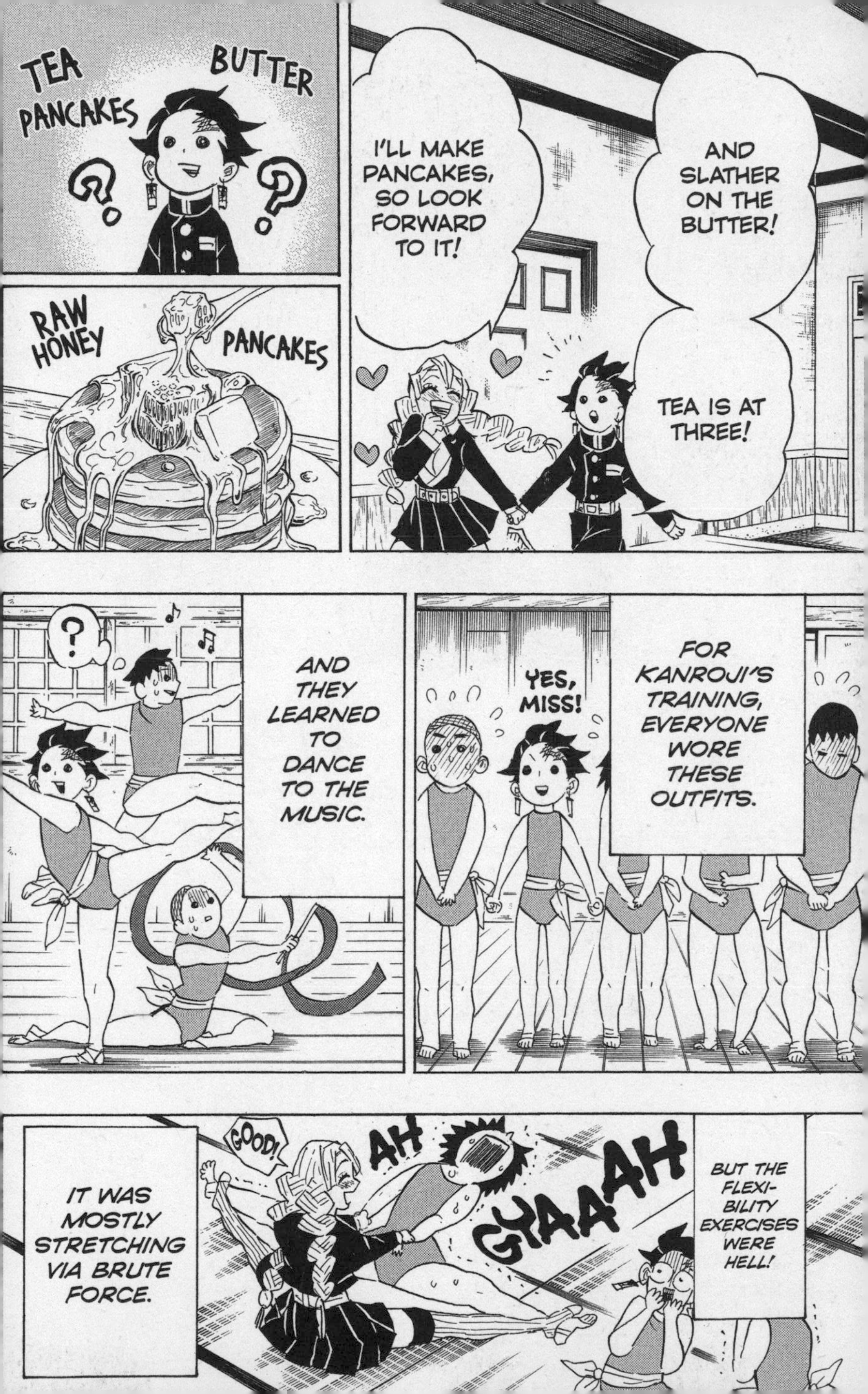
I'LL MAKE PANCAKES, SO LOOK FORWARD TO IT!
AND SLATHER ON THE BUTTER!
TEA IS AT THREE!
BUTTER
TEA
PANCAKES
PANCAKES
RAW HONEY
FOR KANROJI'S TRAINING, EVERYONE WORE THESE OUTFITS.
YES, MISS!
AND THEY LEARNED TO DANCE TO THE MUSIC.
BUT THE FLEXI-BILITY EXERCISES WERE HELL!
GYAAAH
AH
GOOD!
IT WAS MOSTLY STRETCHING VIA BRUTE FORCE.

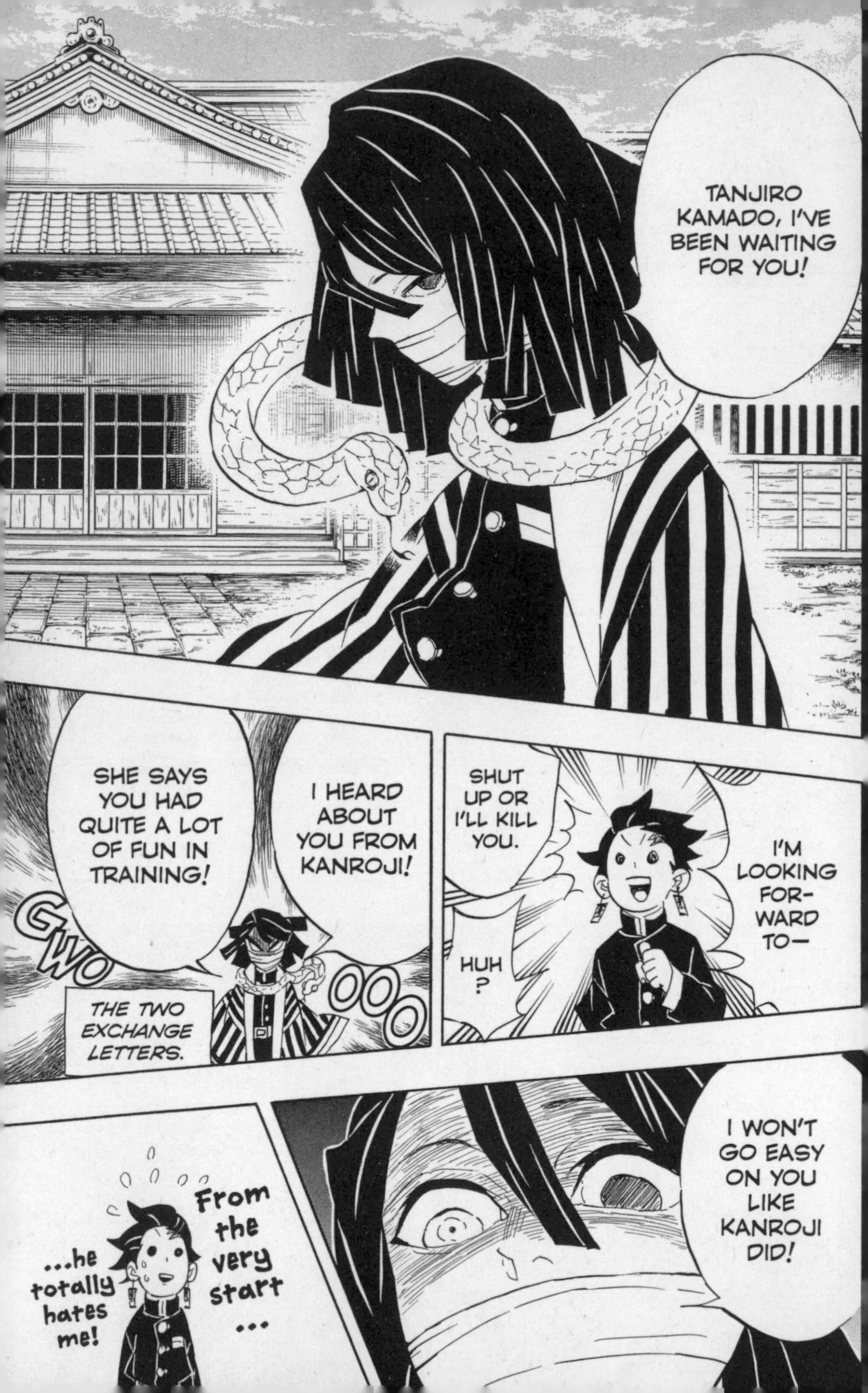
TANJIRO KAMADO, I'VE BEEN WAITING FOR YOU!
I'M LOOKING FOR-WARD TO—
HUH?
SHUT UP OR I'LL KILL YOU.
I HEARD ABOUT YOU FROM KANROJI!
SHE SAYS YOU HAD QUITE A LOT OF FUN IN TRAINING!
GWOOOO
THE TWO EXCHANGE LETTERS.
I WON'T GO EASY ON YOU LIKE KANROJI DID!
From the very start...
...he totally hates me!

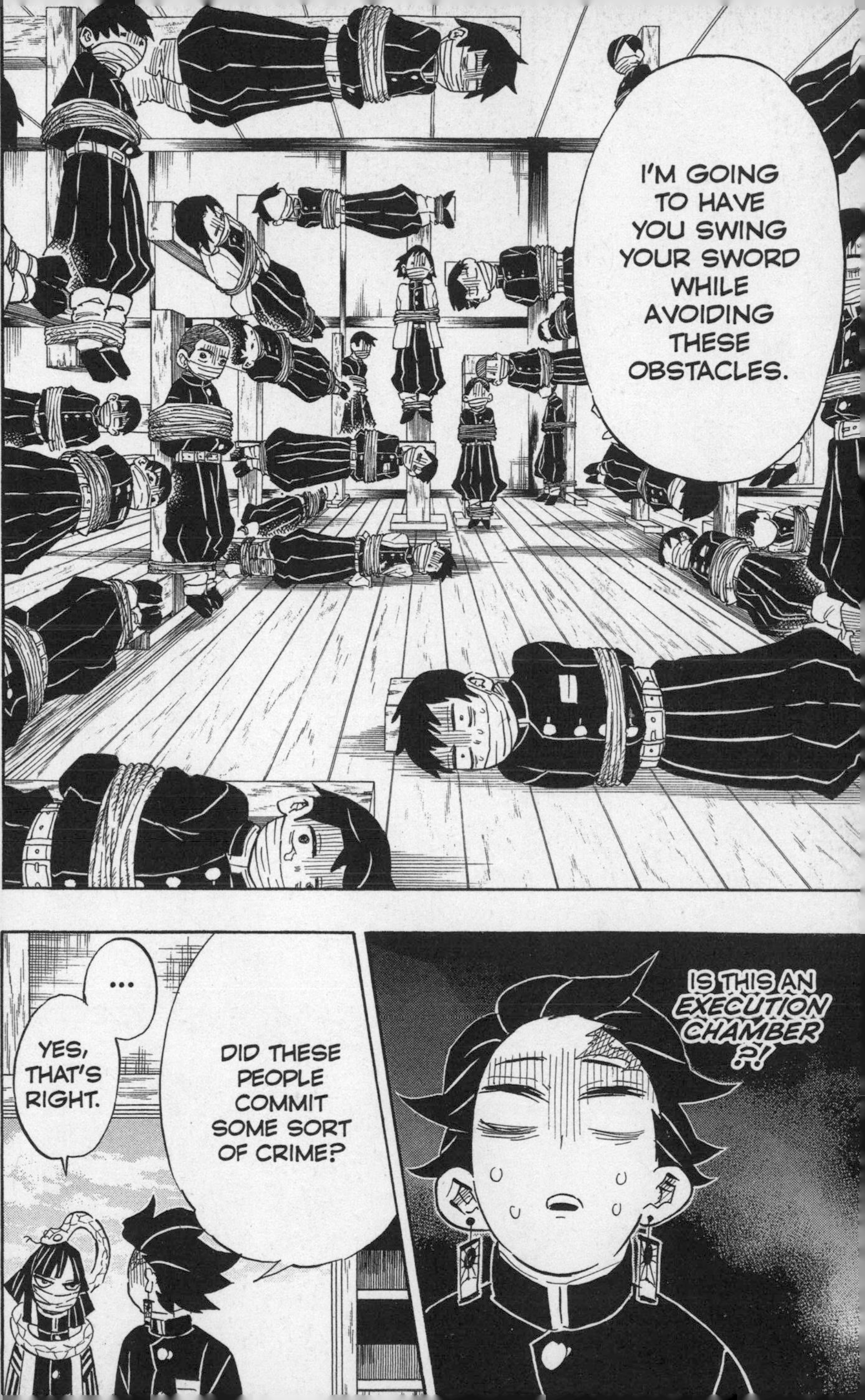
I'M GOING TO HAVE YOU SWING YOUR SWORD WHILE AVOIDING THESE OBSTACLES.
IS THIS AN EXECUTION CHAMBER?!
DID THESE PEOPLE COMMIT SOME SORT OF CRIME?
...
YES, THAT'S RIGHT.

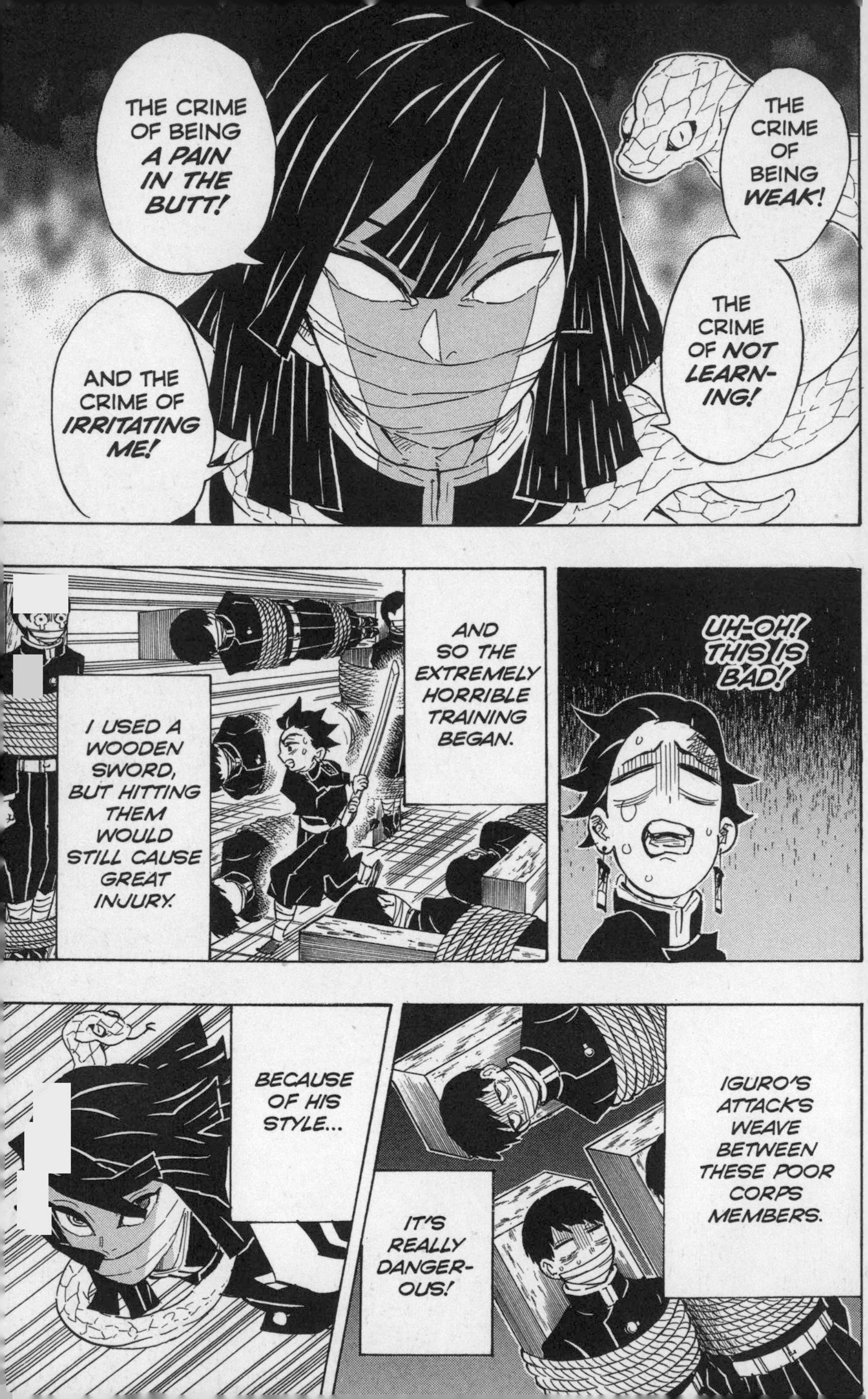
THE CRIME OF BEING WEAK!
THE CRIME OF NOT LEARNING!
THE CRIME OF BEING A PAIN IN THE BUTT!
AND THE CRIME OF IRRITATING ME!
UH-OH! THIS IS BAD!
AND SO THE EXTREMELY HORRIBLE TRAINING BEGAN.
I USED A WOODEN SWORD, BUT HITTING THEM WOULD STILL CAUSE GREAT INJURY.
IGURO'S ATTACKS WEAVE BETWEEN THESE POOR CORPS MEMBERS.
IT'S REALLY DANGEROUS!
BECAUSE OF HIS STYLE...

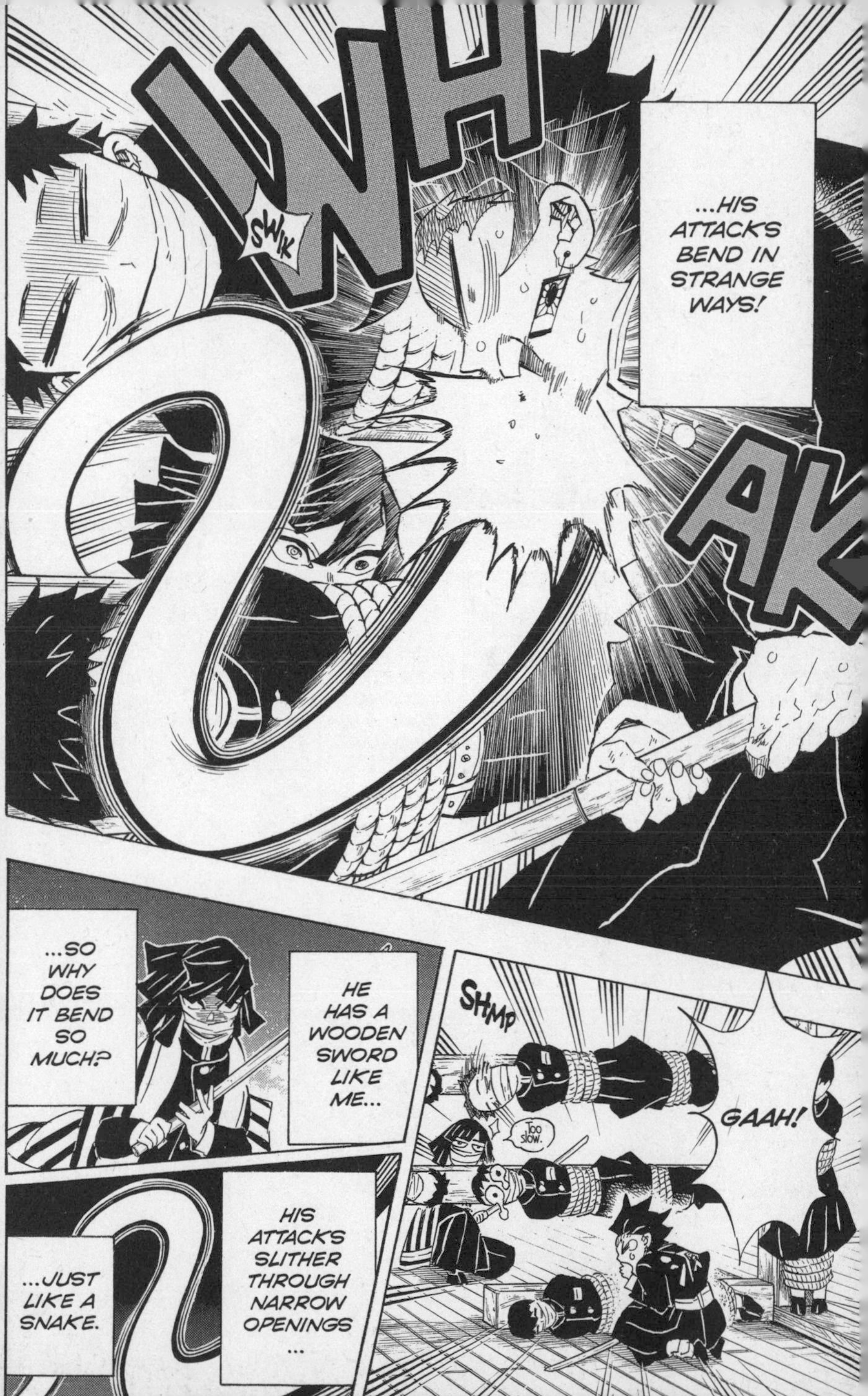
...HIS ATTACKS BEND IN STRANGE WAYS!
WH
AK
SWIK
SHMP
GAAH!
Too slow.
HE HAS A WOODEN SWORD LIKE ME...
...SO WHY DOES IT BEND SO MUCH?
HIS ATTACKS SLITHER THROUGH NARROW OPENINGS ...
...JUST LIKE A SNAKE.

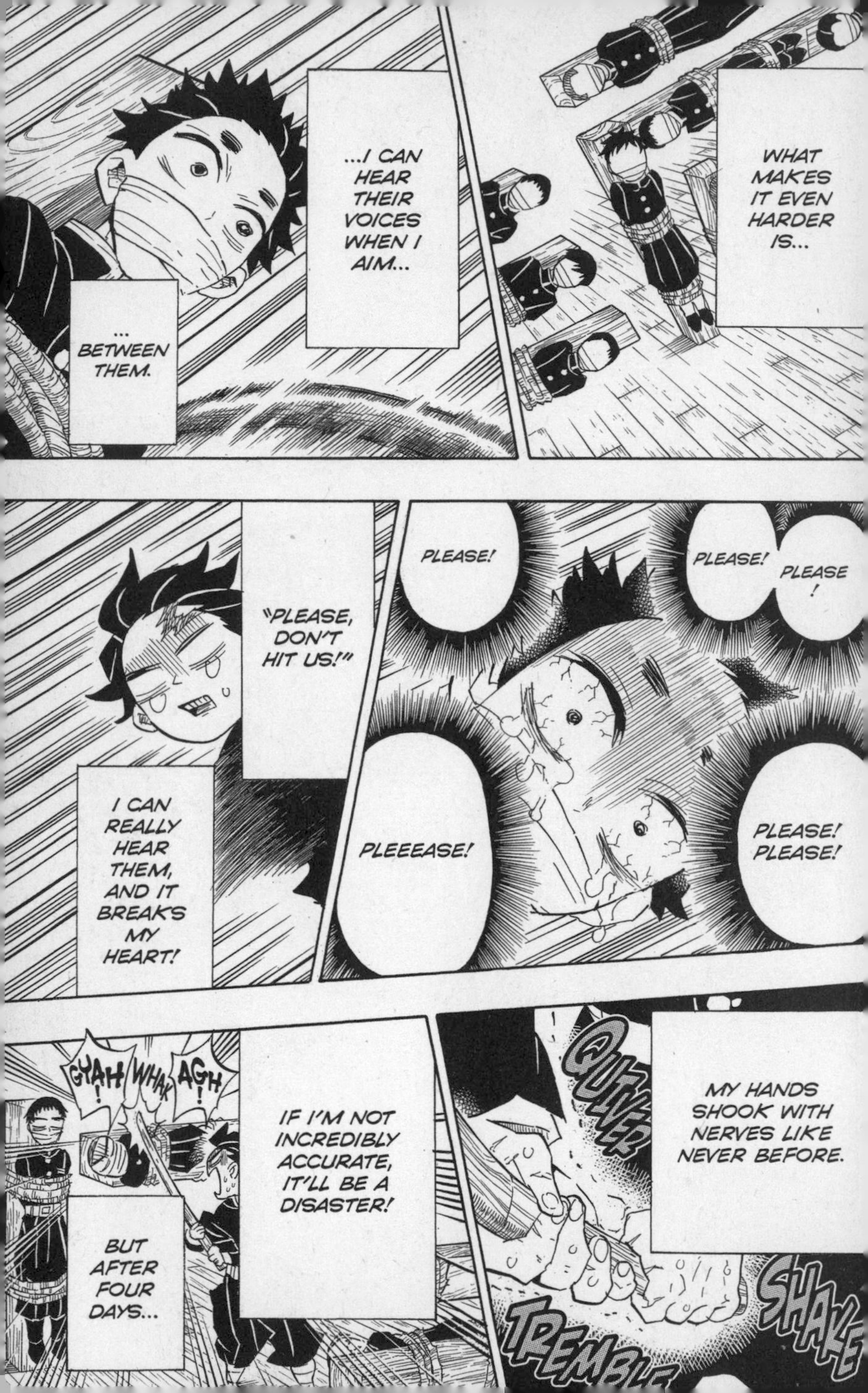
WHAT MAKES IT EVEN HARDER IS...
...I CAN HEAR THEIR VOICES WHEN I AIM...
... BETWEEN THEM.
PLEASE !
PLEASE!
PLEASE!
PLEASE! PLEASE!
PLEEEASE!
"PLEASE, DON'T HIT US!"
I CAN REALLY HEAR THEM, AND IT BREAKS MY HEART!
MY HANDS SHOOK WITH NERVES LIKE NEVER BEFORE.
QUIVER
SHAKE
TREMBLE
IF I'M NOT INCREDIBLY ACCURATE, IT'LL BE A DISASTER!
AGH!
WHAK
GYAH!
BUT AFTER FOUR DAYS...

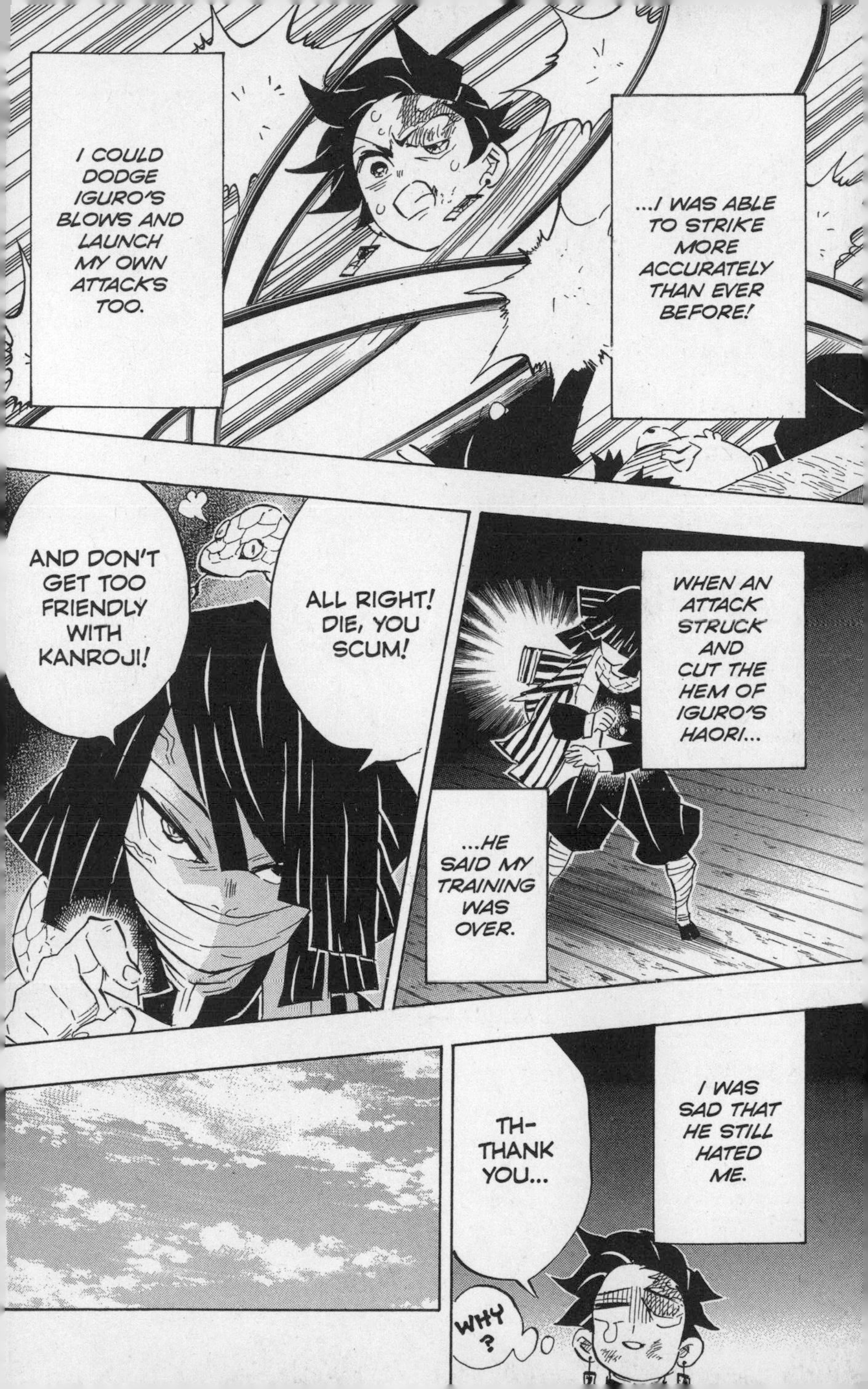
...I WAS ABLE TO STRIKE MORE ACCURATELY THAN EVER BEFORE!
I COULD DODGE IGURO'S BLOWS AND LAUNCH MY OWN ATTACKS TOO.
WHEN AN ATTACK STRUCK AND CUT THE HEM OF IGURO'S HAORI...
...HE SAID MY TRAINING WAS OVER.
ALL RIGHT! DIE, YOU SCUM!
AND DON'T GET TOO FRIENDLY WITH KANROJI!
I WAS SAD THAT HE STILL HATED ME.
TH-THANK YOU...
WHY?

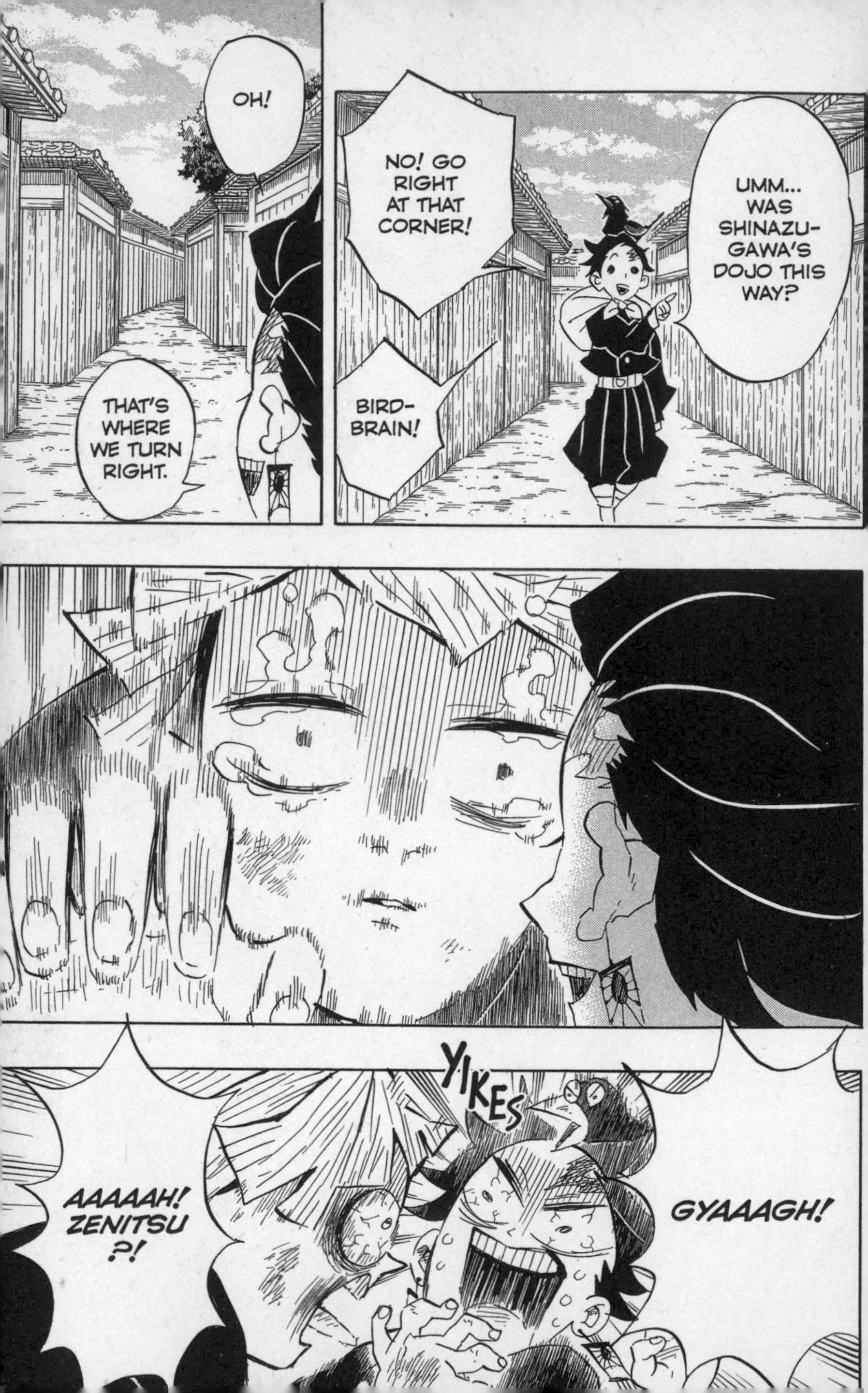
UMM... WAS SHINAZU-GAWA'S DOJO THIS WAY?
NO! GO RIGHT AT THAT CORNER!
BIRD-BRAIN!
OH!
THAT'S WHERE WE TURN RIGHT.
YIKES
GYAAAGH!
AAAAAH! ZENITSU ?!

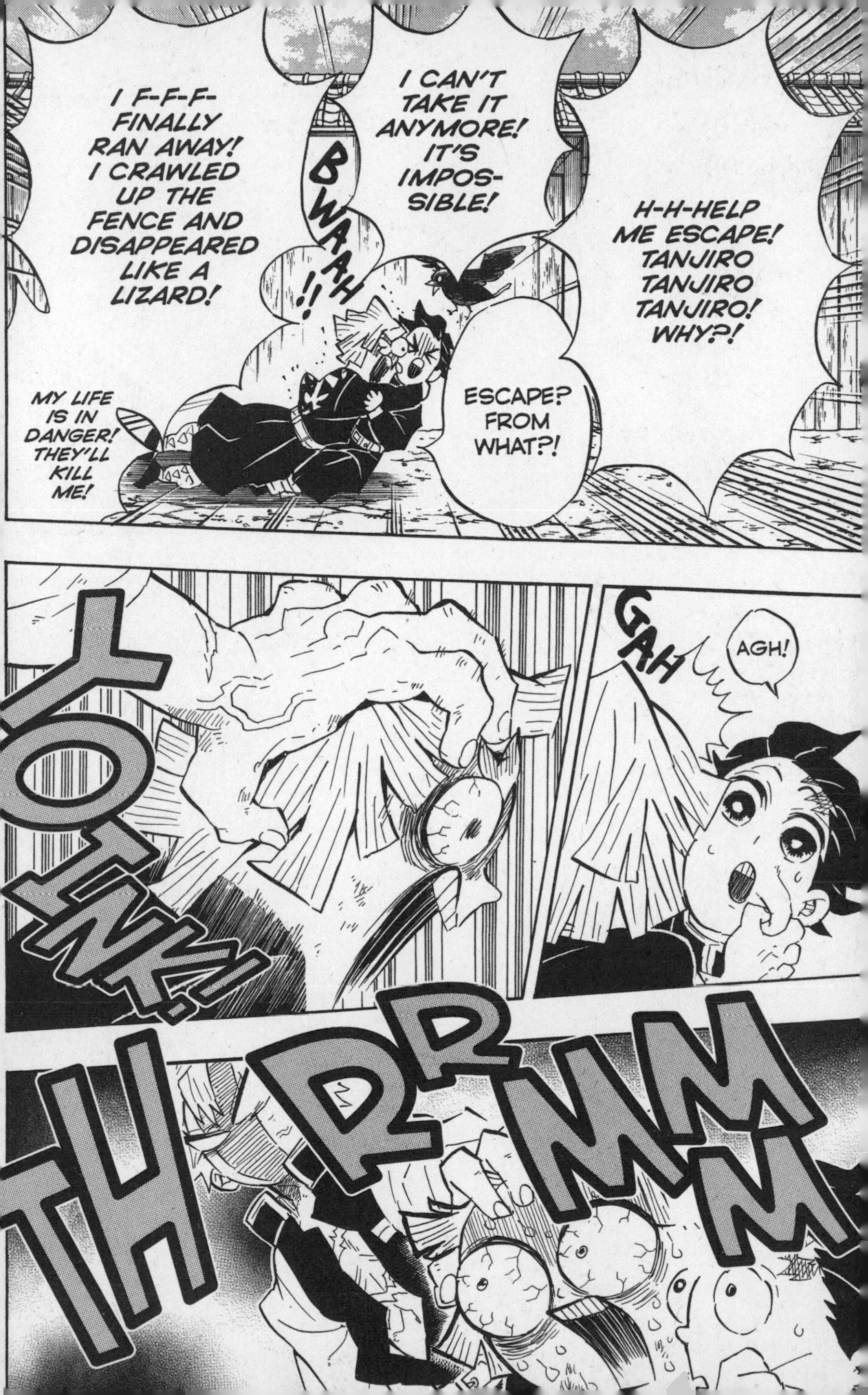
H-H-HELP ME ESCAPE! TANJIRO TANJIRO TANJIRO! WHY?!
I CAN'T TAKE IT ANYMORE! IT'S IMPOS-SIBLE!
BWAAAH!!
I F-F-F-FINALLY RAN AWAY! I CRAWLED UP THE FENCE AND DISAPPEARED LIKE A LIZARD!
ESCAPE? FROM WHAT?!
MY LIFE IS IN DANGER! THEY'LL KILL ME!
GAH
AGH!
YOINK!!
THDRMMM

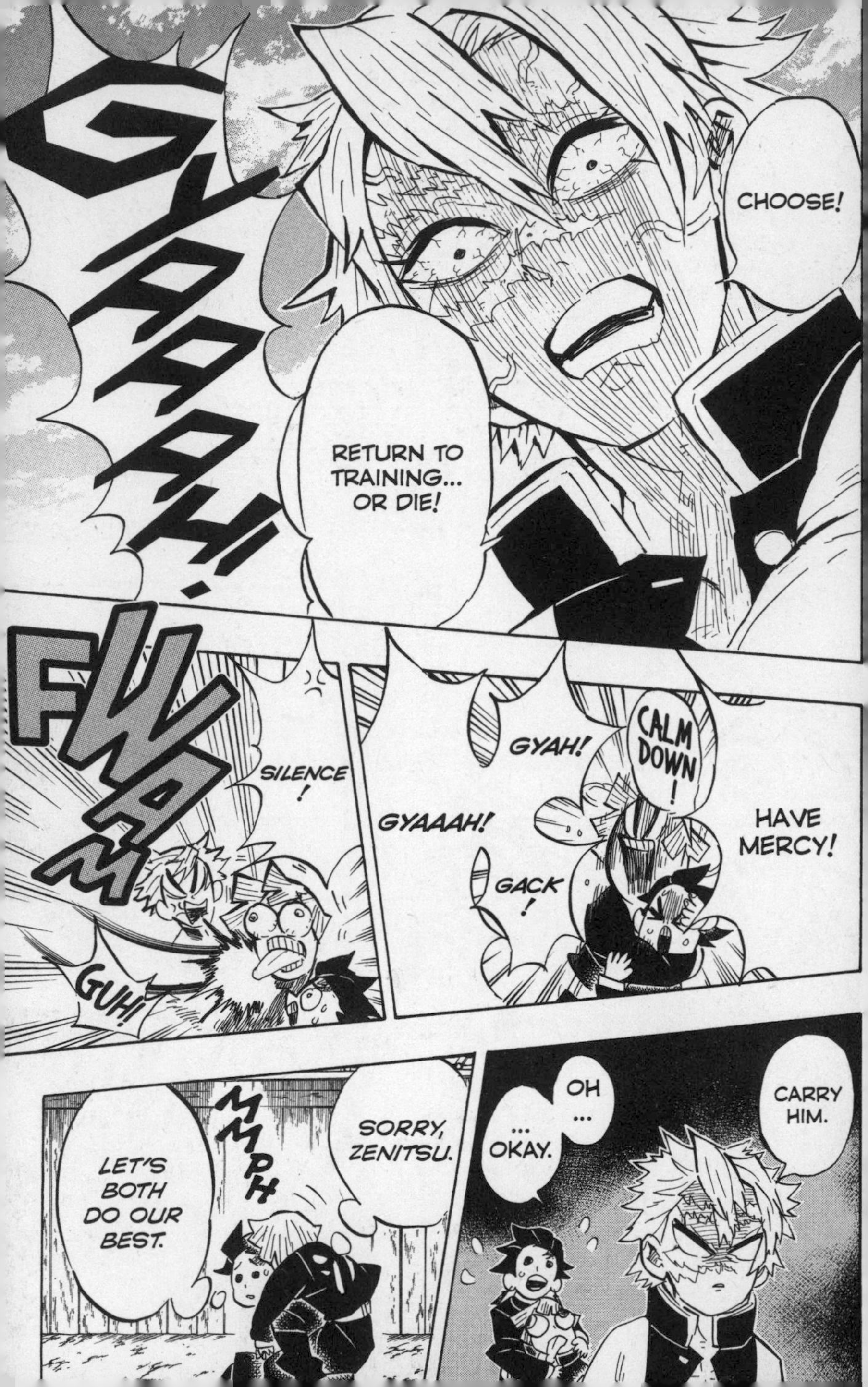
CHOOSE!
RETURN TO TRAINING... OR DIE!
GYAAAH!
CALM DOWN!
HAVE MERCY!
GYAH!
GYAAAH!
GACK!
FWAM
SILENCE!
GUH!
CARRY HIM.
OH...
...OKAY.
SORRY, ZENITSU.
MMPH
LET'S BOTH DO OUR BEST.

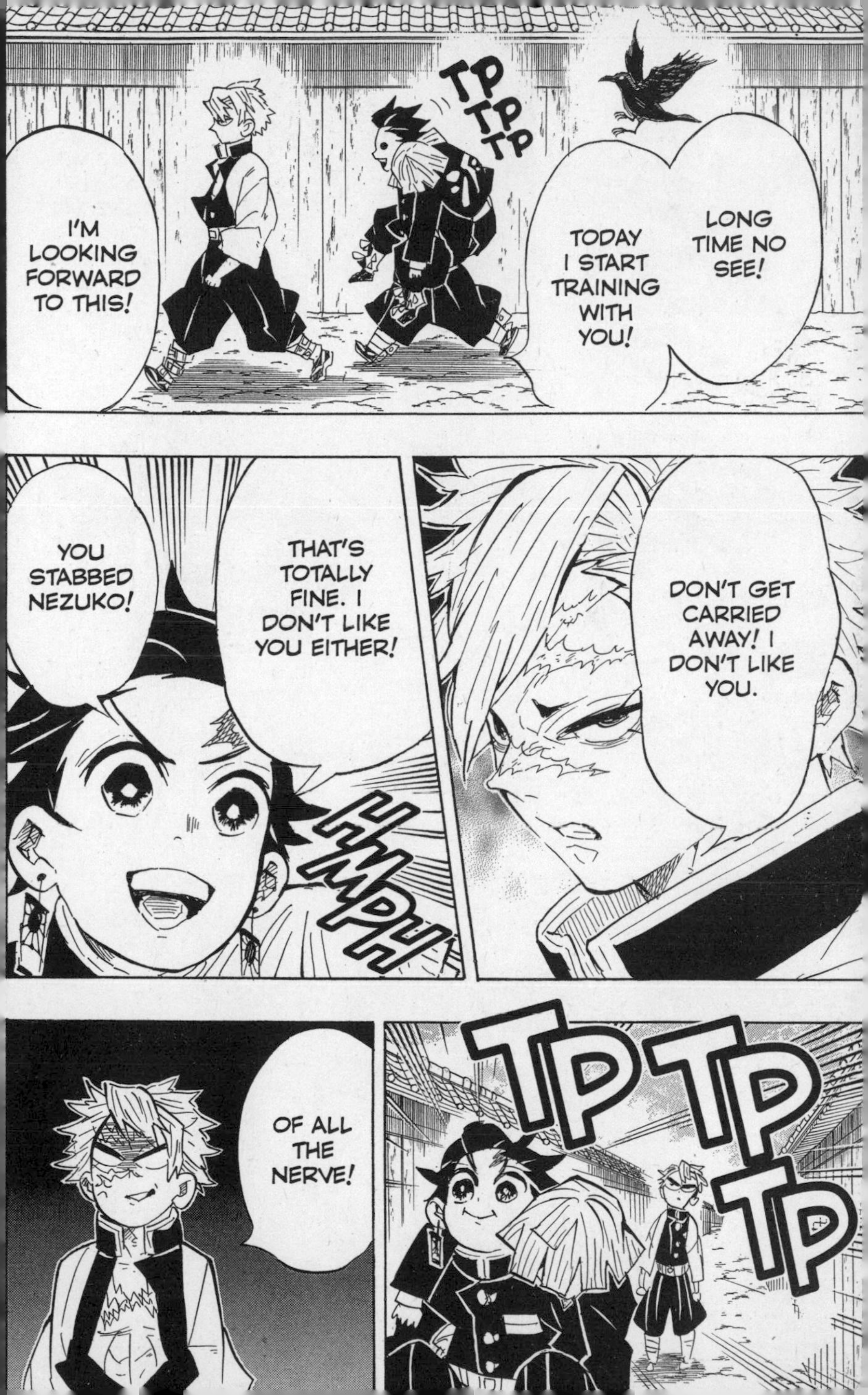
LONG TIME NO SEE!
TODAY I START TRAINING WITH YOU!
TP TP TP
I'M LOOKING FORWARD TO THIS!
DON'T GET CARRIED AWAY! I DON'T LIKE YOU.
THAT'S TOTALLY FINE. I DON'T LIKE YOU EITHER!
YOU STABBED NEZUKO!
HMPH
TP TP TP TP
OF ALL THE NERVE!

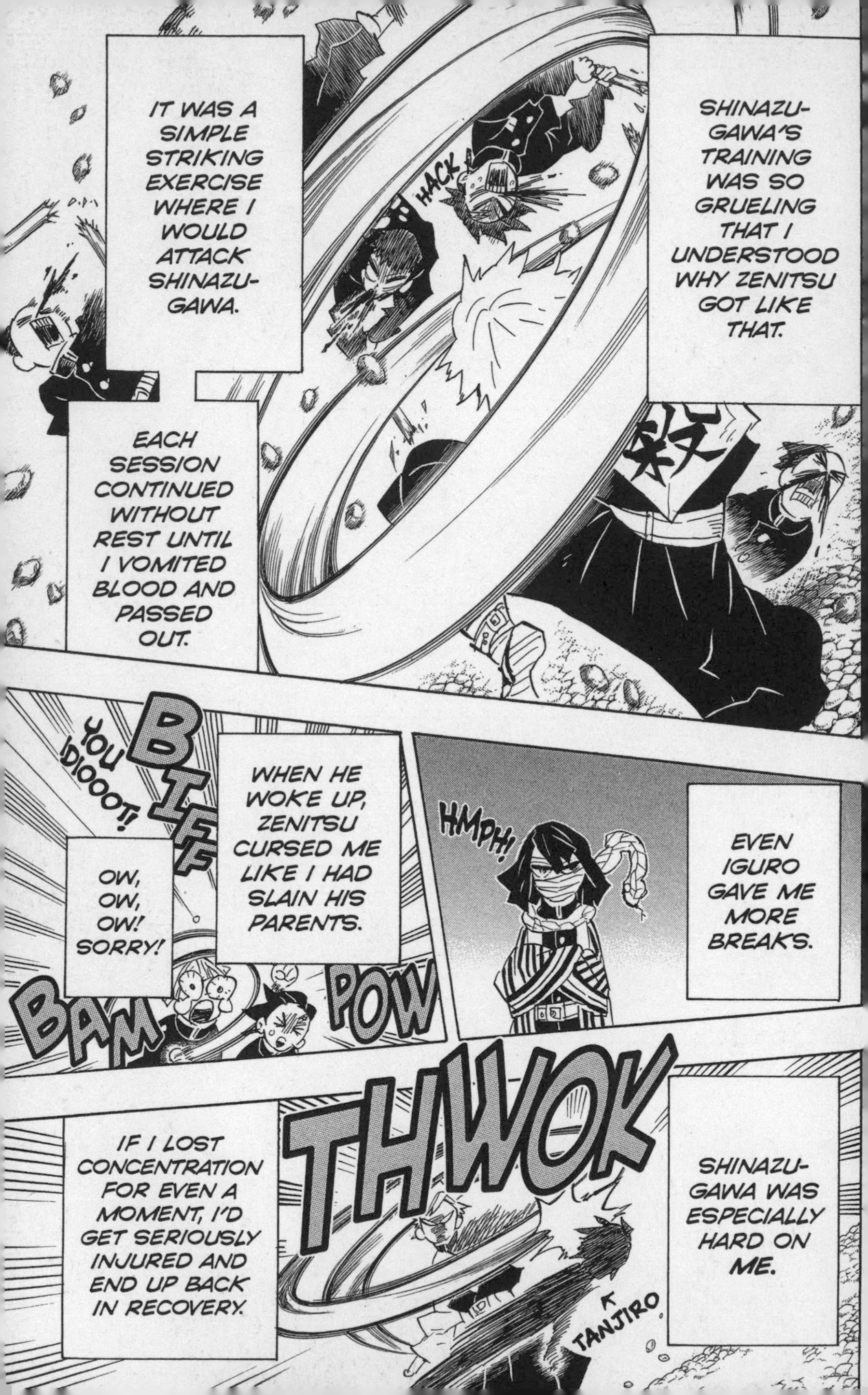

SHINAZU-GAWA'S TRAINING WAS SO GRUELING THAT I UNDERSTOOD WHY ZENITSU GOT LIKE THAT.
HACK
IT WAS A SIMPLE STRIKING EXERCISE WHERE I WOULD ATTACK SHINAZU-GAWA.
EACH SESSION CONTINUED WITHOUT REST UNTIL I VOMITED BLOOD AND PASSED OUT.
EVEN IGURO GAVE ME MORE BREAKS.
HMPH!
WHEN HE WOKE UP, ZENITSU CURSED ME LIKE I HAD SLAIN HIS PARENTS.
BIFF
YOU IDIOOOT!
OW, OW, OW! SORRY!
POW
BAM
SHINAZU-GAWA WAS ESPECIALLY HARD ON ME.
THWOK
TANJIRO
IF I LOST CONCENTRATION FOR EVEN A MOMENT, I'D GET SERIOUSLY INJURED AND END UP BACK IN RECOVERY.

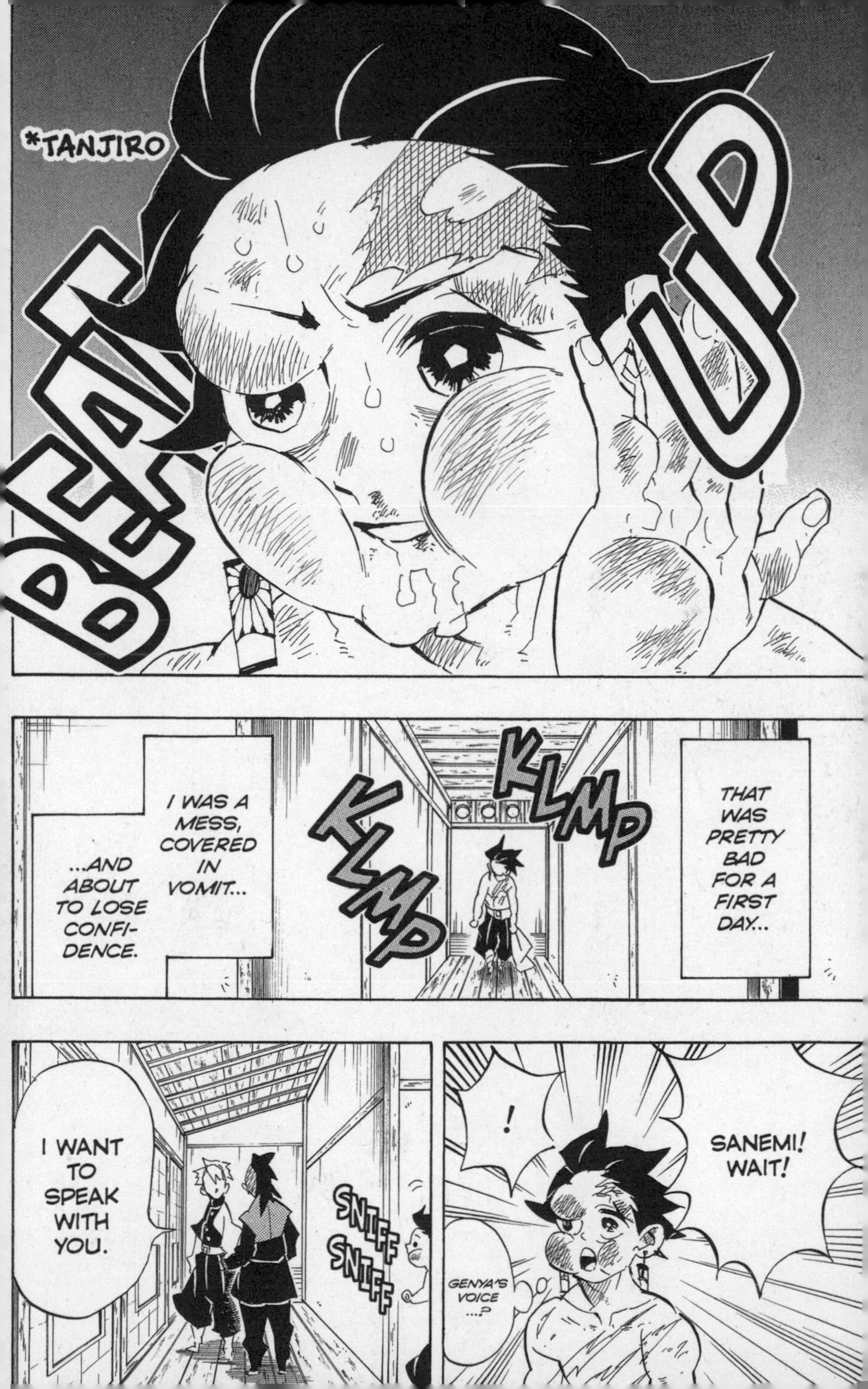

*TANJIRO
BEAT UP
THAT WAS PRETTY BAD FOR A FIRST DAY...
KLMP
KLMP
I WAS A MESS, COVERED IN VOMIT...
...AND ABOUT TO LOSE CONFI-DENCE.
SANEMI! WAIT!
!
GENYA'S VOICE ...?
SNIFF SNIFF
I WANT TO SPEAK WITH YOU.

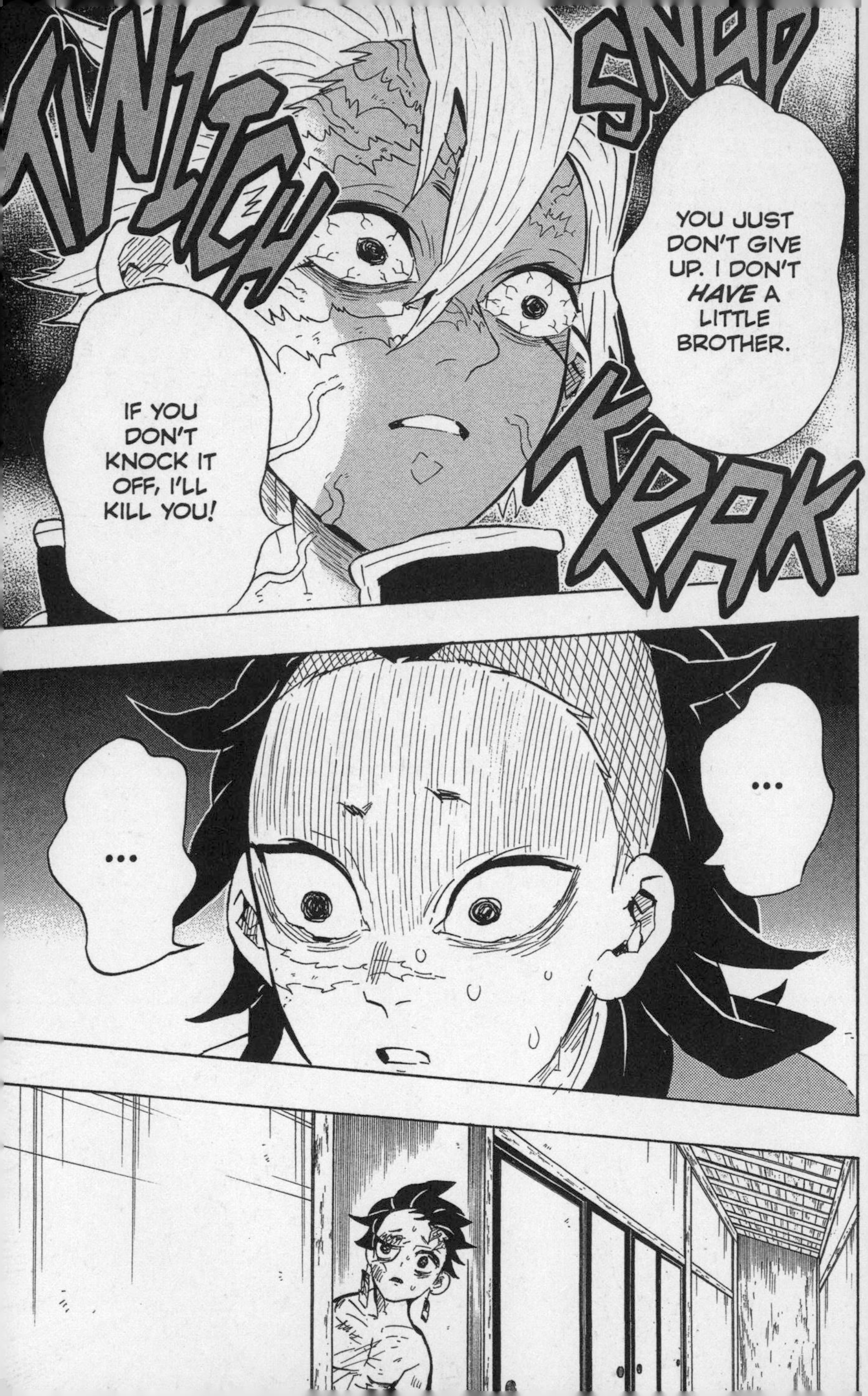
SNAP
YOU JUST DON'T GIVE UP. I DON'T *HAVE* A LITTLE BROTHER.
TWITCH
KRAK
IF YOU DON'T KNOCK IT OFF, I'LL KILL YOU!
...
...

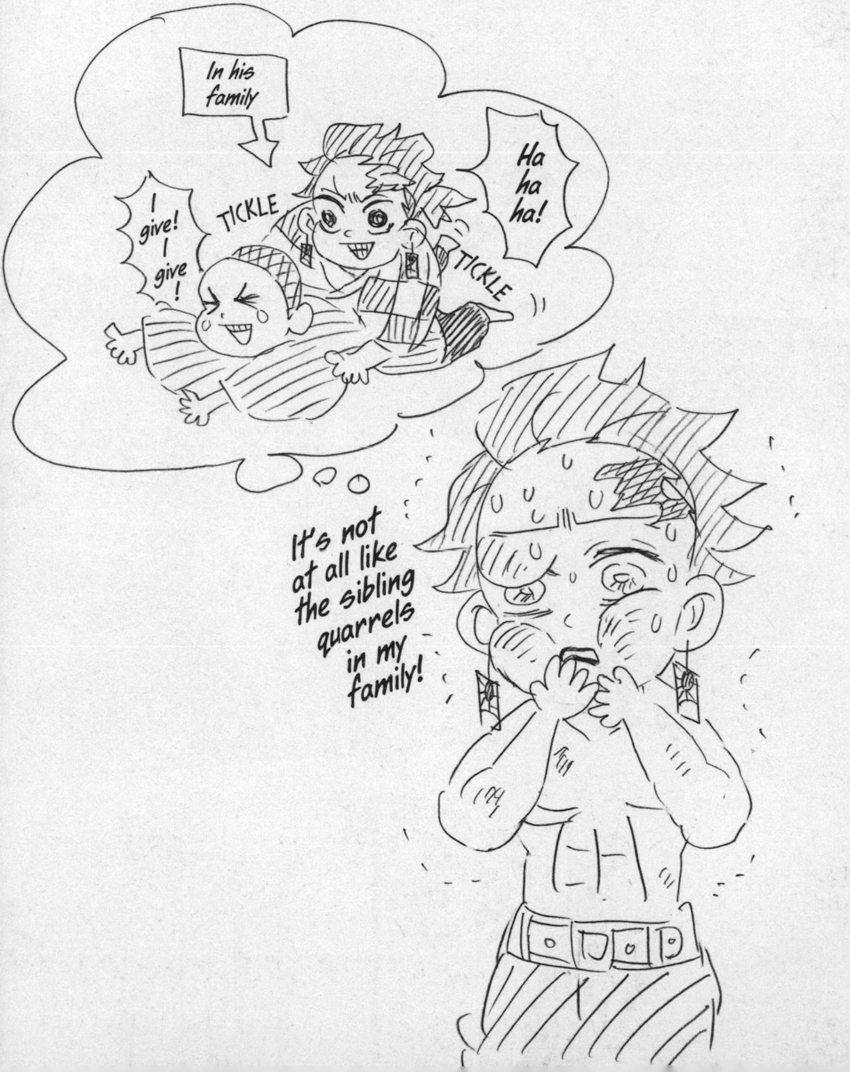
In his family
Ha ha ha!
TICKLE
TICKLE
I give! I give!
It's not at all like the sibling quarrels in my family!

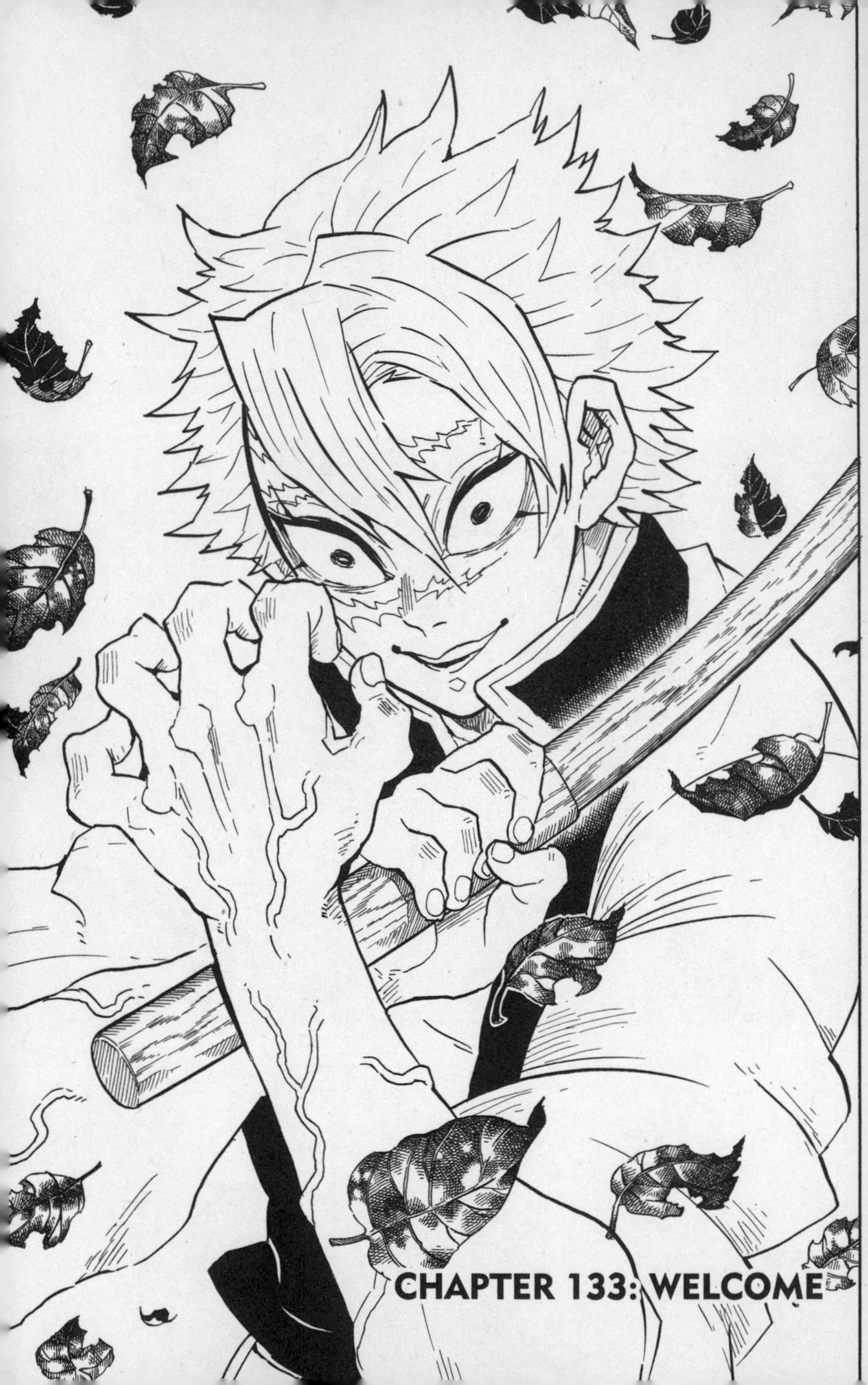
CHAPTER 133: WELCOME

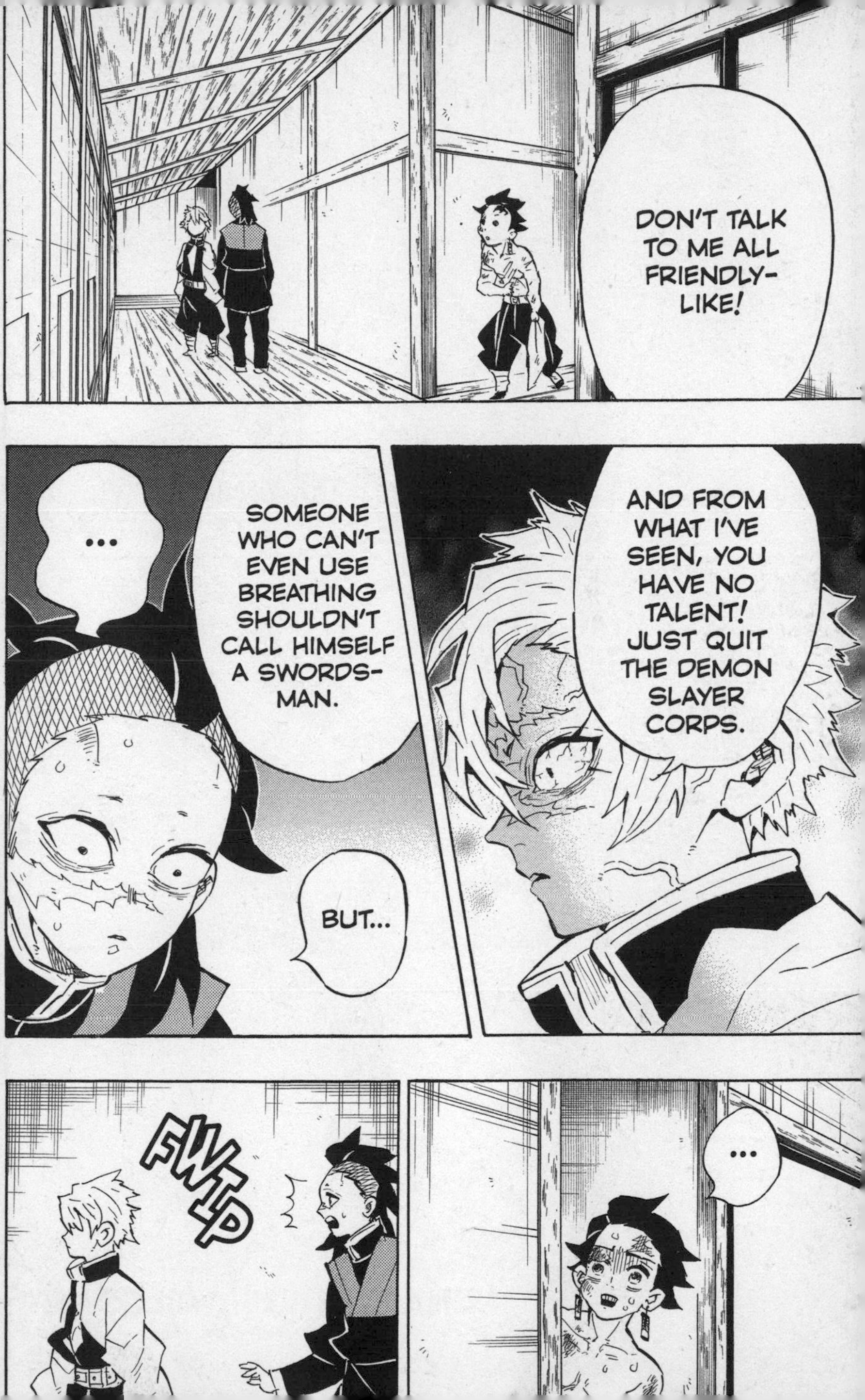
DON'T TALK TO ME ALL FRIENDLY-LIKE!
AND FROM WHAT I'VE SEEN, YOU HAVE NO TALENT! JUST QUIT THE DEMON SLAYER CORPS.
SOMEONE WHO CAN'T EVEN USE BREATHING SHOULDN'T CALL HIMSELF A SWORDS-MAN.
...
BUT...
...
FWIP

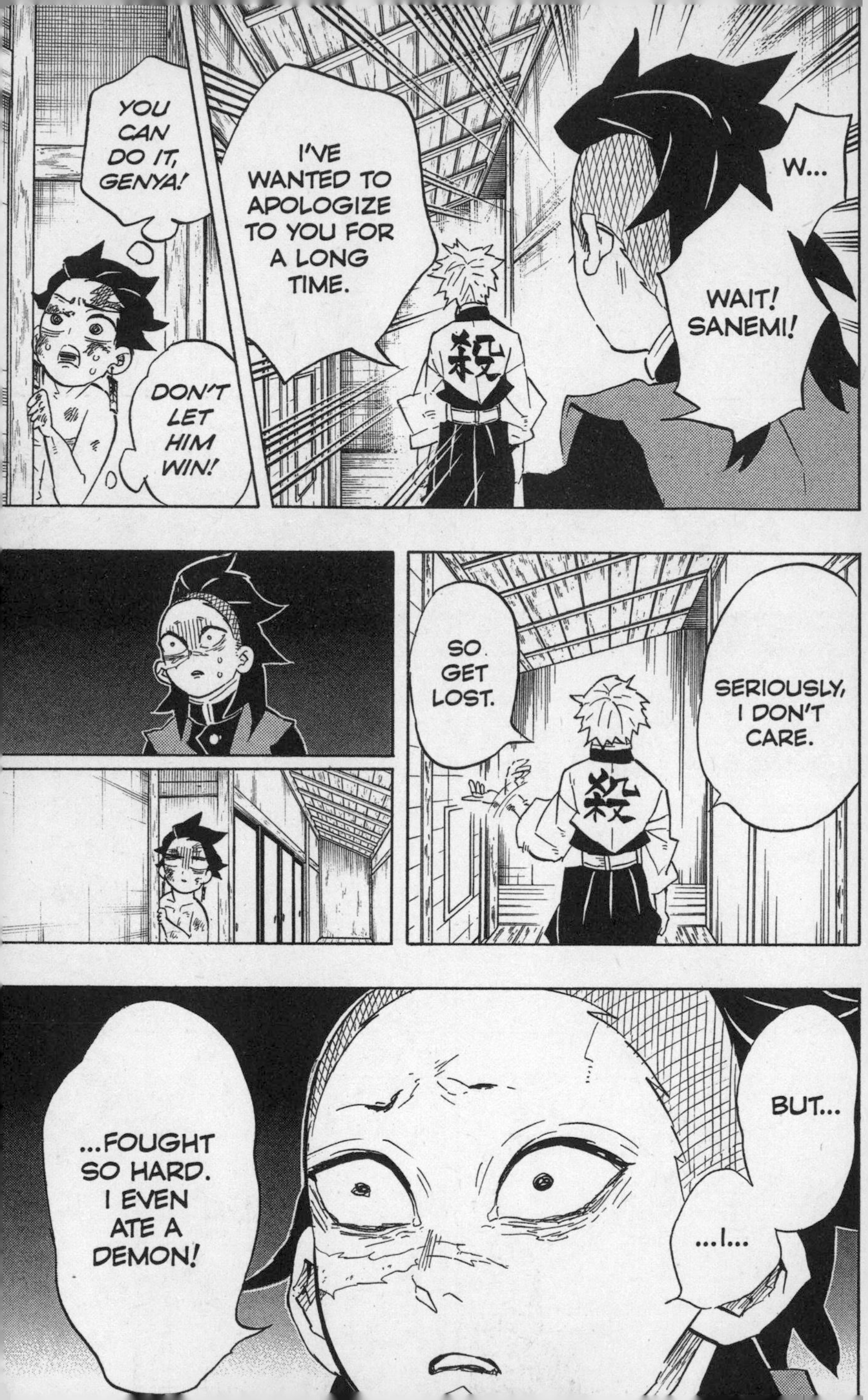
W...
WAIT! SANEMI!
I'VE WANTED TO APOLOGIZE TO YOU FOR A LONG TIME.
YOU CAN DO IT, GENYA!
DON'T LET HIM WIN!
SERIOUSLY, I DON'T CARE.
SO. GET LOST.
BUT...
...I...
...FOUGHT SO HARD. I EVEN ATE A DEMON!

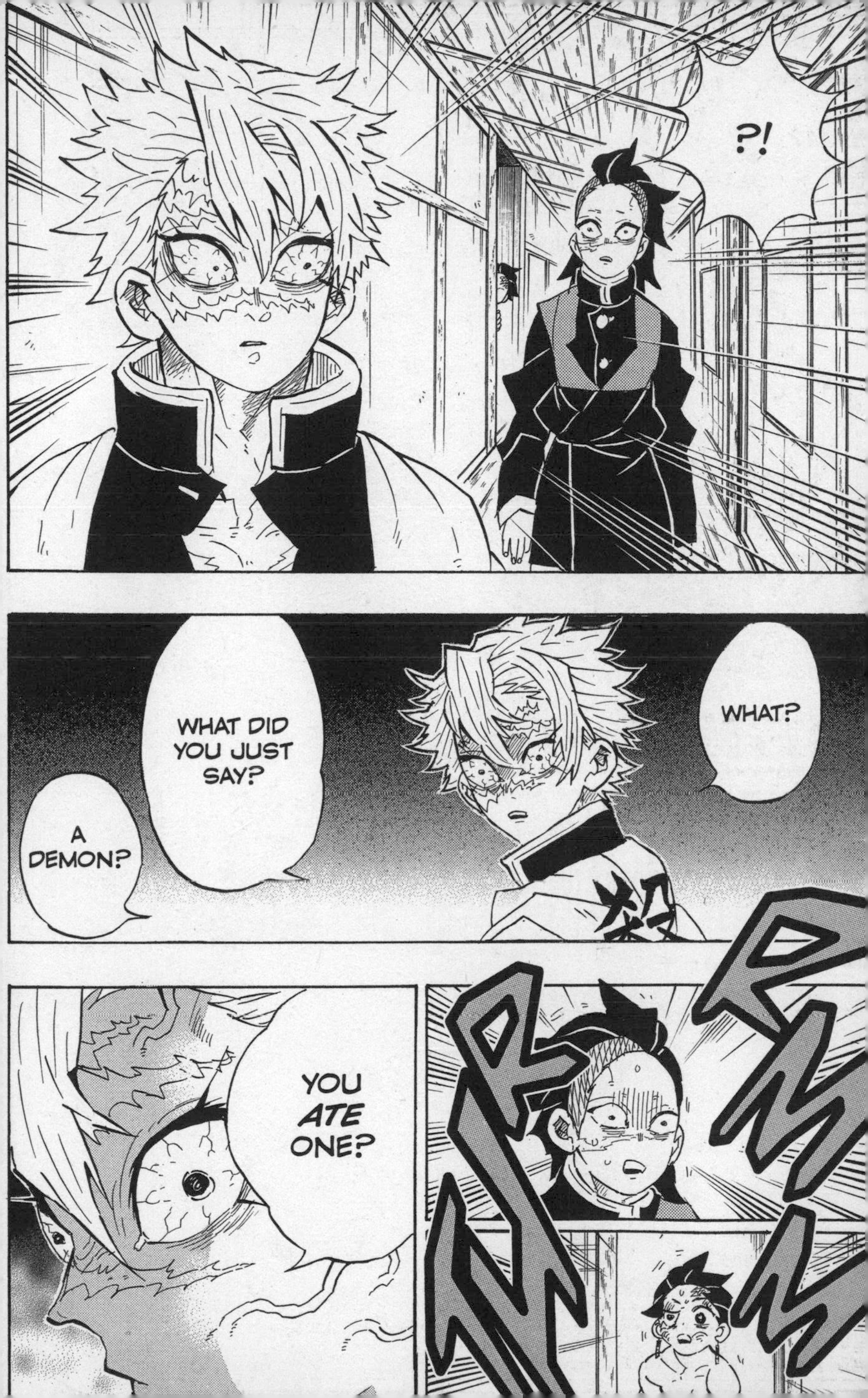
?!
WHAT?
WHAT DID YOU JUST SAY?
A DEMON?
YOU *ATE* ONE?

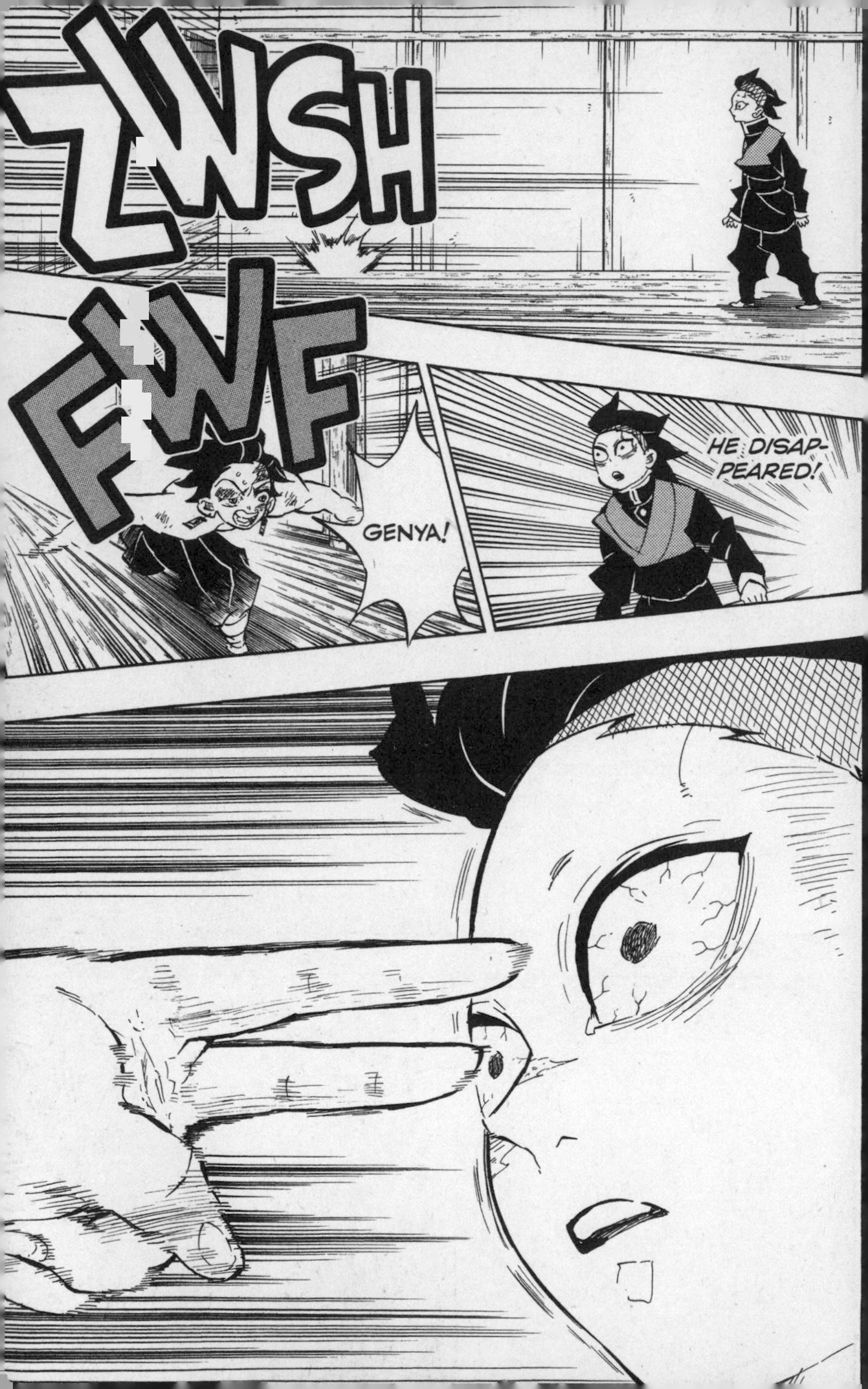
ZWSH
HE DISAP-PEARED!
FWF
GENYA!

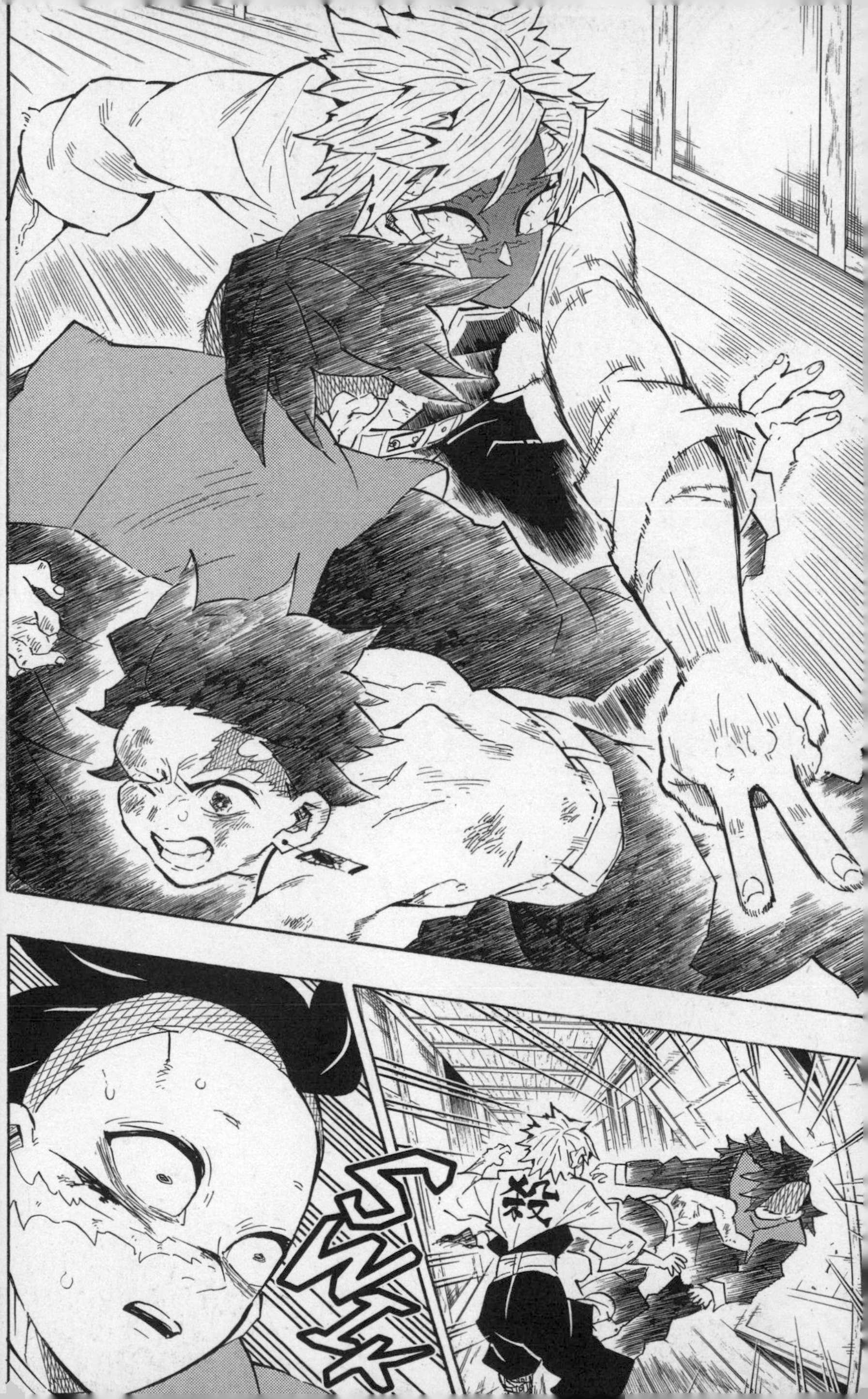
SWISH

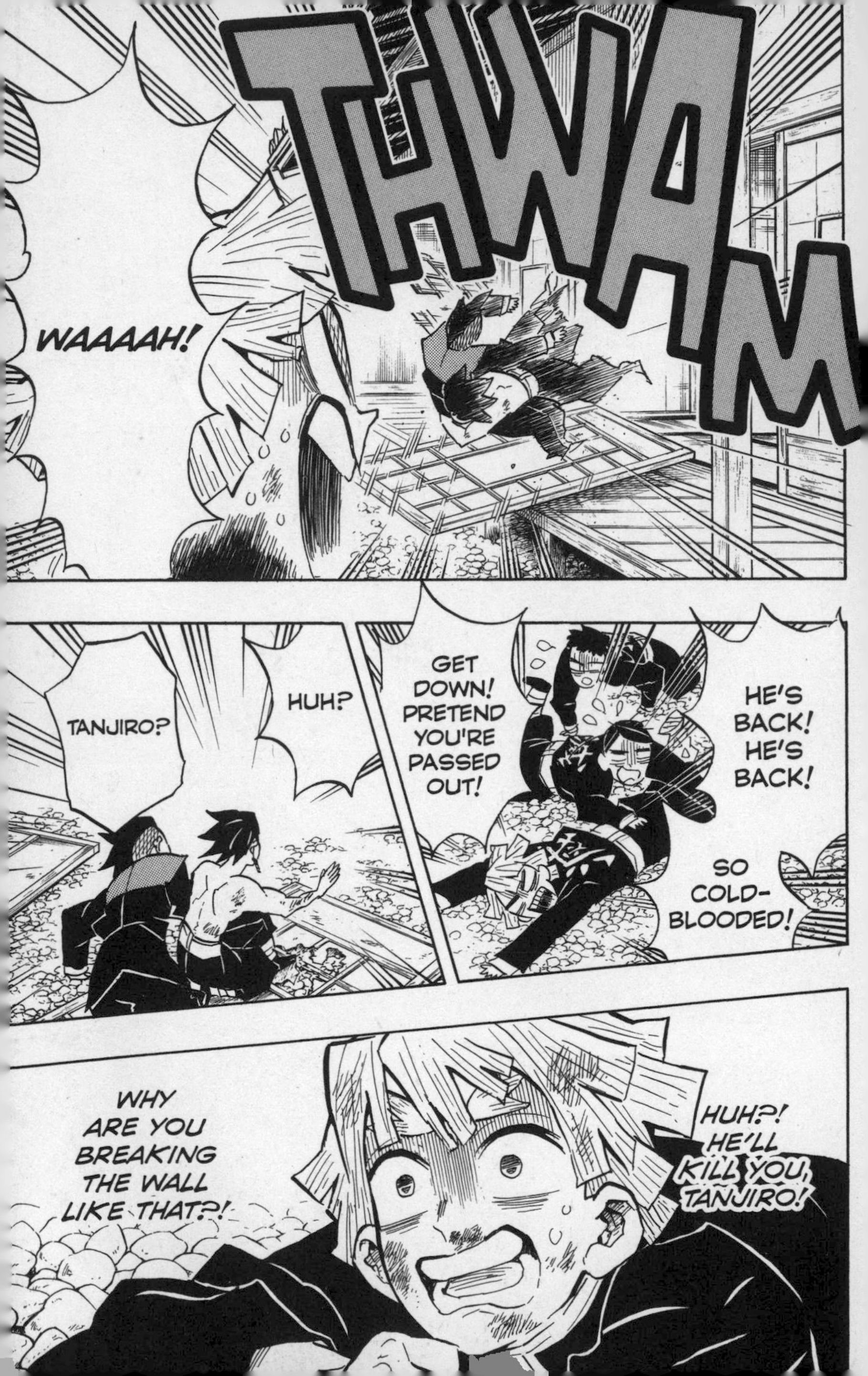
THWAM
WAAAAH!
HE'S BACK! HE'S BACK!
GET DOWN! PRETEND YOU'RE PASSED OUT!
SO COLD-BLOODED!
HUH?
TANJIRO?
HUH?! HE'LL KILL YOU, TANJIRO!
WHY ARE YOU BREAKING THE WALL LIKE THAT?!

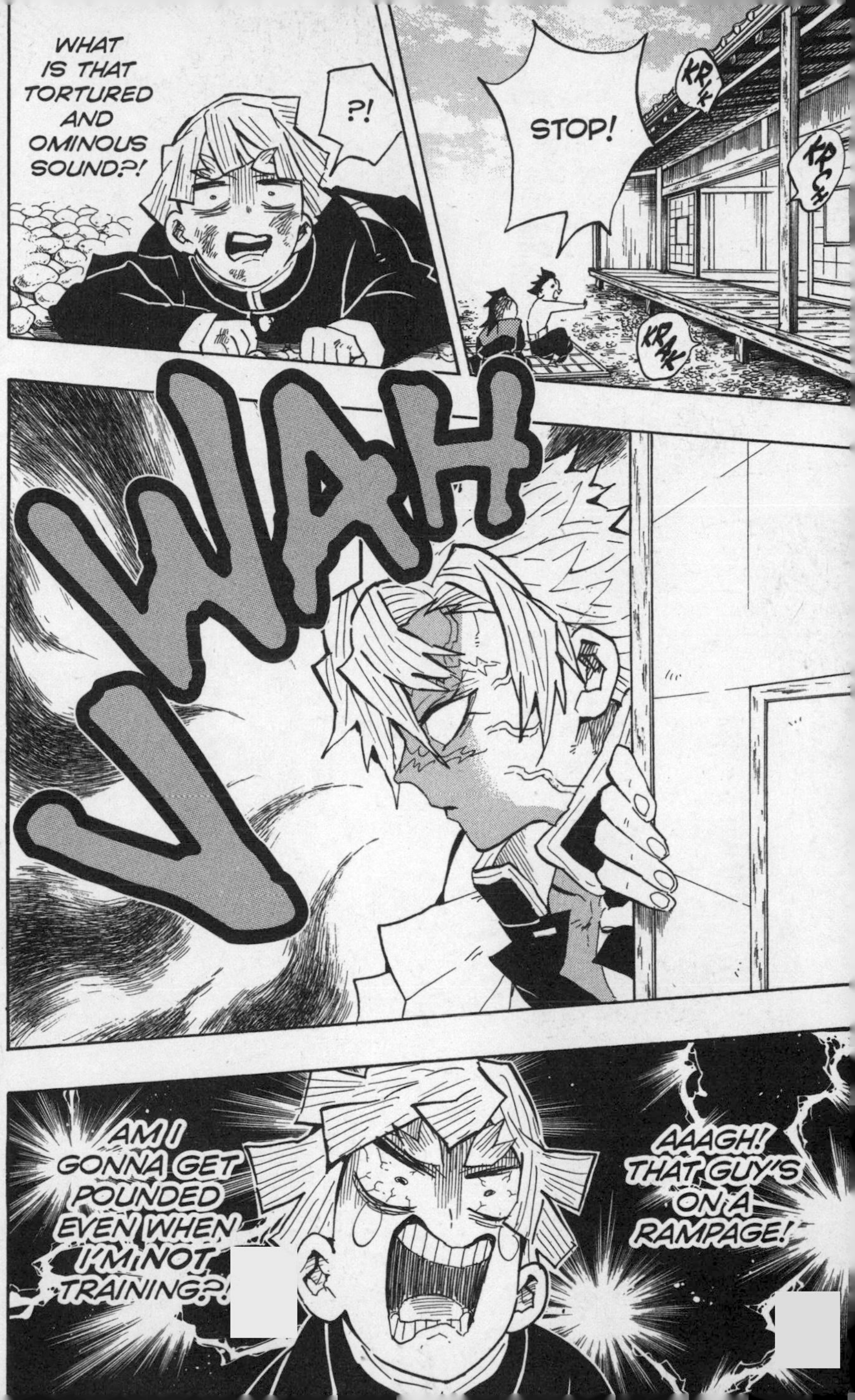
STOP!
KRIK
KRCH
KRAK
?!
WHAT IS THAT TORTURED AND OMINOUS SOUND?!
WAH
AAAGH! THAT GUY'S ON A RAMPAGE!
AM I GONNA GET POUNDED EVEN WHEN I'M NOT TRAINING?!

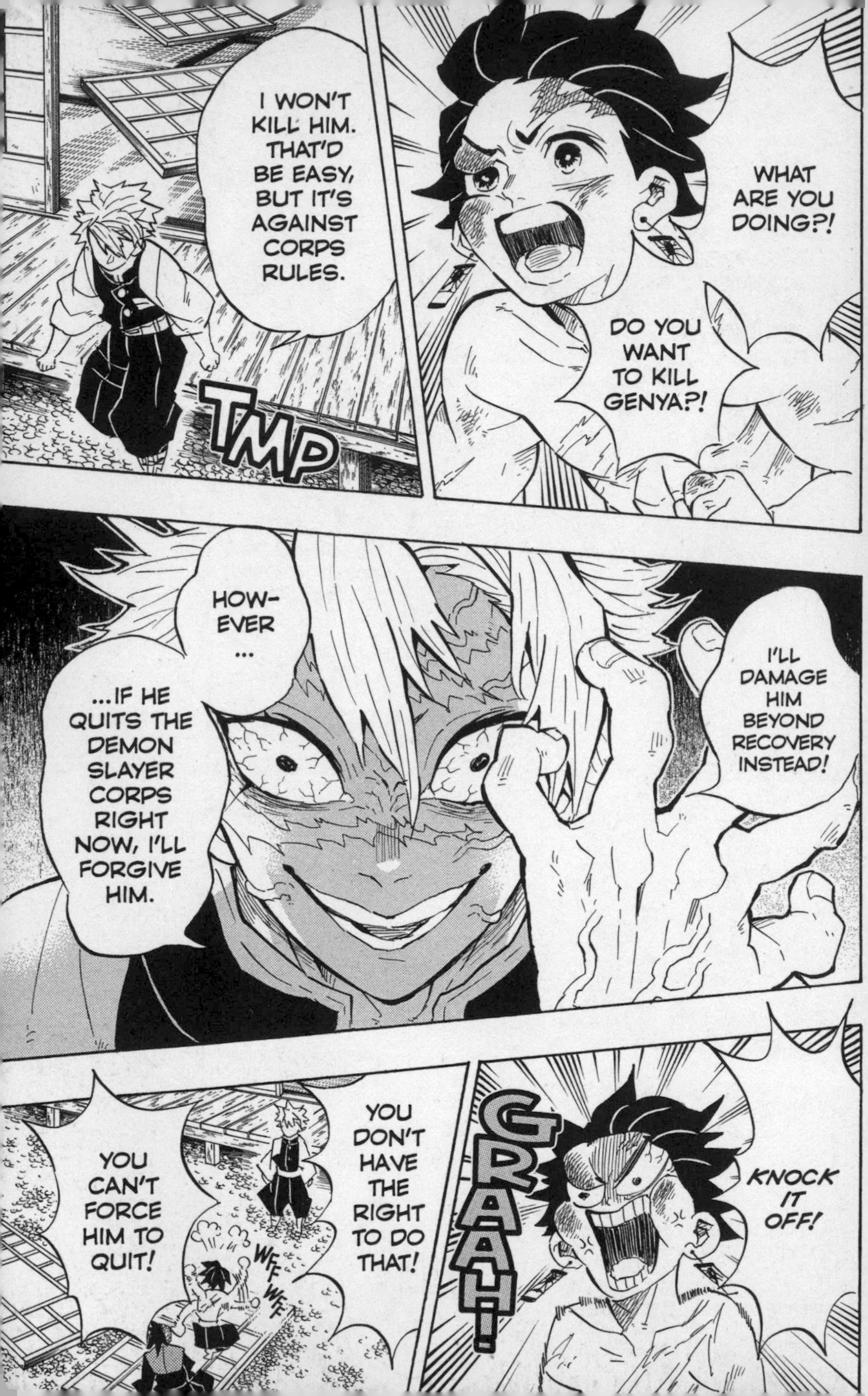
WHAT ARE YOU DOING?!
DO YOU WANT TO KILL GENYA?!
I WON'T KILL HIM. THAT'D BE EASY, BUT IT'S AGAINST CORPS RULES.
TMP
HOW-EVER ...
I'LL DAMAGE HIM BEYOND RECOVERY INSTEAD!
...IF HE QUITS THE DEMON SLAYER CORPS RIGHT NOW, I'LL FORGIVE HIM.
KNOCK IT OFF!
GRAAAH!
YOU DON'T HAVE THE RIGHT TO DO THAT!
YOU CAN'T FORCE HIM TO QUIT!
WFF WFF

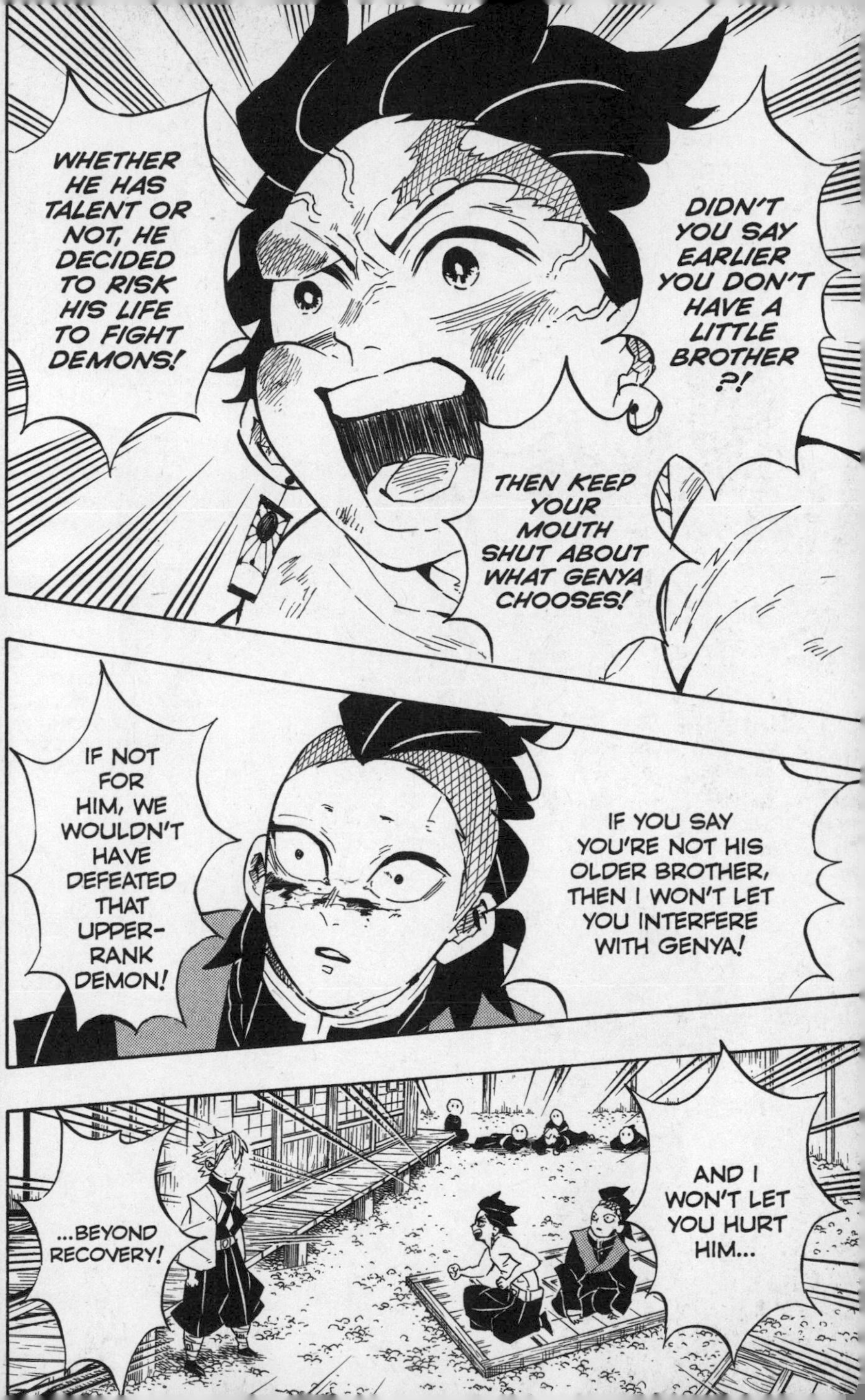
DIDN'T YOU SAY EARLIER YOU DON'T HAVE A LITTLE BROTHER?!
WHETHER HE HAS TALENT OR NOT, HE DECIDED TO RISK HIS LIFE TO FIGHT DEMONS!
THEN KEEP YOUR MOUTH SHUT ABOUT WHAT GENYA CHOOSES!
IF YOU SAY YOU'RE NOT HIS OLDER BROTHER, THEN I WON'T LET YOU INTERFERE WITH GENYA!
IF NOT FOR HIM, WE WOULDN'T HAVE DEFEATED THAT UPPER-RANK DEMON!
AND I WON'T LET YOU HURT HIM...
...BEYOND RECOVERY!

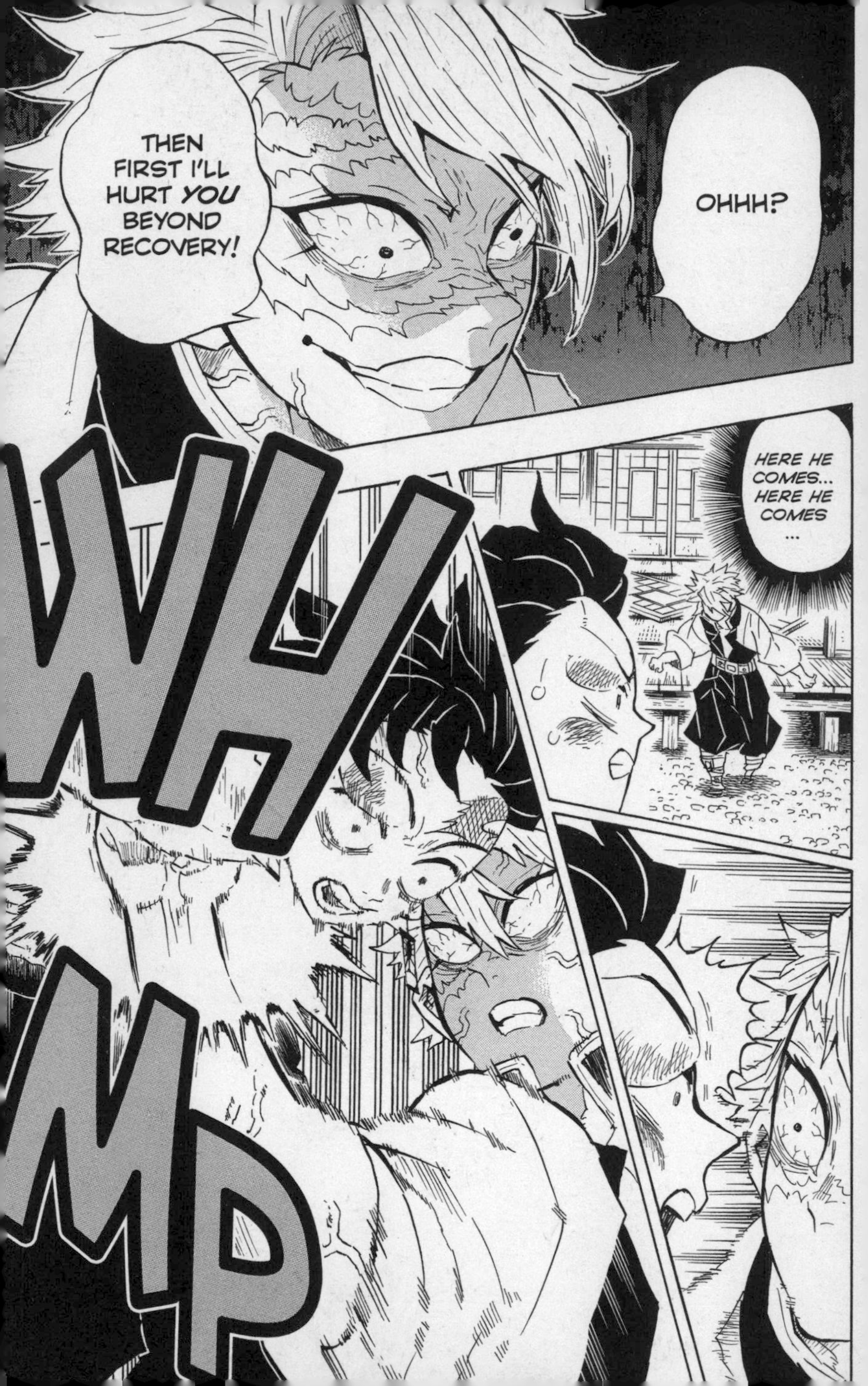
OHHH?
THEN FIRST I'LL HURT *YOU* BEYOND RECOVERY!
HERE HE COMES... HERE HE COMES ...
WHUMP

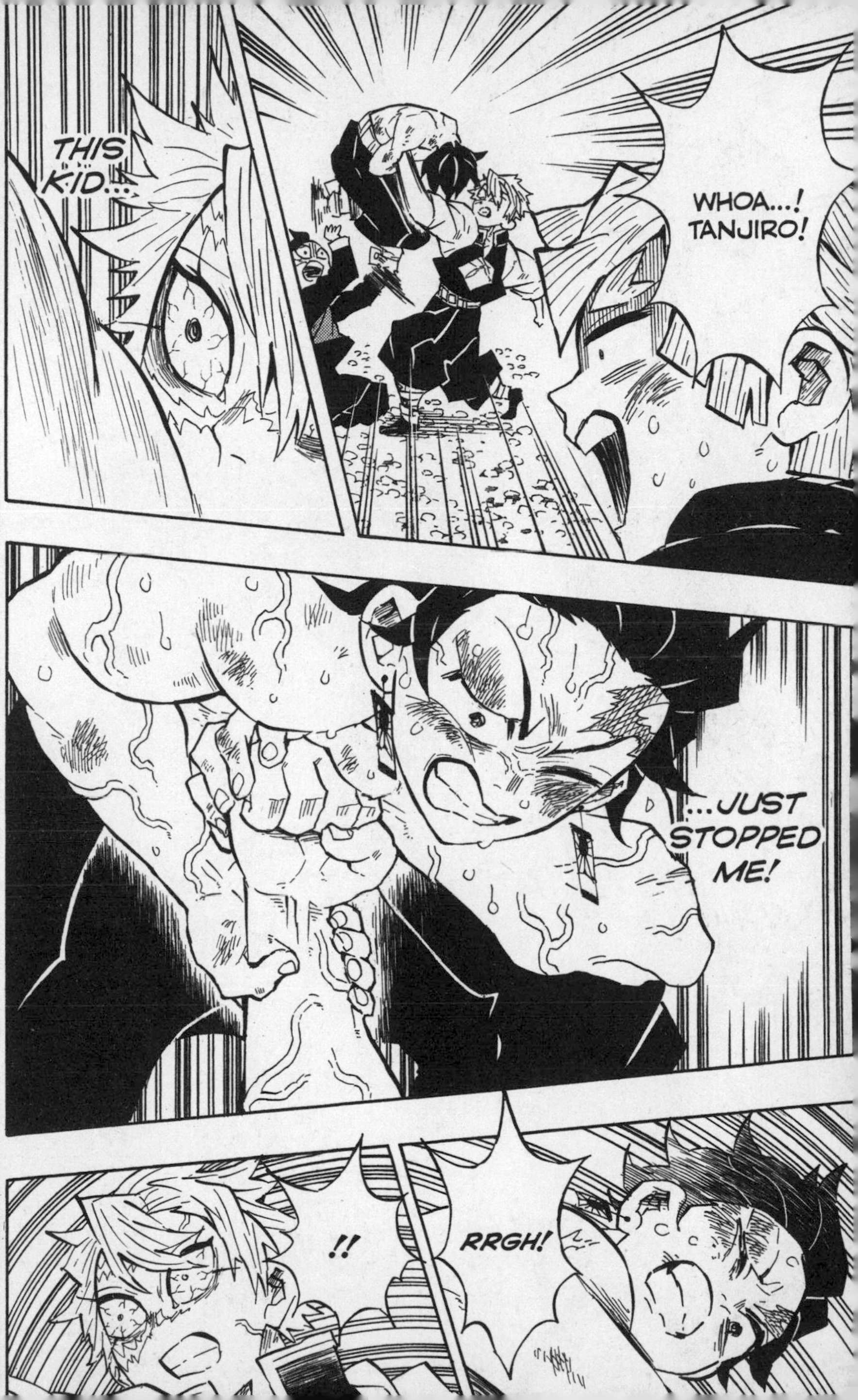
WHOA...! TANJIRO!
THIS KID...
...JUST STOPPED ME!
RRGH!
!!

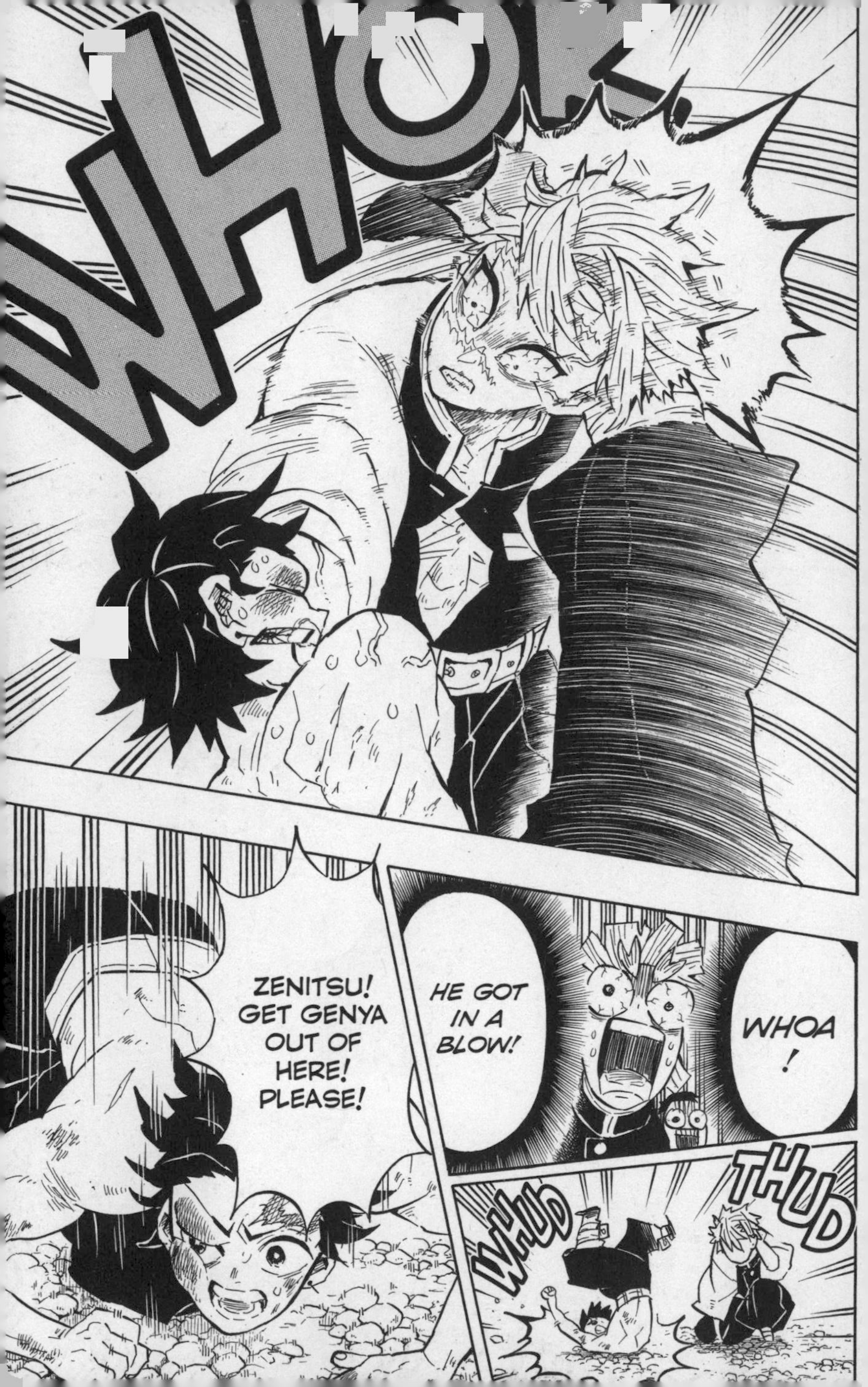
WHOK
WHOA!
HE GOT IN A BLOW!
THUD
WHUD
ZENITSU! GET GENYA OUT OF HERE! PLEASE!

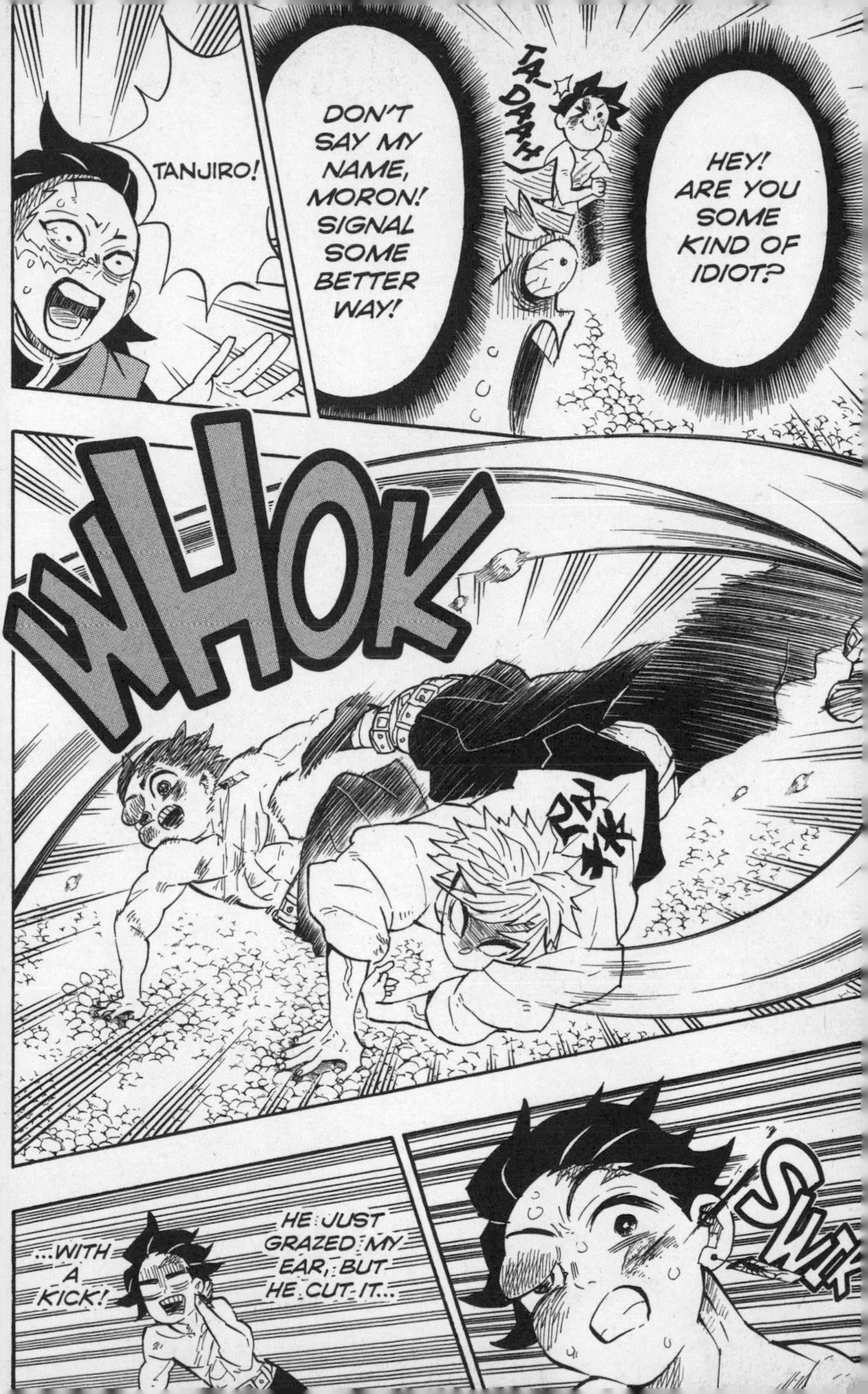
HEY! ARE YOU SOME KIND OF IDIOT?
TA-DAAAH
DON'T SAY MY NAME, MORON! SIGNAL SOME BETTER WAY!
TANJIRO!
WHOK
SWIK
HE JUST GRAZED MY EAR, BUT HE CUT IT...
...WITH A KICK!

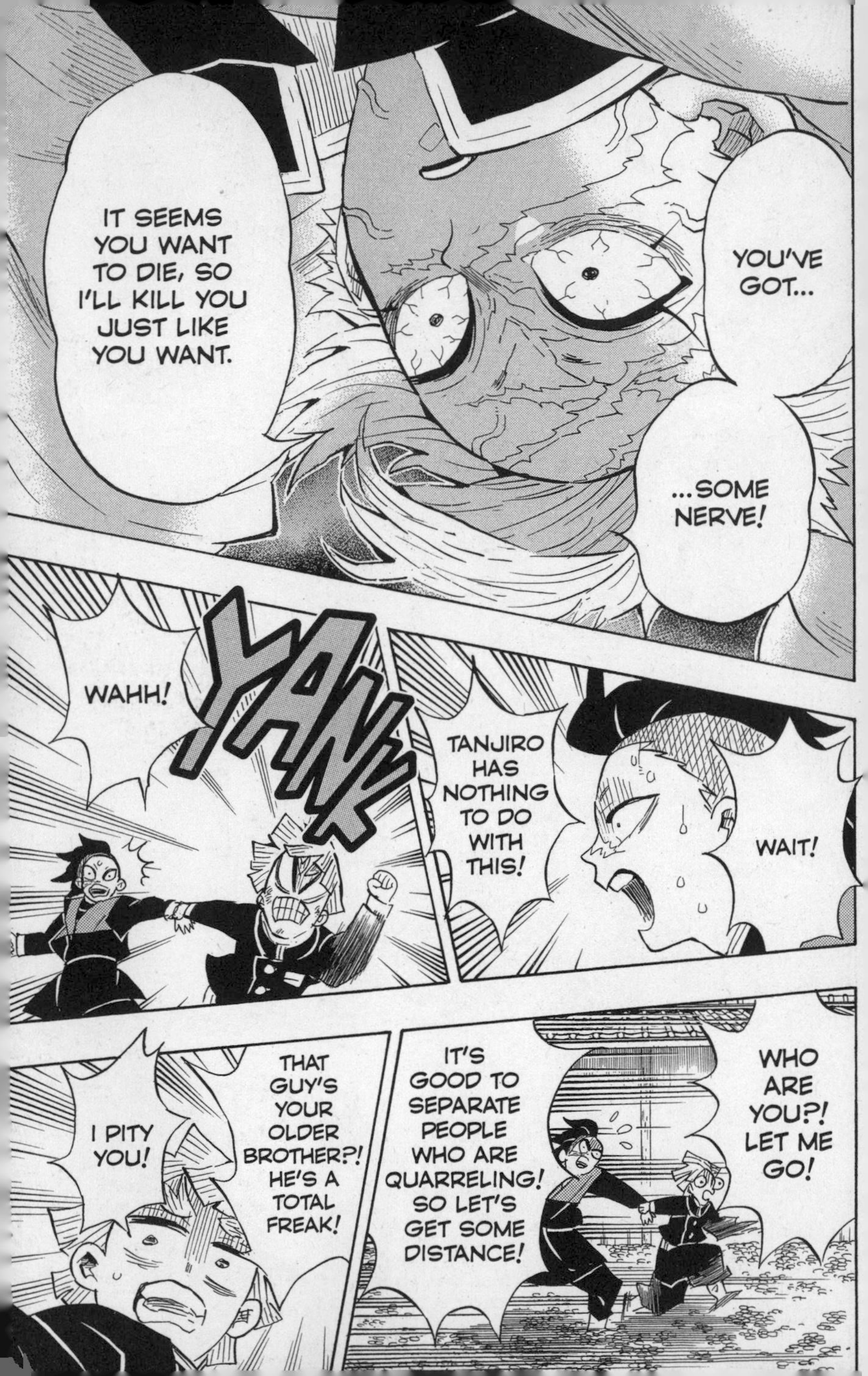
YOU'VE GOT...
...SOME NERVE!
IT SEEMS YOU WANT TO DIE, SO I'LL KILL YOU JUST LIKE YOU WANT.
WAIT!
TANJIRO HAS NOTHING TO DO WITH THIS!
YANK
WAHH!
WHO ARE YOU?! LET ME GO!
IT'S GOOD TO SEPARATE PEOPLE WHO ARE QUARRELING! SO LET'S GET SOME DISTANCE!
THAT GUY'S YOUR OLDER BROTHER?! HE'S A TOTAL FREAK!
I PITY YOU!

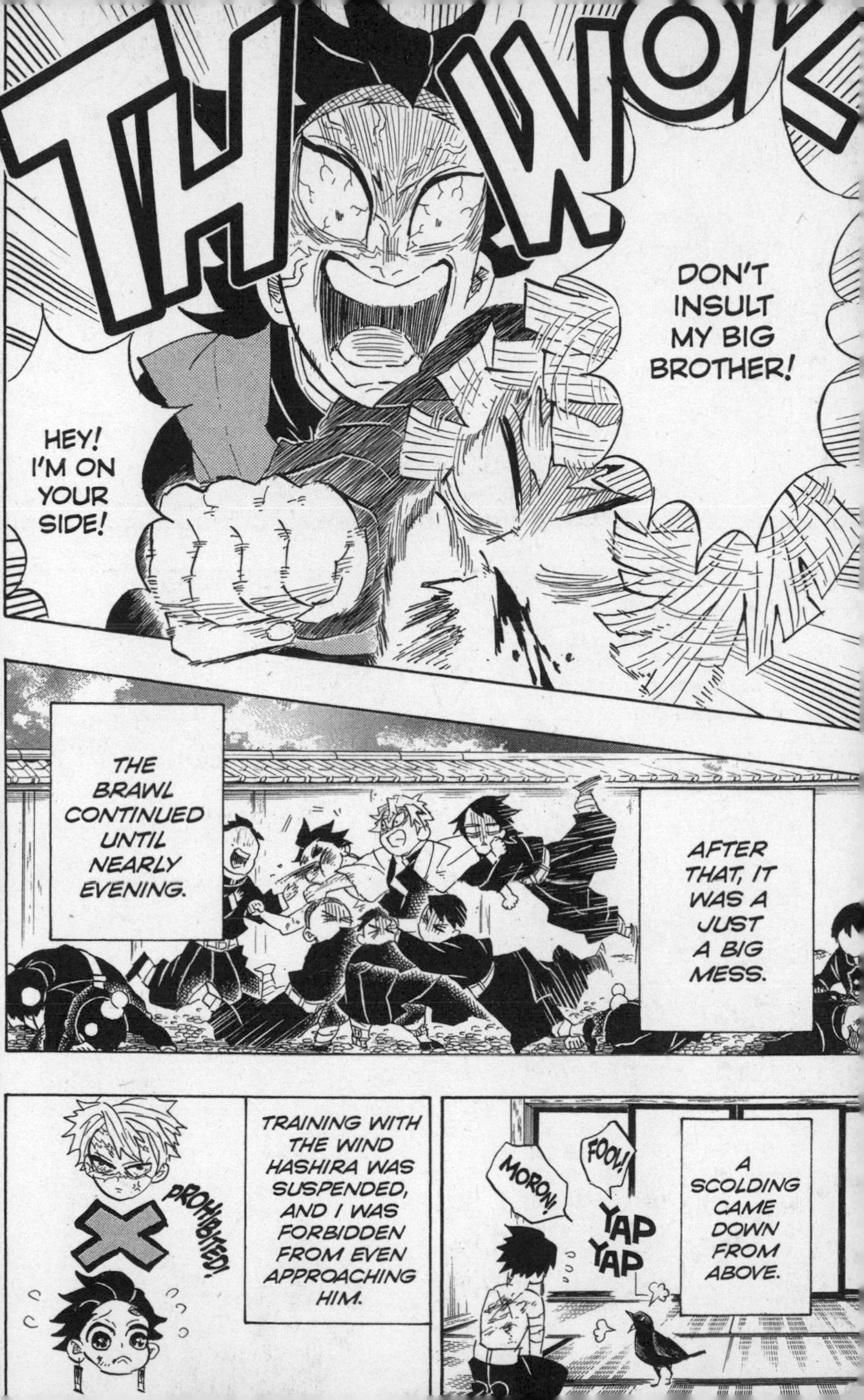
THWOK
DON'T INSULT MY BIG BROTHER!
HEY! I'M ON YOUR SIDE!
AFTER THAT, IT WAS A JUST A BIG MESS.
THE BRAWL CONTINUED UNTIL NEARLY EVENING.
A SCOLDING CAME DOWN FROM ABOVE.
FOOL!
MORON!
YAP YAP
TRAINING WITH THE WIND HASHIRA WAS SUSPENDED, AND I WAS FORBIDDEN FROM EVEN APPROACHING HIM.
PROHIBITED!

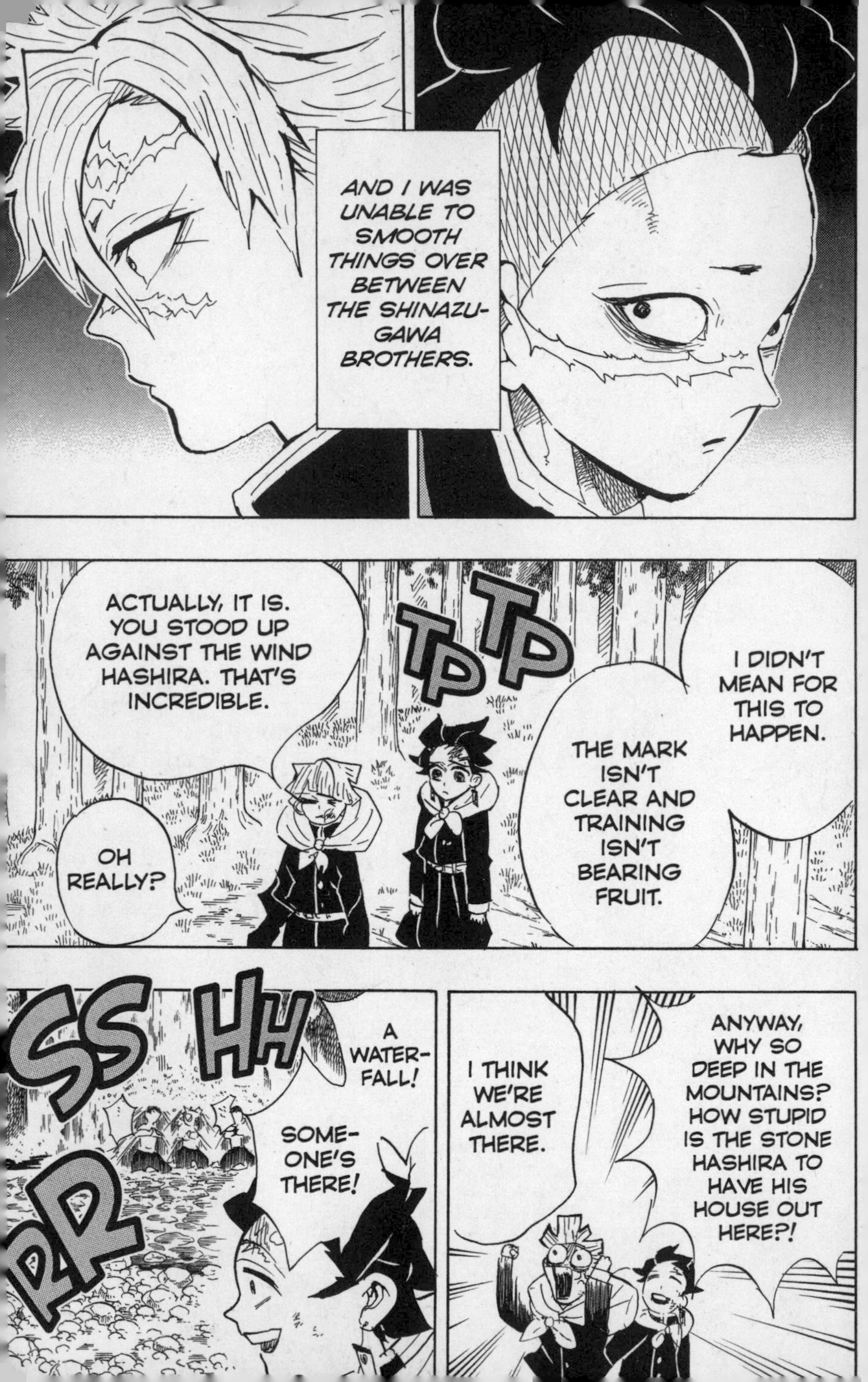
AND I WAS UNABLE TO SMOOTH THINGS OVER BETWEEN THE SHINAZU-GAWA BROTHERS.
I DIDN'T MEAN FOR THIS TO HAPPEN.
THE MARK ISN'T CLEAR AND TRAINING ISN'T BEARING FRUIT.
TP TP TP
ACTUALLY, IT IS. YOU STOOD UP AGAINST THE WIND HASHIRA. THAT'S INCREDIBLE.
OH REALLY?
ANYWAY, WHY SO DEEP IN THE MOUNTAINS? HOW STUPID IS THE STONE HASHIRA TO HAVE HIS HOUSE OUT HERE?!
I THINK WE'RE ALMOST THERE.
A WATER-FALL!
SSHH
SOME-ONE'S THERE!
RR

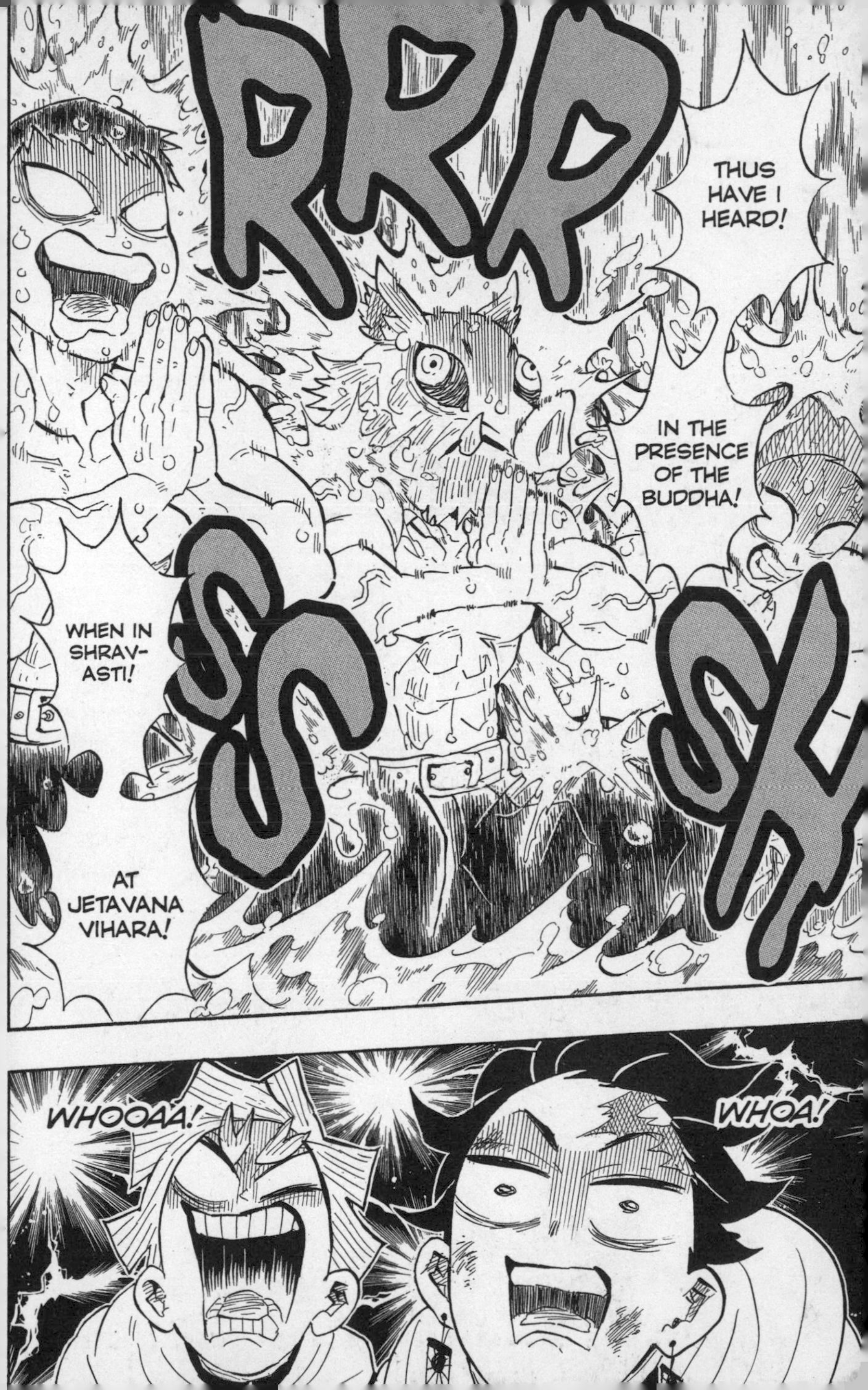
THUS HAVE I HEARD!
IN THE PRESENCE OF THE BUDDHA!
WHEN IN SHRAV-ASTI!
AT JETAVANA VIHARA!
WHOA!
WHOOAA!

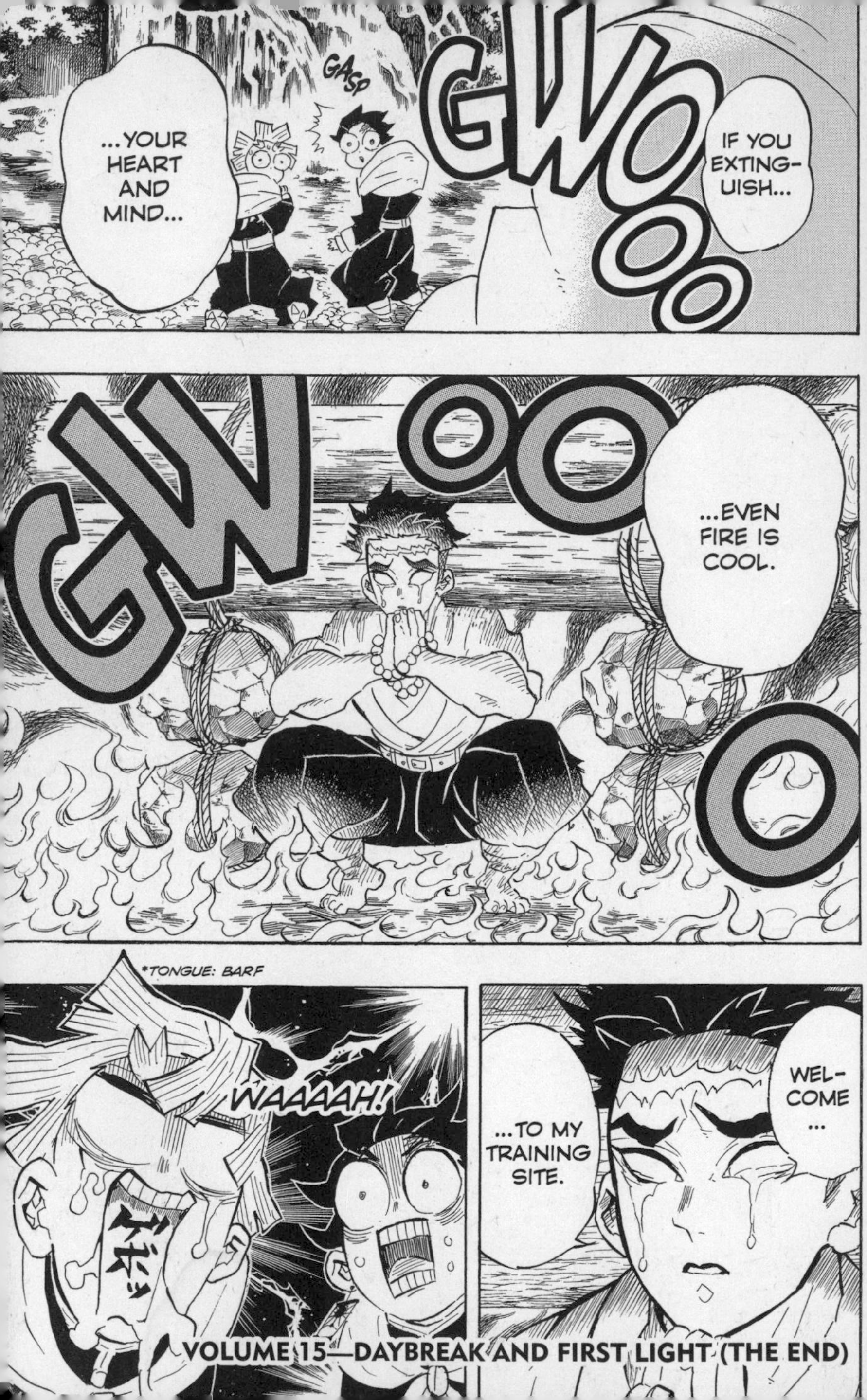
GWOOOO
IF YOU EXTING-UISH...
GASP
...YOUR HEART AND MIND...
GWOOOO
...EVEN FIRE IS COOL.
WEL-COME ...
...TO MY TRAINING SITE.
*TONGUE: BARF
WAAAAH!
VOLUME 15—DAYBREAK AND FIRST LIGHT (THE END)

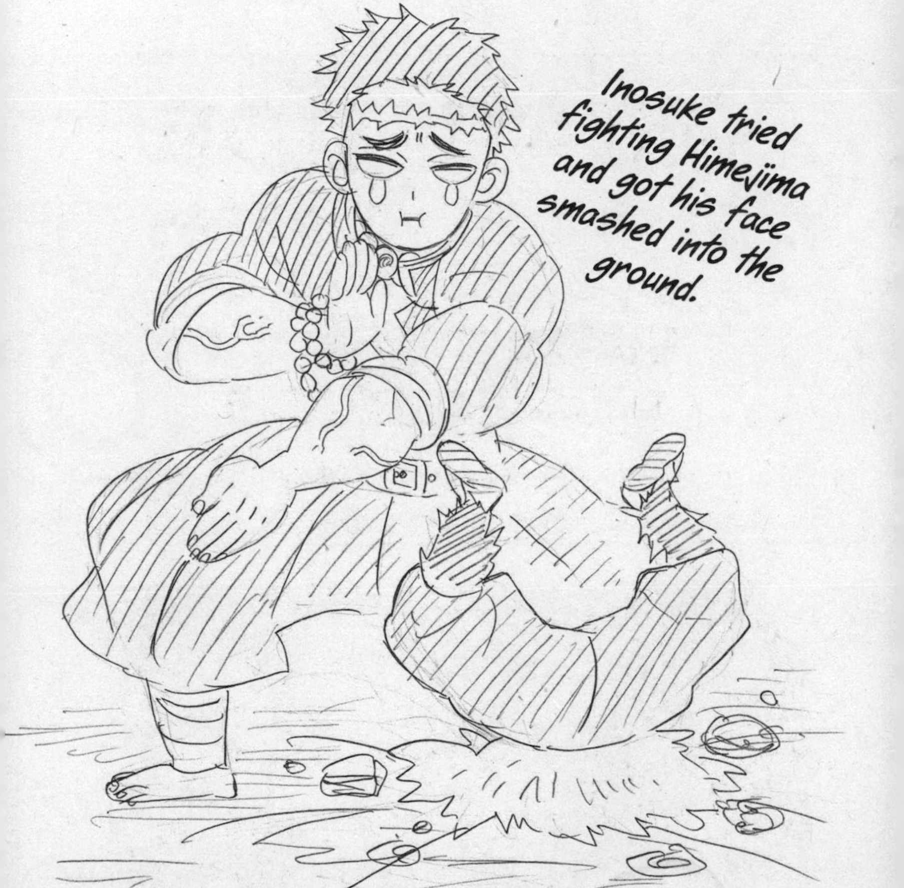
Inosuke tried fighting Himejima and got his face smashed into the ground.

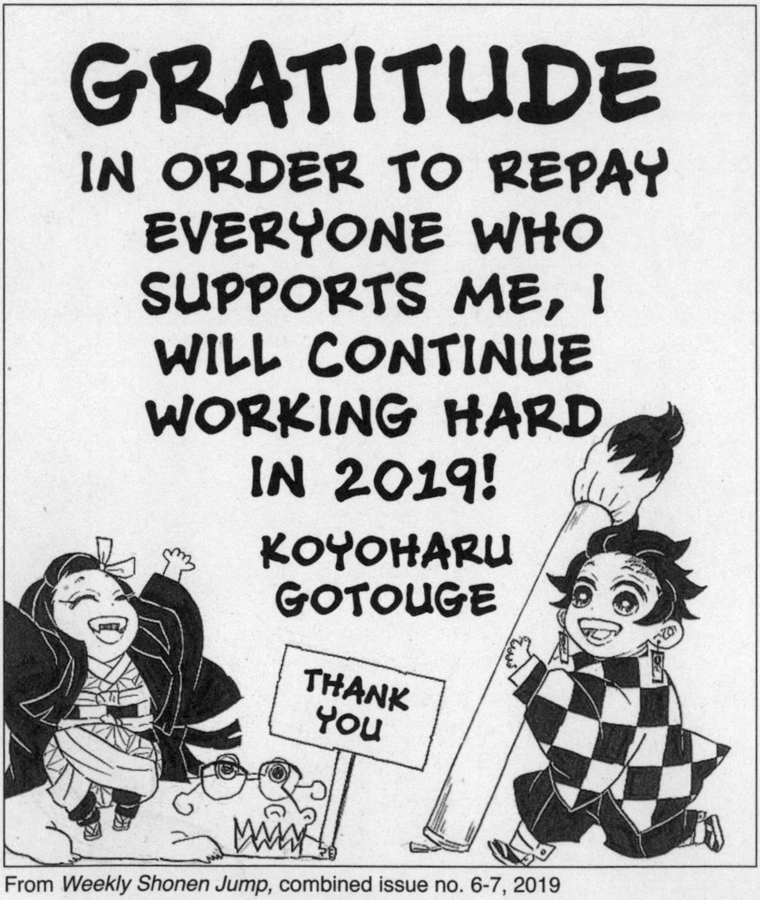
GRATITUDE
IN ORDER TO REPAY EVERYONE WHO SUPPORTS ME, I WILL CONTINUE WORKING HARD IN 2019!
KOYOHARU GOTOUGE
THANK YOU

From *Weekly Shonen Jump,* combined issue no. 6-7, 2019

YOU'RE READING THE
WRONG WAY!

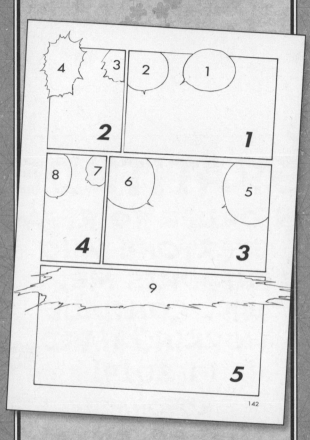

DEMON SLAYER: KIMETSU NO YAIBA reads from right to left, starting in the upper-right corner. Japanese is read from right to left, meaning that action, sound effects and word-balloon order are completely reversed from English order.